AI-Driven Learning and Engagement in Higher Education

Muhammad Usman Tariq
Abu Dhabi School of Management, UAE

IGI Global
Publishing Tomorrow's Research Today

Vice President of Editorial	Melissa Wagner
Managing Editor of Acquisitions	Mikaela Felty
Managing Editor of Book Development	Jocelynn Hessler
Production Manager	Mike Brehm
Cover Design	Phillip Shickler

Published in the United States of America by
IGI Global Scientific Publishing
701 East Chocolate Avenue
Hershey, PA, 17033, USA
Tel: 717-533-8845
Fax: 717-533-8661
Website: https://www.igi-global.com E-mail: cust@igi-global.com

Library of Congress Cataloging-in-Publication Data

Names: Ṭāriq, Muḥammad ʻUs̲mān, author.
Title: AI-driven learning and engagement in higher education / Edited by Muhammad Usman Tariq.
Description: Hershey, PA : IGI Global Scientific Publishing, [2025] | Includes bibliographical references and index. | Summary: "This book provides a comprehensive exploration of these themes and offers insights into the theoretical foundations, practical applications, and ethical implications of AI in education"-- Provided by publisher.
Identifiers: LCCN 2024060580 (print) | LCCN 2024060581 (ebook) | ISBN 9798369340745 (hardcover) | ISBN 9798369350928 (paperback) | ISBN 9798369340752 (ebook)
Subjects: LCSH: Artificial intelligence--Educational applications. | Artificial intelligence--Educational applications--Moral and ethical aspects. | Education, Higher--Effect of technological innovations on.
Classification: LCC LB1028.43 .T38 2025 (print) | LCC LB1028.43 (ebook) | DDC 370.78/563--dc23/eng/20250210
LC record available at https://lccn.loc.gov/2024060580
LC ebook record available at https://lccn.loc.gov/2024060581

British Cataloguing in Publication Data
A Cataloguing in Publication record for this book is available from the British Library.

This book is dedicated to my wife and my family who have sacrificed their time during this book writing journey.

Table of Contents

Preface

OVERVIEW OF THE SUBJECT MATTER

Artificial Intelligence (AI) has rapidly emerged as a revolutionary force across various sectors, with profound influence permeating the domain of higher education. AI in higher education encompasses a wide range of applications designed to enhance teaching methodologies, streamline administrative processes, and personalise learning experiences. The transformative potential of AI lies in its ability to process vast amounts of data, identify patterns, and make intelligent decisions, which can significantly improve educational outcomes.

One of the key areas where AI has made substantial progress is personalised learning. Traditional education models often follow a one-size-fits-all approach, which may not address the diverse needs of individual students effectively. AI technologies, such as adaptive learning platforms and intelligent tutoring systems, enable educators to tailor instructional content and pace to each student's unique learning style and proficiency level. By continuously analysing student performance data, these systems can provide real-time feedback and personalised recommendations, thereby fostering a more engaging and effective learning environment.

In addition to personalised learning, AI has the potential to revolutionise administrative functions within educational institutions. AI-powered tools can automate routine tasks, such as admissions processing, scheduling, and grading, thereby freeing up valuable time for educators and administrators to focus on more strategic initiatives. For instance, AI-driven chatbots can handle student enquiries, provide academic advice, and assist with enrolment procedures, ensuring that students receive timely and accurate information without overwhelming the human staff.

Moreover, AI's role of AI in data analytics cannot be overlooked. Educational institutions generate vast amounts of data, ranging from student attendance and academic performance to campus operations and resource management. AI-driven analytics can shift through these data to uncover insights that inform decision making at all levels. For example, predictive analytics can identify students at risk of dropping out, allowing institutions to intervene proactively through targeted support. Similarly, AI can optimise resource allocation, improve operational efficiency, and enhance overall institutional effectiveness.

AI is instrumental in advancing the research capabilities of higher education. Automated literature reviews, data analysis, and even the generation of research hypotheses are now feasible using AI tools. These advancements not only accelerate the research process, but also enhance the quality and rigor of academic publications. Furthermore, AI-driven plagiarism detection and peer-review systems ensure the integrity and originality of scholarly work.

However, the integration of AI into higher education is challenging. Ethical considerations such as data privacy, algorithmic bias, and transparency are critical issues that institutions must address to ensure responsible AI deployment. The potential of AI to perpetuate or exacerbate existing inequalities necessitates the development of robust ethical frameworks and policies that prioritise fairness and accountability.

This book, *AI-Driven Learning and Engagement in Higher Education*, provides a comprehensive exploration of these themes and offers insights into the theoretical foundations, practical applications, and ethical implications of AI in education. Each chapter delves into specific aspects of AI integration, from personalised learning and intelligent tutoring systems to administrative automation and ethical considerations. By presenting a balanced view of opportunities and challenges, this book aims to equip educators, administrators, policymakers, and researchers with the knowledge and tools necessary to navigate the evolving landscape of AI in higher education.

In summary, AI holds the promise of transforming higher education by making it more personalised, efficient, and effective. Through thoughtful and ethical integration, AI can help institutions meet the needs of their students, enhance the quality of education, and prepare learners for the complexities of the modern world. This book serves as a comprehensive guide for understanding and leveraging the power of AI in the pursuit of educational excellence.

The Role of AI in Today's World

In today's rapidly evolving technological landscape, Artificial Intelligence (AI) has become a pivotal element for enhancing efficiency, accuracy, and personalisation across different domains. This is particularly evident in the realm of higher education, where AI offers unprecedented opportunities to revolutionise teaching methodologies, optimise administrative processes, and foster a more engaging and inclusive learning environment. By leveraging AI, educational institutions can provide tailored learning experiences, streamline administrative tasks, and improve their decision-making processes, ultimately leading to enhanced educational outcomes.

One of the most significant impacts of AI in higher education is its ability to personalise learning experiences. Traditional education models often struggle to accommodate the diverse needs and learning styles of students. AI addresses this challenge by enabling the development of adaptive learning systems that customise educational content to match each student's pace and understanding. These systems use algorithms to analyse a student's performance and learning habits, and adjust the difficulty and style of the material accordingly. This personalised approach helps to ensure that all students, regardless of their starting point, can achieve their full potential.

Furthermore, AI-powered tools such as intelligent tutoring systems provide real-time feedback and support, replicating the benefits of one-on-one tutoring. These systems can identify areas where a student is struggling and offer targeted exercises and resources to address these gaps. This continuous, data-driven feedback loop not only enhances the learning experience, but also helps educators identify and support at-risk students more effectively.

AI's role of AI extends beyond personalised learning to include the automation and optimisation of administrative tasks. Educational institutions handle vast amounts of data and perform numerous routine tasks that are time consuming and prone to human error. AI can automate processes, such as admissions, enrolment, grading, and scheduling, thereby reducing the administrative burden on staff and increasing operational efficiency. For example, AI-driven chatbots can manage student enquiries and provide 24/7 support, freeing up human resources for complex and strategic tasks. These chatbots can answer frequently asked questions, assist with course registration, and even provide personalised academic advice based on students' records and preferences.

In addition to improving efficiency, AI also enhances decision-making processes within educational institutions. AI can provide valuable insights into various aspects of academic and administrative operations by harnessing the power of data analytics. Predictive analytics, for instance, can help institutions forecast enrolment trends, optimise resource allocation, and identify factors that contribute to student success or attrition. This data-driven approach enables administrators to make informed decisions, which enhances the overall effectiveness of their institutions.

Moreover, AI plays a crucial role in advancing higher education research capabilities. The traditional research process can be labour-intensive and time-consuming, but AI technologies such as natural language processing and machine learning can streamline these efforts. Automated literature reviews, data analysis, and even the generation of research hypotheses are now feasible using AI, accelerating the pace of discovery and innovation. AI can also enhance the peer-review process by identifying potential reviewers, detecting plagiarism, and ensuring the originality and quality of academic publications.

The benefits of AI in higher education are not limited to academic realms. AI can also improve overall student experience by enhancing campus services. For instance, AI-driven systems can optimise campus security, manage energy consumption, and enhance facility maintenance. These improvements contribute to the creation of a safer and more efficient learning environment.

However, the integration of AI into higher education brings forth several ethical considerations that must be addressed. Issues, such as data privacy, algorithmic bias, and transparency, are paramount. Educational institutions must develop robust ethical frameworks to ensure that AI is used responsibly and equitably. This includes implementing policies that protect student data, ensuring transparency in how AI systems make decisions, and actively working to mitigate any bias in AI algorithms.

In conclusion, AI holds transformative potential in higher education by enabling personalised learning, optimising administrative processes, and enhancing research capabilities. By thoughtfully integrating AI technologies, educational institutions can improve the quality of education and meet the diverse needs of their students. The responsible and ethical use of AI is crucial in realising these benefits and ensuring that advancements in AI contribute positively to the field of education.

Target Audience

This book is intended for diverse audiences, including educators, administrators, policymakers, researchers, and students in the field of education and technology. It aims to provide valuable insights into the practical applications of AI in higher education by offering both theoretical perspectives and practical guidelines. Whether an academic professional seeks to integrate AI into their teaching practices or a researcher exploring the latest advancements in educational technology, this book will serve as a comprehensive resource.

CHAPTER SUMMARIES

Chapter 1: AI Terminologies

This chapter introduces fundamental AI concepts and terminology, providing a solid foundation for readers to understand the subsequent discussions. It covers key terms, such as machine learning, natural language processing, and neural networks, which are essential for understanding the complexities of AI applications in education.

Chapter 2: Applied vs. Theoretical AI

This chapter differentiates between applied and theoretical AI and highlights their respective roles and contributions to higher education. It discusses practical AI implementation in educational settings and the theoretical underpinnings that drive these innovations.

Chapter 3: Shaping the Future of Higher Education

This chapter explores how AI is poised to shape the future of higher education, focusing on the potential for personalised learning, enhanced student engagement, and improved academic performance. It examines case studies and examples of successful AI integration into educational institutions.

Chapter 4: Artificial Intelligence Challenges in Higher Education

This chapter addresses various challenges associated with implementing AI in higher education, including ethical considerations, data privacy, and algorithmic bias. It provides strategies for overcoming these challenges to ensure responsible and equitable use of AI.

Chapter 5: A General Framework for Artificial Intelligence in Higher Education

This chapter presents a comprehensive framework for integrating AI into higher education, outlining the best practices, governance structures, and implementation strategies. This serves as a guide for institutions seeking to harness the power of AI to enhance their educational offerings.

Chapter 6: AI for Learning Analytics

This chapter delves into the role of AI in learning analytics, discussing how data-driven insights can be used to inform instructional design, track student progress, and personalise learning experiences. This emphasises the importance of ethical data use and privacy considerations.

Chapter 7: Intelligent Tutoring Systems

This chapter explores the development and implementation of intelligent tutoring systems (ITS) that provide personalised tutoring and feedback to students. This highlights the benefits of ITS in improving student learning outcomes and offers practical guidelines for their integration.

Chapter 8: Teaching and Learning Strategies Using AI

This chapter discusses various AI-powered teaching and learning strategies, including adaptive learning platforms, virtual reality, and natural language processing tools. It provides examples of how these technologies can enhance students' engagement and learning effectiveness.

Chapter 9: Ethical and Legal Implications of AI in Education

This chapter examines the ethical and legal implications of using AI in education, focusing on issues such as data privacy, consent, and potential for bias. It offers recommendations for the development of ethical AI policies and practices in educational settings.

Chapter 10: Case Studies of AI Implementation in Higher Education

This chapter presents detailed case studies of AI implementation in higher education institutions, showcasing both the successes and challenges. It provides practical insights and lessons learned from the real-world applications of AI in education.

Chapter 11: AI for Student Support Services

This chapter explores the use of AI in student support services, including academic advice, mental health support, and career counselling. It discusses the benefits of AI-driven support systems in enhancing students' well-being and success.

Chapter 12: AI in Research and Academic Publishing

This chapter examines the impact of AI on research and academic publishing, including its role in automation of literature review, research data analysis, and peer review processes. This highlights the potential of AI to accelerate research and improve the quality of academic publications.

Chapter 13: AI-Enhanced Collaborative Learning

This chapter discusses how AI can facilitate collaborative learning experiences, thereby enabling students to work together more effectively through intelligent collaboration tools and platforms. This emphasises the role of AI in fostering teamwork and communication skills.

Chapter 14: AI for General Administration

This chapter explores the application of AI in general administrative functions within educational institutions such as admissions, enrolment management, and facility management. This highlights the efficiency gains and cost savings that AI can bring to administrative processes.

Chapter 15: AI for Human Resources and Talent Acquisition

This chapter focuses on the use of AI in human resources and talent acquisition and discusses how AI can streamline recruitment processes, improve employee experiences, and enhance workforce planning. It examines ethical considerations and potential biases associated with AI-driven HR practices.

CONCLUSION

The integration of AI into higher education represents a significant paradigm shift, offering transformative potential for teaching, learning, and administrative processes. This book, *AI-Driven Learning and Engagement in Higher Education*, provides a comprehensive exploration of AI applications, challenges, and opportunities in the education sector. By examining theoretical frameworks, practical implementations, and ethical considerations, this book aims to contribute to the ongoing discourse on AI in education and guide institutions in harnessing AI's full potential of AI to create more effective, inclusive, and engaging learning environments. Through thoughtful and responsible AI integration, higher education can meet the diverse needs of students and prepare them for the demands of the future workforce.

Introduction

Artificial Intelligence (AI) is transforming the world at an unprecedented pace, influencing various sectors including healthcare, finance, transportation, and education. The integration of AI into higher education has the potential to revolutionise the learning landscape, providing opportunities for personalised education, efficient administrative processes, and enhanced research capabilities. This book, *AI-Driven Learning and Engagement in Higher Education*, aims to explore the multifaceted impact of AI on higher education, offering insights into both the opportunities and challenges that come with this technological evolution.

The premise of this book is grounded in the belief that AI can serve as a powerful tool to enhance the educational experiences of both students and educators. By leveraging AI technologies, educational institutions can tailor their learning experiences to individual students, ensuring that each learner receives the support they need to succeed. AI powered personalised learning platforms can adapt to a student's unique learning style and pace, providing customised content and feedback. This personalised approach can significantly improve student engagement and outcomes, making learning more effective and enjoyable.

In addition to transforming the learning experience, AI can streamline the administrative functions within educational institutions. Tasks such as admission processing, scheduling, grading, and student support services can be automated using AI, freeing up valuable time for educators and administrators to focus on more strategic activities. AI-powered chatbots and virtual assistants can provide students with 24/7 support, answer queries, guide them through administrative processes, and offer academic advice. This automation not only increases efficiency, but also enhances the overall student experience by providing timely and accurate information.

Another significant aspect of AI in higher education is its role in data analysis. Educational institutions generate vast amounts of data, from student performance metrics to operational statistics. AI-driven analytics can process and analyse these data to uncover patterns and insights that inform decision making. For example, predictive analytics can help to identify students at risk of dropping out, allowing institutions to intervene proactively with targeted support. Data-driven insights can also optimise resource allocation, improve academic planning, and enhance institutional effectiveness.

Ethical considerations regarding the use of AI in education are also a critical focus of this book. Issues such as data privacy, algorithmic bias, and transparency must be addressed to ensure responsible and equitable use of AI technologies. This book provides strategies and frameworks for navigating these ethical challenges, emphasising the importance of developing and implementing AI solutions that uphold ethical standards and promote fairness.

This book is structured into thoughtfully curated chapters, each of which addresses a specific aspect of AI integration in higher education. The chapters offer a comprehensive exploration of the role of AI in education, from foundational concepts and theoretical frameworks to practical applications and case studies. The book also includes discussions on the future trends of AI in higher education, providing readers with a forward-looking perspective of the evolving landscape.

AI-Driven Learning and Engagement in Higher Education is intended for a diverse audience, including educators, administrators, policymakers, researchers, and students. It aims to serve as a valuable resource for those seeking to understand the implications of AI in education and explore innovative ways to harness its potential. By providing a balanced view of opportunities and challenges, this book seeks to equip readers with the knowledge and tools necessary to navigate the complexities of AI integration in higher education.

In conclusion, the integration of AI into higher education presents exciting opportunities and significant challenges. This book offers a thorough examination of these aspects and provides practical insights and ethical considerations to guide the responsible adoption of AI in educational settings. Through thoughtful and informed AI implementation, higher education institutions can enhance their learning experiences, streamline operations, and better prepare students for the future.

Chapter 1
Artificial Intelligence Terminologies

ABSTRACT

The wonders of artificial intelligence are making the world move quickly. Artificial intelligence technology has added innovations and new value to present-day human professional and personal lives. Rapid transformation can sometimes be frightening, but artificial intelligence technology has supplemented human beings with various unique aspects on a positive edge. It added new terminology to the daily vocabulary that had not been heard or read before. Artificial intelligence technology has also added new concepts to the existing terminology. The advantages of artificial intelligence used by the current generation are clear inferences that this technology will help transform lives and will be sustained for sure. This comprehension will allow people to examine the different attributes of the artificial intelligence technology and how it helps its customers to avail benefits.

INTRODUCTION

The proliferation of data from diverse sources, combined with the increased computational power of modern computers, has paved the way for the development of sophisticated data-analysis techniques. These techniques have revolutionized the ability to interpret, predict, and optimize outcomes in numerous domains. For instance, support vector machines have become integral to classification and regression analysis, offering high precision in tasks ranging from image recognition to medical diagnosis. Text analytics has enabled the extraction of meaningful insights from

DOI: 10.4018/979-8-3693-4074-5.ch001

unstructured data, such as social media posts and customer reviews, transforming how businesses understand consumer sentiments and behaviors.

Association rules have provided a method for discovering interesting relationships between variables in large databases, commonly used in market basket analysis, to identify product purchase patterns. Ensemble techniques, which combine multiple models to improve predictive performance, have enhanced accuracy and robustness in various applications ranging from fraud detection to weather forecasting. Subgroup discovery, which focuses on finding interesting patterns in data subsets, has found applications in personalized medicine by identifying patient subgroups that respond differently to treatments. These advanced data analysis techniques have become essential tools in the analytics arsenal across many disciplines. Genetically, they facilitate the identification of genetic markers associated with diseases, leading to personalized treatment plans. In engineering, they optimize the system performance and reliability, from predictive maintenance in manufacturing to the design of smart cities. The medical field leverages these techniques for disease prediction, patient monitoring, and personalized healthcare solutions. Vision systems powered by machine learning algorithms are now integral to facial recognition, autonomous vehicles, and security systems.

Statistics and marketing have also benefited significantly from these advancements. In statistics, these techniques allow for more accurate data modelling and hypothesis testing, leading to deeper insights and better decision-making. In marketing, they enable precise targeting and personalization, improving customer engagement, and campaign effectiveness. Marketers can now harness predictive analytics to forecast trends, segment audiences, and optimize marketing strategies based on real-time data.

The interdisciplinary nature of these techniques underscores their versatility and importance in addressing complex challenges and enhancing the decision-making processes. As businesses and researchers continue to harness the power of data, the integration of these advanced analytical tools will undoubtedly drive innovation, efficiency, and competitive advantage in an evolving digital landscape.

BACKGROUND

This background provides information on various artificial intelligence terminologies.

Algorithm

A set of rules that a machine follows to learn how to perform a task. Even minor artificial intelligence technology design functions require basic instruction. Therefore, the algorithms operate throughout the procedure. Briefly, algorithms are bit-by-bit instructions that support a computer while performing calculations. This is similar to an instruction guide that allows a machine to learn how and when to perform a specific task. A computer may not recognise when it should start functioning or how it should proceed. The coding instructions are becoming more detailed and complex. An algorithm is an expanded subset of machine learning that informs computers to operate independently (Shang et al., 2020). Consequently, the device obtains information to enhance procedures and perform tasks more competently. Artificial intelligence algorithms make it possible to explain the differences between people's voices, learn the names of a particular tune, and then play a song according to a person's streaming music account. A machine learning algorithm uses an artificial intelligence system to perform its functions and forecast the output values from the provided input data. The two basic procedures of machine-learning algorithms are regression and classification. Machine-learning algorithms are generally classified as supervised or unsupervised. Supervised learning algorithms consist of input and preferred output data through labelling, whereas unsupervised algorithms do not function with labelled or classified data (De Stefano, 2019).

Autonomous

Autonomous systems can complete a task, achieve an objective, or work with their surroundings with minimal or no human intervention. It is also vital for these systems to forecast, plan, and become aware of the environment. It is implemented in both autonomous software and hardware systems. Collaborative bots, also known as cobots, are autonomous systems (Bryson & Winfield, 2017). These cobots operate in combination with humans to perform tasks. This is in contrast with industrial robots, which are confined and physically disconnected from humans. Although cobots can function in augmented intelligence, they can function independently of humans. Autonomous systems help minimise human labour and require steadfast, stable, and high standards. The autonomous pattern system of artificial intelligence is perhaps the most difficult to implement and can have a phenomenal impact when performed correctly. The future of autonomous patterns is vivid (Ma et al., 2020).

The development of sophisticated algorithms has enabled the creation of advanced AI applications ranging from simple chatbots to complex neural networks.

- **Supervised Learning Algorithms:** These algorithms rely on labelled data to learn patterns and make predictions. For example, in an educational setting, supervised learning can be used to predict student performance by using historical data.
- **Unsupervised Learning Algorithms:** Unlike supervised learning, unsupervised algorithms operate using unlabelled data. They are used to identify hidden patterns or intrinsic structures within data. Clustering algorithms such as k-means are commonly used in educational data mining.
- **Reinforcement Learning Algorithms:** These algorithms learn by interacting with the environment and receiving feedback in the form of rewards and penalties. In higher education, reinforcement learning can be used to develop personalised learning pathways for students.

Backward chaining

This is also known as backward reasoning or backward deduction when using an inference engine. A backward chaining algorithm is a type of reasoning that begins with an objective and functions backwards, chaining using its rules to explore facts supporting the objective (Janjanam et al., 2021). This is known as the top-down approach. Backward chaining depends on the modus ponens inference instructions. In this method, the model begins with the preferred output and functions in reverse to discover what helps to support it. In backward chaining, the objective is split into sub-goals to verify that the facts are correct. This is known as a goal-driven approach, as an objective list determines which rules are selected and implemented. The backward chaining algorithm is used in proof assistants, game theory, inference engines, automated theorem proving tools, and various artificial intelligence applications. The backward chaining method mostly implements a depth-first search strategy for evidence (Sakharov, 2021).

Bias

In artificial intelligence, bias can take many forms, ranging from ethnic and gender discrimination to hiring inequity and age prejudice. The fundamental reason for artificial intelligence bias lies in unconscious or consciously hidden human bias in artificial intelligence algorithms during their development. Artificial intelligence solutions implement and scale human prejudice. One possible cause of this problem is the biased hypotheses made while developing artificial intelligence models. A model makes assumptions that streamline the learning procedure to perform a designated task. Various supervised machine-learning models perform better with less bias, as these assumptions can adversely affect the outcomes. Another common cause for imitating artificial intelligence bias is the poor quality of data on which artificial intelligence models are skilled (Parikh et al., 2019). Training data may integrate human decisions or echo historical or societal discrimination. No less significant source of artificial intelligence bias is real-world users' feedback networking with models. People may underpin bias baked in already-implemented artificial intelligence frameworks, mostly without recognising it (Nelson, 2019).

Big Data

Artificial Intelligence and big data have collaborative associations. Big data analytics controls artificial intelligence for enhanced data analysis. Consequently, artificial intelligence requires a significant amount of data to learn and improve decision-making procedures. The term big data implies vast, complicated, and high-velocity datasets. Big data act as a fuel that powers the transformation of artificial intelligence's decision-making (Gao et al., 2021). This can be explored and assessed for insights and information. Big data analytics uses procedures and technologies involving machine learning and artificial intelligence to merge and evaluate large datasets to recognise patterns and design actionable understandings. It helps to make fast, better, and data-driven decisions that enhance profits, efficiency, and revenues. Artificial's capabilities function with data analytics is the fundamental reason why big data and artificial intelligence are now apparently indivisible. Artificial intelligence, deep learning, and machine learning draw from each data input and utilise these inputs to create new rules for potential business analytics. However, issues arise when the data used are unacceptable (Yang et al., 2021).

Bounding Box

An imaginary rectangle that serves as a reference point for detecting an object and generating a collision box is called a bounding box. Data annotators create these rectangles over pictures, outlining objects of interest in every image by shaping their X and Y coordinates. This makes it simpler for machine-learning algorithms to identify what they are looking for, decide collision paths, and maintain significant computing resources. Bounding boxes are well-known image annotation methods used in deep learning (Dong et al., 2021). Compared to other image-processing techniques, this process can decrease costs and enhance annotation effectiveness. It is easy to draw and support the annotation of objects of interest in images so that machine vision can identify them. It is utilised for target recognition in a series of applications, including self-driving cars, CCTV cameras, helicopters, autonomous robots, and other machine vision tools. Counting the number of obstacles in a group at the same stage is beneficial. The main objective of deploying this annotation strategy is to decrease the search range for various object elements, preserve computing resources, and resolve computer vision issues (Sunil et al., 2021).

Chatbot

A computer program that imitates human conversation using text messages, voice commands, or both, is known as a chatbot. A chatbot is a short form of a chatterbot, an artificial intelligence factor that can be installed and utilised by a significant messaging app. The continuing advancement of information technology has witnessed growth in firms switching from traditional to digital media to manage customers. Ease through information technology is executed by firms by deploying artificial intelligence techniques on their digital media (Chen et al., 2021). artificial intelligence techniques that are progressing their application are chatterbots. Some instances of chatbot technology are virtual assistants, such as Google Assistant, Siri, Facebook Messenger, We Chat, and Amazon's Alexa. An automated program in the form of a chatbot interacts with consumers and costs less or nothing to communicate with. Chatbots that communicate with consumers are not restricted by their geographical location or time. This makes its deployment attractive to various firms that may not have the human or financial resources to make staff work 24/7 (Cheng & Jiang, 2021).

Cognitive Computing

Cognitive computing explains technologies dependent on the scientific rules behind artificial intelligence and signal processing, incorporating machine learning, data mining, and human-computer interaction. Its objective is to resolve complicated issues classified by ambiguity and vagueness, which means that problems are only resolved by human cognitive thinking. It is commonly assumed that cognitive computing is a part of the artificial intelligence formed to think and function with human beings. With the advancement of computing power, a significant wave of the latest information has come, which is difficult to process manually. Cognitive computing is the ability to broadcast data to assist human beings in decision making. It can assess complicated, contradictory, and varying information contextually to provide an adequate solution–essentially, the most algorithmically correct one (Arabnia et al., 2021). For instance, a cognitive model may offer a practical, attainable weight loss plan to control diabetes over the most useful, still impractical, one. It may also consider financial and age goals while making investment assistance, even if there is a lower rate of return. Derived from the incorporation of cognitive science and dependent on the basic idea of mimicking the human thinking procedure, the view, as well as cognitive computing applications, are sure to have comprehensive effects not only on people's private lives, but also on sectors such as insurance, healthcare, and many more. The benefits of cognitive technology are reasonable and represent a step away from traditional artificial intelligence systems (Lytras & Visvizi, 2021; Tariq, 2024).

Computational Learning Theory

This is a domain of study relevant to the use of proper mathematical procedures implemented in learning systems. Theoretical computer science was used to calculate the learning issues. This involves the characterisation of learning particular functions. Computational learning theory may be believed to be an extension or family of statistical learning theory that utilises formal techniques to assess learning algorithms. The aim of computational learning theory is based on supervised learning tasks. Proper assessment of actual issues and algorithms is difficult (He et al., 2021).

Consequently, it is customary to decrease evaluation complications by emphasising binary classification functions and simple binary-rule-based systems. Therefore, the practical use of theorems may be restricted to explaining the actual algorithms and issues. Moreover, the model's predictive capability and computational learning theory also refer to other vital factors, such as robustness to changes in learning patterns, creating insights into analytically observed occurrences, and simplicity (Al-Sartawi, 2021).

Corpus

A corpus is a compilation of authentic audio or text placed in datasets. Authentics here refers to text written, or audio spoken by a language subject. A corpus is made of recipes, tweets, novels, movies, television shows, newspapers, and radio broadcasts. A corpus consists of speech and text data in natural language processing used to train artificial intelligence and machine-learning systems. If a user wants to address a particular issue or goal, they will require a data collection that supports and is a description of what they are seeking to attain with natural language processing and machine learning. A corpus is a technique that involves computer-based empirical assessment of qualitative and quantitative language used by implementing extensive, electronically accessible collections of naturally appearing written or spoken texts known as corpora (Wang, 2021).

Data Mining

Data mining depends on advanced computing procedures and big data, involving machine learning and other types of artificial intelligence. The main objective was to discover patterns that can lead to forecasts and inferences from otherwise large or unstructured datasets. Data mining apps range from governments attempting to recognise possible security risks to financial segments seeking patterns in the market. Firms, specifically social media and online companies, utilise data mining for their users to generate beneficial marketing and advertising campaigns that target particular users. In data mining, knowledge discovery in databases, machine learning, and artificial intelligence are the practical mining of tacit formerly unidentified and possibly beneficial information from data. Statistical techniques allow trends and other associations to be recognised in large databases. Data mining is the procedure of classifying large sets of data to identify patterns and associations that can help resolve business issues through data assessment. Data-mining tools and methods allow firms to forecast future trends and make better decisions (Dogan and Birant, 2021).

Data Science

Data science is a domain that functions with and assesses large amounts of data to offer important information that can be utilised to solve issues and make decisions. Data science involves computations, programming, statistics, data mining, and analytics. It uses artificial intelligence to create forecasts and emphasises the transformation of data for visualisation and assessment. Machine learning links artificial intelligence and data science. This is because it is the procedure of learning from the data in due course. So artificial intelligence is a technique that supports data science to obtain outcomes and solutions for particular issues. Machine learning helps in attaining this objective. Data science is present at the junction of business, statistics, computer programming, and mathematics. Data science uses these techniques to offer valuable insights from data. Data science is the domain of study that merges domain expertise, mathematics and statistics knowledge, and programming skills to obtain significant perceptions from data. Data science experts implement machine learning algorithms for video, numbers, audio, text, and more to generate artificial intelligence systems to perform functions that commonly require human intelligence (Wong, 2021).

Consequently, these systems provide insights that business users and analysts can transform into substantial business value. Various firms have recognised the significance of machine learning, data science, and artificial intelligence. Irrespective of industry or size, firms that desire to remain competitive in times of big data require effectively creating and applying data science abilities or risk being abandoned (Sarker et al., 2021).

Dataset

A dataset in machine learning is a compilation of data fragments that a computer can consider as a single unit for forecasting and analytics. This means that data collection should be understandable and consistent for a machine that cannot recognise data similar to that of humans. For this purpose, after data collection, it is vital to preprocess it by sorting and completing it, and interpret the data by adding significant labels that are understandable by a computer. Furthermore, a good dataset should be related to specific quantities and quality standards. For fast training and smoothing, firms ensure that their datasets are related and well proportioned. If possible, companies should use live data every time and discuss the data volume and collection sources with experienced specialists. The dataset collection for an artificial intelligence project might seem easy, which can be done in the background, while the firm uses most of its time and resources to develop the machine learning model. However, as proven repeatedly, coping with data might take most of the firm's time because of the absolute scale that this task might end up. Therefore, it is important to recognise what a dataset in machine learning is, how to accumulate it, and what factors a proper dataset has (Finlayson et al., 2021).

Deep Learning

Deep learning, known as artificial neural networks, is a subdivision of machine learning relevant to algorithms influenced by the function and structure of the brain. It is a machine-learning technique that trains computers to do what humans can think naturally, such as learning. Deep learning is a fundamental technology behind driverless vehicles, allowing them to identify stop signs or differentiate pedestrians from streetlights. Voice control is crucial in customer devices such as mobile phones, hands-free speakers, and television. Deep learning has received much attention recently. It is obtaining outcomes that were not possible before. In deep learning, a computer model learns to perform classification functions directly from sounds, images, or text. Deep-learning models can attain state-of-the-art precision, sometimes beyond human-level work. The models are instructed to use a large set of tagged data and neural network designs that may consist of several layers (Jena et al., 2021).

Entity Annotation

Creating an artificial intelligence or machine learning model that works like a person requires large volumes of training data. It should be trained to recognise certain information so that a model can take action and make decisions. Data annotation is the classification and cataloguing of data and artificial intelligence applications, and data training should be correctly classified and annotated for a particular use case. Firms can create and deploy artificial intelligence applications with high-level, human-powered data annotations. The outcome is an improved customer experience solution, such as product suggestions, related search engine results, computer vision, chatbots, and computer vision. Data labelling or annotation is a procedure that makes data with particular objects understandable by machines to forecast the result. Processing, tagging, or transcribing objects in textual scans or images allows algorithms to understand the tagged data and obtain training to resolve actual business cases on their own without human interference (Chen et al., 2021).

Entity Extraction

Entity extraction, also called named-entity recognition, and entity chunking is a subactivity of information mining that categorises and detects phrases in a text into predefined groups. While identifying entities in an automated manner is beneficial, it mainly serves as a preprocessing step for complicated tasks, such as relationship extraction. For instance, biomedicine entity extraction is crucial for recognising the connections between various entity types, drug-disease associations, and gene-protein associations. Feature generation for such functions is complicated and time consuming. Neural networks can preclude feature engineering requirements and utilise actual data as input. Entity extraction models understand detailed data in the target firms based on their business requirements; the model recognises prime aspects in the text and then categorises them into predetermined groups. It can support the transformation of unstructured data into structured data that can be read by machines. Various preprocessing functions should be completed before there is a probability of extracting entities from textual material (Zhao et al., 2021; Tariq, 2024).

Forward Chaining

Forward chaining is a procedure based on accessible data for making specific decisions. This is the procedure for chaining the data in the forward direction. Firms can start with accessible data in forwarding chaining and use implication rules to extract data until the objective is not attained. This is the idea of decision and data. From the accessible data, develop until a decision is not made. In artificial intelligence, forward chaining is a technique in which inference rules are implemented in the previous data to extract supplementary data until an end objective is attained. The inference engine first assesses previous facts, conditions, and derivations in this type of chaining before determining new information. An objective is attained by manipulating the knowledge present in the knowledge base. It streamlines a complicated task by splitting it into various easy tasks that a computer may commence either sequentially or synchronously, primarily as a chain of procedures. The logical or data-driven approach to forwarding chaining is generally applied to expert systems and production rules. Forward chaining helps a program in artificial intelligence develop a solution by assessing identified data and positioning it with predetermined factors (Anwar, 2021).

General Artificial Intelligence

General artificial intelligence is as good as human abilities; for example, artificial general intelligence can perform any job that a human being can perform. Although artificial general intelligence can perform tasks with enhanced efficiency compared to human beings for a specific task, they cannot perform any task that is not allocated to them. Conversely, a human performs a task with less competence but can perform a wider series of functions than any of the previous artificial intelligence apps of the present age. Artificial general intelligence is a type of artificial intelligence used in films. An artificial general intelligence is a system that is more like a human to resolve any problem. Artificial general intelligence is also known as deep or strong artificial intelligence (AI). It is an idea of machine and general intelligence that imitates human intelligence, with capabilities to implement, think, learn, and understand its intelligence to resolve any problem as human beings in any given circumstance. It uses the concept of the mind artificial intelligence model not to repeat or mimic; it is about training systems to recognise human beings to distinguish requirements, thought procedures, beliefs, or emotions (Zhang & Lu, 2021).

Hyperparameter

A machine learning parameter, whose value is selected before training a learning algorithm, is known as a hyperparameter. The parameters should not be confused with hyperparameters. The label parameter is used to recognise the variables in machine learning, whose values are implemented during the training procedures. A hyperparameter is a parameter whose value is not fixed before the machine-learning procedure commences. In contrast, other parameter values were extracted through training. The algorithm hyperparameters affect the quality and speed of the learning procedure. Hyperparameters are vital because they can directly affect the behaviour of the training algorithm and have an essential effect on the operation of the trained model. Opting suitable hyperparameters plays a crucial part in the progress of the neural network architecture and significantly affects the model that has been learned. For instance, the model will miss significant patterns in the data if learning is low. It may collide if it is high (Ahmed et al., 2021).

Intent

Intent refers to a consumer's objective while typing a query or comment within a chatbot. Intent is a crucial element in chatbot functionality, because the chatbot's capability to analyse intent eventually defines the progress of the interaction. It must be trained and programmed with a beneficial model that includes a large amount of training data, and it should take the benefit of machine learning for constant improvement and advancement for a chatbot to be efficient at this— chatbots based on the intent function on a case-by-case basis. Every interaction is different from the previous interaction. Natural language processing is required to provide this type of scope. This is a factor in artificial intelligence that permits machines to extract understanding from language, as it is applied in regular conversation. Specifically, intent-based chatbots search for entities or critical terms in the received messages. Generally used in the training data of natural language processing tasks or chatbots, it is a label that describes the objective or purpose of what is communicated. For instance, the intent for the instruction “turn down the volume” maybe “reduce the volume.” (Choi & Lee, 2021).

Label

It is part of the training data that recognises the required output for that specific data segment. Data labelling is the procedure of identifying raw data, such as videos, images, or text files, and adding one or more significant or instructive labels to offer ideas so that the machine learning model can learn from it. For instance, labels might suggest whether an image consists of a car or bird, which words are spoken in an audio recording, or whether an X-ray consists of a tumour. Data labelling is required for various applications involving speech recognition, computer vision, and natural processing. Most functional machine learning models use supervised learning in the present age, which implements an algorithm to plan one input to one output. There is a requirement for a labelled dataset for supervised learning so that the model can learn to make the right decisions. Data labelling primarily begins by asking humans to judge a segment of unlabelled data. For instance, labellers may be requested to tag all pictures in a dataset where “does the image contain an animal” is correct. The tagging can be rough as yes or no or recognising particular pixels in the photo linked with the animal. The machine learning model utilises human-given labels to understand fundamental patterns in the model training procedure. The outcome was a trained model that could predict new data. A correctly labelled dataset, seen as an excellent standard in machine learning for training and assessing a provided model, is mainly known as the ground truth. The precision of the trained model will rely on the precision of the ground truth; therefore, spending resources and time to guarantee exact data labelling is vital (Ren et al., 2022).

Linguistic Annotation

Linguistic annotation includes any analytic or descriptive notation implemented in the raw language data. The fundamental data may be in time functions, such as audio, physiological, textual, or video recordings. The added notations may involve transcriptions of all types from discourse structures or phonetic features, syntactic assessment, sense tagging, part-of-speech, co-reference annotation, and entity identification. The emphasis is on tools that have been broadly used for constructing annotated linguistic databases, and on the systems generally implemented by such databases and tools. Linguistic annotation involves tagging a dataset sentence with the subject of every sentence ready for assessment or analysis. The general benefits of linguistically annotated data include natural language processing and sentiment assessment (Garcia-Silva et al., 2021).

Machine Intelligence

Machine intelligence is innovative computing that allows technology, an algorithm, a machine, or a device to connect with its environment intelligently, which means it can make decisions to increase its chances of productively achieving its objectives. The concept of machine intelligence pinpoints the junction of artificial intelligence and machine learning, as well as the broad spectrum of approaches and opportunities in the domain. Machine learning is an umbrella term used to determine the precision of machine learning, classical algorithm output, or deep learning. In business-to-business marketing, the phrase is also being utilised to determine a progressing market domain for information technology supplier experts in artificial intelligence and machine learning as a service. Machine intelligence is developed when machines are programmed with certain characteristics of human intelligence such as learning, prioritisation, and problem solving. With these restricted capabilities, machines can handle complicated sets of problems. Machine intelligence includes deductive logic. For instance, systems depicting actual machine intelligence come to recognise when they have made errors look for similar data that may end up in the same error the next time and evade doing so. This means that machine intelligence will have a set of diversified machine-learning methods accessible to it and a battery of automation methods. It will efficiently prioritise and implement a sequence of them correctly, with the proper time to attain particular business objectives. Machine learning can be thought of as a higher advancement of machine learning with prioritisation and objectives added in a striding stone on the route to actual artificial intelligence (Gupta et al., 2021).

Machine Learning

The subset of artificial intelligence is specifically focused on creating algorithms that will support machines to change and learn new data without the intervention of a human being. Machine learning is a type of artificial intelligence that permits software applications to become more precise in forecasting results without being programmed to do so. Machine-learning algorithms utilise previous data as inputs to forecast new output values. The daily use of machine learning is a recommendation engine. Other well-known benefits include predictive maintenance, spam filtering, business-process automation, fraud detection, and malware risk detection. Machine learning is significant because it provides firms with an opinion of trends in consumer behaviour and business function patterns and helps create the latest products. Many of the present-day top firms, for example, Uber, Google, and Facebook, make machine learning a prime part of their functions. Machine learning has become a vital competitive discriminator for various types of firms. Conventional machine learning is mainly classified based on how precise an algorithm becomes in its forecasts. There are four primary approaches to machine learning: unsupervised, semi-supervised, and reinforcement. The type of algorithm data researchers opt to utilise relies on the type of data they want to forecast (Sircar et al., 2021).

Machine Translation

Machine translation is the procedure of utilising artificial intelligence to translate words automatically from one language that is the source to another, which is the target without any human intervention. Translation was one of the earliest applications of computational power in the early 1950s. Unfortunately, the complexity of the task was much higher than the estimations of former computer scientists, requiring immense data processing power and storage capacity far beyond the abilities of early systems. At the beginning of the 2000s, the software, hardware, and required data were able to perform basic machine translation. Former developers have utilised statistical databases of languages to train computers to translate content. The training of these systems included manual labour and every added language needed, starting with the progress of that language. In 2016, Google had an investigational team that examined the use of neural learning frameworks and artificial intelligence to teach translation engines. The small group's method was examined against Google's fundamental statistical machine translation engine, which proved fast and efficient across various languages. In addition, it was utilised to generate a continuous enhancement in quality. Neural machine translation was also efficient because Google altered its course and implemented it as a fundamental development framework. Other significant providers such as Amazon and Microsoft soon followed, and contemporary machine translation became a feasible addition to translation technology. Various technology management systems now integrate machine translation into their programs for their users' plans (Hasyim et al., 2021).

Model

This is a wide-ranging term concerning artificial intelligence developed by running a machine algorithm on training data. Artificial intelligence is a subdomain in computer science linked with the creation of machines that can imitate human intelligence. An artificial intelligence model is a program that uses a dataset that allows it to understand certain patterns. It permits it to reach a conclusion or make forecasts when given adequate information. Artificial intelligence models use different algorithms to learn and reason from these data, with the primary objective of resolving business issues. Various domains utilise artificial intelligence models with diverse goals and complexities involving computer vision, natural language processing, and robotics. Ultimately, an artificial intelligence model is an artificial intelligence algorithm that runs on training data. It signifies the numbers, rules, or other algorithm-specific data structures needed to forecast untested test data. For example, the decision tree algorithm develops a model containing a tree of if-them assertions, with each forecast on particular values. Currently, deep neural network algorithms develop models with a graph structure consisting of various diversified weights or vectors with specific values (Reis et al., 2021).

Neural Network

Neural networks are also known as neural nets and computer systems that operate similarly to the human mind. Although scientists are still struggling to develop a machine model of a human being's mind, previous neural networks can perform various tasks, such as vision, board game strategy, and vision. A neural network is a system hardware or software that functions similarly to the jobs performed by human brain neurones. Neural networks involve different technologies such as machine learning and deep learning as a segment of artificial intelligence. Many business applications and commercial firms have used these technologies. Their fundamental objective is to resolve complicated problems, such as pattern or facial recognition, and some other apps involve speech-to-text transcription, signal processing, data assessment, weather forecasting, and handwriting recognition for check processing. Neural networks have the extraordinary capability to recover profound data from inaccurate data used to identify exact patterns and trends that are difficult to recognise by humans or computers. A well-trained neural network can be made a specialist in the information that has been provided to assess and can be used to give forecasts (Samek et al., 2021).

Natural Language Generation

It refers to the procedure by which a machine changes structured data to speech or text that human beings can recognise. Natural language generation involves what a machine says or writes as the last segment of a communication procedure. Natural language generation is the process of converting data into natural language. This is done using statistical methods, which assess massive datasets and utilise them to create natural-sounding sentences. Natural language processing can be used in customer service, journalism, financial reporting, and marketing. These systems have the objective of generating text from structured information or knowledge such as ontologies or databases. These systems create natural language in various formats. They can change numbers into narratives depending on preset patterns. They can forecast words that should be generated next. Alternatively, modern systems can create complete summaries, responses, or articles (Meera and Geerthik, 2022). With accurate data in the proper format, a natural language generation system can automatically turn numbers in an Excel spreadsheet narrative or utilise links between words to generate fully or partially machine-generated texts. Natural language generation has been a domain of artificial intelligence research for years, but the most remarkable and beneficial advancements in technology have only recently occurred. A system such as Gmail's Smart Compose now recommends what a person should write next to the email. Subsequently, it learns every time a person selects one of the recommendations. It utilises advanced natural language generation and natural language processing to read emails when a person types them, and then forecasts what the person is trying to write next in actual time (Locke et al., 2021; Tariq, 2024).

Natural Language Processing (NLP)

Natural language processing is an umbrella term for a system's ability to do conversational jobs, such as understanding what is being said, recognising the deliberate context, and replying intelligently. It is a part of artificial intelligence in computer science that emphasises supporting computers in identifying the way human beings speak and write. This is challenging, because it includes a large set of unstructured data. The pattern in which human beings write and take, sometimes known as the tone of voice, is distinctive and consistently changing, reflecting common usage. Comprehending this perspective also requires a semantic assessment for machine learning to manage it. Natural language understanding is a sub-segment of natural language processing that handles these subtleties through machine reading comprehension instead of understanding the exact meanings. The objective of natural language processing and natural language is to support systems that properly recognise human language and communicate naturally. Real-world use cases and applications of natural language processing involve the following:

- Voice-operated virtual assistants such as Alexa or Siri
- Natural language generation for queries replying by customer service chatbots
- Simplifying the hiring procedure on websites such as LinkedIn by scanning through people's abilities and expertise
- Some tools such as Grammarly use natural language processing to assist in the correction of errors and make recommendations for simplifying complicated writing
- Language models, such as autocomplete, are skilled in forecasting successive words, depending on what has already been written (Chen et al., 2021).

All these features enhance the more spoken, written, and communicated with systems, and they keep learning constantly. An excellent example of iterative learning is a feature like Google Translate, which utilises a system known as Google Neural Machine Translate (GNMT). It is a technique that utilises a vast artificial neural network to enhance precision and fluency across languages. Instead of translating one segment of text at a time, GNMT helps translate complete sentences. As GNMT searches millions of examples, it uses a broader context to extract the most appropriate translation. It also explores the similarities between languages instead of developing their universal interlanguage. It is not like the original Google Translate that kept using the lengthy translation procedure from the base language to English before translation to the objective language; GNMT makes use of zero-short translate, which translates directly from the base to the target. Google Translate may not be a good option for medical suggestions; however, natural language processing is broadly used in medical care. This is specifically beneficial for collecting information from electronic health record systems filled with unstructured data. Because of its unstructured nature and the difficulties of using sometimes bulky media, doctors' case comments may be conflicting and naturally utilise many keywords. Natural language processing can support the discovery of improperly coded and missed conditions (Lauriola et al., 2022).

Natural language understanding (NLU)

It is a sub-branch of natural language processing and assists machines in comprehending the intended context of a language, including grammatical mistakes and subtle nuances. Natural-language understanding uses computer software to recognise input sentences using speech or text. Natural language understanding allows for a human-computer interface. Understanding human languages such as English, French, and Spanish permits computers to recognise commands without the syntax of formal computer languages. Natural language understanding also allows computers to interact with humans in their preferred languages. The prime objective of natural language understanding is to develop chat- and voice-enabled bots that can communicate with individuals without guidance. Natural language understanding assesses data to define its context using algorithms to decrease human speech into a structured ontology, a data frame containing pragmatic and semantic definitions. The two primary concepts of natural language understanding are entity and intent recognition (Chen et al., 2021; Tariq, 2024).

Overfitting

Overfitting, an important artificial intelligence terminology, indicates machine learning training in which an algorithm can work on or recognize particular instances existing in the training data. A working framework should use the common trends behind the data to function in new instances. Overfitting occurs when a machine learning framework has become too accustomed to the data on which it is skilled, and hence loses its pertinence to any other dataset. A framework that is overfitted when it is particularly relevant to the actual data that applies it to data collected in the future would result in erroneous or problematic results and make less-than-optimal decisions. Overfitting causes the framework to falsify the data from which it learns. An overfitted model will be less precise on new, same data than a more commonly fitted framework; however, the overfitted model will enhance precision when implemented on the training data. With no safety against overfitting, model creators might train and implement a model they contemplate is highly precise; in fact, it will drift in manufacturing when provided with the new data. Implementing an overfitted model can create all types of issues (Bejani and Ghatee, 2021).

Parameter

Parameter is a variable inside the model that assists in forecasting. Its value can be assessed through data and is mostly not fixed by the individual running the model. In programming, a parameter can be passed on to a function. Parameters may consist of a range of values that are known as a parameter. In machine learning, the model being used is a function that forecasts new data; whether a framework has a variable or fixed number of parameters determines whether it may be known as parametric or nonparametric. Some instances of the model parameters include the following:

- Weights in artificial neural network
- Support vectors in a support vector system
- This involves the coefficients of logistic or linear regression (Danesh, 2021).

Pattern Recognition

The difference between machine learning and pattern recognition is primarily blurry; however, this domain is involved in discovering patterns and trends in data. Pattern recognition is a procedure for finding similarities and regularities in data by utilizing machine-learning information. These similarities can depend on the statistical assessment, previous data, or knowledge previously attained by the machine itself. A pattern is a constancy in the world, or conceptual notion. If sports are discussed, the description is a pattern. If an individual scrolls videos relevant to the cricket, YouTube will not suggest chess tutorials (Prakash & Kanagachidambaresan, 2021). Some examples include speech recognition, automatic medical diagnosis, multimedia document recognition, and speaker identification. Before looking for a pattern, there are some specific steps, the first of which is to accumulate data from the actual world. The accumulated data must be preprocessed and filtered to deduce features from the data. Then, depending on the type of data system, we will opt for a suitable algorithm for classification and regression to understand the pattern. Pattern recognition features are as follows: speed and precision for the familiar object are high-pitched, and they can understand the unknown object. It can recognize various objects and shapes from all angles. It can identify objects and patterns when they are hidden, and during the assessment, they swiftly grab the patterns automatically (Bai et al., 2021).

Predictive Analytics

The type of analytics created to predict what will happen in a given timeline, dependent on previous trends and data, by combining machine learning and data mining is known as predictive analytics. It is a branch of advanced analytics that forecasts future results by utilizing previous data merged with data modelling, data mining methods, and machine learning. Firms implement predictive analytics to discover patterns in these data and recognize opportunities and risks. Predictive analytics is mainly linked to data science and big data. Firms in the present age are spinning data that exist across transactional databases, sensors, pictures, equipment log files, videos, and other data sources. Data experts utilize deep learning and machine learning algorithms to obtain insights from the data, recognize patterns, and forecast future events. These involve linear and nonlinear regression, decision trees, neural networks, and support vector systems. Learnings attained through predictive analysis can be further utilized in perspective analytics to carry out actions dependent on predictive perceptions (Souza & Leung, 2021).

Python

Python is a well-known programming language that is used for general programming. Although it is a common purpose language, Python has made its route into the most complicated technologies, such as machine learning, artificial intelligence, and deep learning. It is a sophisticated language, meaning that tasks can be conceptually developed. Generally, it is lengthy and challenging to recognize that an overview of semantic structures substitutes for programming code structures. A programmer can explain the functions of data structures through the human language, mainly English, using Python. A considerable benefit of Python is that compared to some other programming languages, algorithms have already been prepared, and the language is accessible to people who have never developed any code for artificial intelligence. Python's syntax is clear, and the code is well coordinated. For some individuals, it may look like it is slow, but the primary technique is that most required algorithms for programming have already been developed, and Python makes it more straightforward and quicker to integrate libraries. Artificial intelligence was the main reason for using Python. The advantage of Python is that developers create a program from already functional segments, and these segments are also added. Other languages use the development situation to prepare a project (Shu, 2021). Python is a universal language for artificial intelligence software development, and by using it, a code can be written for Android and iOS, PCs, and smartphones, creating applications and different projects. It does not rely on media and program architecture. Python is a perfect programming language for machine learning. By utilizing various language libraries, beginners can create artificial intelligence. The demand for artificial intelligence software creation and development is progressing each year, suggesting that Python is improving its reputation and enhancing it rapidly. The latest languages that evolve as programming languages cannot drive Python down, possibly because of the number of user-friendly libraries, among other factors. With ever-evolving technology, novel Python libraries have emerged, which is why they are among the leaders in data science development, machine learning, and artificial intelligence (Kumar et al., 2021).

FUTURE RESEARCH DIRECTIONS

Future research in artificial intelligence (AI) and data analysis should focus on several critical areas to enhance the technology's effectiveness and ethical deployment. Key areas include developing methods to detect and mitigate biases in AI algorithms, ensuring fairness and equity across diverse demographic groups, and establishing robust ethical frameworks for responsible AI use. Additionally, advancing explainable AI (XAI) will be crucial for creating models that are transparent and interpretable, fostering trust in AI systems. Research should also prioritize improving the safety and reliability of autonomous systems and enhancing human-AI collaboration. In natural language processing (NLP), efforts should be directed towards better contextual understanding and expanding multilingual capabilities. AI's role in healthcare can be furthered through personalized medicine and predictive analytics. Ensuring data privacy and security, particularly through secure data handling and privacy-preserving algorithms, remains essential. Integrating big data from diverse sources for real-time analytics, enhancing AI-IoT interactions, and focusing on human-centric AI to improve user experience and emotional intelligence will drive the next wave of AI innovations.

CONCLUSION

In this chapter, we have explored various terminologies and concepts related to artificial intelligence, highlighting the profound impact AI has on modern professional and personal lives. The rapid advancements in AI technologies are reshaping industries and daily routines, introducing new vocabulary and concepts that are now integral to our understanding of the digital world. From algorithms and autonomous systems to machine learning and natural language processing, AI continues to drive innovation and efficiency across multiple domains. The integration of big data and AI has revolutionized data analysis, enabling the extraction of valuable insights and the development of predictive models that inform decision-making processes. As AI systems become more sophisticated, they increasingly mimic human cognitive functions, offering solutions to complex problems with unprecedented accuracy and efficiency.

Despite the many benefits, challenges such as bias in AI algorithms and the risk of overfitting highlight the need for careful and ethical implementation of these technologies. The continuous evolution of AI, driven by advancements in computational power and data availability, promises a future where AI not only augments human capabilities but also transforms how we interact with technology and each other. This comprehension of AI's diverse attributes and applications underscores its potential to shape the future positively, ensuring that it remains a pivotal tool in various sectors, from healthcare and finance to education and beyond. As we embrace these innovations, it is crucial to remain vigilant about the ethical implications and strive for AI systems that are fair, transparent, and beneficial to all.

REFERENCES

Ahmed, S. I., Radhakrishnan, S., Nair, B. B., & Thiruvengadathan, R. (2021). Efficient hyperparameter-tuned machine learning approach for estimation of supercapacitor performance attributes. *Journal of Physics Communications*, 5(11), 115011. DOI:10.1088/2399-6528/ac3574

Al-Sartawi, M. (2021). *Big Data-Driven Digital Economy: Artificial and Computational Intelligence*. Springer. DOI:10.1007/978-3-030-73057-4

Anwar, M. (2021). Designing an expert system for determining student learning styles using forward chaining in engineering education. *Jurnal Konseling dan Pendidikan, 9*(1), 93-101.

Arabnia, H. R., Ferens, K., de la Fuente, D., Kozerenko, E. B., Varela, J. A. O., & Tinetti, F. G. (2021). *Advances in Artificial Intelligence and Applied Cognitive Computing*. Springer International Publishing. DOI:10.1007/978-3-030-70296-0

Bai, X., Wang, X., Liu, X., Liu, Q., Song, J., Sebe, N., & Kim, B. (2021). Explainable deep learning for efficient and robust pattern recognition: A survey of recent developments. *Pattern Recognition*, 120, 108102. DOI:10.1016/j.patcog.2021.108102

Bejani, M. M., & Ghatee, M. (2021). A systematic review on overfitting control in shallow and deep neural networks. *Artificial Intelligence Review*, 54(8), 6391–6438. DOI:10.1007/s10462-021-09975-1

Bryson, J., & Winfield, A. (2017). Standardizing ethical design for artificial intelligence and autonomous systems. *Computer*, 50(5), 116–119. DOI:10.1109/MC.2017.154

Chen, J. S., Tran-Thien-Y, L., & Florence, D. (2021). Usability and responsiveness of artificial intelligence chatbot on online customer experience in e-retailing. *International Journal of Retail & Distribution Management*, 49(11), 1512–1531. DOI:10.1108/IJRDM-08-2020-0312

Chen, M., Zhang, H., Ning, Q., Li, M., Ji, H., McKeown, K., & Roth, D. (2021). Event-centric natural language understanding. *Proceedings of the 59th Annual Meeting of the Association for Computational Linguistics.*

Chen, Q., Leaman, R., Allot, A., Luo, L., Wei, C. H., Yan, S., & Lu, Z. (2021). Artificial intelligence in action: Addressing the COVID-19 pandemic with natural language processing. *Annual Review of Biomedical Data Science*, 4(1), 313–339. DOI:10.1146/annurev-biodatasci-021821-061045 PMID:34465169

Cheng, Y., & Jiang, H. (2021). Customer–brand relationship in the era of artificial intelligence: Understanding the role of chatbot marketing efforts. *Journal of Product and Brand Management*.

Choi, D., & Lee, S. (2021). Comparison of machine learning algorithms for predicting lane changing intent. *International Journal of Automotive Technology*, 22(2), 507–518. DOI:10.1007/s12239-021-0047-x

Danesh, M. H. (2021, May). Reducing Neural Network Parameter Initialization Into an SMT Problem (Student Abstract). *Proceedings of the AAAI Conference on Artificial Intelligence*, 35(18), 15775–15776. DOI:10.1609/aaai.v35i18.17884

De Stefano, V. (2019). "Negotiating the Algorithm": Automation, Artificial Intelligence, and Labor Protection. *Comp. Lab. L. & Pol'y J.*, 41, 15.

Dogan, A., & Birant, D. (2021). Machine learning and data mining in manufacturing. *Expert Systems with Applications*, 166, 114060. DOI:10.1016/j.eswa.2020.114060

Dong, B., Huang, Z., Guo, Y., Wang, Q., Niu, Z., & Zuo, W. (2021). Boosting Weakly Supervised Object Detection via Learning Bounding Box Adjusters. In *Proceedings of the IEEE/CVF International Conference on Computer Vision* (pp. 2876-2885). DOI:10.1109/ICCV48922.2021.00287

Finlayson, S. G., Subbaswamy, A., Singh, K., Bowers, J., Kupke, A., Zittrain, J., Kohane, I. S., & Saria, S. (2021). The clinician and dataset shift in artificial intelligence. *The New England Journal of Medicine*, 385(3), 283–286. DOI:10.1056/NEJMc2104626 PMID:34260843

Gao, P., Li, J., & Liu, S. (2021). An introduction to key technology in artificial intelligence and big data driven e-learning and e-education. *Mobile Networks and Applications*, 26(5), 2123–2126. DOI:10.1007/s11036-021-01777-7

Garcia-Silva, A., Denaux, R., & Gomez-Perez, J. M. (2021). On the impact of knowledge-based linguistic annotations in the quality of scientific embeddings. *Future Generation Computer Systems*, 120, 26–35. DOI:10.1016/j.future.2021.02.019

Gupta, R., Srivastava, D., Sahu, M., Tiwari, S., Ambasta, R. K., & Kumar, P. (2021). Artificial intelligence to deep learning: Machine intelligence approach for drug discovery. *Molecular Diversity*, 25(3), 1315–1360. DOI:10.1007/s11030-021-10217-3 PMID:33844136

Hasyim, M., Saleh, F., Yusuf, R., & Abbas, A. (2021). Artificial Intelligence: Machine Translation Accuracy in Translating French-Indonesian Culinary Texts. *Available atSSRN* 3816594.

He, L., Bai, L., Dionysiou, D. D., Wei, Z., Spinney, R., Chu, C., Lin, Z., & Xiao, R. (2021). Applications of computational chemistry, artificial intelligence, and machine learning in aquatic chemistry research. *Chemical Engineering Journal*, 426, 131810. DOI:10.1016/j.cej.2021.131810

Janjanam, D., Ganesh, B., & Manjunatha, L. (2021, February). Design of an expert system architecture: An overview. *Journal of Physics: Conference Series*, 1767(1), 012036. DOI:10.1088/1742-6596/1767/1/012036

Jena, B., Saxena, S., Nayak, G. K., Saba, L., Sharma, N., & Suri, J. S. (2021). Artificial intelligence-based hybrid deep learning models for image classification: The first narrative review. *Computers in Biology and Medicine*, 137, 104803. DOI:10.1016/j.compbiomed.2021.104803 PMID:34536856

Kumar, M., Sharma, S., Chaudhary, D., & Prakash, S. (2021, March). Image Recognition Using Artificial Intelligence. In *2021 International Conference on Advance Computing and Innovative Technologies in Engineering (ICACITE)* (pp. 760-763). IEEE.

Lauriola, I., Lavelli, A., & Aiolli, F. (2022). An introduction to deep learning in natural language processing: Models, techniques, and tools. *Neurocomputing*, 470, 443–456. DOI:10.1016/j.neucom.2021.05.103

Locke, S., Bashall, A., Al-Adely, S., Moore, J., Wilson, A., & Kitchen, G. B. (2021). Natural language processing in medicine: A review. *Trends in Anaesthesia & Critical Care*, 38, 4–9. DOI:10.1016/j.tacc.2021.02.007

Lytras, M. D., & Visvizi, A. (2021). Artificial intelligence and cognitive computing: Methods, technologies, systems, applications and policy making. *Sustainability (Basel)*, 13(7), 3598. DOI:10.3390/su13073598

Ma, Y., Wang, Z., Yang, H., & Yang, L. (2020). Artificial intelligence applications in the development of autonomous vehicles: a survey. *IEEE/CAA Journal of Automatica Sinica,* 7(2), 315-329.

Meera, S., & Geerthik, S. (2022). Natural language processing. *Artificial Intelligent Techniques for Wireless Communication and Networking*, 139-153.

Nelson, G. S. (2019). Bias in artificial intelligence. *North Carolina Medical Journal*, 80(4), 220–222. DOI:10.18043/ncm.80.4.220 PMID:31278182

Parikh, R. B., Teeple, S., & Navathe, A. S. (2019). Addressing bias in artificial intelligence in health care. *Journal of the American Medical Association*, 322(24), 2377–2378. DOI:10.1001/jama.2019.18058 PMID:31755905

Prakash, K. B., & Kanagachidambaresan, G. R. (2021). Pattern Recognition and Machine Learning. In *Programming with TensorFlow* (pp. 105–144). Springer. DOI:10.1007/978-3-030-57077-4

Reis, T., Bornschlegl, M. X., & Hemmje, M. L. (2021). Toward a Reference Model for Artificial Intelligence Supporting Big Data Analysis. In *Advances in Data Science and Information Engineering* (pp. 561–572). Springer. DOI:10.1007/978-3-030-71704-9_38

Ren, Y., Xu, N., Ling, M., & Geng, X. (2022). Label distribution for multimodal machine learning. *Frontiers of Computer Science*, 16(1), 1–11. DOI:10.1007/s11704-021-0611-6

Sakharov, A. (2021). A Best-first Backward-chaining Search Strategy based on Learned Predicate Representations. In *ICAART (2)* (pp. 982-989). DOI:10.5220/0010299209820989

Samek, W., Montavon, G., Lapuschkin, S., Anders, C. J., & Müller, K. R. (2021). Explaining deep neural networks and beyond: A review of methods and applications. *Proceedings of the IEEE*, 109(3), 247–278. DOI:10.1109/JPROC.2021.3060483

Sarker, I. H., Hoque, M. M., Uddin, M., & Alsanoosy, T. (2021). Mobile data science and intelligent apps: Concepts, ai-based modeling and research directions. *Mobile Networks and Applications*, 26(1), 285–303. DOI:10.1007/s11036-020-01650-z

Shang, Y., Nguyen, H., Bui, X. N., Tran, Q. H., & Moayedi, H. (2020). A novel artificial intelligence approach to predict blast-induced ground vibration in open-pit mines based on the firefly algorithm and artificial neural network. *Natural Resources Research*, 29(2), 723–737. DOI:10.1007/s11053-019-09503-7

Shu, W. (2021, April). Combined Forecasting Model Method Based on Python and Artificial Intelligence Algorithm. In *International Conference on Application of Intelligent Systems in Multi-modal Information Analytics* (pp. 636-643). Springer, Cham. DOI:10.1007/978-3-030-74811-1_91

Sircar, A., Yadav, K., Rayavarapu, K., Bist, N., & Oza, H. (2021). *Application of machine learning and artificial intelligence in oil and gas industry*. Petroleum Research. DOI:10.1016/j.ptlrs.2021.05.009

Souza, J., & Leung, C. K. (2021). Explainable Artificial Intelligence for Predictive Analytics on Customer Turnover: A User-Friendly Interface for Non-expert Users. In *Explainable AI Within the Digital Transformation and Cyber Physical Systems* (pp. 47–67). Springer. DOI:10.1007/978-3-030-76409-8_4

Sunil, A., Sheth, M. H., & Shreyas, E. (2021, September). Usual and Unusual Human Activity Recognition in Video using Deep Learning and Artificial Intelligence for Security Applications. In *2021 Fourth International Conference on Electrical, Computer and Communication Technologies (ICECCT)* (pp. 1-6). IEEE. DOI:10.1109/ICECCT52121.2021.9616791

Tariq, M. U. (2024). Multi-Agent Models in Healthcare System Design. In Dall'Acqua, L. (Ed.), *Bioethics of Cognitive Ergonomics and Digital Transition* (pp. 143–170). IGI Global. DOI:10.4018/979-8-3693-2667-1.ch008

Wang, D. (2021, March). Construction of Knowledge Graph Corpus Under the Framework of Artificial Intelligence. In *The International Conference on Cyber Security Intelligence and Analytics* (pp. 41-48). Springer. DOI:10.1007/978-3-030-69999-4_6

Wong, C. H. (2021). *Applications of Data Science and Artificial Intelligence to Decision Making in Healthcare and Finance* (Doctoral dissertation, Massachusetts Institute of Technology).

Yang, Y. C., Islam, S. U., Noor, A., Khan, S., Afsar, W., & Nazir, S. (2021). Influential usage of big data and artificial intelligence in healthcare. *Computational and Mathematical Methods in Medicine*, 2021, 2021. DOI:10.1155/2021/5812499 PMID:34527076

Zhang, C., & Lu, Y. (2021). Study on artificial intelligence: The state of the art and future prospects. *Journal of Industrial Information Integration*, 23, 100224. DOI:10.1016/j.jii.2021.100224

Zhao, T., Yan, Z., Cao, Y., & Li, Z. (2021, January). Asking effective and diverse questions: a machine reading comprehension based framework for joint entity-relation extraction. In *Proceedings of the Twenty-Ninth International Conference on International Joint Conferences on Artificial Intelligence* (pp. 3948-3954).

ADDITIONAL READING

Abonamah, A. A., Tariq, M. U., & Shilbayeh, S. (2021). On the commoditization of artificial intelligence. *Frontiers in Psychology*, 12, 696346. Advance online publication. DOI:10.3389/fpsyg.2021.696346 PMID:34659012

Ashfaq, M., Khan, I., Alzahrani, A., Tariq, M. U., Khan, H., & Ghani, A. (2024). Accurate wheat yield prediction using machine learning and climate-NDVI data fusion. *IEEE Access : Practical Innovations, Open Solutions*, 12, 40947–40961. DOI:10.1109/ACCESS.2024.3376735

Babar, M., Khattak, A. S., Jan, M. A., & Tariq, M. U. (2021). Energy aware smart city management system using data analytics and internet of things. *Sustainable Energy Technologies and Assessments*, 44, 100992. Advance online publication. DOI:10.1016/j.seta.2021.100992

Chapter 2
Applied AI vs. Theoretical AI

ABSTRACT

Artificial intelligence (AI) has become a powerful force in today's society, economy, and industry. In this chapter, the authors set out to investigate the dynamic interaction between two essential components of artificial intelligence: theoretical AI and applied AI. The chapter begins with an introduction to the fundamental ideas behind artificial intelligence (AI), tracing its roots back to Alan Turing's ground-breaking work and the continuing impact of the Turing Test. It clarifies the various definitions and objectives of AI, separating systems that imitate human knowledge and thought from those more concerned with imitating human behaviour. The investigation of Applied AI, an area of AI that focuses on real-world problem solving, is a key theme of this chapter. In this study, the authors clarify the essential rules governing the application of AI concepts and technology to actual business problems. This chapter emphasises the crucial abilities and knowledge needed to succeed in this discipline. In essence, applied AI converts theoretical knowledge into useful solutions.

INTRODUCTION

Artificial intelligence (AI), a fast-developing field, aims to create intelligent computers with cognitive capacities similar to those of humans. It includes a variety of methods, strategies, and algorithms that allow computers to carry out operations such as speech recognition, problem solving, and learning that otherwise require human intellect. The work of British mathematician and computer scientist Alan Turing is responsible for one of the turning points in the development of artificial intelligence. 1950 In his seminal work "Computing Machinery and Intelligence", Turing laid the groundwork for the development of artificial intelligence. Turing explored the potential of machines to exhibit intelligent behaviour and introduced

DOI: 10.4018/979-8-3693-4074-5.ch002

the concept of a test that could determine the machine's ability to mimic human intelligence. The Turing Test constituted a crucial turning point in the advancement of AI. According to the Turing Test, a computer is deemed artificially intelligent if it can behave intelligently during a conversation that cannot be distinguished from that of a person. This examination spurred discussions about the definition of intelligence and established a standard for assessing AI programs.

Thinking Humanly

This viewpoint attempts to create AI systems that can imitate human thoughts and reasoning. It aims to comprehend and imitate human intelligence to build robots that can think, comprehend, and solve problems comparable to those of humans.

Acting Humanly

This concept of AI focuses on creating systems capable of carrying out activities or displaying behaviours identical to those of humans. To enable seamless contact between humans and robots, machines can be built to mimic human movements, emotions, and reactions.

Reasoning Logically

This approach to AI strongly emphasises the creation of systems that can logically reason. It focuses on formalising human thinking into logical frameworks and algorithms so that robots can make defensible conclusions and handle challenging issues.

Behaving Rationally

This definition of AI emphasises the creation of systems that can act reasonably, even when the behaviour differs from that of humans. It does not matter if the outcomes resemble human behaviour; the goal is to build robots to make the best choices possible in light of information and objectives. These four AI definitions and aims emphasise the many viewpoints and goals of the area. While some researchers prioritise imitating human intellect, others prioritise creating systems that behave logically or successfully carry out particular jobs. The ultimate objective of artificial intelligence is to build smart machines that can supplement human talents, increase productivity, and spur innovation in various fields.

BACKGROUND OF APPLIED AI THEORETICAL AI

Artificial intelligence (AI) has become a powerful force for change, transforming many sectors and altering how people live and work. There is a division between theoretical AI and applied AI within artificial intelligence. While theoretical AI focuses on the underlying ideas and concepts that underlie AI algorithms and models, applied AI concentrates on practically using AI approaches to address real-world issues. This essay examines the distinctions between theoretical and applied artificial intelligence (AI), emphasizing each field's advantages and disadvantages and the critical need to close the gap between theory and application (Tariq, 2024).

Recognising Applied AI

Applied AI uses AI technologies to provide workable answers to problems in various fields. This area of artificial intelligence utilizes current AI models and algorithms to address real-world challenges. To create systems that can perform tasks, such as picture recognition, voice synthesis, recommendation systems, autonomous cars, machine learning, natural language processing, computer vision, and other AI approaches are applied. The application of AI-powered chatbots to customer service is a famous example of Applied AI. Chatbots are used by businesses such as Amazon, Apple, and Google to answer consumer questions, provide tailored suggestions, and speed up online transactions. To comprehend and respond to user enquiries, these chatbots use natural language processing algorithms. This improves customer experience and streamlines company processes.

Exposing Theoretical AI

The development of AI algorithms and models is guided by the theoretical foundations and principles, which are the focus of theoretical AI. It seeks to comprehend the basic ideas that underlie AI, including machine learning algorithms, neural networks, and optimization methods. The study of theoretical AI explores the underlying mathematical, statistical, and computational ideas. Theoretical research on deep learning has improved speech recognition, natural language processing, and computer vision. The theoretical foundation of deep learning has enabled real-world applications such as autonomous driving and medical diagnostics.

AI-Driven Personalised Learning

Personalised learning refers to instructional approaches tailored to the unique needs, interests, and abilities of students. AI-driven personalised learning systems adapt content delivery based on real-time data on a student's performance, providing a customised learning experience. Platforms such as Knewton and DreamBox use complex algorithms to analyse student interactions and adapt the content accordingly. These systems assess student performance, identify learning gaps, and adjust the level of difficulty of optimising learning (Tariq, 2024; Raimi et al., 2022).

Knewton's adaptive learning technology has been implemented in various educational institutions and has demonstrated improved engagement and academic outcomes. By tailoring the educational content to individual needs, Knewton ensures that students receive an appropriate level of challenge and support. ITS, such as Carnegie Learning and ALEKS, offer personalised tutoring by providing immediate feedback and tailored hints. These systems use AI to simulate the benefits of one-on-one tutoring, thereby enhancing learning efficiency. For example, Carnegie Learning's ITS analyzes student responses to provide instant feedback and customised hints, helping students understand complex concepts more thoroughly.

Real-Time Feedback and Assessment

Real-time feedback and assessments are critical components of effective teaching and learning. AI technologies enable educators to provide instant feedback, helping students correct errors and improve their understanding immediately. Tools, such as Gradescope and Turnitin, use AI to automate the grading process and provide timely feedback to students. These systems not only save time for educators but also ensure consistency and objectivity in grading. Gradescope's AI-driven grading system allows educators to grade assignments quickly and consistently, providing students with detailed feedback that helps them learn from their mistakes (Tariq, 2024).

AI-powered formative assessments offer a continuous evaluation of student performance, allowing for timely intervention. These assessments help educators identify at-risk students and provide targeted support to improve learning outcomes. ALEKS uses AI to deliver formative assessments that adapt to each student's knowledge level, providing personalised learning paths and immediate feedback (Niemine et al., 2023).

Collaborative Learning Environments

AI fosters collaborative learning environments by enabling communication and interaction between students. AI-driven tools support group work, discussions, and collaborative projects, thus enhancing peer-to-peer learning. Platforms, such as Zoom and Microsoft Teams, integrate AI features to facilitate virtual classrooms, enabling real-time interaction and collaboration among students and instructors. Zoom's AI capabilities include automated transcription and real-time language translation, which makes virtual classrooms more accessible and inclusive. AI-powered discussion forums, such as those integrated into learning management systems like Edmodo and Moodle, promote collaborative learning by allowing students to share ideas, ask questions, and engage in academic discussions. Edmodo's discussion forums enable students to collaborate on assignments, share resources, and provide peer feedback, thus fostering a sense of community and engagement (Deeva et al., 2021).

Closing the Gap: The Importance of Cooperation

It is critical to close the gap between theory and practice, even if Applied AI and Theoretical AI are distinct. Cooperation between researchers, practitioners, and industry specialists is crucial to ensure that theoretical developments are transferred into practical applications. A few factors make closing the gap important:

1. Practical Implementation: To obtain real-world advantages, theoretical developments in AI must be transformed into usable applications. Cooperation between theorists and practitioners creates effective, scalable, and dependable AI systems.
2. Ethical Considerations: As AI develops, ethical questions regarding its use have become more apparent. By bridging the theoretical and practical divide, the ethical implications of AI can be fully understood, allowing for the creation of fair and impartial AI systems. Collaboration between theorists and practitioners promotes innovation and creation of new AI methodologies.
3. Innovation and Adaptability. Theoretical developments can spark new applications and theoretical research can be steered by practical knowledge to address pressing issues.

Case Studies: Successful Fusion of Theoretical and Applied AI

Let us look at a few example studies where the merging of Applied AI and Theoretical AI has produced remarkable results to further highlight the significance of closing the gap between the two:

a. AlphaGo: In 2016, Lee Sedol, the reigning world champion of Go, was beaten by DeepMind's AlphaGo. The combination of theoretical developments in deep learning and reinforcement learning with actual implementation has led to the success of AlphaGo. Theoretical research on deep learning was the basis for building the neural network, whereas practical approaches allowed the machine to play the game well. AlphaGo's success was rooted in advancements in deep learning and reinforcement learning. Deep learning, a branch of machine learning based on neural networks, provided the theoretical framework for AlphaGo. This approach involves training artificial neural networks on vast amounts of data, allowing the system to learn complex patterns and make informed decisions. For Go, a game known for its complexity and strategic depth, this meant AlphaGo could evaluate numerous potentials moves and their outcomes far more effectively than traditional methods.
b. Healthcare Diagnostics: Theoretical and Applied AI have been integrated to completely transform medical diagnostics. Researchers have created AI models that can accurately identify illnesses by analyzing medical images such as X-rays and MRIs. Deep learning algorithms have advanced tremendously, and their application in healthcare facilities has resulted in earlier identification and better patient outcomes. For instance, deep learning algorithms can analyze imaging data to spot early stages of diseases like cancer, often before they are visible to radiologists. This capability is particularly valuable in detecting conditions at a stage when treatment options are more effective, thereby improving patient outcomes and potentially saving lives. The practical application of these AI technologies in healthcare settings has led to a new era of diagnostic accuracy and efficiency. Hospitals and clinics are increasingly employing AI-powered tools to support radiologists and clinicians, enabling them to make informed decisions and tailor treatments to individual patient needs.

HUMAN APPROACH TO AI

Understanding how artificial intelligence (AI) systems imitate human cognitive processes and behaviours is essential for the constantly developing field of AI. Systems thinking and acting as humans are two key facets of the Human Approach to AI. These aspects provide insight into the subtleties of human-AI interaction and illuminate how AI aims to mimic the cognitive and behavioural features of human intelligence.

Systems Thinking as Humans

The concept of Systems Thinking as Humans delves into the cognitive processes AI systems aim to emulate. It revolves around the idea that AI should possess the capacity to think and reason like humans do. This facet of AI explores the depth of human cognition from logical reasoning to abstract thinking, and seeks to imbue AI systems with similar capabilities. At its core, Systems Thinking as Humans is about endowing AI with the ability to analyse complex problems, make decisions based on available data, and adapt to changing circumstances. It encompasses various cognitive functions, including problem-solving, critical thinking, and pattern recognition. By replicating these cognitive processes, AI systems can navigate uncertain and dynamic environments, making them indispensable in various domains from healthcare to finance.

At its core, Systems Thinking as Humans is about endowing AI with the ability to analyse complex problems, make decisions based on available data, and adapt to changing circumstances. It encompasses various cognitive functions, including problem-solving, critical thinking, and pattern recognition. By replicating these cognitive processes, AI systems can navigate uncertain and dynamic environments, making them indispensable in various domains from healthcare to finance. AI systems can traverse unpredictable and dynamic settings by simulating these cognitive processes, making them important in various industries from banking to healthcare. Utilising the capabilities of deep learning models, neural networks, and machine learning algorithms is essential in the quest for systems thinking like humans. With the aid of these technologies, AI systems can recognise subtle patterns, learn from massive amounts of information, and act independently. AI systems can help people solve complicated issues by providing insightful information and suggestions to exploit their superior cognitive abilities.

Nevertheless, it is not as easy to achieve Systems Thinking as Humans. However, it is still extremely difficult to replicate the complex and context-sensitive characteristics of human cognition. Artificial intelligence (AI) systems must contend with the ambiguity that permeates human decision making, where elements such as emotions and ethical concerns frequently emerge. AI research is always working to find a balance between simulating human-like reasoning and guaranteeing impartial and reasonable results.

Systems Acting as Humans

Systems Acting as Humans examine the behavioral component of AI, whereas Systems Thinking as Humans focuses on its cognitive elements. This aspect of AI is concerned with allowing robots to interact with the environment and people in a way similar to human actions and behaviors. It includes a wide spectrum of applications, ranging from virtual assistants to robots, and systems Acting as Humans aims to provide AI systems with the ability to properly detect and react to their surroundings. This covers activities such as comprehending a normal language, recognizing gestures, and even physical dexterity. The objective is to develop AI systems that can interact with people and traverse the real world, thereby bridging the gap between machines and people. These AI-powered machines can comprehend spoken language, determine user intent, and carry out orders that mimic how people communicate with one another. Similarly, AI-driven robots in robotics are designed to carry out jobs that require manual dexterity, such as helping with hospital surgery or assembling items in manufacturing facilities.

Importantly, systems that act as humans go beyond simple imitation. AI systems must comprehend the context, adjust to user preferences, and deliver individualized experiences. With this degree of sophistication, AI can improve user utility and engagement across various applications, from customer care chatbots offering personalized suggestions to autonomous cars safely negotiating complex traffic conditions. However, attaining systems that act as humans has their own unique set of difficulties. To interpret natural language, AI systems must recognize the subtleties of human speech, such as slang, humor, and cultural allusions. Similarly, a thorough examination of ethical and social ramifications is necessary to ensure safe and ethical deployment of AI-driven robots in real-world settings. The Human Approach to AI, which includes Systems Thinking as Humans and Systems Acting as Humans, reflects a multifaceted effort to mimic the subtleties of human cognition and behavior in robots. The potential of AI systems to comprehend people and interact with them in more complicated and meaningful ways is held by the harmonious integration of these aspects, even if advancements are still being made in this area.

Ideal Approach

The definition provided by Alan Turing falls under a group of systems acting like humans. In its basic form, artificial intelligence is a domain that merges robust datasets and computer science for problem-solving (Ouyang & Jiao, 2021). It also includes subdomains of deep learning and machine learning, which are often mentioned in combination with artificial intelligence. These subjects are encompassed by artificial intelligence algorithms that seek to create expert systems that can classify and predict according to the input data. Currently, artificial intelligence is still surrounded by much hype, which is anticipated to be a novel emerging technology in the market. Product innovations such as personal assistants and self-driving cars follow a steady evolution of innovation from fanatism through a period of discouragement to an ultimate recognition of the innovation's significance and role in a domain or market (Cui & Zhang, 2021). Pursuing the Ideal Approach in artificial intelligence (AI) comprises two essential dimensions: rational thinking and acting. These features encapsulate the desire to develop AI systems with high efficiency and logic in addition to cognitive and behavioral characteristics similar to those of humans.

Systems Rational Thinking

The system-rational approach to AI is based on rational thinking. The basic idea is to provide AI systems with the ability to reason logically and rationally. By enabling AI to reason perfectly, accurately analyze massive datasets, and find the best answers, this dimension aims to go beyond the constraints of human cognition. Systems Rational Thinking is fundamentally about using AI's computing capability to carry out tasks beyond human ability. This involves real-time processing and interpretation of enormous amounts of data, pattern recognition of sophisticated patterns, and decision making based on statistical probability. AI systems perform best in financial markets, medical diagnosis, and scientific research, where logical data-driven analysis is crucial.

The capacity of AI in Systems Rational Thinking to eliminate subjectivity and prejudice from decision-making processes is one of its main advantages. AI systems may reach objective conclusions by relying on actual data and mathematical models, which minimize the influence of human cognitive biases and mistakes. This aspect emphasizes how AI has the power to improve decision-making across a variety of fields. Systems Rational Thinking, however, does not come without difficulties. Particularly in situations where the results are probabilistic rather than deterministic, AI systems must deal with the complexities of uncertainty and probabilistic reasoning. As rationality must align with ethical norms and societal values, assuring the ethical use of AI-driven decision making also remains an issue.

Systems Rational Acting

Associated Systems Systems Rational acting, a dimension that emphasizes the behavioral features of AI, is rational thinking. Systems' Rational Acting adopts a more practical approach, whereas Systems Acting as Humans attempt to mimic human behavior. It entails creating AI systems with high effectiveness, accuracy, and purpose, motivated by logical decision making. In autonomous systems and robotics, AI-driven entities perform tasks with the greatest precision and the least amount of resource waste. This is an example of a system's rational actions. For instance, autonomous cars use the best paths to negotiate difficult traffic circumstances while using the least amount of fuel and time possible. Robots driven by AI in manufacturing perform jobs with millimeter-level accuracy and streamline production procedures.

Additionally, systems rational accounting in business and logistics entails coordinating resources such as supply chain optimization and resource allocation. Complex logistical processes are expertly managed by AI systems, making real-time decisions to maximize effectiveness, reduce costs, and improve overall performance. However, implementing rational accounting systems has challenges. AI algorithms must be adjusted to balance effectiveness and flexibility, as inflexible optimization may impede responses to changing settings. Additionally, ethical issues must be considered since AI systems must follow moral standards while pursuing logical goals.

The search for AI systems that combine cognitive capacities akin to those of humans, with an increased sense of rationality and efficiency, is symbolized by the Ideal Approach to AI, which entails systems of rational thinking and systems of rational accounting. This method emphasizes the potential of AI to improve rational decision-making and optimize processes across various disciplines, eventually transforming how humans engage with and utilize technology reasonably and effectively, even as it continues to develop.

TYPES OF ARTIFICIAL INTELLIGENCE–STRONG ARTIFICIAL INTELLIGENCE AND WEAK ARTIFICIAL INTELLIGENCE

Narrow Artificial Intelligence, also known as weak artificial intelligence, is an artificial intelligence focused on and trained to perform particular tasks. Weak artificial intelligence derives much of the artificial intelligence in the present world. Narrow is a much correct signifier for this kind of artificial intelligence as it is whatsoever but weak; it allows some very robust applications, such as Amazon's Alexa, autonomous vehicles, Apple's Siri, and IBM Watson. Strong artificial intelligence has evolved from artificial intelligence (ASI) and Artificial General

Intelligence (AGI). General Artificial Intelligence is a theoretical form of artificial intelligence in which a machine may consist of intelligence similar to humans (Saheb et al., 2022). It would have a consciousness about self-awareness that can solve problems, learn, and make plans for the future. Artificial super-intelligence, known as super-intelligence-would, exceeds the intelligence and capability of the human brain. However, strong artificial intelligence is still completely theoretical with no applied instances in use in the present world, which does not mean artificial intelligence scholars are not discovering its development (Gunasekeran et al., 2021).

Machine Learning vs. Deep Learning

As machine learning and deep learning are utilised interchangeably, it is worth noting the shades between them. As stated above, both machine learning and deep learning are subdomains of deep learning, and artificial intelligence is a subdomain of machine learning. Deep learning consists of neural networks (NNs). The term "deep" in deep learning denotes a neural network consisting of more than three layers, which would be all-encompassing of the output, and inputs can be considered as a deep learning algorithm (Berente et al., 2021). It is commonly represented by the following equation:

How does machine learning and deep learning vary? The answer to this question is how each algorithm learns. Deep learning automates the feature extraction part of the procedure, eradicating some of the manual human involvement needed and allowing the use of big data sets. Deep learning can be considered as scalable machine learning (Eltweri, 2021). Nondeep or classical machine learning is more reliable for human involvement in learning. Human specialists regulate the pyramid of features to recognise alterations between data inputs, mostly requiring more structured data to learn. Deep machine learning can control labelled datasets, also called supervised learning, to notify its algorithm; however, it does not require a labelled dataset. It can use unstructured data in its raw forms, such as images and text, and it can automatically determine the pyramid of features that differentiate various data types from each other. In contrast to machine learning, human involvement is not required to work on data, permitting people to take advantage of machine learning in more compelling ways (Finlayson et al., 2021).

Applications of Artificial Intelligence

Currently, there are various real-world applications of Artificial Intelligence systems in the present world. The following are some of the most well-known examples:

Speech Recognition

This is also called automatic speech recognition (ASR), speech-to-text recognition, or computer speech recognition. It is an ability that utilises natural language processing to process human language in a written format. Various smartphones integrate speech recognition into their systems to conduct voice searches, such as Siri, or offer more approachability around texting (Crawford, 2021).

Customer Service

Web-based virtual agents substitute for human representatives during their consumer journey. They reply to frequently asked questions (FAQs) about subjects such as shipping or offering customised advice, cross-selling products, and recommending sizes for customers, altering the method of thinking about customer engagement across social media podiums and websites. Instances involve messaging bots on e-business websites with virtual agents, messaging applications such as Facebook Messenger and Slack, and tasks mostly performed by virtual and voice assistants (Zeba et al., 2021).

Computer Vision

Artificial intelligence technology allows systems and computers to extract evocative information from digital videos, images, and other visual inputs and can take action depending on those inputs. This capability to offer suggestions differentiates it from image recognition tasks. Power-driven by convolutional neural networks, computer vision has applications in photo tagging on social media websites, self-driving cars in the automobile industry, and radiology imaging in medical care (Gupta et al., 2021).

Suggestion Engines

Artificial intelligence algorithms can help discover data trends using past consumption behaviour data, which can help develop more efficient cross-selling strategies. It is used to provide optional suggestions to consumers in the checkout process for online retailers (Thiebes et al., 2021).

Automated Stock Trading

Artificial Intelligence-driven high-frequency trading media make thousands and millions of trades daily with no human involvement, designed to enhance stock portfolios (Ahmad et al., 2021). However, the concept of intelligence involves various identifications. Logical properties, even though they affect the subject of human thought of intelligence. Therefore, Artificial Intelligence theory requires determining the boundary of its empirical evidence directly related to Artificial Intelligence and which of them are not (Pan & Zhang, 2021).

Applied Artificial Intelligence

Among the flourishing domains in the subject of Data Science is Artificial Intelligence. Although familiarity with the mathematical and theoretical characteristics of Artificial Intelligence is not sufficient to emerge with any perceptible outcomes, it is domineering to know how to use Artificial Intelligence. As the subject of Statistics, Applied Statistics manages the practical use of all its ideas. Similarly, when it comes to artificial intelligence, there is a distinct domain of study called Applied Artificial Intelligence that works by utilising the different concepts of artificial intelligence and emerging with diversified programs, software, and applications that resolve several business problems (Alhayani et al., 2021). The precondition for understanding applied artificial intelligence is to first know about it. Among the millions of definitions available, the basic knowledge of artificial intelligence is a subset of Data Science that attempts to resolve many business problems that are mostly predictive by nature with the use of Machine Learning and Deep Learning. Suppose the Artificial Intelligence model utilises Deep Learning, and this is something that Artificial Intelligence is relevant most of the time (Santoro et al., 2021). In this case, the idea of multilayered numeral networks emerges, where different weights are utilised to twist the model and make it more exact. At this point, a layout that imitates the functioning of the human mind was used. Therefore, instead of statistical, rule-based, problematic, or traditional models (hyperplane-based methods), deep learning algorithms utilise neurones to generate results. Even though a person should remember that Machine Learning which is mostly treated as a distinct domain of study, can also create a part of Artificial Intelligence, as is most of the time quoted, when people discuss machine learning in a broad context, they are discussing artificial intelligence only. The framework functions under supervised, unsupervised, and semi-supervised learning setups, unlike deep learning frameworks that function in a reinforcement learning setup (Roberts et al., 2022).

With the definition of Artificial Intelligence being clear, it has become much simpler to recognise the definition of applied artificial intelligence (Rana et al., 2021). Knowledge of the different and most commercial uses of Artificial Intelligence models can be recognised as Applied Artificial Intelligence. Here, it is anticipated that the individual has a simple understanding of the theoretical characteristics of Artificial Intelligence, Machine Learning, and Deep Learning Algorithms, and the emphasis is on the domains of the application, where, and how it can be applied. Artificial Intelligence has shifted from programming everything called the top-down or symbolic approach to offering answers to the machine and allowing the machine to emerge with a set of programs that it utilises to emerge with a result called the bottom-up approach or connectionist (Huang et al., 2021).

Currently, the last approach is considered identical to Artificial Intelligence, which has triggered such a progression in the domain of Artificial Intelligence, mostly because of the current revolution in the introduction of powerful GPUs and computing power. Primarily, the basic and primitive Artificial Intelligence models utilised more of a brute-force method, where all the blends were tried to come up with an outcome. The initial instance of this was Alan Turning's Bombe which supported decoding German Engima-machine-encrypted secret messages during the Second World War (J.K et al., 2022). It was anticipated that by turning that one day, the computer would be able to beat humans in a game of chess and almost in less than six decades. In 1997, Deep Blue developed a chess computer that could beat the ruling world champion Garry Kasparov in a match of six games. It was only possible if the computer could narrow down the probable number of moves and learn from previous experiences. The method still depends on brute force and may not be known as Artificial Intelligence by modern standards, although it unlocked the world of probabilities of Artificial Intelligence. With this, particularly after the uprising in computing power, the commercial use of Artificial Intelligence has come into the limelight (Xu et al., 2021).

ARTIFICIAL INTELLIGENCE STRATEGIES AND SOLUTIONS

As mentioned above, the study of the application and usage aspect of Artificial Intelligence is based on applied intelligence, and there are numerous domains where artificial intelligence can be applied. These include Chatbots, Sentiment Analysis, Natural Language Generation, and Image or Speech Recognition. In the present world, the use of artificial intelligence is mostly omnipresent. It is utilised by several business firms to develop CRM media that permits better consumer handling and enhances consumer satisfaction (Demlehner et al., 2021). Artificial intelligence also sustains its conventional application domains of automation, where monotonous tasks must be performed. Here, Artificial Intelligence can do so more effectively than simply hard-coding everything (Nguyen et al., 2022). Artificial Intelligence domains now involve those areas where its use was previously ignored, such as marketing, where it is utilised to forecast the correct advertisement, among other things, education where it supports in deciding the course curriculum, solving preliminary questions, where the usage of Chatbots is in high demand among other areas involving Cyber Security for threat detection, finance for the analysis of the trade trends, production and manufacturing for logistic support, medical care for initial detection, and prompt diagnoses of disease. Other firms manufacture dedicated software that exclusively depends on Artificial Intelligence, such as motion detection sensors, image recognition software utilised by law enforcement agencies, and self-driving vehicles that utilise motion detection with image recognition (Yu et al., 2021).

Technological Development Using Artificial Intelligence

The Artificial Intelligence application areas mentioned above have led to the creation of different technologies that are utilised to resolve different business issues. Among these, the most well-known are Natural Language Processing, Computer Vision, and Machine Learning (Wu & Dai, 2021). Artificial Intelligence consists of machine learning and deep learning. While discussing machine learning as a technology, the machine learning features of remembering, continuous enhancement, memorising previous behaviour, and adjustment to novel scenarios are utilised. Unlike computer vision which mainly utilises deep learning methods, machine learning units are predominantly utilised (Borges et al., 2021). Application domains involve anything where the previous behaviour of people or any other subject is utilised to forecast the future for them or similar subjects. For instance, to forecast whether a specific individual will have the ability to repay the loan, machine learning technology is implemented where various machine learning algorithms are used to detect the pattern among historical consumers and their ultimate loan repayment (Ameen et al., 2021). Here, instead of hard-coding some regulations, the machine is prepared to learn from previous experiences and forecast whether a specific individual will have the ability to repay a loan depending on his or her authorisations. The best part of this is that as the trends in the population change, so do the technique of predictions as nothing is hardcoded which is permanent or fixed, although re-training of the model is needed. Machine learning units are rightly used as a segment of Applied Artificial Intelligence in several machine learning algorithms, such as logistic regression and linear regression. K-support Vector Machines were utilised to learn the machine from the data. To the extent that deep learning methods are concerned, Artificial Neural Network is the most known Deep learning algorithm utilized in machine learning technology (Angelov et al., 2021). Natural language processing is one of the most widely available technologies for applied artificial intelligence. Unlike computer vision, which utilises a camera and performs analogue-to-digital conversions and image processing, natural language processing must handle this conversion. The text ranges from numbers to characters which can be used to represent the text implicitly. Natural language processing is the knowledge of languages, vocabulary, standard terms, and grammar, along with assessing a text for meaningful outcomes. Its application domains involve chatbots, which are now applied in almost all business sectors, sentiment analysis, and text generation. The most general algorithms that work with natural language processing are recursive neural networks and naïve Bayes (Galaz et al., 2021).

The Method to Learn Applied Artificial Intelligence

It is vital to know the language in which these algorithms can be prewritten and written to be implemented to apply artificial intelligence-based algorithms. Among several languages, Python is the most widely used language, particularly in data science. A large number of Artificial Intelligence algorithms are accessible in Python and have been developed in Python on a broad level, making it even more vital. Therefore, to begin with applied artificial intelligence, the preliminary step would be to start with learning Python (Pena et al., 2021). As mentioned above, to understand applied Artificial Intelligence, one must know Artificial Intelligence, and for recognising artificial intelligence, the two fundamental components are Deep Learning and Machine Learning. The preliminary step after having some Python knowledge was to learn the machine-learning concepts. Here, one must search for an effective machine-learning course that suits the applicant. It covers all the features of machine learning algorithms that are theoretical, intuitive, and mathematical as the application part (implementing machine learning algorithms utilising languages such as Python) (Puente-Castro et al., 2021). After learning Python Programming for Data Science and using machine learning algorithms, the Deep Learning architecture and mechanisms of an algorithm that functions in a reinforcement learning setup can be emphasised. A better course would be to clarify the different frameworks of Artificial Neural Networks, Convolutional Neural Networks, and Recurrent Neural Networks (Narkhede et al., 2021). An effective applied artificial intelligence course would particularly ask the applicant to know all the prerequisites which are mentioned above, which are knowledge of deep and machine learning units and Python for Data Science, or it describes all of this from the start by describing the different domains of artificial intelligence and some technologies linked with it. Here, a course should have the ability to offer the applicant a comprehensive mathematical and statistical background of the algorithms with the instinct behind them, the right way of performing Data Mining, Data Cleaning, and Exploratory Data Analysis. When discussing various application domains and technologies linked with it, the course should have the ability to offer a common workflow for managing all the problems, the general mistakes that individuals might make, and adequate knowledge of the final objective so that the application is effective. In addition, projects, case studies, assignments, and placement support should be of excellent quality (Bag et al., 2021). Understanding a computer language, theoretical understanding of the machine and deep learning algorithms, or knowledge of the different application areas of artificial intelligence is not enough in the present age. The requirement is to merge all this knowledge. Without this, no one can understand applied artificial, as having a secluded understanding can be useless. Once the various characteristics of artificial intelligence are applied, one can then opt to go in-depth into a specific domain, such as self-driving cars, computer vision, machine learning for forecasts, natural language processing, and robotics (Han, 2021).

Applied Artificial Intelligence Principles

When there is a discussion about artificial intelligence, business applications are examined with the following:

- An enhanced emphasis on end-to-end process automation
- Enhanced expressed performance goals and model accuracy
- Usage of enhanced machine learning methods
- Suitable usage of human decision and automatic forecasts
- Constant learning and transformation through feedback loops
- Methods to restrict the effect of model biases and error

Many firms find it difficult to start with artificial intelligence as it is such a complicated subject, and there are so many domains where it can support it (Kuang et al., 2021).

Theoretical Artificial Intelligence

Theoretical artificial intelligence has balanced, on the margin of this broad green field, learning logical, analytical, and experience-based problem solving as if these special mind activities were the whole story. However, people will never recognise human thoughts or develop a computer that can imitate them until the definition is deepened and broadened. Science needs that people generalise, and in a specific situation, it is easy to capture the dispersed thought facts and fix the jigsaw pieces into a clear picture. Theoretical artificial intelligence follows the theory of mind artificial intelligence framework, through which it is anticipated to be able to reason, make decisions, solve complicated problems under undefined situations, plan, attain learning about cognitive skills, incorporate previous knowledge in decision making or get precision, and be inventive, creative, and imaginative. Theoretical artificial intelligence involves training machines to recognise human behaviour completely and the ability to recognise perception. The human mind is the execution of a model behind the development of theoretical artificial intelligence. Thus, it is the lack of all-inclusive knowledge and cognitive abilities that are the challenge for attaining it in contrast to the working of a human mind, which has made scholars put huge efforts into imitating the simplest functionalities of movement and slight movement with perception perspective being covered (Trocin et al., 2021). Theoretical artificial intelligence can be used to resolve huge problems, and it could also be utilized to plan out the financial crisis and take rigorous actions against it. Artificial general intelligence or theoretical intelligence can influence humanity for financial gains. With theoretical artificial intelligence, machines can imitate the human brain and behaviour to solve complicated problems (Jelonek et al., 2020).

The functionality of these machines is identical to that of humans and has been developed to have all-inclusive knowledge and cognitive computing abilities. Artificial general intelligence is depending on the theory of the artificial intelligence framework of the brain. Primarily, the theory of mind-level artificial intelligence deals with training machines to recognise and learn human behaviour and basic concepts of consciousness. Various approaches have been developed and assessed to attain human-like intelligence (Frolov et al., 2021). The following are some of these approaches:

Symbolic Approach

The symbolic approach explains the usage of logic networks, for example, if-then statements and symbols, to learn and create an all-inclusive knowledge base, which is further broadened by deploying these symbols on behalf of the physical world's important aspects. This approach replicates higher levels in the thoughts of the human mind (Kitsios & Kamariotou, 2021).

General Artificial Intelligence Symbolic Approach.

Theoretically, the symbolic approach can perform higher-level thinking and logic, but it lacks the ability to learn low-level tasks such as perception (Stepin et al., 2021).

Connectionist Approach

The connectionist approach is a sub-symbolic method that uses frameworks such as the human mind and neural nets to develop general intelligence. This method expects the evolution of higher-level intelligence for low-level symbolic systems, such as neural nets, which still has to happen. Convolutional neural networks and deep learning networks, such as DeepMind's AlphaGo, are the best instances of the connectionist approach (Behl et al., 2021).

Hybrid Approach

The hybrid approach is a The hybrid approach is the combination of symbolic and connectionist approaches. Leading general artificial intelligence frameworks use a hybrid approach, such as the CogPrime framework. It signifies sub-symbolic and symbolic knowledge through a single understanding representation, known as AtomsSpace (Huang et al., 2021).

Whole-Organisation Framework

Scholars assume that an actual theoretical artificial intelligence system should hold a physical body and attain an understanding of physical interactions. Although there are no such systems, the closest is Sophia. This humanoid robot mimics human facial expressions and gestures, and involves discussions on predefined subjects (Gaur et al., 2021).

KEY CHALLENGES OF THEORETICAL ARTIFICIAL INTELLIGENCE

Although theoretical artificial intelligence has not gained much significance, it signifies various prospects which can help in the revolution of the Artificial Intelligence domain. Artificial Intelligence is presently flawed by some challenges and barricades, delaying its progress (Grundner & Neuhofer, 2021).

Problems in Grasping Human-Like Ability

Theoretical artificial intelligence must grasp some human-like abilities to attain actual human-level intelligence, such as:

Sensory Observation

Although deep learning systems have made significant progress in computer vision, artificial intelligence systems lack human-like sensory observation abilities. For instance, trained deep learning systems still possess poor colour observations. It is clear that self-driving vehicles are easily tricked by small black tape pieces or stickers on the red stop signal. The same situation was observed for sound recognition. Current artificial intelligence systems cannot mimic and perceive different human sound perceptions (Neuhofer et al., 2021).

Motor Skills

Humans can effortlessly retrieve items from their pockets because of their good motor skills. A recent advancement applied reinforcement learning to train a robotic hand to solve Rubik's block. Even though the demo is prominent, it discloses the issues involved in programming the robot's fingers on a single hand to operate small objects such as keys (Dwivedi et al., 2021).

Natural Language Knowledge

Humans share knowledge through blog posts, books, videos, and articles. Afterwards, when humans write, they are inclined to think of it as the reader's general knowledge, and, as such, much information is unstated in writing (Han et al., 2021). To begin with, the present Artificial Intelligence requires obtaining a huge amount of knowledge from all information sources, which is a crucial task. If Artificial Intelligence has less understood of common sense, it will be difficult for these systems to understand real-world cases and functions (Nagy & Hajdú, 2021).

Problem-Solving

If we consider an instance where a home robot must understand that the house's LED bulb is damaged and either change it with a new one or notify someone, the robot must have common sense to perform this task. Alternatively, the robot should be capable of simulating all combinations and permutations that determine the probabilities, possibilities, and plausibility. Currently, artificial intelligence lacks both simulation and sensing abilities (Mikalef & Gupta, 2021).

Human-like Creativity

Artificial intelligence systems can enhance their intelligence if they recognise the huge amounts of code written by humans, recognise new approaches that need improvement, and then rewrite the recognised code. Even though artificial intelligence machines can compose tunes and draw pictures, signifying human-like creativity for self-optimisation requires further progress in artificial intelligence (Yousra & Khalid, 2021).

Emotional and Social Connection

Human interaction is unavoidable for artificial intelligence-enabled robots worldwide. Consequently, these robots require recognising humans, tones, and facial expression variations to understand real emotions. Artificial intelligence systems that empathise with emotionally connected systems seem to be a reality. As artificial intelligence progress takes centre stage within the global pandemic COVID-19, the creation of human-like intelligence has been developing more quickly than ever (Rust & Huang, 2021).

Ethical Considerations and Data Privacy

The use of AI in education involves the collection and analysis of vast amounts of data, which raises important ethical considerations regarding data privacy and security. Ensuring the protection of student data is essential to maintaining trust and compliance with legal standards.

Data Governance

Educational institutions must implement robust data-governance frameworks to safeguard student information. This includes adhering to legal regulations such as the GDPR in Europe, which sets strict guidelines for data privacy. Under the GDPR, institutions must obtain explicit consent from students before collecting and processing their data to ensure transparency and accountability in data handling (Chou et al., 2022).

Bias and Fairness

AI systems can inadvertently perpetuate the biases present in the data on which they are trained. It is crucial to develop fair and unbiased algorithms to ensure equitable educational outcomes. Researchers are developing fairness-aware algorithms that aim to reduce bias in AI systems, ensuring that all students have equal opportunities for success.

Challenges of Integrating AI in Education

Despite its potential benefits, integrating AI into educational systems presents several challenges. These include the high cost of implementation, need for technical expertise, and resistance to change from educators and students.

Cost of Implementation

Developing and maintaining AI-driven educational platforms can be expensive, limiting their adoption in institutions with limited budget. Smaller institutions may struggle to invest in AI technologies due to financial constraints, potentially widening the gap between well-funded and underfunded schools.

Technical Expertise

The effective implementation of AI requires educators and administrators to possess a certain level of technical expertise. Professional development and training programs are necessary to equip staff with the skills needed to effectively use AI tools. Institutions may offer workshops and training sessions to help educators integrate AI technology into their teaching practices.

Resistance to Change

Some educators and students may be resistant to adopting new technologies and preferring traditional teaching methods. Addressing this resistance requires demonstrating the benefits of AI and providing support during transition. Pilot programs and success stories can help to illustrate the positive impact of AI on student engagement and learning outcomes, thus encouraging wider adoption.

Global Perspectives

The adoption and implementation of AI in education varies globally, reflecting different educational priorities, resources, and regulatory environments. Understanding these differences is crucial for developing effective AI strategies. The U.S. is a leader in integrating AI into education, with a focus on personalised learning and smart classrooms. Initiatives such as AI in the Education pilot program aim to enhance learning experiences and improve student outcomes. The AI in Education initiative in the U.S. supports the development of AI-driven educational technologies, providing funding and resources to schools and universities. China is rapidly advancing AI education, emphasising the use of AI for administrative efficiency and personalised learning. Government support and significant investments in AI research and development have positioned China as a global leader in AI education. The Chinese government's AI in Education programs aims to integrate AI technologies into classrooms across the country, thereby enhancing personalised learning and administrative efficiency. European countries have focused on data privacy and ethical considerations for the implementation of AI. Regulations such as the GDPR ensure that AI applications in education adhere to high standards for data protection and ethical use. The European Commission's Ethical Guidelines for Trustworthy AI provide a framework for developing and implementing AI technologies that respects fundamental rights and promotes transparency and accountability.

CONCLUSION

In conclusion, the dynamic interaction between theoretical and applied AI captures the story of the development of AI. Numerous sectors, including healthcare, banking, customer service, and autonomous cars, have already been transformed by AI and its useful uses. Unquestionably, Applied AI positively impacts our daily lives, making it more convenient, effective, and secure. However, the enormous importance of theoretical AI cannot be ignored. It continues to be a subject of speculation and ambition, but motivates our unrelenting search for artificial intelligence. Theoretical AI forces us to reflect on the nature of consciousness, intelligence, and limits of what is possible for robots. It stands for the pursuit of genuine artificial general intelligence, the so-called "Holy Grail," which, if attained, could bring about a new era of knowledge and technology. These two concepts will likely coexist peacefully in the future. Theoretical AI will motivate us to delve into the depths of human cognition, while Applied AI will continue to spur innovation and address real-world problems. How well will these techniques work together to shape the future AI environment? We are reminded of the enormous potential of human intellect and the seemingly limitless possibilities ahead, as we consider the journey of Applied AI versus Theoretical AI. Artificial intelligence (AI) continues to be a strong force that influences our environment and challenges our views of what is possible, whether improving consumer experiences through virtual assistants or pushing the bounds of machine learning. One thing is certain: the voyage of AI is far from complete, and its biggest revelations may still be in store. Only time will indicate how these two sides of the AI will intersect.

REFERENCES

Ahmed, S. I., Radhakrishnan, S., Nair, B. B., & Thiruvengadathan, R. (2021). Efficient hyperparameter-tuned machine learning approach for estimation of supercapacitor performance attributes. *Journal of Physics Communications*, 5(11), 115011. DOI:10.1088/2399-6528/ac3574

Albert, E. T. (2019). AI in talent acquisition: A review of AI-applications used in recruitment and selection. *Strategic HR Review*, 18(5), 215–221. DOI:10.1108/SHR-04-2019-0024

Arora, M., Prakash, A., Mittal, A., & Singh, S. (2021, December). HR analytics and artificial intelligence-transforming human resource management. In *2021 International Conference on Decision Aid Sciences and Application (DASA)* (pp. 288-293). IEEE. DOI:10.1109/DASA53625.2021.9682325

Chou, Y. L., Moreira, C., Bruza, P., Ouyang, C., & Jorge, J. (2022). Counterfactuals and causability in explainable artificial intelligence: Theory, algorithms, and applications. *Information Fusion*, 81, 59–83. DOI:10.1016/j.inffus.2021.11.003

Chowdhury, S., Dey, P., Joel-Edgar, S., Bhattacharya, S., Rodriguez-Espindola, O., Abadie, A., & Truong, L. (2023). Unlocking the value of artificial intelligence in human resource management through AI capability framework. *Human Resource Management Review*, 33(1), 100899. DOI:10.1016/j.hrmr.2022.100899

Deeva, G., Bogdanova, D., Serral, E., Snoeck, M., & De Weerdt, J. (2021). A review of automated feedback systems for learners: Classification framework, challenges and opportunities. *Computers & Education*, 162, 104094. DOI:10.1016/j.compedu.2020.104094

Gethe, R. K. (2022). Extrapolation of talent acquisition in AI aided professional environment. *International Journal of Business Innovation and Research*, 27(4), 462–479. DOI:10.1504/IJBIR.2022.122510

Jelonek, D., Mesjasz-Lech, A., Stępniak, C., Turek, T., & Ziora, L. (2020). The artificial intelligence application in the management of contemporary organization: Theoretical assumptions, current practices and research review. In *Advances in Information and Communication:Proceedings of the 2019 Future of Information and Communication Conference (FICC),* Volume 1 (pp. 319-327). Springer International Publishing.

Johnson, R. D., Stone, D. L., & Lukaszewski, K. M. (2020). The benefits of eHRM and AI for talent acquisition. *Journal ofTourism Futures*, 7(1), 40–52. DOI:10.1108/JTF-02-2020-0013

Kinkel, S., Baumgartner, M., & Cherubini, E. (2022). Prerequisites for the adoption of AI technologies in manufacturing–Evidence from a worldwide sample of manufacturing companies. *Technovation*, 110, 102375. DOI:10.1016/j.technovation.2021.102375

Nieminen, J. H., Bearman, M., & Tai, J. (2023). How is theory used in assessment and feedback research? A critical review. *Assessment & Evaluation in Higher Education*, 48(1), 77–94. DOI:10.1080/02602938.2022.2047154

Paramita, D. (2020). Digitalization in talent acquisition: A case study of AI in recruitment.

Pillai, R., & Sivathanu, B. (2020). Adoption of artificial intelligence (AI) for talent acquisition in IT/ITeS organizations. *Benchmarking*, 27(9), 2599–2629. DOI:10.1108/BIJ-04-2020-0186

Ramesh, S., & Das, S. (2022, January). Adoption of AI in Talent Acquisition: A Conceptual Framework. In *International Conference on Digital Technologies and Applications* (pp. 12-20). Cham: Springer International Publishing. DOI:10.1007/978-3-031-01942-5_2

Rao, R., & Hill, B. (2019). How is the Role of AI in Talent Acquisition Evolving?

Tariq, M. U. (2024). Leveraging AI for Entrepreneurial Innovation in Healthcare. In Özsungur, F. (Ed.), *Generating Entrepreneurial Ideas With AI* (pp. 192–216). IGI Global. DOI:10.4018/979-8-3693-3498-0.ch009

Tariq, M. U. (2024). Leading Smart Technologies and Innovations for E-Business 5.0: Applications and Management Frameworks. In Popkova, E. (Ed.), *Smart Technologies and Innovations in E-Business* (pp. 25–46). IGI Global. DOI:10.4018/978-1-6684-7840-0.ch002

ADDITIONAL READING

Babar, M., Ahmad, A., Tariq, M. U., & Kaleem, S. (2023). Real-time fake news detection using big data analytics and deep neural network. *IEEE Transactions on Computational Social Systems*. Advance online publication. DOI:10.1109/TCSS.2023.3309704

Babar, M., Jan, M. A., He, X., Tariq, M. U., Mastorakis, S., & Alturki, R. (2023). An optimized IoT-enabled big data analytics architecture for edge–cloud computing. *IEEE Internet of Things Journal*, 10(5), 3995–4005. DOI:10.1109/JIOT.2022.3157552 PMID:38046398

Babar, M., Tariq, M. U., & Jan, M. A. (2020). Secure and resilient demand side management engine using machine learning for IoT-enabled smart grid. *Sustainable Cities and Society*, 62, 102370. Advance online publication. DOI:10.1016/j.scs.2020.102370

KEY TERMS AND DEFINITIONS

Applied AI: The practical use of AI technologies and algorithms to solve real-world problems and perform specific tasks, such as speech recognition and image analysis.

Artificial General Intelligence (AGI): A theoretical form of AI that possesses the ability to understand, learn, and apply intelligence across a broad range of tasks at a human-like level.

Artificial Intelligence (AI): The field of computer science dedicated to creating machines capable of performing tasks that typically require human intelligence, such as learning, reasoning, and problem-solving.

Artificial Superintelligence (ASI): A hypothetical AI that surpasses human intelligence across all domains, including creativity, problem-solving, and emotional intelligence.

Autonomous Vehicles: Vehicles equipped with AI systems that can operate and navigate without human intervention, using sensors and algorithms to interpret data from the environment.

Deep Learning: A subset of machine learning involving neural networks with multiple layers (deep networks) that can automatically extract features and learn from large datasets.

Narrow AI (Weak AI): AI systems designed to perform specific tasks or functions, often without general intelligence or awareness, such as virtual assistants and recommendation systems.

Reinforcement Learning: A type of machine learning where an agent learns to make decisions by receiving rewards or penalties based on its actions within an environment.

Strong AI: A term for AI systems with general intelligence comparable to human cognition, theoretically capable of understanding and reasoning across various domains.

Theoretical AI: The study of the foundational concepts and principles behind AI algorithms and models, focusing on mathematical and computational theories.

Turing Test: A test proposed by Alan Turing to determine if a machine's behaviour is indistinguishable from that of a human, thus indicating the machine exhibits intelligent behaviour.

Chapter 3
Shaping the Future of Higher Education:
Emerging Trends and Technologies

ABSTRACT

In the contemporary scene, advanced education remains at a basic point, ready for custom and development, confronting extraordinary difficulties and opening doors. The conjunction of globalization, mechanical headways, segment moves, and developing educational standards has catalyzed an extraordinary excursion in advanced education. This chapter fills an exhaustive outline of the arising patterns and advancements that are reshaping the fate of advanced education, explaining their suggestions, possibilities, and difficulties. Globalization has created a borderless world portrayed by interconnectedness and relationships. In the domain of advanced education, globalization has introduced another period of internationalization set apart by the portability of understudies, researchers, and information across topographical limits. Colleges are progressively captivating in cross-line coordinated efforts, shaping key organizations, and laying out branch grounds to upgrade their worldwide impressions.

INTRODUCTION

The rapid speed of mechanical development has catalysed significant changes in advanced education, upsetting education, learning, and exploring ideal models. Advanced innovations, such as man-made brainpower (computer-based intelligence), AI, augmented reality (AR), augmented reality (VR), and blockchain, have upset customary instructive models, offering new roads for customised, intuitive, and vivid

DOI: 10.4018/979-8-3693-4074-5.ch003

growth opportunities. In addition, web-based learning stages, huge open web-based courses (MOOCs), and learning the executive frameworks (LMS) have democratised admittance to schooling, rising above fleeting and spatial requirements. Segment Movements and Variety in Advanced education segment shifts, portrayed by changing populace elements, generational advances, and expanding variety, present two difficulties and valuable open doors for advanced education establishments. The flood of different understudy accomplices, including people from changed financial, social, and instructive foundations, requires the reception of comprehensive practices and arrangement of custom-made help systems to guarantee impartial access and achievement (De Wit and Altbach, 2021).

Moreover, the maturing labour force and rise of modern students highlight the fundamentals of deep-rooted learning drives and adaptable instructive pathways. The development of instructive standards and hypotheses mirrors a shift from customary instructional methodologies towards understudy-focused, experiential, and request-based learning procedures. Constructivist hypotheses such as social constructivism and connectivism underscore the significance of dynamic commitment, cooperation, and information development within credible settings. Moreover, the coordination of experiential learning, project-based learning, and issue-based learning encourages decisive reasoning, imagination, and certifiable use of information, and planning understudies the intricacies of the contemporary labour force. While rising patterns and innovations hold enormous commitment to the fate of advanced education, they are accompanied by a number of difficulties and intricacies. Issues relating to advanced value, protection, and security highlight the requirement for moral structures, and computerised education is driven to relieve aberrations and defend information honesty (Cesco et al., 2021).

Moreover, concerns regarding the commodification of instruction, the disintegration of scholastic opportunities, and the corporatisation of colleges warrant basic examination and consultation. Nonetheless, in the midst of these difficulties lies open doors for advancement, joint effort, and re-evaluation, as advanced education partners explore the development scene with flexibility and versatility. The fate of advanced education is being formed by a combination of arising patterns and advancements impelled by globalisation, mechanical progressions, segment moves, and developing academic standards. As we set out in this extraordinary excursion, it is basic to embrace advancement, cultivate inclusivity, and maintain the fundamental beliefs of scholastic trustworthiness, value, and greatness. By utilising the capability of arising advances, supporting variety and consideration, and rethinking instructive practices, we can explore the intricacies representing things to come to an advanced educational scene and enable students to flourish in a quickly impacting world.

BACKGROUND

The coronavirus pandemic has caused exceptional interruptions across different areas, including advanced education. With the unexpected beginning of lockdowns and social separation measures, instructive foundations were constrained to change to remote helping and learning modalities to guarantee quick progression amid the emergency. This rapid shift uncovered the weaknesses of customary instructive models and catalysed a rush of mechanical developments and changes in the learning scene (Tariq, 2024). One of the most prompt and substantial impacts of the Coronavirus pandemic on advanced education was the inescapable reception of remote learning modalities. Short-term homerooms were supplanted by virtual gathering stages, and close and personal collaborations gave way to online conversations. Foundations mixed to convey Learning: The executive's Frameworks (LMS), video conferencing apparatuses, and other advanced stages of working with far-off guidance. For instance, colleges such as Harvard and MIT quickly changed their educational program to online arrangements, utilizing stages such as Zoom and Material to convey addresses and draw in understudies (Lauder, 2020).

This rapid shift to remote learning empowered instructive congruity and featured the capability of innovation to rise above geological boundaries and extend admittance to training. Understudies from distant regions or those with versatility limitations found themselves ready to partake in classes and seek degrees from renowned establishments, without the requirement for actual migration. For example, people recently confronted moving to nearby classes because of work or family responsibilities viewed remote learning choices as obligatory and adaptable (Rasul et al., 2023).

The difficulties of the pandemic have led advanced education organizations to investigate and embrace many mechanical developments to improve remote opportunities for growth. For example, artificial consciousness (computer-based intelligence) has emerged as an important device for customizing guidance, mechanizing regulatory errands, and providing ideal criticism for understudies. Versatile learning stages controlled by artificial intelligence calculations were used to fit instructive substance and evaluations of individual understudies' learning styles and speed, consequently improving the learning results. In addition, advancements in computer-generated reality (VR) and expanded reality (AR) have gained momentum for their capability to establish vivid learning conditions and mimic true encounters (Govindarajan and Srivastava, 2020).

Organizations utilized VR recreation to prepare medical services experts, permitting clinical understudies to rehearse surgeries and analyze patients in virtual settings. In addition, AR applications have been utilized to upgrade learning in fields such as design and engineering, empowering understudies to imagine complex ideas and designs in three-layered spaces. Furthermore, blockchain innovation collected consideration for its capacity to obtain scholastic certifications, smooth accreditation confirmation cycles, and battle issues of qualification misrepresentation. Blockchain-based stages gave computerized endorsements and identifications, providing a sealed record of understudies' accomplishments and skills. This upgraded the uprightness and transportability of scholarly qualifications and worked with deep-rooted acquiring and acknowledgement of abilities in advanced age.

Despite the extraordinary capabilities of mechanical developments in advanced education, the rapid shift to remote picking up during the pandemic likewise led to difficulties and contemplations. One of the essential concerns was the computerized partition, which exacerbated variations in admittance to innovation and web networks among the understudies. Understudies from low-pay families or rustic regions frequently require dependable web access and fitting gadgets, blocking their ability to participate in remote learning exercises.

In addition, the abrupt shift to online guidance required critical educational changes and personnel preparing to use advanced devices and stages. Numerous teachers wrestled with issues, such as keeping up with understudy commitment, encouraging cooperative learning conditions, and moderating deceiving in web-based appraisals. Moreover, concerns have been raised regarding the disintegration of customary grounds in social and local areas, as understudies wrestled with sensations of disengagement and separation in remote learning conditions (Eringfeld, 2021).

Moreover, the expanded dependence on advanced stages and information examination has resulted in significant issues regarding understudy protection, information security, and moral contemplations. Organizations must explore the intricacies of information assortment, use, and capacity while guaranteeing consistency with protection guidelines and defending the delicate data of understudies. Moreover, the commodification of instruction and the expansion of the for-benefit Internet learning stages raised concerns about value, quality affirmation, and the disintegration of scholarly guidelines. As the world rises bit by bit out of the grasp of the Coronavirus pandemic, the significant effect on advanced education resonates, molding the direction of the learning scene into the indefinite future. While the pandemic uncovered the innate weaknesses and imbalances in customary instructive models, it led to a flood of development, trial and error, and cooperation in advanced education. Organizations that effectively explored the difficulties of the pandemic and embraced mechanical progressions are ready to flourish in the post-pandemic period, utilizing advanced devices and academic ways to convey more comprehensive, drawing in, and customized growth opportunities (Crompton and Burke, 2023).

Looking forward, the mix of rising advancements such as computer-based intelligence, VR, AR, and blockchain is supposed to additionally change the advanced education biological system, obscuring the limits of physical and virtual learning conditions. Cross-breed models of guidance that join the web and up close and personal components will probably become progressively pervasive, offering understudied adaptability and independence in their learning processes. In addition, the pandemic has highlighted the significance of strength, flexibility, and development in advanced education, provoking establishments to re-examine customary standards and embrace a culture of consistent improvement and trial and error. Overall, the Coronavirus pandemic lastingly affects advanced education, speeding up mechanical progressions, and catalyzing extraordinary changes in the learning scene. While the difficulties and intricacies of the pandemic are evident, they have prepared for advancement, flexibility, and transformation in advanced education. By utilizing examples gained from the pandemic and saddling the force of innovation, establishments can rethink the eventual fate of schooling and endeavor towards a more open, evenhanded, and comprehensive learning environment (Tariq, 2024).

Indeed, 2020 has been a significant year of massive revolution and transformation, leading to the emergence of a "new normal" across various industries. The worldwide COVID-19 pandemic has compelled the adoption of remote working, schooling, and management, and higher education is no exception. The sudden demand for technological capabilities and solutions, particularly in the context of distance learning, has been unpredictable, although not entirely unexpected, considering the need for such alternatives two years ago (Alt et al., 2023).

Currently, in the era of digital literacy, it is unsurprising to see students' increasing familiarity with technology. Younger students, who have grown up with tablets, the Internet, and computers, have now transitioned into college students who are well equipped to navigate this modern digital landscape. They have become discerning customers who expect the same level of convenience and flexibility in their university experiences. The need for improved technology-based learning alternatives has always been present, and the pandemic has accelerated pre-existing trends. Many other educational institutions have successfully tackled the challenges of online learning over the past two years and universities have progressively implemented enhanced technology-based models. For instance, our university has a proven track record of providing live online learning experiences for students at all levels, from bachelor's degree seekers to PhD candidates. We are fully committed to meeting the requirements of our students and possess the expertise to transition seamlessly into this new normal.

The higher education landscape is currently undergoing rapid and unpredictable change. The evolving diversity of higher education institutes, competitive environment, and cultural ecosystem have created dynamic domains of potential evolution. These changes are as ground-breaking as those witnessed in previous decades.

FORECASTS FOR THE FUTURE OF HIGHER EDUCATION

Consequently, the following are five forecasts for the future of higher education, technology solutions, and student experience:

1. Students have never had much control over their learning experience. The COVID-19 pandemic has been a significant catalyst for this shift, as students now have a greater say in higher education. With remote, online, and distance learning becoming widely accepted across all education levels, traditional in-person teaching models may become less common. To thrive, educational institutions must prioritize the needs of their students in all decision-making processes (Neuwirth et al., 2021).
2. Education plays a crucial role in reducing social and political divisions. The importance of education and the consequences of underinvestment will become even more relevant in a world that is being increasingly divided economically, socially, and politically. The prevalence of fake news and misinformation has created a crisis of trust in information for both the society and students. Educational institutions, students, industry leaders, and policymakers must engage in thoughtful deliberation to address these concerns and pave the way for a future characterized by common ground and mutual understanding.
3. Universities must embrace agility and adapt to a new definition of higher education. Institutions of higher learning need to embark on a transformative journey necessitated by the COVID-19 pandemic, challenging rigid norms and remaining adaptable to change. Holding rigidly to pre-pandemic practices will leave universities lagging behind, as the concept of a "return to normal" is no longer feasible. Those who rely on outdated experiences or learning frameworks that no longer meet the evolving needs of students will hinder university progress in the post-pandemic future (Looi, 2024).
4. Short-term accreditations shape the higher-education landscape. In today's world, employers increasingly value skills over degrees; this trend is likely to become more prevalent in the post-pandemic era. Students will recognize the benefits of stackable credentials and obtain certifications for specific skills while pursuing their undergraduate or graduate degrees. With rising unemployment and job displacement due to the pandemic, the value of certifications is evident, enabling individuals to explore new employment opportunities without needing to complete a two- or four-year degree. Traditional college students no longer have to view experience and learning as mutually exclusive; forward-thinking universities provide students with the opportunity to earn certifications while pursuing their degrees and offer flexible class schedules that allow them to gain valuable skills and credentials while working (Toquero, 2020).

5. The approach to student well-being and health in higher education must undergo radical change. With the growth of remote online education, students are constantly connected virtually, posing new and diverse challenges that can hinder the learning process and overall quality of life. This continuous connectivity creates a level of complexity never encountered before, particularly when considering how students can disconnect and prioritize self-care. The blending of online classrooms, workspaces, and leisure activities further complicates this situation. Educational institutions must proactively explore and implement methods to support the health and well-being of their students as their personal and academic lives increasingly overlap.

Future university experiences for incoming learners, especially high school graduates, may appear significantly different because of the need for adaptability on the part of educational institutions and the contemporary educational solutions available to students. In the short term, the success or failure of many institutions will depend on their ability to meet the needs of their students while still recognising the importance of maintaining some elements of normalcy. The next generation of post-secondary students has been exposed to new possibilities and possesses a more diverse set of skills relevant to education. Universities must be equipped to cater to students' expectations. While experienced college students may yearn for familiar aspects, such as physical campus settings, in-person lectures, and campus activities, new students will be accustomed to the structure of distance and remote learning (Tariq, 2024).

Online teaching platforms, such as Zoom, are expected to become increasingly common. There may have been some leniency during the initial learning curve for institutes to adapt to new technologies, but incoming college students in the future expect universities to have the necessary arrangements and technology in place. If institutions fail to meet these expectations, it is uncertain whether they will choose to stay. Digital generation value technology meets their needs and expects universities to embrace digital proficiency. There are still many uncertainties regarding the future of higher education, particularly regarding the changes imposed by the global pandemic. University administrators can only anticipate what is expected in terms of the ongoing impact of the pandemic and its effects on learning models. In 2020, students at all levels of education were thrust into the role of remote learners. It is now more crucial than ever for educational institutions to adapt and respond effectively to students' varying needs (Guàrdia et al., 2020).

Reasons That Shift Higher Education Forward to the Novel Landscape

Higher education institutions offer concurrent distance and face-to-face learning models, known as hybrid instruction, to cater to a wider range of learners. These models allow faculties to meet instructional objectives while accommodating the needs and preferences of students. Implementing hybrid courses requires additional effort from teachers and increases the technological and financial resources of institutions. Universities should invest in faculty assistance in course design, dynamic and inclusive instruction, and the use of learning management systems and other technological solutions. Examples of such support include free micro-boot camps during summer breaks, extensive assistance for faculty, faculty learning communities for analysing online teaching, one-on-one discussions, and toolkits. Providing adequate faculty support is crucial to ensuring high-quality hybrid courses, regardless of the instructional modality (El Said, 2021).

To enable access to hybrid teaching modes, it is essential for learners to have affordable and versatile technologies at their disposal. Universities collaborate across the campus community to make Wi-Fi, laptops, and other necessary technologies available to students at little or no cost. They established Wi-Fi hotspots in parking areas and repurposed vacant classrooms as student spaces, providing students with a place to participate in virtual sessions. Collaboration with libraries, industry partners, and non-profit organisations further expands public access to Wi-Fi networks, increasing the availability of the community. Offering low-cost or borrowable tools is crucial for ensuring equitable accessibility for students, faculty, and staff. In cases where universities did not have these resources, they sought gifts and grants from regional agencies and communities to acquire the necessary technology in response to the global pandemic (Gallagher and Savage, 2023).

The pandemic has introduced various challenges to the physical and mental well-being of students, staff, and faculty in higher education institutions. Members of these institutions now face additional difficulties, including increased childcare and eldercare responsibilities, underemployment, unemployment, social distancing measures, and disruptions to their eating, drinking, and sleeping routines. Universities recognize the importance of maintaining healthy routines and prioritizing support for the well-being of their campus communities.

To promote well-being, universities offer incentives and resources, such as workshops and classes on topics such as meditation, mindfulness, social media use, news consumption, and exercise. These workshops can be conducted in multiple formats including asynchronous and synchronous sessions to accommodate different schedules and preferences. Such provisions prove particularly effective for individuals, especially those from moderate- and low-income backgrounds, who may lack access to external resources. Human resource management skills play a vital role in delivering workshops and training sessions to support the community members (Chatterjee and Bhattacharjee, 2020).

Furthermore, institutional policies are reviewed to ensure that they account for the global pandemic and incorporate necessary flexibility. These policy adjustments encompass strategies related to remote work, leave policies, tenure, and promotion. By adapting policies to address the unique challenges brought about by the pandemic, higher education institutions can better support the health and well-being of their staff, faculty, and students.

Lessons From Modifications Only Valid During the Pandemic

Higher education institutions have recognized the value of online classes for students, staff, and faculty during the pandemic. Universities swiftly transitioned to remote learning in the early stages of the global crisis and utilized their expertise to ensure student success. However, this shift revealed that an all-online teaching format may not be suitable for all students, particularly those who thrive in in-person learning experiences and community-building activities that are typically found on campus. Traditional-age learners transitioning from high school experienced a loss of the campus-based experience, leading to feelings of being deferred between being a college student and a high school student.

Many students face various challenges in a virtual learning environment, including limited economic and technological resources, social distancing measures, and family responsibilities. It has become clear that a "one-size-fits-all" approach to education is not effective in meeting the needs of today's diverse student population. Consequently, universities have recognized the limitations of exclusively virtual classes and have adopted a more strategic approach. They differentiated between courses that require campus-based settings and those that can be effectively delivered remotely (Salas-Pilco et al., 2022).

Faculty members have implemented innovative strategies to enhance students' performance and engagement in virtual settings. For example, some universities have emphasized individual video feedback to provide personalized guidance. The faculty has also created online collaborative practices, such as remote newsrooms and studios in journalism departments, to facilitate dynamic interactions between students and their instructors.

While virtual field-based experiences were introduced to provide the necessary learning opportunities during the pandemic, feedback indicated that these experiences did not fully capture the immersive nature of face-to-face interactions. Institutions that hosted students in settings such as schools, hospitals, laboratories, and clinics acknowledged that these virtual appointments may have limited the impact of these experiences. To address this limitation, universities have started adopting video assessment software that enables students to showcase their skills through joint video assignments while faculty and clinical administrators provide personalized feedback (Chan and Hu, 2023).

Higher education institutions should deliberately assess and refine virtual field-based experiences to better replicate the engaging and impactful nature of face-to-face interactions.

Personal Association Is a Requirement Factor Irrespective of Work Modality

During the global pandemic, many administrators, staff, and faculty quickly adapted to virtual conferences to effectively fulfil their services, scholarships, and teaching responsibilities. They put significant effort into ensuring student success in an online format. While virtual conferences supported the professional objectives of universities during the pandemic, many faculty, administrators, and staff deeply missed the informal interactions and socialization opportunities provided by in-person meetings. Virtual conferences lack meaningful socialization among students, staff, and faculty, which contributes to a sense of community and fosters a culture of connections.

To address these challenges, administrators and faculty members should arrange smaller groups and individual meetings to address the limitations of virtual meetings. Creating opportunities for socializing in a non-work environment, such as organizing happy virtual hours, can also help foster personal connections. Some staff members may choose to limit the number of daily conferences to reduce burnout and ensure meaningful participation in meetings (Duran et al., 2020). Recognizing the importance of personal associations and actively finding ways to nurture them within a virtual setting is crucial for maintaining a sense of community and fostering a positive working environment in higher education institutions.

In the rapidly developing field of advanced education, the customary worldview of latent learning and one-size-fits-all guidance provides a more powerful and understudy-driven approach. Vital to this change, acknowledges the significance of understudy strengthening and customized opportunities for growth. Enabling understudies to take responsibility for learning excursions and fitting instructive encounters to their singular requirements, interests, and goals are the basic objectives for cultivating commitment, inspiration, and scholarly achievement. This paper investigates the meaning of understudy strengthening and customized growth opportunities regarding advanced education, inspecting their effect on understudy results, institutional viability, and a more extensive instructive biological system (Rudolph et al., 2023).

Understudy strengthening in advanced education involves giving students the information, abilities, and organization to effectively mold their instructive encounters and accomplish their scholastic objectives. It includes encouraging independence, self-viability, and obligation among understudies, enabling them to pursue informed choices, set significant learning goals, and take responsibility for their educational experiences. Enabled understudies are proactive colleagues in their schooling, participating in basic requests, intelligent practice, and independent learning. Strengthening advanced education stretches out past scholarly accomplishments to envelop individual and expert development, a comprehensive turn of events, and long-lasting learning. This includes developing the certainty, versatility, and flexibility of understudies, outfitting them with the capabilities and attitudes expected to flourish in a steadily impacting world. Engaged graduates are not just beneficiaries of information, but also dynamic supporters of society, fit for positive change, and make significant commitments to their networks.

Fitting schools to individual necessities customized gaining addresses a takeoff from the conventional one-size-fits-all informative model, wherein instructive encounters are custom-made to the extraordinary qualities, interests, and learning styles of every understudy. It includes utilizing innovation, information investigation, and student-focused teaching methods to provide tweaked pathways, assets, and supports that address individual students' requirements and inclinations. Customized learning incorporates a range of approaches, from separated guidance- and capability-based schooling to versatile learning stages, and experiential learning opens doors. One illustration of customized learning in advanced education is skill-based training (CBE), wherein understudies progress through their coursework in light of the authority of explicit capabilities, as opposed to the end of foreordained time-sensitive units. CBE permits students to progress at their speed, obtain designated help and input, and exhibit capability through legitimate appraisals lined up with true assumptions. Versatile learning stages use calculations to powerfully change the speed, content, and trouble of guidance given the reactions and execution of understudies, working with customized growth opportunities at scale (Ortagus et al., 2020).

The huge understudy strengthening, and customized growth opportunities hold significant ramifications for the understudy results, institutional viability, and a more extensive instructive biological system. Research demonstrates that enabled understudies show more significant levels of inspiration, commitment, and scholastic accomplishment than their sabotaged partners do. When understudies feel a sense of responsibility and organization in their learning, they are bound to persevere notwithstanding difficulties, put forth aggressive objectives, and step up in chasing after their instructive goals. In addition, customized learning has been shown to upgrade learning results, encourage further reasonable comprehension, and advance the dominance of center skills. By fitting guidance to understudies' singular necessities and inclinations, customized learning mitigates the restrictions of customary one-size-fits-all methodologies, taking care of assorted learning styles, capacities and interests. For instance, understudies who battle with specific ideas can obtain designated intercessions and remediation, while those who succeed can seek further developed or advanced learning that opens doors (Bashir et al., 2021).

Institutionally, understudy strengthening and customized learning development align with more extensive endeavors to improve understudy achievement, maintenance, and fulfilment. Enabled understudies are bound to effectively participate in their surroundings, participate in curricular exercises, and search for potential open doors for administration and urban commitment. In addition, foundations that focus on customized learning drives show a pledge to development, responsiveness, and persistent improvement in gathering the development requirements of their different understudy bodies. Difficulties and Contemplations Regardless of the possible advantages, understudy strengthening and customized learning approaches in advanced education present different difficulties and contemplations. One huge test is the requirement for personnel advancement and backing to configure, execute, and evaluate customized opportunities for growth. Numerous instructors might miss the mark on educational mastery, innovative capability, and institutional help expected to incorporate customized learning techniques into their practice. Furthermore, the versatility and supportability of customized learning drives requires cautious preparation, asset designation, and arrangements with institutional objectives and needs.

Moreover, guaranteeing value and inclusivity in customized learning conditions is crucial for addressing differences in access, opportunity, and results among different study populations. There is a gamble that customized learning draws near, if not carried out nicely, may compound existing imbalances and minimize generally underserved understudies. Organizations should focus on value-disapproved practices, socially responsive teaching methods, and proactive help components to guarantee that all understudies have evenhanded admittances to customized growth opportunities. Future Bearings and Suggestions As advanced education continues to develop because of moving cultural, mechanical, and financial elements, the basics of understudy strengthening and customized opportunities for growth will be important. Organizations that focus on understudy organization, independence, and individualization are better suited to meet the assorted requirements and earnings of their inexorably heterogeneous understudy body. Additionally, as headways in innovation and information examination continue to increase, the potential for personalization and customization in training will extend, offering new opportunities to improve learning results and enhance under-study insight. Overall, understudy strengthening and customized growth opportunities are necessary for advancing advanced education, filling in impetuses for commitment, inspiration, and scholarly achievement. By encouraging a culture of strengthening and embracing customized learning draws near, foundations can develop an age of engaged students who are outfitted with information, abilities, and organization to flourish in a complex and quickly impacting world.

The higher education landscape is continuously evolving due to technological advancements, the changing demands of employees and students, increased competition, and shifts in student demographics. In response to these changes, institutional supervisors can focus on three key initiatives to position their institutions effectively.

- Increasing accessibility to new students
- Addressing faculty concerns related to technology
- Supporting and enhancing the learner journey

The future of higher education relies on the ability of institutions to be agile, adaptable, and flexible in their approach to supporting, offering, and developing educational programs and learning designs.

Increasing Accessibility to New Students

Student demographics in higher education have undergone significant changes, with increased accessibility leading to a diverse range of learners seeking advanced degrees. Many working professionals return to educational institutions to obtain higher-level qualifications. To effectively respond to these evolving demographics and attract new students, educational institutions must consider providing scalable and strategic learning options that align with the demands of the job market and prospective students.

This involves considering the types of learning alternatives that employers and students seek, such as specialised programs, certifications, and industry-relevant courses, as well as the different modalities of learning, including online, hybrid, and on-campus learning. By strategically aligning their program offerings with market requirements, educational institutions can attract a broader range of students and extend their reach beyond traditional metro regions to audiences who may be unable to travel to the campus.

However, implementing a market-focused strategy to enhance accessibility to new students can be resource-intensive and time consuming. Educational institutions may consider adopting a forward-thinking program-planning approach known as Strategic Portfolio Development (SPD) to address this challenge. SPD allows institutions to maximise resource utilisation, rapidly expand program offerings, establish a strong digital presence, align program outcomes with employer expectations, and enhance enrolment by offering programs that emphasise market-relevant expertise (Fitzgerlad et al., 2020).

SPD supports institutions in effectively targeting future markets by identifying scalable and strategically aligned digital programme offerings. It enables the development of program suites that build upon each other, potentially integrating the current and future program and content domains. This approach allows the reuse of existing courses and subjects in other in-demand learning provisions, enabling institutions to enhance accessibility to students more efficiently. By continuously assessing trends in the industry and market, and identifying gaps in learning opportunities, institutions can create flexible online curricula that meet the needs of today's learners and prepare them for future employment opportunities.

By adopting a market-oriented approach and leveraging SPD, educational institution supervisors can enhance accessibility to new students, better align their offerings with the demands of the job market, and support learners in acquiring the skills and knowledge needed for success in their chosen career.

Incapacitating Faculty Technological Concerns

Despite the stimulating effects of technology on student engagement in learning, many teachers still have reservations regarding the online learning environment. Some experts argue that the traditional classroom setting, with physical teacher presence, offers greater value than virtual engagement. To address these concerns and obtain faculty support for virtual learning initiatives, school administrators must take deliberate steps (Hong and Ma, 2020).

It is crucial for administrators to fully understand, acknowledge, and address the concerns raised by the faculty, which typically fall into three main domains: incentives, support, and quality. By carefully planning and taking action in these areas, administrators can navigate the development of high-quality and successful online or hybrid initiatives, avoiding conflicts and negative consequences on campuses.

It is understandable that faculty members may feel uncertain and have concerns about the outcomes and quality of virtual education. However, administrators have an opportunity to assist faculty in embracing new technologies, as their alignment with these technologies ultimately impacts the overall quality of courses and educational experience.

By actively addressing faculty concerns, providing incentives to engage with technology, offering comprehensive support, and ensuring a focus on quality, administrators can alleviate faculty technological concerns and create an environment in which faculty members feel confident and supported in adopting and integrating technology into their teaching practices.

Supporting and Refining the Learner Journey

The proliferation of e-commerce businesses such as Amazon has significantly influenced learners' expectations regarding their experiences with educational institutions. Students now approach their education with a consumer-service-like mindset. If their expectations of attention and assistance are not met, they are more likely to seek alternatives elsewhere. To differentiate themselves, increase enrolment, and retain students, universities and colleges must place a strong emphasis on enhancing student experiences throughout the entire educational journey, from the initial stages to graduation.

This emphasis on enhancing the learner journey requires institutions to go beyond simply providing education and to focus on delivering a comprehensive and personalised experience. From the moment students consider enrolling in a program, they expect prompt and relevant information, efficient application processes, and support for navigating their educational options. Once enrolled, students seek engaging and interactive learning experiences, access to resources and support services, opportunities for personal and professional growth, and clear pathways to their desired careers. Institutions must also provide effective mechanisms for feedback and continuous improvement, ensuring that students' voices are heard, and their needs addressed throughout their educational journey.

By prioritising the enhancement of student experiences, institutions can distinguish themselves in a competitive landscape, attract and retain students, and foster a strong sense of loyalty and connection. This requires a student-centric approach that involves proactive communication, personalised support, innovative teaching methods, and commitment to continuous improvement. Through these efforts, institutions can create an environment where students feel valued, supported, and empowered.

THE ROLE OF HIGHER EDUCATION IN ADDRESSING SOCIAL AND POLITICAL DIVISIONS AND PROMOTING TRUST IN INFORMATION

Advanced education plays a significant role in tending toward social and political divisions and advancing confidence in data through different channels, including educational plan improvement, examination, and local area commitment. By encouraging decisive reasoning, urban proficiency, and a promise of prove-based thinking, advanced education organizations add to the development of educated and connected residents to explore complex cultural issues and knowledge of solid data from falsehood. One way in which advanced education foundations address social and political divisions is through the reconciliation of city schooling and popularity-based standards into their educational plans. Courses in political theory, human science, history, and correspondence furnish understudies with a more profound comprehension of the political cycle, social elements, and the media's role in forming a general assessment. For instance, seminars on media education outfit understudies with the ability to fundamentally assess the well-being of data, recognize inclination, and recognize truth and assessment (Sherman et al., 2022).

Moreover, interdisciplinary projects emphasizing metro commitment, civil rights, and local area sorting enable understudies to become dynamic members in the vote-based cycle and specialists in positive change inside their networks. Advanced educational establishments add to social and political divisions through examination and information creation. Employees participate in interdisciplinary exploration that reveals insights into squeezing cultural issues, illuminates public approach discussions, and advances proof-based navigation. For instance, political theory, brain science, and correspondence scientists concentrate on the elements that add to polarization, deception, and doubt in organizations, giving bits of knowledge to powerful procedures to cultivate social unions and advance confidence in data.

Additionally, colleges act as centers for discourse, discussion, and coordinated effort, uniting researchers, policymakers, and local-area individuals to trade thoughts, share viewpoints, and foster inventive answers to complex difficulties. Even with scholastic undertakings, advanced education establishments participate in local area efforts, and government-funded training drives pointed toward connecting social and political partitions and advancing confidence in data. Through associations with nearby associations, government offices, and local area pioneers, colleges work with exchanges, local area discussions, and arrange occasions that advance common talk, shared understanding, and joint effort. For instance, colleges might have municipal events, board conversations, and studios on points such as media proficiency, political polarization, and productive compromise, furnishing individuals from the local area with opportunities to participate in deferential and helpful exchanges.

In addition, advanced education organizations are critical in advancing variety, value, and consideration, which are fundamental to cultivating social unions and building trust in data. By embracing a variety of structures and establishing comprehensive learning conditions, colleges develop a culture of regard, sympathy, and appreciation from different points of view. This inclusivity reaches out to the educational program, personnel enlistment, and under-study support administrations, guaranteeing that all individuals from the college's local area feel esteemed, heard, and addressed. Through drives, for example, coaching in racial awareness, social capability studios, value-disapproved strategies, and advanced education foundations endeavors to destroy fundamental hindrances, advance civil rights, and make a more impartial society.

Advanced education displays a complex parole tending to social and political divisions and advancing confidence in data. Through educational plan improvement, research, local area commitment, and a guarantee of variety, value, and consideration, colleges add to the development of educated, connected with, and communally proficient residents to explore complex cultural issues and take part definitively in the majority rule process. By cultivating decisive reasoning, advancing proof-based thinking, and working with discourse and coordinated effort, advanced education organizations act as impetuses for positive social change and drivers of progress towards a stronger, comprehensive, and majority-rule society.

RECOGNIZING THE NEED FOR AGILITY AND ADAPTABILITY IN HIGHER EDUCATION INSTITUTIONS

In a period set apart by fast mechanical progressions, moving socioeconomics, and developing cultural necessities, advanced education establishments face developing strains to adjust and improve to live up to the understudies' changing assumptions and requirements. The basis for nimbleness and versatility in advanced education originates from the acknowledgement that customary education and learning models may never again do the trick to prepare understudies for progress in an undeniable mind-boggling and dynamic world. One of the main reasons for the requirement for dexterity and versatility in advanced education organizations is the changing assumptions for understudies. The present understudies, frequently referred to as computerized locals, have experienced childhood at an advanced age, portrayed by moment admittance to data, customized encounters, and adaptable learning modalities.

Accordingly, they anticipate that advanced educational establishments should connect with intelligent and innovatively upgraded growth opportunities that are significant, adaptable, and receptive to their singular necessities and inclinations. For instance, understudies progressively look for open doors for experiential learning, certifiable applications, and interdisciplinary cooperation that overcomes any issues between hypotheses and practice. They esteem instructive encounters that allow them to foster decisive reasoning, critical thinking, and adaptable relational abilities in assorted settings. Advanced education establishments should be deft and versatile in planning educational plans, templates, and curricular exercises that align developing assumptions and prepare understudies for outcomes in the 21st-century labor force (Blankenberger and Williams, 2020).

Readiness and versatility in advanced education are also fundamental to saddling the capability of arising patterns and advancements to upgrade education and learning. The rapid speed of mechanical development presents two amazing open doors and difficulties for advanced education establishments using computerized apparatuses, information investigation, and artificial brainpower to work on instructive results and upgrade their understudy insight. Establishments that embrace lithe practices can rapidly adjust to mechanical headways, explore different avenues regarding new showing systems, and coordinate inventive learning advances into informative practices. For example, versatile learning stages use calculations to customize guidance, provide prompt input, and adjust to the understudies' singular advancing necessities and inclinations. Additionally, advancements in computer-generated reality (VR) and expanded reality (AR) offer vivid growth opportunities that mimic certifiable conditions and draw in understudies of intelligent reproduction and virtual field trips. By embracing a dexterous way of dealing with an innovation mix, advanced education organizations can keep up-to-date with arising patterns, explore different avenues regarding new apparatuses and techniques, and constantly work on the quality and pertinence of the instructive encounters they propose to understudy. In addition, market requests and worldwide contests drive the requirements for nimbleness and versatility in advanced education organizations. In an undeniably cutthroat scene, establishments should be receptive to changing business sector elements, segment shifts, and financial patterns to draw in and hold understudies, staff, and subsidies. Foundations that exhibit nimbleness in responding to business sector requests can separate themselves by offering creative projects, adaptable booking choices, and experiential learning, thus opening doors that meet understudies' assorted requirements and inclinations.

In addition, globalization has strengthened the contest among advanced education establishments for worldwide understudies, workforce abilities, and examination associations. Establishments that show spryness in adjusting to worldwide patterns and cultivating culturally diverse coordinated efforts are better situated to profit by opening doors for internationalization, cooperation, and information trade. By embracing variety, inclusivity, and worldwide perspectives, advanced education establishments can improve the instructive experience for all understudies and set them up for progress in an interconnected and reliant world. The requirement for spryness and flexibility in advanced education establishments is fundamental in gathering the developing necessities and assumptions for understudies in the present dynamic and rapidly evolving scene. By perceiving and responding to changing understudy assumptions, arising patterns and advancements, market requests, and worldwide rivalry, foundations can remain important, imaginative, and receptive to the necessities of their partners. Through essential preparation, coordinated effort, and a promise for constant improvement, advanced education establishments can adjust to the difficulties and opportunities of the 21st century and maintain their main goal of teaching, enabling the upcoming age of pioneers, trailblazers, and worldwide residents.

EXAMINING THE POTENTIAL OF SHORT-TERM ACCREDITATION AND STACKABLE CREDENTIALS

Transient licenses and stackable accreditations have arisen as creative answers to overcome any barrier between advanced education degrees and occupation market requests by giving people designated abilities and qualifications aligned with industry needs. These adaptable, skill-based approaches offer pathways for students to gain applicable abilities and accreditations steadily, permitting them to enter or progress inside the labor force all the more rapidly and really. One of the key difficulties confronting advanced education is the ability crisscross between what understudies realize in customary degree programs and the abilities requested by businesses in the present rapidly developing position market. Transient licenses and stackable certifications offer a more coordinated and responsive way to deal with ability improvement, permitting people to secure industry-explicit abilities and capabilities within a more limited period than customary degree programs. For instance, in momentary authentication programs in fields such as network safety, information examination, and projects, executives furnish students with designated preparation and active involvement with appeal regions, setting them up for section-level positions or professional success valuable open doors.

One of the critical benefits of momentary licenses and stackable accreditations is their adaptability and customization, which allows students to fit their instructive pathways to their particular objectives, interests, and professional desires. Instead of focusing on an extended-degree program, people can seek momentary endorsements or miniature qualifications pertinent to their ideal vocation. These certifications can be procured part-time or full-time, permitting people to offset their schooling with work and other responsibilities.

Furthermore, stackable certifications empower students to expand their current abilities and accreditations over the long run, continuously advancing towards further developed capabilities and professional amazing open doors. Transient authorization and stackable qualifications are planned in close cooperation with industry accomplices, guaranteeing that the abilities and capabilities shown in these projects are pertinent to the present place of employment market requests.

By integrating input from businesses, industry affiliations, and labor force improvement offices, credentialing projects can adjust their educational plans to industry guidelines, arising patterns, and mechanical progressions. This industry arrangement improves the employability of certification workers, as managers perceive the pertinence and money of these accreditations in the work market. For instance, confirmations, such as CompTIA A+ for IT experts or AWS-Ensured Arrangements Planner for distributed computing, are exceptionally esteemed by bosses looking for competitors with explicit specialized mastery.

Momentary certification and stackable accreditations additionally advance deep-rooted advancement by giving people valuable opportunities to refresh and grow their abilities throughout their profession. In the present quickly evolving economy, where mechanical progressions and market disturbances are steady, the capacity to adjust and gain new abilities is fundamental for the remaining cutthroat in the labor force. Transient certifications offer an adaptable and open pathway for people to obtain new abilities, turn to new professional ways, or reskill because of changing market position requests. Besides, stackable certifications empower students to amass credits and qualifications over the long haul, prompting numerous passage and leave focuses along their instructive excursion

Overall, momentary certification and stackable accreditations hold enormous potential in overcoming barriers between advanced education degrees and occupation market requests by offering adaptable, industry-adjusted pathways for ability improvement and professional success. By furnishing students with designated preparation and industry-perceived accreditations and opening doors for long-lasting learning, these imaginative methodologies engage people to obtain the abilities and capabilities expected to prevail in the present dynamic and cutthroat labor force. As the interest in gifted laborers develops and the idea of work advances, transient authorization and stackable accreditations are ready to assume an undeniably significant part in planning people for progress in the 21st-century economy.

STRATEGIES FOR SUPPORTING THE WELL-BEING AND HEALTH OF STUDENTS IN THE VIRTUAL LEARNING ENVIRONMENT

As training progressively moves towards virtual learning conditions, addressing the prosperity and soundness of understudies in these settings becomes basic. The change to Internet learning, advanced by variables such as the Coronavirus pandemic, presents extraordinary difficulties that can influence understudies' psychological, physical, and close-to-home well-being. Teachers and foundations should investigate techniques to advance prosperity and cultivate a strong and helpful climate for learning. This paper examines different methodologies and drives that support understudies' prosperity and well-being in the virtual learning climate, taking into account both proactive measures and responsive mediations. Virtual learning conditions represent a few difficulties that can influence understudies' prosperity and well-being (Tariq, 2024; Babar et al., 2023).

The absence of close and personal cooperation and actual presence can add to the sensations of detachment, forlornness, and disengagement among understudies. In addition, delayed screen time and stationary behavior related to web-based earnings can prompt medical problems, such as eye strain, outer muscle issues, and diminished active work. Furthermore, obscuring the limits between home and school life in a virtual climate can lead to increased pressure, burnout, and trouble balancing serious and fun activities.

Moreover, computerized partitioning worsens variations in admittance to innovation and web availability, restricting understudies' capacity to participate completely in web-based learning exercises. Understudies from minimized or underserved networks might confront difficulties in obtaining vital equipment, programming, and dependable web access, further fueling existing imbalances.

Tending these difficulties requires a comprehensive methodology that considers the interconnectedness of the physical, mental, profound, and social aspects of prosperity. One vital procedure for supporting understudies' prosperity in a virtual learning climate is advancing emotional well-being and close-to-home prosperity. This can be accomplished through different drives, encouraging a feeling of local area, association, and place among understudies. For instance, teachers can integrate amazing open doors for social associations, peer-coordinated efforts, and conversations into web-based learning exercises.

Virtual review gatherings, conversation discussions, and cooperative activities allow understudies to interface with companions, share encounters, and assemble steady connections. In addition, proactive measures such as normal registrations, overviews, and evaluations can assist teachers in recognizing understudies who might be battling psychological wellness issues or encountering uplifted feelings of anxiety. Admittance to emotional wellbeing assets, directing administrations, and encouraging groups of people can engage in understudies to look for help and access the help they need (Kaleem et al., 2024).

Moreover, integrating care rehearses, unwinding procedures, and stressing the executive's techniques into the educational program can furnish understudies with the ability to adapt to difficulties and assemble versatility. In addition to advancing psychological wellness and close-to-home prosperity, addressing acts of well-being once they belong well to the virtual toning climate is crucial. Teachers can urge understudies to pursue sound routines, such as enjoying customary reprieves, remaining hydrated, and participating in daily work.

Integrating development breaks, extending activities, and care exercises into online classes can assist in reducing actual strain and advancing general prosperity. In addition, bringing issues to light about ergonomics, legitimate stance, and screen ergonomics can assist in moderating outer muscle issues and lessen the gambling of dreary strain wounds. Giving direction to setting up ergonomic workstations and changing guest plans can engage understudies to establish a helpful learning climate that upholds their well-being and solace. Guaranteeing value and access in a virtual learning climate are pivotal for supporting prosperity and soundness, as everything is equal (Raimi et al. 2022).

Organizations should effectively attempt to connect computerized partitions by giving admittance to vital innovation, web availability, and specialized help administrations. This might include giving loaner gadgets, portable areas of interest, and advanced education to understudy from underserved networks. In addition, planning the web courses and materials considering openness can guarantee that all understudies, incorporating those with handicaps or different advancing requirements, can completely partake and participate in virtual learning exercises. Subtitling recordings, giving elective text to pictures, and utilizing available learning-the-board frameworks advances inclusivity and availability in web-based schooling. Establishing a strong learning climate is fundamental for advancing the prosperity and well-being of understudies in virtual homeroom (Mateev et al., 2023).

Instructors can cultivate peace and mental security by exhibiting sympathy, understanding, and adaptability towards the singular conditions and needs of understudies. Being receptive to under-study input, concerns, and demands for facilities can assist in developing a culture of care and backing inside the Internet learning local area. In addition, encouraging a feeling of independence, organization, and strengthening among understudies can upgrade their inspiration, commitment, and self-viability in the virtual learning climate. Giving open doors to understudy decisions, independence, and privately managed learning can cultivate feelings of responsibility and interest in the educational experience (Raimi et al. 2022).

Moreover, straightforward correspondence, clear assumptions, and customary input can assist understudies by exploring difficulties, overseeing assumptions, and remaining roused through their web-based learning ventures. Overall, supporting the prosperity and strength of understudies in the virtual learning climate requires a far-reaching and multilayered approach that addresses the physical, mental, profound, and social components of prosperity. By advancing psychological wellness, tending to actual well-being concerns, guaranteeing value and access, and developing a strong learning climate, instructors and establishments can make conditions helpful for understudy achievement, commitment, and all-encompassing turns of events. As virtual learning continues, it is fundamental to focus on understudies' prosperity and well-being as the central components of compelling and comprehensive instruction (Rahman et al., 2023).

LESSON LEARNED BUT MISSED OBJECTIVE

During the global pandemic, many staff, students, and faculty have embraced synchronous online experiences and courses as alternatives to in-person education. However, it soon became apparent that such educational approaches demanded extensive planning and sufficient resources to ensure student success. Students facing financial and family constraints often struggle to meet designated time requirements without additional support, such as elder care or childcare. The varying care needs and capacity of the marketplace to address them pose significant challenges. Faculty members also faced similar constraints and had to make adjustments to course requirements and schedules because of their own shifting care responsibilities (Tariq, 2024).

To accommodate these challenges, the faculty implemented measures such as offering flexible due dates for assessments and extending office hours to accommodate students who belonged to vulnerable population groups. While some faculty members found it difficult to allocate additional resources, they recognized the importance of addressing the diverse needs of students. Faculty members in higher education institutions have made efforts to develop equitable grading procedures across their courses and design assignments that align with curricular objectives and promote fairness. Overall, university faculty members have embraced a deeper understanding of the challenges faced by the current student demographics. They have shown the ability to incorporate flexibility into course preparation without compromising learning outcomes. This experience underscores the importance of being responsive to the varying needs of students and ensuring equity in educational practices.

Virtual assignments in universities pose various challenges for the staff, faculty, and students. Some faculty members and students encounter issues related to Internet connectivity, especially during critical testing times. Others face complications due to elderly care, childcare, and other responsibilities during exam sessions. Additionally, some students struggle to find a quiet environment for exams or experience a combination of these difficulties. Recognising these factors, faculties have emphasised flexibility in virtual assignments by considering alternative assignments, testing locations, and procedures. For example, assessing the details in large graphics on small screens during student presentations and examinations can be challenging. Faculty members address this issue by providing detailed feedback and suggestions based on a comparative assessment of images and graphics. They often provide more extensive written feedback to compensate for the inability to comment directly on visuals. This requires increased effort from the faculty and support from strategic and online learning departments.

Certain subjects who rely heavily on hands-on use and training with equipment face limitations in virtual settings. Many students encounter obstacles in obtaining the desired learning experiences in these hands-on subjects and require additional assistance to visualise working with the equipment. Virtual environments often fail to replicate physical and intellectual aspects of these disciplines. Faculty members are now recognising these limitations and are implementing and developing technology boxes that can be shipped to students. These boxes contain equipment, videos, or laboratories that provide the necessary software and hardware for students to engage in projects or courses. Students living on campus can collect these boxes in a contactless manner, whereas institutions can deliver them to students who require them through philanthropic and funding resources. Socially distanced workstations and labs that require physical presence on campus have also been established, requiring institutions to think creatively and adapt to students' needs. This may involve expanding the class timings to weekends and later hours on weekdays.

CONCLUSION

A crucial aspect of enhancing student experience is customisation, as each student has unique behaviours, responses, and thought processes. The challenge lies in how institutions can develop high-quality and customised experiences with limited resources, considering the individuality of each student. It is important to recognise students' goals, aspirations, and reasons for choosing to pursue higher education. Supporting students throughout their educational journey and helping them understand the value that an educational institution provides are paramount. Offering the necessary assistance and resources to students as they navigate their educational journey is especially crucial, as institutions continue to expand their presence in the virtual space and demonstrate the value of higher education.

Many administrators have recognised the significance of establishing strategic partnerships to support recruitment and marketing strategies. By forging these associations, institutions can better meet students' expectations, attract new students, and showcase their unique offerings and benefits. In summary, the key to simplifying students' experiences lies in customisation, understanding their individual needs, and providing tailored support. While it may be challenging to achieve this with limited resources, institutions must prioritise recognising students' aims and desires, and assisting them in recognising the value of higher education. By offering necessary assistance and resources throughout the student journey, institutions can continue to expand in the virtual space and highlight the importance of higher education. Administrators can play a vital role in creating strategic partnerships that support recruitment and marketing efforts, ultimately contributing to the success and satisfaction of students.

REFERENCES

Alt, D., Kapshuk, Y., & Dekel, H. (2023). Promoting perceived creativity and innovative behavior: Benefits of future problem-solving programs for higher education students. *Thinking Skills and Creativity*, 47, 101201. DOI:10.1016/j.tsc.2022.101201

Bashir, A., Bashir, S., Rana, K., Lambert, P., & Vernallis, A. (2021, August). Post-COVID-19 adaptations; the shifts towards online learning, hybrid course delivery and the implications for biosciences courses in the higher education setting. *Frontiers in Education*, 6, 711619. DOI:10.3389/feduc.2021.711619

Blankenberger, B., & Williams, A. M. (2020). COVID and the impact on higher education: The essential role of integrity and accountability. *Administrative Theory & Praxis*, 42(3), 404–423. DOI:10.1080/10841806.2020.1771907

Cesco, S., Zara, V., De Toni, A. F., Lugli, P., Betta, G., Evans, A. C., & Orzes, G. (2021). Higher education in the first year of COVID-19: Thoughts and perspectives for the future. *International Journal of Higher Education*, 10(3), 285–294. DOI:10.5430/ijhe.v10n3p285

Chan, C. K. Y., & Hu, W. (2023). Students' voices on generative AI: Perceptions, benefits, and challenges in higher education. *International Journal of Educational Technology in Higher Education*, 20(1), 43. DOI:10.1186/s41239-023-00411-8

Chatterjee, S., & Bhattacharjee, K. K. (2020). Adoption of artificial intelligence in higher education: A quantitative analysis using structural equation modelling. *Education and Information Technologies*, 25(5), 3443–3463. DOI:10.1007/s10639-020-10159-7

Crompton, H., & Burke, D. (2023). Artificial intelligence in higher education: The state of the field. *International Journal of Educational Technology in Higher Education*, 20(1), 22. DOI:10.1186/s41239-023-00392-8

De Wit, H., & Altbach, P. G. (2021). Internationalization in higher education: Global trends and recommendations for its future. *Policy Reviews in Higher Education*, 5(1), 28–46. DOI:10.1080/23322969.2020.1820898

Duran, A., Orozco, R. C., & Gonzalez, S. A. (2020). Imagining the future of jotería studies as a framework in the field of higher education. *Association of Mexican American Educators Journal*, 14(2), 67–86. DOI:10.24974/amae.14.2.360

El Said, G. R. (2021). How Did the COVID-19 Pandemic Affect Higher Education Learning Experience? An Empirical Investigation of Learners' Academic Performance at a University in a Developing Country. *Advances in Human-Computer Interaction*, 2021(1), 6649524. DOI:10.1155/2021/6649524

Eringfeld, S. (2021). Higher education and its post-coronial future: Utopian hopes and dystopian fears at Cambridge University during Covid-19. *Studies in Higher Education*, 46(1), 146–157. DOI:10.1080/03075079.2020.1859681

Fitzgerald, H. E., Karen, B., Sonka, S. T., Furco, A., & Swanson, L. (2020). The centrality of engagement in higher education. In *Building the field of higher education engagement* (pp. 201–219). Routledge.

Gallagher, S. E., & Savage, T. (2023). Challenge-based learning in higher education: An exploratory literature review. *Teaching in Higher Education*, 28(6), 1135–1157. DOI:10.1080/13562517.2020.1863354

Govindarajan, V., & Srivastava, A. (2020). What the shift to virtual learning could mean for the future of higher ed. *Harvard Business Review*, 31(1), 3–8.

Guàrdia, L., Crisp, G., & Alsina, I. (2020). Trends and challenges of e-assessment to enhance student learning in higher education. *Learning and Performance Assessment: Concepts, Methodologies, Tools, and Applications*, 1575-1595.

Hong, C., & Ma, W. W. (2020). Introduction: Education 4.0: Applied degree education and the future of work. In *Applied Degree Education and the Future of Work: Education 4.0* (pp. 1–13). Springer Singapore. DOI:10.1007/978-981-15-3142-2_1

Lauder, H. (2020). The roles of higher education, further education and lifelong learning in the future economy. *Journal of Education and Work*, 33(7-8), 460–467. DOI:10.1080/13639080.2020.1852499

Looi, K. H. (2024). Ameliorating emergency Web-enabled teaching in higher education institutions and implications for future emergencies. *Information Discovery and Delivery*, 52(3), 289–304. DOI:10.1108/IDD-01-2023-0005

Neuwirth, L. S., Jović, S., & Mukherji, B. R. (2021). Reimagining higher education during and post-COVID-19: Challenges and opportunities. *Journal of Adult and Continuing Education*, 27(2), 141–156. DOI:10.1177/1477971420947738

Ortagus, J. C., Kelchen, R., Rosinger, K., & Voorhees, N. (2020). Performance-based funding in American higher education: A systematic synthesis of the intended and unintended consequences. *Educational Evaluation and Policy Analysis*, 42(4), 520–550. DOI:10.3102/0162373720953128

Rasul, T., Nair, S., Kalendra, D., Robin, M., de Oliveira Santini, F., Ladeira, W. J., & Heathcote, L. (2023). The role of ChatGPT in higher education: Benefits, challenges, and future research directions. *Journal of Applied Learning and Teaching*, 6(1), 41–56.

Rudolph, J., Tan, S., & Tan, S. (2023). ChatGPT: Bullshit spewer or the end of traditional assessments in higher education? *Journal of Applied Learning and Teaching, 6*(1), 342-363.

Salas-Pilco, S. Z., Yang, Y., & Zhang, Z. (2022). Student engagement in online learning in Latin American higher education during the COVID-19 pandemic: A systematic review. *British Journal of Educational Technology*, 53(3), 593–619. DOI:10.1111/bjet.13190 PMID:35600418

Sherman, M., Puhovskiy, E., Kambalova, Y., & Kdyrova, I. (2022). The future of distance education in war or the education of the future (the Ukrainian case study). *Futurity Education*, 2(3), 15–24.

Tariq, M. U. (2024). Crafting Authentic Narratives for Sustainable Branding. In *Compelling Storytelling Narratives for Sustainable Branding* (pp. 194–229). IGI Global. DOI:10.4018/979-8-3693-3326-6.ch011

Tariq, M. U. (2024). The role of AI in skilling, upskilling, and reskilling the workforce. In Doshi, R., Dadhich, M., Poddar, S., & Hiran, K. (Eds.), *Integrating generative AI in education to achieve sustainable development goals* (pp. 421–433). IGI Global. DOI:10.4018/979-8-3693-2440-0.ch023

Toquero, C. M. (2020). Challenges and opportunities for higher education amid the COVID-19 pandemic: The Philippine context. *Pedagogical Research, 5*(4). Applications and Management Frameworks. In Popkova, E. (Ed.), *Smart Technologies and Innovations in E-Business* (pp. 25–46). IGI Global. DOI:10.4018/978-1-6684-7840-0.ch002

ADDITIONAL READING

Babar, M., Alshehri, M. D., Tariq, M. U., Ullah, F., Khan, A., Uddin, M. I., & Almasoud, A. S. (2021). IoT-enabled big data analytics architecture for multimedia data communications. *Wireless Communications and Mobile Computing*, 2021(1), 1–9. DOI:10.1155/2021/5283309

Babar, M., Tariq, M. U., Almasoud, A. S., & Alshehri, M. D. (2021). Privacy-aware data forensics of VRUs using machine learning and big data analytics. *Security and Communication Networks*, 2021, 1–9. DOI:10.1155/2021/3320436

Babar, M., Tariq, M. U., Alshehri, M. D., Ullah, F., & Uddin, M. I. (2022). Smart teledentistry healthcare architecture for medical big data analysis using IoT-enabled environment. *Sustainable Computing : Informatics and Systems*, 35, 100719. DOI:10.1016/j.suscom.2022.100719

Banu, S. R., Thulasi, V. V. Y. R., Tariq, M. U., & Sethi, S. (2023). Relationship between leadership effectiveness and organizational performance and its effect on human resource management. *Journal of Informatics Education and Research*, 3(2).

Bhardwaj, S., Nair, K., Tariq, M. U., Ahmad, A., & Chitnis, A. (2023). The state of research in green marketing: A bibliometric review from 2005 to 2022. *Sustainability (Basel)*, 15(4), 2988. DOI:10.3390/su15042988

Mateev, M., Tariq, M. U., & Sahyouni, A. (2023). Efficiency, market concentration and bank performance during the COVID-19 outbreak: Evidence from the MENA region. *PLoS One*, 18(5), e0285403. DOI:10.1371/journal.pone.0285403 PMID:37163516

Raimi, L., Kah, J. M., & Tariq, M. U. (2022). The discourse of blue economy definitions, measurements, and theories: Implications for strengthening academic research and industry practice. In Raimi, L., & Kah, J. (Eds.), *Implications for entrepreneurship and enterprise development in the blue economy* (pp. 1–17). IGI Global. DOI:10.4018/978-1-6684-3393-5.ch001

Raimi, L., Tariq, M. U., & Kah, J. M. (2022). Diversity, equity, and inclusion as the future workplace ethics: Theoretical review. In Raimi, L., & Kah, J. (Eds.), *Mainstreaming diversity, equity, and inclusion as future workplace ethics* (pp. 1–27). IGI Global. DOI:10.4018/978-1-6684-3657-8.ch001

KEY TERMS AND DEFINITIONS

Adaptive Learning Technologies: Educational technologies that use algorithms to personalize the learning experience by adjusting the content, pace, and difficulty level to meet the individual needs.

Competency-Based Education (CBE): An approach where students progress through their coursework based on their demonstration of mastery of specific skills or competencies.

Data Privacy: The branch of data management that deals with the proper handling, processing, storage, and usage of personal data to ensure it is protected from unauthorized access and misuse.

Stackable Credentials: Certifications that can be accumulated over time to build up an individual's qualifications and help them progress in their careers by gaining new skills and competencies relevant to their job market.

Chapter 4
Artificial Intelligence Challenges in Higher Education

ABSTRACT

This chapter focuses on the intricacies and future possibilities of coordinating computerised reasoning (artificial intelligence) innovations in the advanced education scene. It investigates the multi-layered difficulties faced by establishments, instructors, and partners in utilising artificial intelligence to upgrade education, learning, and regulatory cycles. Ethical considerations, algorithmic bias, data privacy and security, faculty development and support, integration with existing systems, equity and access, and other key topics are also discussed. Through a complete examination, this part features the basics of addressing these difficulties to guarantee the viable and moral execution of artificial intelligence in advanced education. By taking into account assorted points of view and embracing proactive measures, organisations can saddle the extraordinary capability of artificial intelligence to progress instructive results and encourage comprehensive, even-handed learning conditions for all understudies.

INTRODUCTION

Artificial intelligence in higher education systems is a widely discussed subject worldwide. However, this perspective differs across developing and developed countries. Researchers have elaborated on the widespread problems faced by the higher education sector worldwide while implementing artificial intelligence. The implementation of artificial intelligence systems and algorithms in education has progressed each year. As education progresses, researchers are implementing ad-

DOI: 10.4018/979-8-3693-4074-5.ch004

vanced artificial intelligence techniques such as data mining, deep learning, and big data to manage complicated learning problems and personalise teaching methods for individual learners. The COVID-19 pandemic has augmented the procedure by taking online classes, assessments, and lectures. Artificial intelligence is already added value to the educational sector. Implementing artificial intelligence can be an intimidating challenge for educational institutions which lack time, resources, and expertise to discover its many benefits. Higher education does not leverage artificial intelligence at a formal level. The present usage of artificial intelligence is inch-deep and milli-wide. It is not difficult to determine why. Artificial intelligence is a highly imprecise concept and is mainly exhibited in such a theoretical, future-oriented way that one may attempt to comprehend it as something that can be categorically implemented in their firm or job (Zawacki-Richter et al., 2019).

Artificial Intelligence has become an extraordinary power across different areas, including advanced education. Recently, instructive establishments had progressively incorporated computer-based intelligence advances to improve education, learning, regulatory cycles, and understudy support administrations. Despite the promising possibilities of computer-based intelligence, its execution in advanced education is challenging. This acquaintance points out that the complex difficulties presented by the reception of simulated intelligence in advanced education settings should be investigated and resolved. One of the essential difficulties in carrying out artificial intelligence in advanced education is the moral ramifications that encompassss itutilisationon. As artificial intelligence calculations become more refined, information protection, value, and predisposition concerns emerge. For example, simulated intelligence-controlled confirmation frameworks can unintentionally propagate predispositions to authentic information, prompting out-of-line results for specific segment gatherings (Chen & Johri, 2020). Besides, the assortment and usage of understudied information brings up moral issues concerning assent, straightforwardness, and the expected abuse of individual data (Selwyn, 2020). Another huge test relates to the variation of artificial intelligence advances to the special setting of advanced education. Unlike different areas where computer-based intelligence applications are clearer, the intricacies of instructive conditions present additional obstacles. For instance, creating simulated intelligence-driven coaching frameworks requires a profound comprehension of teaching methods, understudy of educational experiences, and informative plan standards (VanLehn et al., 2007).

Consequently, coordinating computer-based intelligence successfully in instructive settings requires a joint effort between technologists, teachers, and scientists to guarantee arrangements with instructive objectives and practices. In addition, computerised partitioning worsens the difficulties related to computer-based intelligence execution in advanced education. While simulated intelligence can democratise admittance to schooling by offering customised growth opportunities, aberrations in admittance to innovation and advanced proficiency abilities frustrate fair support (Gonzalez et al., 2019). Understudies from oppressed foundations might be short on fundamental assets or support to connect definitively with artificial intelligence-empowered instructive apparatuses, broadening existing instructive imbalances. In addition, keeping faculty and staff up-to-date on AI developments and proficient in their use is challenging, given the rapid pace of technological advancement.

According to Wawacki-Richter et al. (2019), educational institutions must invest in ongoing professional development programs to provide faculty members with the knowledge and abilities necessary to effectively use AI in teaching and research. With satisfactory preparation and backing, teachers might feel energised to incorporate artificial intelligence into their work, blocking broad reception. Although the combination of computer-based intelligence in advanced education holds enormous potential for further developing learning results, improving managerial productivity, and cultivating development, it also presents various difficulties. Adjusting artificial intelligence to instructive settings, spanning the computerised partition, and guaranteeing workforce status are among the key snags that instructive establishments should explore to bridge the full advantages of artificial intelligence in advanced education.

An astonishing number of leaders in institutions do not recognise how artificial intelligence is implemented across different parts of their institutions. Some are unaware of using artificial intelligence for higher education instructional tasks, such as tutoring and plagiarism detection. Some do not recognise that artificial intelligence is utilised for institutional tasks, such as fundraising, planning support, resources, and development. Some leaders are unaware of how artificial intelligence should be used for student support and success (Hwang et al., 2020).

In contemporary instruction, the mix of Artificial Intelligence reasoning (Artificial intelligence) has become progressively predominant, offering commitment to proficiency, development, and further learning results. Be that as it may, notwithstanding its likely advantages, there remains a prominent role in understanding among advanced education pioneers regarding the degree to which computer-based intelligence is being used inside their organizations. This paper aims to investigate this phenomenon by examining the factors contributing to leaders' scepticism regarding the adoption of AI, its repercussions, and potential solutions to this knowledge gap. Through a broad survey of writing and experimental proof, this study aims to provide some knowledge into the present status of artificial intelligence use in advanced education authorities and provide suggestions for upgrading mindfulness and understanding.

Artificial Intelligence has arisen as a groundbreaking power in different areas, including schooling, with the possibility of changing education, learning, and regulatory cycles. In advanced education, simulated intelligence applications range from customised learning stages to prescient examinations for understudied achievement. Despite the rising predominance of advances in simulated intelligence in instructive settings, there exists an outstanding error in mindfulness and understanding among advanced education pioneers regarding the degree to which artificial intelligence is being used inside their establishments. This paper digs into this peculiarity, investigating the explanations for pioneers' vulnerability in computer-based intelligence reception, its suggestions, and possible procedures for tending to this information hole.

A few variables add to the vulnerability of pioneers in advanced education regarding the use of computer-based intelligence. The fast speed of innovative progression, first and foremost, frequently outperforms pioneers' comprehension and attention to emerging advances (Delen & Lassoued, 2017). As artificial intelligence advances and new applications arise, pioneers might battle to stay informed about the most recent events and their expected ramifications in advanced education.

Besides, the intricacy of artificial intelligence advancements presents difficulties for pioneers in understanding their functionalities and applications inside instructive settings (Zawacki-Richter et al., 2019). Unlike conventional apparatuses and frameworks, artificial intelligence frequently works through calculations and AI models, which might be dark and challenging to decipher for those without specialised ability. This absence of straightforwardness can add to the vulnerability of pioneers to how artificial intelligence is used inside their organisations. In addition, the decentralised idea of dynamics in advanced education foundations can block pioneers' capacity to acquire far-reaching comprehension of computer-based intelligence use (Chen & Johri, 2020). With numerous divisions and units freely investigating and executing artificial intelligence drives, pioneers might battle to facilitate endeavours and obtain an all-encompassing perspective on artificial intelligence reception across the organisation.

The vulnerability of pioneers in advanced education concerning computer-based intelligence usage has a few ramifications for institutional viability and development. This may impede key preparation and dynamic cycles as pioneers might disregard the chances of computer-based intelligence working on instructive results and functional effectiveness (Gonzalez et al., 2019). Without a reasonable comprehension of intelligence's likely advantages and limits, establishments risk falling behind their companions in bridging the extraordinary force of computer-based intelligence. In addition, pioneers' vulnerability regarding artificial intelligence reception might fuel concerns connected with moral and capable artificial intelligence use (Selwyn, 2020). Without sufficient oversight and administrative systems, foundations may incidentally sustain predisposition or security infringement through artificial intelligence applications. In addition, pioneers' absence of mindfulness about artificial intelligence drives inside their foundations might ruin endeavours to guarantee value and consideration in artificial intelligence improvement and execution processes.

Moreover, the shortfall of informed authority might obstruct the workforce and staff's capacity to successfully coordinate artificial intelligence in educating and learning rehabilitation (Zawacki-Richter et al., 2019). Pioneers assume an urgent part in giving direction, assets, and backing to employees keen on investigating artificial intelligence-empowered teaching methods. Without a clear course from authority, personnel may battle to explore the intricacies of simulated intelligence reception and execution in instructive settings. A few systems can be utilised to address the information hole regarding artificial intelligence usage in advanced education authorities. Right off the bat, organisations can focus on proficient improvement drives toward upgrading comprehension. pioneers might interpret the advances in simulated intelligence and their likely applications (Delen & Lassoued, 2017). This might incorporate studios, courses, or chief schooling programs zeroed in computer-based intelligence proficiency and suggestions for advanced education.

BACKGROUND ON ARTIFICIAL INTELLIGENCE CHALLENGES IN HIGHER EDUCATION

Artificial Intelligence, a powerful tool in advanced education, offers unprecedented opportunities for growth, efficiency, and enhancement. Despite these challenges, the potential benefits of AI in enhancing teaching, learning, and administrative processes remain immense. To fully harness these benefits, educational institutions must navigate the complexities of integrating AI technology into their settings. The rapid pace of technological advancement is a significant hurdle for incorporating AI into higher education. For instance, new AI algorithms for personalized learning and automated grading are constantly being developed. Staying abreast of these advancements and understanding their implications for teaching, learning, and institutional management are major challenges for educators, administrators, and policymakers. As new simulated intelligence calculations for customized learning or mechanized reviewing are created, advanced educational establishments should assess their viability, dependability, and versatility before executing them for an enormous scope. This requires proficient turns of events, exploration, and cooperation with specialists in artificial intelligence and instructive innovation.

Ethical Considerations and Algorithmic Bias

Addressing ethical considerations and the risk of algorithmic bias is a crucial part of implementing advances in AI in higher education. AI systems rely on algorithms to analyze data, make predictions, and generate recommendations. However, these algorithms may unintentionally perpetuate biases in training data, leading to unfair or discriminatory outcomes. It is our responsibility to ensure transparency, accountability, and fairness in AI-driven decision-making processes, especially in areas such as admissions where AI algorithms may unintentionally discriminate against certain demographic groups based on race, gender, or financial status.

Information Protection and Security

The joining of artificial intelligence advances in advanced education requires assortment, stockpiling, and examination of tremendous measures of understudy information. Guaranteeing this information's security is foremost to safeguard understudy secrecy and conform to guidelines, such as the Family Instructive Freedoms and Protection Act (FERPA) (Zawacki-Richter et al., 2019). For example, in computer-based intelligence-fueled learning, the executive's frameworks might follow under-study communications, execution information, and individual data to customize growth opportunities. Advanced education establishments should execute hearty information administration approaches, encryption instruments, and access controls to shield under-study information from unapproved access or breaks.

Staff Support and Development

Staff readiness and support in integrating AI technologies into teaching and research are crucial in higher education. Many employees lack the necessary knowledge, skills, and resources to use AI tools in their courses and research projects. It is important to recognize their concerns about job displacement and the perceived complexity of AI technologies. By providing comprehensive professional development opportunities, technical support, and incentives, we can empower staff to explore innovative ways to integrate AI into their academic work, making them feel valued and integral to the process.

Specialized Framework and Asset Requirements

Constructing and keeping up with the specialised foundation expected to help intelligence drives in advanced education can be asset-escalated. Foundations might confront difficulties related to financing, admittance to skill, and similarity with existing frameworks and work processes (UNESCO, 2019). Model: Carrying out artificial intelligence-controlled arrangements, such as versatile learning stages or robotized evaluating frameworks, may require interest in equipment, programming licenses, and staff preparation. Advanced education establishments should cautiously evaluate their specialised abilities and dispense assets decisively to uphold artificial intelligence drivers.

The reconciliation of computer-based intelligence advances into advanced education and holds a tremendous commitment to changing instructing, learning, and managerial cycles. Nonetheless, establishments should address difficulties related to mechanical headways, moral contemplations, information security, personnel availability, and asset requirements to understand the maximum capacity of artificial intelligence in upgrading instructive results. Higher education institutions can harness the power of AI to prepare students for the demands of the workforce and society of the 21st century by proactively addressing these issues and cultivating a culture of innovation and collaboration.

Defining Artificial Intelligence and Its Uses

Artificial Intelligence alludes to the reenactment of human knowledge processes by machines, especially PC frameworks. These cycles incorporate learning (securing data and rules for utilizing them), thinking (utilizing rules to arrive at resolutions), and self-revision. *Simulated Intelligence* is an expansive field that incorporates different subfields such as AI, normal language handling, mechanical technology, and master frameworks. A definitive objective of artificial intelligence is to create machines that can perform undertakings that require human insight. Grasping artificial Intelligence: Simulated intelligence frameworks are intended to imitate human mental capabilities, empowering them to perform undertakings such as critical thinking, direction, and language understanding. These frameworks depend on calculations and information to dissect designs, generate expectations, and create reactions.

Computer-based intelligence calculations can be arranged into three classes: administered learning, solo learning, and supportive learning. Managed learning includes preparing a model on marked information, whereas solo learning includes finding designs in unlabeled information. Training an agent to interact with the environment and learn from feedback is a part of reinforcement learning. Healthcare, finance, transportation, manufacturing, and education are just a few of the fields in which AI can be used. In medical services, artificial intelligence is utilized for clinical picture examination, drug disclosure, customized medication, and current investigation. In finance, computer-based intelligence powers algorithmic exchange, extortion identification, credit scoring, and client-care chatbots. AI makes it possible to use traffic management systems, autonomous vehicles, and route optimization in transportation. In assembly, computer-based intelligence is utilized for prescient upkeep, quality control, and store network enhancement.

Artificial Intelligence is progressively incorporated into instructive settings to improve education, learning, and regulatory cycles. A portion of the critical utilization of computer-based intelligence in training includes adaptive learning platforms powered by AI, which personalize learning experiences based on individual student preferences, needs, and learning styles. These stages examine under-study information, distinguish qualities and shortcomings, and convey customized guidance and assets to improve learning results. ITS influences artificial intelligence advancements to provide customized mentoring and input for understudies. These frameworks examine under-study execution information, analyze areas of trouble, and convey designated intercessions to help learn and dominate ideas.

Artificial intelligence-driven reviewing frameworks robotize the appraisal of understudy tasks, tests, and tests. These frameworks examine under-study reactions, assess accuracy, and give moment input to the two under-studies and teachers, empowering more productive and reliable evaluation processes. Artificial intelligence-controlled remote helpers and chatbots offer moment help and help understudies, personnel, and staff. To enhance the access to resources and services, these systems answer questions, provide information, and direct users through various processes and tasks. AI has many advantages for education but raises ethical issues and challenges. These incorporate concerns about information protection and security, algorithmic predisposition, work uprooting, and the moral utilization of simulated intelligence in dynamic cycles. Establishments should focus on moral artificial intelligence standards, straightforwardness, and responsibility to guarantee that simulated intelligence advancements are utilized dependably and fairly.

Artificial Intelligence is a rapidly developing field with different applications and suggestions across different areas, including training. AI can transform administrative, educational, and teaching processes by enhancing decision making, automating tasks, and providing personalized experiences. Notwithstanding, it is fundamental to approach the events and organization of artificial intelligence advancements with alertness, considering moral contemplations, security concerns, and possible cultural effects. Educators can use AI's capabilities to improve educational outcomes and empower students if they use it ethically and responsibly.

Technical Characteristics of Artificial Intelligence in the Higher Education System

Artificial Intelligence has become progressively incorporated into different parts of advanced education, offering potential advantages, such as customized opportunities for growth, authoritative productivity, and prescient examination for understudy achievement. This paper examines the specialised qualities of artificial intelligence in an advanced education framework, including AI calculations, normal language handling, information examination, and wise mentoring frameworks. Through an exhaustive survey of writing and observational proof, this study will provide some knowledge into the specialised groundwork of simulated intelligence in advanced education and its suggestions for instructing, learning, and institutional administration.

Manmade brainpower (simulated intelligence) has become an extraordinary power in advanced education, upsetting conventional instruction and learning standards. The specialised qualities of simulated intelligence envelop many innovations and approaches, each adding to the headway of instructive practices and institutional administration. This paper investigates these specialised attributes, revealing insights into their functionalities, applications, and suggestions within the advanced education framework.

AI CALCULATIONS

One critical attribute of computer-based intelligence in advanced education is the use of AI calculations. AI empowers computer-based intelligence frameworks to examine large datasets, recognize examples, and make expectations or suggestions without unequivocal programming (Chen & Johri, 2020). In advanced education, AI calculations are utilized in different applications, such as ancient examinations for understudy maintenance, versatile learning stages, and literary theft discovery frameworks. For instance, colleges might utilize AI models to break down under-study information and distinguish in-danger under-studies needing extra help or mediation.

Processing of Natural Language (NLP)

Normal Language Handling (NLP) is an urgent part of artificial intelligence in advanced education, empowering PCs to comprehend, decipher, and produce human language. NLP technologies enable applications like chatbots, virtual assistants, and automated essay grading systems to facilitate communication between humans and machines (Gonzalez et al., 2019). In an advanced education setting, NLP-fueled chatbots can provide customized help to understudy, respond to questions, give direction, and work with admittance to assets. In addition, computerized paper-reviewing frameworks influence NLP calculations to evaluate understudy composing, giving the two understudies and educators opportune input.

Information Investigation

Information examination is essential for utilizing artificial intelligence advancements to separate bits of knowledge from instructive information. By dissecting huge datasets from different sources, such as learning board frameworks, understudy data frameworks, and online associations, foundations can acquire significant knowledge about understudy conduct, learning inclinations, and execution patterns (Zawacki-Richter et al., 2019). Institutions can use data analytics methods such as clustering, classification, and regression to find patterns, trends, and correlations in data. This helps them decide on the curriculum design, instructional strategies, and student support services.

Systems for Intelligent Teaching (ITS)

Savvy Mentoring Frameworks (ITS) address a refined utilization of artificial intelligence in advanced education, offering customized and versatile growth opportunities to understudies. ITS influences artificial intelligence innovations, such as AI, NLP, and mental display, to imitate human coaches, giving individualized guidance, criticism, and backing (VanLehn et al., 2007). These frameworks dissect under-study execution information progressively, adjusting the educational substance and speed to address the issues of every student. For instance, an ITS may progressively change the trouble of training practices given under-study execution or give designated remediation to weak spots.

The landscape of higher education has been fundamentally altered by the technical characteristics of Artificial Intelligence (AI), which provides unprecedented opportunities for innovation, efficiency, and improvement. AI calculations, regular language handling, information examination, and canny mentoring frameworks address only a few instances of the different scopes of artificial intelligence innovations, such as instructing, learning, and institutional administration in advanced education. As foundations embrace simulated intelligence, understanding these specialised attributes and their suggestions is fundamental for bridging the maximum capacity of artificial intelligence to improve instructive results and understudy achievements.

ANALYSIS OF THE EFFICIENCY OF ARTIFICIAL INTELLIGENCE-POWERED EDUCATION SYSTEMS FROM DIVERSIFIED VISIONS

Artificial Intelligence, a pervasive force in contemporary culture, has made significant inroads into education, promising to revolutionize traditional teaching methods and enhance learning experiences. This study focuses on the efficiency of AI-powered educational systems, a topic of paramount interest and debate. Proponents cite benefits, such as personalized learning, automated grading, and adaptive tutoring systems. However, a comprehensive analysis of AI's effectiveness of AI in education must encompass a broad spectrum of stakeholders, perspectives, and contexts to provide a nuanced understanding of its impact.

Student-Centric Perspective

From a student-centric viewpoint, the power of AI-driven education systems lies in their ability to tailor opportunities for growth and cater to individual students' needs and preferences. AI algorithms analyze student data such as learning patterns, performance metrics, and preferences to deliver personalized instruction, feedback, and support. For instance, adaptive learning platforms adjust patterns' speed, content, and difficulty level based on real-time feedback and assessment results, allowing students to progress at their pace and focus on weak areas. Example: A student struggling with mathematical concepts may benefit from an AI-powered tutoring system that offers targeted remediation activities, explanations, and feedback tailored to their learning style and pace. AI-powered systems can enhance student engagement, motivation, and learning outcomes by addressing specific areas of difficulty and adapting instructions to individual needs.

Teacher's Perspective

From a teacher's viewpoint, the effectiveness of AI-powered education systems lies in their ability to streamline administrative tasks, automate routine processes, and provide meaningful insights into students' progress and performance. AI algorithms can automate grading, generate analysis reports, and identify trends and patterns in the student data. This allows teachers to focus their time and effort on more important tasks such as curriculum, tutoring, and intervention. Example: A teacher using an AI-powered learning management system can use automated grading features to assess student assignments, quizzes, and tests more efficiently. The system can provide instant feedback to students, flag areas of concern for further attention, and generate detailed analytical reports to inform instructional planning and navigation.

By automating routine tasks, teachers can devote more time to offering personalized support and guidance to their students.

Institutional Viewpoint

From an institutional perspective, the productivity of artificial intelligence-controlled schooling systems lies in their capacity to streamline asset designation, develop maintenance and graduation rates, and upgrade institutional standing and seriousness. Artificial intelligence calculations can dissect enormous volumes of information connected with understudy socioeconomics, scholarly execution, and commitment measurements to recognize dangers to understudies, foresee results, and carry out designated mediations (Cook et al., 2010). Model: An advanced education establishment utilizing prescient examinations fueled by artificial intelligence can distinguish understudies in danger of exiting given elements, such as course execution, participation designs, and financial foundation. By interceding early and offering customized help administrations, such as scholarly exhorting, coaching, and monetary help, organisations can further develop understudy degrees of consistency and upgrade in general institutional viability.

Cultural Point of View

From a cultural viewpoint, the efficiency of computer-based intelligence-fueled schooling systems lies in their potential to address broader societal challenges, such as educational inequality, workforce development, and lifelong learning. Artificial intelligence algorithms can democratize access to quality education by creating affordable and scalable learning solutions and bridging gaps in access, affordability, and quality (UNESCO, 2019). AI-powered adaptive learning platforms can provide personalized instruction and support to students in underserved communities, remote areas, or developing countries, where access to traditional educational resources is limited. By harnessing AI technologies, policymakers and education stakeholders can promote lifelong learning, upskilling, and reskilling initiatives to prepare individuals for future demands in management and society.

Exploring the efficiency of AI-powered education systems from diverse perspectives underscores the complexity of their impact on teaching, learning, and institutional management. By integrating the viewpoints of students, teachers, institutions, and society, stakeholders can gain a comprehensive understanding of AI's potential benefits and challenges of AI in education. While AI holds promise for enhancing educational outcomes and addressing societal needs, it is of utmost importance to approach its implementation ethically, responsibly, and inclusively to maximize its positive impact on students and society at large.

RE-ASSESSING AND RE-DEFINING PREVIOUS EDUCATIONAL MODELS

Recently, the infusion of artificial intelligence into education has sparked the re-evaluation and redefinition of traditional instructional models. The potential of AI technologies to revolutionize teaching, learning, and administrative procedures in educational institutions is immense. This definitive note delves into the transformative impact of AI in education, and the imperative to reassess and redefine past instructional models to effectively harness the diverse roles of artificial intelligence.

AI's Impact on Education

Artificial intelligence encompasses various technologies, including AI, natural language processing, and robotics, each playing a specific role in education. AI algorithms power adaptive learning platforms, personalized tutoring systems, and predictive analytics, thereby offering tailored growth opportunities for students (Koedinger et al., 2012). Natural language processing, as noted by Gikandi et al. (2011), facilitates communication between intelligent tutoring systems, chatbots, and virtual assistants, thus enhancing student support services. Advanced robotic technologies enable interactive growth opportunities, active experimentation, and immersive simulations, fostering engagement and creativity among students (UNESCO, 2019). Traditional educational models often adhere to a one-size-fits-all approach with standardized curricula, assessments, and instructional methods. However, the advent of artificial intelligence has challenged this paradigm by offering personalized, adaptive, and flexible growth opportunities tailored to individual student needs and preferences. Therefore, there is an urgent need to re-evaluate traditional educational models to accommodate the various roles of artificial intelligence and harness its potential to enhance student outcomes.

Redefining Educational Models With Artificial Intelligence

Redefining educational models with artificial intelligence involves adopting student-driven approaches, leveraging data-driven insights, and embracing technology-enabled instructional methods. Teachers should transition from the passive transmission of knowledge to the active facilitation of learning, using AI as a tool to personalize instruction, assess student progress, and provide timely feedback (Baker et al., 2010). This redefinition of educational models necessitates a holistic approach that seamlessly integrates AI into curriculum design, pedagogical practices, and institutional strategies. For instance, in a new educational model, teachers and AI systems collaborate to create personalized learning pathways that incorporate a variety of instructional modalities such as videos, games, simulations, and real-world projects.

Artificial intelligence algorithms continuously analyze student data to identify confusion, learning gaps, and areas of interest, guiding teachers in adjusting instruction and interventions. This dynamic collaboration among educators, students, and AI creates a fun, interactive, and inclusive learning environment that fosters student success. While the reevaluation and redefinition of instructional models with AI holds immense promise, they also present several challenges and considerations. Ethical concerns related to data privacy, algorithmic bias, and equity must be addressed to ensure responsible use of artificial intelligence in education. Readiness and support of educators are crucial in enabling them to use AI effectively and ethically in their teaching practice.

Moreover, the framework, asset distribution, and institutional culture are vital for joining artificial intelligence into instructive models (Gonzalez et al., 2019). Re-evaluating and characterizing past instructive models with the thought of different jobs of man-made brainpower in training addresses a change in perspective towards student-driven, information-driven, and innovation-empowered ways of dealing with education and learning. By embracing simulated intelligence as an impetus for development and change, instructive establishments can create dynamic, versatile, and comprehensive learning conditions that enable understudies to flourish in the computer age.

INNOVATIVE ARTIFICIAL INTELLIGENCE-BASED ASSESSING AND LEARNING STRATEGIES

Integrating the latest technologies into pedagogical settings implies the latest ideas of educational design. Therefore, it is favourable to review and re-assess current assessments and learning strategies. A challenging instance is that if competition-based education is implemented in classrooms, instructors must re-assess student assessments manually. This method infers that the instructor will declare the winner after students submit their assessments. In an artificial-intelligence-powered education design, an artificial-intelligence system could dynamically work as an intelligent report and assessment reviewer in such an activity based on competition, inferring that educational design or competition policies could differ. One new policy could be that learners can review and resubmit their assessments after receiving feedback and re-assessing results from the artificial intelligence reviewer before the time is over (Alexander et al., 2019).

Artificial Intelligence is altering training by offering creative appraisal and learning procedures that address individual understudy needs, upgrade commitment, and further develop learning results. This paper investigates the capability of computer-based intelligence in proposing novel evaluation and learning procedures, including versatile learning frameworks, mechanized reviewing, customized criticism components, and savvy mentoring frameworks. Through a complete survey of writing and observational proof, this study aimed to clarify the advantages, difficulties, and ramifications of simulated intelligence-based approaches in training and provide proposals for their viable execution. Customary ways to deal with evaluation and learning in school frequently depend on state-sanctioned tests, manual reviewing, and a one-size-fits-every single educational strategy. Nonetheless, computerized reasoning (computer-based intelligence) presents a change in the training outlook by offering creative procedures that adjust to individual understudy needs, inclinations, and capacities. This study investigates the groundbreaking capability of simulated intelligence in proposing novel appraisal and learning techniques that influence AI, regular language handling, and astute coaching frameworks to improve instructive encounters.

An imaginative AI-based method to deal with instruction is a versatile learning framework that customizes growth opportunities based on the individual attributes of understudy, execution, and progress. These frameworks use AI calculations to investigate under-study information, distinguish learning designs, and powerfully change the educational substance, speed, and trouble levels (Cortez & Ramos, 2017). For instance, versatile learning stages give modified learning methods to every understudy, offering extra help or difficulties depending on the situation to streamline learning results. Robotized Reviewing: Computer-based intelligence-fueled robotized reviewing frameworks offer a more proficient and reliable option than manual evaluation processes, especially for genuine evaluations such as various decision questions or coding tasks. These frameworks influence AI calculations to break down understudied reactions, survey their exactness, and give moment inputs (Gikandi et al., 2011). Students can receive timely feedback on their work because automated grading systems can identify typical errors, provide explanations, and offer suggestions for improvement.

Simulated intelligence empowers the improvement of customized input components that address designated directions and support individual understudies. According to Altrabsheh et al. (2015), AI systems can analyze student responses, identify misconceptions, and generate real-time personalized feedback using Natural Language Processing (NLP) technologies. Customized criticism components can take different structures, including text-based remarks, sound accounts, or intuitive recreation, contingent upon the idea of learning undertaking and understudy inclinations.

Systems for Intelligent Teaching (ITS) address a modern simulated intelligence-based method of discovering giandigivedualized guidance, backing, and criticism of understudies. ITS influences AI, NLP, and mental display methods to copy human mentors by adjusting the educational substance and speed to address the issues of every student (VanLehn et al., 2007). For instance, an ITS might dissect under-study execution information, analyze weak spots, and give designated remediation through intelligent activities, reproductions, or sight and sound introductions.

While AI-based assessment and learning strategies have a lot of potential advantages, they also have many problems and things to think about. Right off the bat, guaranteeing the decency and legitimacy of computer-based intelligence-driven appraisals requires cautious thoughtfulness regarding algorithmic predisposition, information security, and moral contemplations (Fletcher et al., 2018). Furthermore, incorporating computer-based intelligence advances into instructive settings requires a sufficient framework, assets, and preparation for teachers and understudies (Zawacki-Richter et al., 2019). In addition, worrying about work removal and the job of human educators in simulated intelligence-empowered homerooms is fundamental for encouraging the acknowledgement and reception of artificial intelligence-based approaches. Artificial Intelligence(computer-based intelligence) has a huge commitment to changing evaluation and learning in schooling through creative techniques that customize guidance, upgrade criticism, and enhance learning results. Among the many AI-based strategies that reshape educational practices are adaptive learning systems, automated grading, personalized feedback mechanisms, and intelligent tutoring systems. By utilizing artificial intelligence, teachers can create captivating, powerful, and comprehensive learning conditions that take special care of the necessities and goals of every understudy.

AI IN HIGHER EDUCATION: CHALLENGES TO OVERCOME

The following are the various challenges in the adoption of artificial intelligence for higher education:

Comprehensive Public Policy on Artificial Intelligence for Growth

Although artificial intelligence includes the possibility of enhancing higher education systems, the all-encompassing inclusion of artificial intelligence in higher education requires tough policy assistance. Higher education leaders should be supported financially and ethically to emphasise moulding students with the skills to flourish in the artificial intelligence society. Artificial intelligence enhancements in schooling are emerging from the private sector, while the government is attempting to manage them. The creation of public policy for artificial intelligence in higher education at its initial level is anticipated to progress in the next ten years. Government policies should solve queries to propose solutions and procedures and assist innovative ecosystems in recognising the prospects of artificial intelligence in higher education. Various countries have already made substantial financial obligations to develop artificial intelligence research centres and prepare and employ artificial intelligence experts. Governments also finance advanced training and research in artificial intelligence by forming academic centres of excellence, research institute networks, and scholarships. Associations between research institutes and universities nurture combined research and intra-sector associations and advance academia-industry associations (Ilkka, 2018).

Equity and Inclusion in Artificial Intelligence in Education

Artificial intelligence may expand inequities and splits because deprived populations might be omitted from AI-driven higher education, ensuing in a digital divide. It is a new digital divide with a divide present in using data-based knowledge for smart decision-making. Inclusion and equity should become fundamental when planning policies. Administrators should consider the following aspects:

- Insistence of setup in developing states
- Lessons from previous experiences in the context of digital privileges
- Artificial intelligence helps the lacking population and groups
- Bridge the learning gap between financially poor and rich students
- Eliminate gender gaps

Some of the challenges to overcome include the following.

- Electrical accessibility
- Information and communications technology hardware availability
- Internet dependability
- Data expenses
- Insufficiency of fundamental information and communication technology skills
- Language
- Insufficiency of culturally applicable content

Numerous policies must be implemented to address fundamental challenges. It is vital to consider the Internet as a human right and develop several global associations to create a basic setup even in the most deprived sectors of developing countries (Sun & Medaglia, 2019).

Preparing Instructors for Artificial Intelligence-Driven Higher Education

It is extremely important to address current issues faced by instructors. Instructors remain at the forefront of higher education, as social-emotional and creative aspects of teaching in higher education can never be deserted. In this respect, artificial intelligence-driven software in higher education must formulate solid support in cognition, large-scale test scores, and classrooms. Various countries are preparing strategies to assist the national higher educational technology sector in its attempts to stimulate innovation and deepen attempts to enable schools and teachers. An evident recognition of how artificial-intelligence-powered systems can simplify learning provisions to make value decisions should be considered.

The training should focus on the following:

- Data and research analytical abilities to infer data offered by the artificial intelligence-powered systems
- Novel management abilities to handle artificial intelligence and human resources at their clearance
- Crucial perception of how artificial intelligence technologies impact human lives
- Take benefits of artificial intelligence doing repetitious tasks
- Support students attain new competencies and skills that machines cannot substitute

An all-inclusive functional data analytics system can provide prospects for artificial intelligence-powered machine learning and predictive algorithms. However, technologies for apprehending data might prove expensive for middle- and low-income states. Expenses must be measured against these advantages (Maddox et al., 2019).

Transparency and Ethics

Ethical and societal concerns must be addressed when adopting artificial intelligence. Technology is being enhanced swiftly; what is impractical today can become possible? Data security and privacy are abrupt queries that have emerged in any debate on data ethics. The challenge is to utilise personal data while guaranteeing the safety of individual privacy inclinations and personally recognisable information. The use and collection of data must be secured through express and informed consent, fairness, and transparency (Greene et al., 2019).

Inefficient Data Integration, Management, and Data Governance

Researchers suggest that inefficient data integration and management provide at least an average challenge for artificial intelligence adoption. This is undoubtedly an issue, and the first higher education institutions must address it. Poor data can only generate flawed assessments or, as in computing science, garbage in and garbage out. Insufficient integration worsens this issue. If a higher education institution is struggling with integration, governance, and management, it might need to consider progressing the digital transformation program sooner rather than later. Beginning with systems that develop the institution's available foundations is the only method that guarantees efficient data management and capture. No matter how much data are being generated, only precise, rough data gathered rationally can engender actionable and precise visions. With a robust set of regulations and procedures in the capture phase, innovation decays as it becomes unbearable to track and benchmark enhancements logically. Typically, it is primarily the situation that this challenge to artificial intelligence implementation should be mitigated, at least by utilising artificial intelligence itself. Utilising machine learning for the primary capture of transactional data can enhance precision, which is the basis of enhanced perceptions (Dignum, 2019).

Lack of Technical Knowledge

Researchers have witnessed insufficient expertise as a moderate obstacle to the implementation of AI. It can look like a chicken-and-egg issue, but artificial intelligence can realistically support higher education institutions to control the lack of artificial intelligence knowledge. As artificial intelligence's actual job is to manage things humans used to do manually, it should not be a centralised job but a complex centralised command system.

Higher education institutions can be both prevalent and dispersed. To some extent, this is already the circumstance in the applications of artificial intelligence, which are already being used, such as frequently asked questions chatbots to financial support assessment tools. Higher education institutions must hire artificial intelligence experts in information technology to automate the jobs of other individuals. Rather, institutions provide people with the prospect of developing automated solutions that support them in performing their tasks more efficiently. This gives them the authority to fix procedures they know properly, and that work automatically can save focus and time on more vital aspects.

Developing this type of distributed artificial setting does not have essential technical requirements. Higher education institutions' systems must be flexible enough to allow artificial intelligence models to drag and drop, with user-friendly interfaces that do not require afresh coding. These systems will also require supporting higher education institutions to incorporate other data sources and solutions to generate an all-inclusive picture and pivot to deal with future mysteries. This type of microservice design is adequately demonstrated by the Microsoft Azure medium's capability to use current technologies as services within itself. Universities have allowed this functionality in their institutional solutions. For example, virtual assistants can be preconfigured by integration with other systems to support people submitting leaves or expenses or obtaining performance perceptions via natural language communications through chat applications they already utilise rather than having to log into human resources and finance systems. Higher education institutions use artificial intelligence to automate inbound invoice registrations (Chang & Fang, 2020).

Algorithmic Bias and Ethical Concerns

Ethical and algorithmic bias concerns are vital challenges to artificial intelligence adoption. This is a vital concern, and higher education institutes cannot ignore it. Artificial intelligence can learn from previous experiences, and if what it learns is already dependent on biased details, its outcomes will also be biased. Efficient use cases for artificial intelligence are less about predicting and replacing human behaviour, and more about identifying repetitious, time-consuming sections of workflows can be forecasted, recommended, and established. Higher education institutes can leave users to reject, amend, or accept suggestions made by artificial intelligence, so people have more time to participate creatively with improved tasks they are assigned. Another advantage of promoting a culture of artificial intelligence usage throughout higher education institutes relates to the initial point of providing people with the prospect of developing their artificial intelligence solutions. Business procedures and technology democratisation can support everyone in comprehending the most vital aspects of their working ecosystem instead of leaving it as a black box that only the information technology team can use. The user remains in charge- they control the artificial intelligence and not the other aspects (Chassignol et al., 2018). By overcoming these challenges, artificial intelligence can act as an opportunity to advance higher education in the following ways:

ARTIFICIAL INTELLIGENCE AND INSTRUCTORS

The first aspect is that artificial intelligence can never replace instructors in higher education systems. However, this will allow teachers to spend more time connecting with their students virtually or in person. With a decrease in their workload, instructors can be spared to focus on high-priority tasks, leading to better results and a more efficient and fulfilling experience for students (Dignum, 2019).

Artificial Intelligence Can Offer Customised Experiences to Students

As observed in their daily routines, students are already witnessing the advantages of artificial intelligence such as adaptive learning techniques. The future challenge is to assess how to commence using this capability to offer more benefits. Digital chatbots and assistants presently function in universities and colleges, assisting staff and students similarly. Digital assistants and chatbot sessions with firms across the educational sector have underlined the prospect of using artificial intelligence to assist students with the application until graduation. Induction and enrolment for students can mostly be manual, complex, and take more time to finish efficaciously. If educational institutions have a clear and smooth journey, they will provide support to students and avoid early dropouts (Chassignol et al., 2018).

Artificial Intelligence Can Make Higher Education Accessible and Inclusive

Artificial intelligence will also make higher education more accessible and inclusive for students who are especially abled or have language barriers. People will progressively be able to utilise artificial intelligence to offer access to higher education in a formatted and customised manner according to the requirements of the student, for instance. The same material could be given as video, text, or audio, all of which were discussed correctly. Artificial intelligence allows the development of tools such as virtual assistants that offer supplementary support and supervision to students with particular requirements. Artificial intelligence assistance that helps learners at any time of the day offers great prospects as it utilises artificial intelligence to customise students' learning experiences. However, there is a requirement to ensure that this type of progress includes stakeholders and is not technology powered (Dignum, 2019). Some queries need to be answered: How can the concept of learning content and enhancing and maintaining learner agency be balanced?

Use of Data to Drive Accurate Outcomes

Advancements in artificial intelligence, along with an increase in accessible data, offer new prospects in domains such as educational analytics solutions which offer suggestions for students who are dropping out or are at risk of failure. Presently, working on the outputs of predictive frameworks, as these have black-box technologies, it can be observed that inference has been attained by an artificial intelligence framework, but not why. Advancements in artificial intelligence explainability are being witnessed, which infers a significant perception of the aspect impacting any specific situation. The value of having the ability to extract perceptions from this implies that enhancing analytics and data is a priority for universities and colleges (Sun & Medaglia, 2019).

RECOMMENDATIONS ON ETHICAL USAGE OF ARTIFICIAL INTELLIGENCE

Techniques and tools offering specific ethical challenges are evolving. For instance, numerous artificial intelligence methods aim to recognise human emotions, and institutions may want to start contemplating and discussing the position of these types of techniques and tools in higher education. For example, artificial intelligence systems can be trained to identify emotions in human speech and expressions. These techniques and tills may be developed into video-conferencing solutions in the coming years. Artificial intelligence could recognise students' emotional and sentiment aspects from analysis outcomes, social media platforms, discussion forums, and student teamwork. The data could then be utilised to determine performance and detect domains for enhancement, a job done manually at present (Sun & Medaglia, 2019).

Some instances of artificial intelligence can be used to develop a better working setting for higher education institutions, allowing institutes to work more effectively and eventually enhance student experiences.

- Chatbots based on natural language processing (NLP)
- Financial modelling based on machine learning
- Expense prediction
- Program profitability assessment
- Data anomaly recognition
- Smart receipt and invoice detection

In the future, there will be more capabilities in progress in research and development, such as intelligent student reliability ratings dependent on available receipts, payment behaviour, invoices, and external sources (Chen et al., 2020).

Future Challenges of Artificial Intelligence in Higher Education

While Artificial Intelligence continues to progress quickly, its combination with advanced education presents two open doors and difficulties. While artificial intelligence can change instruction, learning, and regulatory cycles, a few future difficulties should be addressed to guarantee its powerful and moral execution in advanced education organisations. One of the essential future difficulties of artificial intelligence in advanced education is its tendency to moral contemplate and alleviate the gamble of algorithmic predisposition. Artificial intelligence calculations depend on information to make expectations and proposals, and assuming that the information utilized for preparation is one-sided, it can prompt unjustifiable or oppressive results (Chen & Johri, 2020). Guaranteeing straightforwardness, decency, and responsibility in artificial intelligence dynamic cycles is fundamental to maintaining moral standards and forestalling mischief to understudy. For instance, historical biases in admission data may cause AI algorithms to favor some demographic groups over others in the admission process. Auditing algorithms, diversifying training data, and involving stakeholders in decision making are all actions that higher education institutions must take to identify and reduce algorithmic bias.

As AI systems in higher education use student data, protecting and maintaining data safety is a big challenge. To safeguard student privacy and prevent unauthorized access or breach, educational establishments must adhere to regulations such as the Family Educational Rights and Privacy Act (FERPA) and General Data Protection Regulation (GDPR) (Selwyn, 2020). For instance, learning management systems that AI powers might obtain sensitive student data such as grades, attendance records, and behavioral information. Advanced education organisations should execute hearty information administration approaches, encryption components, and access controls to protect under-study information and maintain trust with under-studies, staff, and partners.

Another future test of artificial intelligence in advanced education is providing staff improvement and backing to empower teachers to use simulated intelligence innovations in instruction and research. Numerous employees might need more fundamental information, abilities, and assets to incorporate artificial intelligence into their courses and adjust their instructive practices appropriately (Zawacki-Richter et al., 2019). Advanced education foundations should put resources into proficient improvement projects and studios and prepare opportunities to engage the workforce to investigate imaginative approaches to integrating artificial intelligence into instruction. Offering continuous specialised help, assets, and motivation can support staff reception and upgrade the nature of simulated intelligence-empowered guidance.

Coordinating computer-based intelligence innovations into existing frameworks and work processes represents a huge future for advanced education foundations. Artificial intelligence frameworks must consistently coordinate with learning board frameworks, understudy data frameworks, and other institutional stages to guarantee interoperability and limit interruption to existing cycles (UNESCO, 2019). Executing simulated intelligence-fueled arrangements, such as versatile learning stages or robotized reviewing frameworks, might require broad customization, combination, and testing to align with institutional necessities and prerequisites. Advanced education foundations should collaborate with sellers, IT offices, and partners to foster execution plans and address specialised difficulties.

Guaranteeing the value and admittance to simulated intelligence-controlled training innovations for all understudies is a basic future test. While computer-based intelligence can customize growth opportunities and back different under-study needs, there is a gamble of worsening existing imbalances if admittance to simulated intelligence advancements is restricted or inconsistent (Gonzalez et al., 2019). Understudies from impeded foundations or underrepresented gatherings may have restricted admittance to innovation or web availability, blocking their capacity to profit from artificial intelligence-controlled instructive assets. Advanced education organizations should address computerized partition issues by providing evenhanded admittance to gadgets, web frameworks, and backing administrations to guarantee that all understudies can completely partake in simulated intelligence-empowered learning conditions.

The challenges that Artificial Intelligence will pose to higher education in the future emphasize the need for proactive measures, strategic planning, and stakeholder collaboration to guarantee its ethical implementation. By tending to moral contemplations, protecting information security, giving workforce advancement and backing, incorporating computer-based intelligence with existing frameworks, and advancing value and access, advanced education organisations can outfit the groundbreaking capability of artificial intelligence to improve instruction, learning, and institutional adequacy.

CASE STUDY

Stanford University, renowned for its commitment to innovation and academic excellence, embarked on a transformative journey to incorporate artificial intelligence (AI) into various aspects of its operations. This contextual analysis investigates the difficulties faced by Stanford College in implementing computer-based intelligence advances across education, learning, and regulatory cycles. By assessing the foundation's encounters, this contextual investigation explains reasonable obstacles, moral situations, and key contemplations related to simulated intelligence reception in advanced education.

Stanford College in California's Silicon Valley is an esteemed examination foundation known for its commitment to innovation and schooling. Trying to use simulated intelligence to improve instructive encounters and institutional viability, Stanford set out an extensive drive to incorporate simulated intelligence innovations into its different scholarly projects and managerial capabilities.

Challenges Experienced

One of the first difficulties experienced by Stanford College in executing simulated intelligence advancements was moral contemplations and moderating the gamble of algorithmic predisposition. As the foundation tried to convey artificial intelligence-driven apparatuses for errands, for example, affirmation screening, scholastic prompting, and customised learning, concerns emerged with regard to the potential for predisposition in algorithmic navigation (Chen & Johri, 2020). Stanford College perceived the significance of guaranteeing decency, straightforwardness, and responsibility in simulated intelligence frameworks for maintaining value and civil rights standards. Stanford College teamed up with driving specialists in man-made intelligence morals and algorithmic reasonableness to conduct thorough reviews of its artificial intelligence calculations. Through careful assessment of preparing information, algorithmic rationale, and choice results, the establishment distinguished and tended to likely wellsprings of predisposition, guaranteeing that artificial intelligence-driven processes were fair, straightforward, and lined up with moral standards (Alexander et al., 2019).

Information Protection and Security

Another huge test, Stanford College, explored information protection and security concerns related to artificial intelligence execution. As AI systems rely on student data to make predictions and recommendations, protecting sensitive information and complying with privacy laws such as the Family Educational Rights and Privacy Act (FERPA) has become very important (Selwyn, 2020). Stanford College created complete information administration approaches and conventions to safeguard understudied security and privacy. The foundation implemented powerful encryption components, access controls, and information anonymisation practices to relieve the gamble of unapproved access or information breaks. Furthermore, Stanford College gave broad preparation to staff and personnel on information protection guidelines and best practices to advance the culture of information stewardship and consistency.

Workforce Reception and Backing

A critical obstacle in Stanford College's artificial intelligence venture was the cultivation of personnel reception and backing for artificial intelligence innovations in education and research. Numerous employees complained about the apparent intricacy of simulated intelligence, misgiving about work relocation, and doubts about the adequacy of simulated intelligence-driven instruments (Zawacki-Richter et al., 2019). Stanford College executed a multilayered workforce improvement program zeroed in on man-made intelligence proficiency and educational systems and involved preparing with artificial intelligence devices. The institution held workshops, seminars, and initiatives led by the faculty to empower educators to incorporate AI into their courses and research projects. Stanford College developed a committed help group to provide specialised help, direction, and assets to employees exploring computer-based intelligence reception.

Specialized Foundation and Asset Design

Stanford College confronted difficulties with the specialised foundation and asset distribution expected for artificial intelligence execution. Fabricating and maintaining with artificial intelligence frameworks requires significant interest in equipment, programming, ability, and progressing support, presenting monetary and strategic difficulties for the organisation (Gonzalez et al., 2019). To address asset requirements, Stanford College utilised distributed computing administrations and key associations with artificial intelligence sellers to obtain adaptable and savvy man-made intelligence arrangements. The institution has also established collaborative initiatives and interdisciplinary research centres to pool resources, expertise, and funding for AI projects. By cultivating coordinated efforts with industry accomplices and government organisations, Stanford College had the option of obtaining extra assets and backing computer-based intelligence drives.

The difficulties, opportunities, and complexities of implementing AI technologies in higher education were clarified through Stanford University's experiences. Through proactive measures, vital organisations, and a pledge to moral artificial intelligence standards, the establishment explored the landscape of artificial intelligence execution. This bridged the groundbreaking capability of artificial intelligence to improve education, learning, and institutional administration. By sharing its encounters and illustrations learned, Stanford College plans to illuminate and rouse other advanced education organisations, leaving behind comparative artificial intelligence attempts.

CONCLUSION

The significant challenge facing artificial intelligence usage for enhanced higher education functions is that it is not formally an aspect of any person's job description presently. Artificial intelligence can help people to perform their jobs more efficiently. This means that culture requires transformation to incentivise and prioritise innovative artificial intelligence driven by individuals who know their procedures efficiently. There is a requirement to guarantee that the initial systems are sufficiently versatile in this innovative working culture. Technology giants and the private sector are prominent in many countries. The growth of technology start-ups also plays a substantial role in maximising artificial intelligence implementation. Many states have national artificial intelligence policies in which higher education is an aspect by default. Debate and implementation are restricted in developing regions. The implementation artificial intelligence in higher education should become a constant and regular procedure. The sky is now becoming clearer. The progress is so promising that artificial intelligence higher education is not so distant. There is a requirement to start preparing data and systems to assist incorporation and permit the future progress of these systems. Chatbots and digital assistants are placed in the higher education sector to allow institutes to strategize how they will effectively, ethically, and efficiently utilise artificial intelligence. Artificial intelligence has witnessed numerous innovations in recent times and exhibits an evolving technology that will modernise the methods in which humans live. Technology is already present in the domain of higher education. The rise in the use and implementation of artificial intelligence in higher education has opened new prospects and challenges. Artificial intelligence will drive efficient governance changes in the entire internal structure of higher education institutions. The opportunity to use artificial intelligence involves assessing educational inferences regarding how instructors would supplement them, how learners would learn, and how precise and instant decisions can be taken in higher education institutions. This is vital as workload increases because of higher education massification. In such a situation, the assistance of artificial intelligence is exceptionally vital; artificial intelligence could play different roles in higher education setups. The progress of evolving computer technologies such as wearable devices, sensing devices, quantum computing, robot control, and the acceptance of 5G wireless and mobile communication technologies has offered novel prospects and appearance for implementing artificial intelligence in learning and teaching design. Therefore, it is vital for scholars to consider how this can be implemented. Innovation in artificial intelligence has made computer-powered higher education a new era. A computer system can work as a smart tutor, tutee, or tool, simplifying decision-making in higher educational setups and integrating human intelligence. The incorporation artificial intelligence and higher education will offer new prospects for enhancing learning and teaching. Instructors can take advantage of smart systems that help with data collection and assessments, improve learning progress, and create novel strategies. Students should take advantage of asynchronous learning and intelligent tutors to improve learning outcomes

Additional aspects that should be considered

- Big data analytics for significant data sources in higher education contexts and learning systems
- Creating large-scale learning structures
- Generating ethical practices and regulations for implementing artificial intelligence applications and technologies in higher education
- Human-artificial intelligence association

The rise of cloud computing, machine learning, big data, and artificial neural networks has helped engineers develop machines that can imitate human intelligence. The method of recognising, perceiving, learning, and resolving issues using artificial intelligence builds on these technologies. Indeed, such intelligent technologies will modernise workplaces in the coming years. Thus, although artificial intelligence can integrate and support human work at higher levels, it is progressing as a significant future innovation. Artificial intelligence is currently observed as a driver that is essential to the fourth industrial revolution, and it may generate the fourth revolution in higher education (Chassignol et al., 2018).

REFERENCES

Alam, A. (2022). Employing Adaptive Learning and Intelligent Tutoring Robots for Virtual Classrooms and Smart Campuses: Reforming Education in the Age of Artificial Intelligence. In *Advanced Computing and Intelligent Technologies* (pp. 395–406). Springer. DOI:10.1007/978-981-19-2980-9_32

Alexander, B., Ashford-Rowe, K., Barajas-Murph, N., Dobbin, G., Knott, J., McCormack, M., . . . Weber, N. (2019). *Horizon report 2019 higher education edition* (pp. 3-41). EDU19.

Chan, K. S., & Zary, N. (2019). Applications and challenges of implementing artificial intelligence in medical education: Integrative review. *JMIR Medical Education*, 5(1), e13930. DOI:10.2196/13930 PMID:31199295

Chang, C. L., & Fang, M. (2020, June). E-Learning and online instructions of higher education during the 2019 novel coronavirus diseases (COVID-19) epidemic. *Journal of Physics: Conference Series*, 1574(1), 012166. DOI:10.1088/1742-6596/1574/1/012166

Chassignol, M., Khoroshavin, A., Klimova, A., & Bilyatdinova, A. (2018). Artificial Intelligence trends in education: A narrative overview. *Procedia Computer Science*, 136, 16–24. DOI:10.1016/j.procs.2018.08.233

Chen, X., Xie, H., Zou, D., & Hwang, G. J. (2020). Application and theory gaps during the rise of artificial intelligence in education. *Computers and Education: Artificial Intelligence*, 1, 100002. DOI:10.1016/j.caeai.2020.100002

Dignum, V. (2019). *Responsible artificial intelligence: how to develop and use AI in a responsible way*. Springer Nature. DOI:10.1007/978-3-030-30371-6

Greene, D., Hoffmann, A. L., & Stark, L. (2019). Better, nicer, clearer, fairer: A critical assessment of the movement for ethical artificial intelligence and machine learning.

Hwang, G. J., Xie, H., Wah, B. W., & Gašević, D. (2020). Vision, challenges, roles and research issues of Artificial Intelligence in Education. *Computers and Education: Artificial Intelligence*, 1, 100001. DOI:10.1016/j.caeai.2020.100001

Ilkka, T. (2018). The impact of artificial intelligence on learning, teaching, and education. *European Union*.

Kaplan, A., & Haenlein, M. (2020). Rulers of the world, unite! The challenges and opportunities of artificial intelligence. *Business Horizons*, 63(1), 37–50. DOI:10.1016/j.bushor.2019.09.003

Maddox, T. M., Rumsfeld, J. S., & Payne, P. R. (2019). Questions for artificial intelligence in health care. *Journal of the American Medical Association*, 321(1), 31–32. DOI:10.1001/jama.2018.18932 PMID:30535130

Pedro, F., Subosa, M., Rivas, A., & Valverde, P. (2019). Artificial intelligence in education: Challenges and opportunities for sustainable development.

Sun, T. Q., & Medaglia, R. (2019). Mapping the challenges of Artificial Intelligence in the public sector: Evidence from public healthcare. *Government Information Quarterly*, 36(2), 368–383. DOI:10.1016/j.giq.2018.09.008

Tariq, M. U. (2024). Smart Transportation Systems: Paving the Way for Sustainable Urban Mobility. In Munuhwa, S. (Ed.), *Contemporary Solutions for Sustainable Transportation Practices* (pp. 254–283). IGI Global., DOI:10.4018/979-8-3693-3755-4.ch010

Tariq, M. U. (2024). Integration of IoMT for Enhanced Healthcare: Sleep Monitoring, Body Movement Detection, and Rehabilitation Evaluation. In Liu, H., Tripathy, R., & Bhattacharya, P. (Eds.), *Clinical Practice and Unmet Challenges in AI-Enhanced Healthcare Systems* (pp. 70–95). IGI Global. DOI:10.4018/979-8-3693-2703-6.ch004

Tariq, M. U. (2024). Cybersecurity Risk Assessment Models and Theories in the Travel and Tourism Industry. In Thealla, P., Nadda, V., Dadwal, S., Oztosun, L., & Cantafio, G. (Eds.), *Corporate Cybersecurity in the Aviation, Tourism, and Hospitality Sector* (pp. 1–17). IGI Global. DOI:10.4018/979-8-3693-2715-9.ch001

Tariq, M. U. (2024). Data Breach Incidents and Prevention in the Hospitality Industry. In Thealla, P., Nadda, V., Dadwal, S., Oztosun, L., & Cantafio, G. (Eds.), *Corporate Cybersecurity in the Aviation, Tourism, and Hospitality Sector* (pp. 181–199). IGI Global. DOI:10.4018/979-8-3693-2715-9.ch010

Tariq, M. U. (2024). Navigating the Personalization Pathway: Implementing Adaptive Learning Technologies in Higher Education. In Minh Tung, T. (Ed.), *Adaptive Learning Technologies for Higher Education* (pp. 265–291). IGI Global. DOI:10.4018/979-8-3693-3641-0.ch012

Zawacki-Richter, O., Marín, V. I., Bond, M., & Gouverneur, F. (2019). Systematic review of research on artificial intelligence applications in higher education–where are the educators? *International Journal of Educational Technology in Higher Education*, 16(1), 1–27. DOI:10.1186/s41239-019-0171-0

ADDITIONAL READING

Babar, M., Ahmad, A., Tariq, M. U., & Kaleem, S. (2023). Real-time fake news detection using big data analytics and deep neural network. *IEEE Transactions on Computational Social Systems*. Advance online publication. DOI:10.1109/TCSS.2023.3309704

Babar, M., Jan, M. A., He, X., Tariq, M. U., Mastorakis, S., & Alturki, R. (2023). An optimized IoT-enabled big data analytics architecture for edge–cloud computing. *IEEE Internet of Things Journal*, 10(5), 3995–4005. DOI:10.1109/JIOT.2022.3157552 PMID:38046398

Babar, M., Khattak, A. S., Jan, M. A., & Tariq, M. U. (2021). Energy aware smart city management system using data analytics and internet of things. *Sustainable Energy Technologies and Assessments*, 44, 100992. Advance online publication. DOI:10.1016/j.seta.2021.100992

Kaleem, S., Sohail, A., Babar, M., Ahmad, A., & Tariq, M. U. (2023). Ensemble learning for multi-class COVID-19 detection from big data. *PLoS One*, 18(10), e0292587. DOI:10.1371/journal.pone.0292587 PMID:37819992

KEY TERMS AND DEFINITIONS

Adaptive Learning Platforms: AI-powered systems that personalize learning experiences based on individual student preferences, needs, and learning styles.

Algorithmic Bias: The phenomenon where AI algorithms produce biased outcomes due to prejudices present in the training data or the design of the algorithm.

Artificial Intelligence (AI): The simulation of human intelligence processes by machines, particularly computer systems.

Automated Grading Systems: AI systems that automate the assessment of student assignments, tests, and quizzes.

Intelligent Tutoring Systems (ITS): AI-driven systems that offer personalized tutoring and feedback to students.

Machine Learning (ML): A subset of AI that involves the development of algorithms that allow computers to learn from and make predictions or decisions based on data.

Natural Language Processing (NLP): A field of AI that focuses on the interaction between computers and humans through natural language. NLP technologies enable machines to understand, interpret, and generate human language. Applications in higher education include chatbots, virtual assistants, and automated essay grading systems .

Professional Development in AI: Continuous training and support provided to educators and staff to help them integrate AI technologies into their teaching and research.

Chapter 5
A General Framework for Artificial Intelligence in Higher Education

ABSTRACT

Artificial intelligence is reforming different areas, including training, with commitments to upgrading opportunities for growth, further developing effectiveness, and customising instruction. In advanced education, a combination of simulated intelligence presents two amazing open doors and difficulties. This writing survey aimed to investigate the present status of simulated intelligence execution in advanced education, zeroing in on an overall system that envelops different computer-based intelligence applications and their suggestions for instructing, learning, and managerial cycles. One of the essential areas of artificial intelligence execution in advanced education is the upgrade of education and growing experiences.

INTRODUCTION

Computer-based intelligence in advanced education envelops a wide cluster of advances and applications, going from savvy coaching frameworks to a prescient examination of understudy achievement. These advancements will help educators, overseers, and understudies in different parts of the instructive environment. For example, astute mentoring frameworks use man-made intelligence calculations to adjust learning materials and provide customised criticism to understudies, thus improving their understanding and maintenance (Woolf, 2010). In addition, recent investigations influence simulated intelligence to dissect enormous datasets and recognise designs that can help establishments mediate early and support danger understudies (Arnold and Pistilli, 2012). One of the essential areas of artificial

DOI: 10.4018/979-8-3693-4074-5.ch005

intelligence execution in advanced education is the upgrade of education and growing experiences. Man-made intelligence-driven devices, such as remote helpers and chatbots, can offer prompt help to understudy beyond class hours, respond to questions, give assets, and work with correspondence with teachers (Holotescu and Grosseck, 2017). For instance, a remote helper coordinated into a learning the board framework (LMS) can direct understudies through course materials, suggest valuable assets in view of their learning inclinations, and deal with customised plans. Moreover, computer-based intelligence-controlled versatile learning stages offer customised growth opportunities by changing the speed, trouble, and content of instructive materials to match individual under-study needs (Bread cook, 2010). For example, versatile learning stages can powerfully produce tests and tasks custom-made to every understudy's capability level, guaranteeing that they get designated help in regions where they battle, while permitting progressed students to advance at a sped up pace (VanLehn et al., 2007).

In addition to supporting instruction and learning, simulated intelligence innovations hold critical potential for advancing authoritative cycles in advanced educational organisations. For instance, computer-based intelligence-controlled frameworks can robotise routine regulatory errands such as planning, reviewing, and information passage, permitting personnel and staff to zero in their significant investment in more complicated and esteem added exercises (Blikstein, 2013). In addition, simulated intelligence calculations can examine institutional information to recognise patterns, estimate future necessities, and illuminate vital dynamic cycles (Siemens & Long, 2011; Tariq, 2024). While the joining of artificial intelligence in advanced education offers various advantages, it also raises moral and social concerns that warrant cautious thought. One concern is the potential for predisposition in artificial intelligence calculations, which can propagate imbalances and impede certain gatherings of understudies (Selwyn, 2017). For instance, if current investigation calculations depend exclusively on verifiable information, they may unintentionally support existing differences by excessively hailing understudies from underrepresented foundations as in danger, disregarding relevant variables or fundamental obstructions. Another moral thought is the effect of computer-based intelligence on protection and information security. As advanced education establishments gather and investigate expanding measures of under-study information, there is a gamble of unapproved access, abuse, or penetrates that could think twice about classification and trust (Lomas, 2019). In this manner, it is fundamental for foundations to carry out strong information administration approaches and components to shield delicate data and guarantee consistency with applicable guidelines, such as the Overall Information Assurance Guideline (GDPR) in Europe or the Family Instructive Freedoms and Protection Act (FERPA) in the US.

Taking everything into account, computer-based intelligence holds tremendous potential to change advanced education by upgrading instruction and opportunities for growth, enhancing regulatory cycles, and working in an information-driven direction. Nevertheless, understanding this potential requires an insightful and comprehensive methodology that tends toward moral, social, and specialised contemplations. Pushing ahead, future exploration ought to zero in creating comprehensive and straightforward simulated intelligence frameworks, cultivating interdisciplinary coordinated efforts between instructors, technologists, and policymakers, and assessing the effects of man-made intelligence execution on quality, understudy results, and institutional viability.

BACKGROUND

Artificial intelligence is a concept that characterizes a system that can perform various human cognitive skills, such as thinking, speaking, problem-solving, and learning. This is a broad concept that includes various algorithms and technologies. Previously, during its development, artificial intelligence in education was most characteristically associated with smart tutoring systems that attempted to automatically address challenges, such as boosting operator competence. The progress in information and computing techniques has accelerated the advancement of artificial intelligence, which attempts to allow computers to perform tasks by imitating smart human behaviours such as decision-making, inference, and analysis. Scholars who have assessed artificial intelligence have made substantial advancements. Many products offer intelligence services by understanding or acting like humans, utilising traditional machine learning or contemporary deep learning methods. Artificial intelligence is utilised in various domains, such as voice recognition and visual, language translation, decision-making, and natural language processing. This comes in several ways, involving computer programs and embedded control systems in robots and equipment. Some medical systems can support human specialists in recognising possible infections or in making decisions by dealing with a broad range of data. Some robots can cooperate with humans using audio and visual monitoring technologies. Artificial intelligence has been used to innovate various businesses in today's society. Artificial intelligence adoptions in higher education are divided into learner-oriented artificial intelligence in higher education, instructor-oriented artificial intelligence in higher education, and institutional system-oriented higher education. Students can use learner-oriented artificial intelligence in higher education to research a topic, generally called a customised or adaptive learning management system. Administrative procedures, feedback provision, plagiarism detection, and reviews can be automated by using an instructor-oriented tool. These systems may also support instructors in keeping track of their students' progress so that pre-emptive interventions can be provided. With enhancements such as information technology services, support systems becoming more refined, and instructor bots, artificial intelligence in higher education has validated its capability to support students in comprehending knowledge gaps and acquiring personalised assistance, relieving instructors from routine tedious tasks, and permitting them to attend to students more efficiently. Eventually, artificial intelligence in higher education resources may offer valuable information to institutional administrators and decision-makers, such as retention and enrolment rates across universities and courses. Artificial intelligence in higher education implementation remains a trending subject among the departments. It has unlocked novel opportunities for creating more progressive learning practices and enhanced technology improvement environments and applications. Most experts and researchers in the domains of education and computers, on the contrary, commence struggling to apply relevant programs and practices. Intelligent tutoring and innovative learning systems face complications regarding computer programming capabilities and policies to imitate the intelligence of human specialists. Human instructors' understanding and knowledge were used to make decisions and assessments based on the best available data to support overcoming obstacles and improve learning for specific students. Robust dependence on technologies and the cross-curricular structure of artificial intelligence in higher education create these obstacles. Suppose scholars do not understand the functions of artificial intelligence in higher education and how artificial intelligence program's function.

In this case, they will not efficiently integrate artificial intelligence in higher education practices and applications and improve and assess it in higher education research concerns. For instance, an artificial intelligence implementation works as a mentor, observing student learning procedures, analysing results, and providing on-demand support. Multidisciplinary groups can create innovative teaching programs focused on their students' requirements, supporting students to study, interact, and practice with tutors or colleagues, while providing supervision, assistance, and support to those who follow their needs or situations. In contrast, the knowledge and features of artificial intelligence technology permit instructors to utilise efficient classroom implementation to enhance inspiration, learning outcomes, and student involvement as researchers. The design of artificial intelligence algorithms for humanity is the primary concern for the artificial intelligence of human beings. This artificial intelligence includes interpretable and explanatory procedures for decisions and computations and constant amendments of artificial intelligence algorithms through human and social perspectives to augment human minds through machines and enhance human well-being (Zawacki-Richter et al., 2019).

GENERAL FRAMEWORK FOR ARTIFICIAL INTELLIGENCE IN HIGHER EDUCATION

User Interactive Technology and Components of Artificial Intelligence

Regarding information systems that involve sophisticated algorithms, such as artificial intelligence, there are more or less challenges to deal with than for systems that are simpler. Reinventing analyses and methods could be vital for creating artificial intelligence-powered websites. The outcome of these challenges should not condemn educational institutes; rather, it should boost the enhancement of human-computer collaborations. The evolution of these subjects would be helpful for non-iterative methods (Dilmurod and Fazliddin, 2021).

Technology and Components of Artificial Intelligence

Even though the database accumulates valuable information to fulfil the institution's demands and allows more people to attain its accessibility, it can also be used. Proposals and ideas can be raw data or general data, such as sound, texts, maps, and photographs that can be developed from abstractions or concrete. Data can be classified into three categories: personal, internal, and off-site data. Storage approach: The data configuration of a database can be roughly classified as network, relational, or hierarchical. Most management information is saved in relational databases, such as Microsoft SQL and Oracle, as with NoSQL, such as CSV and MongoDB (Hinojo-Lucena et al., 2019). Database management uses, handles, modifies, and constructs user databases. A worthy database and its effective administration can simplify managerial practices. Predictive modelling includes three usual activities: browsing documents, managing and establishing complicated associations, and generating reports (Holmes et al., 2022). Data catalogues are an all-inclusive listing of the information in the database. Where the data saves the information, involving data files and tables, is mainly known as database storage, and is the segment of the database concept. The fundamental role is to offer descriptions relevant to the data sources. It also boosts the addition, recovery, and removal of artefacts with exclusive dislikes and likes (Abad-Segura et al., 2020). Much of the work, such as obtaining, retrieving, and processing the results. Other constituents determine how data are attained, directly express how the results are attained, and pass them on those particulars to the individual who requested them (Ciolacu et al., 2018).

Data Warehouse

Data sources are generated from various distribution systems, involving web transactions and operating databases as external sources, making them data warehouse sources (Dilmurod and Fazliddin, 2021). The objective of data collection from the sources, validation, arrangement, and processing in the data warehouse, and ultimately loading it from the database (Abad-Segura et al., 2020). This creates a knowledge framework for the source data warehouse and provides a precise illustration of the data in the objective. This contains the information required to save and handle data models as metadata. The metadata signifies the details in the source data warehouse, which can be utilised to realise the source data and support the recognition of the tool using which it will be moved to the target. For specific significant adoptions, dedicated multidimensional databases can offer benefits for complicated decision support. DSS programs should be part of the data mart. The aspects of the data centre were sustained even when the data in the data centre were not (Castro, 2019). The objective of the target database is to possess, assess, process, and arrange information (Ejdys et al., 2019). Information on the front-end user interface offers market thinkers' and leaders' accessibility to data for more inclusive research (Holmes et al., 2022). Information processing involves data security, computer protection, and other challenges (Ejdys et al., 2019).

Predictive, quantitative, qualitative, management, and general models are presented in the library. These mathematical models possess DSS. The model consists of four bases: prepare, act, work on, interpret, design, and assess models. There are theoretical, practical, and strategic models as well as substructure projects and programming matters (Gaebel et al., 2021; Tariq, 2024). In semi-structured or unstructured issues, templates such as Java, OLAP applications, or worksheets, specific mode-specific tools such as programming models or database modelling are also required (Gaebel et al., 2021). DSS tools are utilised to develop the latest programs, enhance them, and deploy data by utilising programming languages and low-level building blocks (Ciolacu et al., 2018). In addition, the catalogue can work for the same goal as the reference model, categorising all models. The fundamental purpose of a model is to observe how well the design idea works in the actual world (Alyahyan & Düştegör, 2020). Models have real-world restrictions on processes. It integrates models that can be incorporated as required (for instance, handling the output of a model; for instance, forecasts are processed by another model, such as a linear programming framework (Ejdys et al., 2019).

Knowledge Management Subsystem

Knowledge acquisition: The conversion, accumulation, translation, and transmission of information from archives and knowledge experts to computers for novel systems or databases are critical work operations in the creative range. Possible intelligence information sources include private and public video archives, textbooks, databases, and researchers. The most challenging aspect of obtaining information is convincing experts about price. A massive infrastructure cannot be developed without someone who converses with human specialists. Although in practical information engineering solutions, replies to human problems are explainable, analogies for other issues have been developed, and obstacles have been constructed to offer counter-examples to describe the differences (Alyahyan & Düştegör, 2020). The database has the required information to demonstrate, decode, and solve problems. It comprises two fundamental segments: exploration and skill. A comprehensive fact is the solution of a specific domain, whereas a specific exploratory or guiding regulation is a particular solution to a specific application domain (Ejdys et al., 2019). Brains are regulated structures in expert systems, also called rule-makers, that have their working frameworks, which are known as inference engines (Hinojo-Lucena et al., 2019). A machine with an expert system can support the disintegration of issues into a simple form that allows individuals to better comprehend, permitting them to communicate more efficiently. It can be completed using standard language. Because contemporary communication technologies cannot be assimilated to meet all needs, most apps depend on customers to ask queries to explore what they want. Supplementary time-sensitive tools, such as graphs, spreadsheets, brochures, and menus, may enhance productivity (Holmes et al., 2022). Blackboard design is utilised in work-memory computing. The worksheet is utilised to depict the present problem using data. It is used to compute decisions and expectations. The capability to track conclusions back to their background is vital to exploring issues and deductions. Interpretation subsystems can support users in making sense of their plans and decisions through interactive enquiries (Alyahyan & Düştegör, 2020). Human experts have a method that can critically assess their progress and human methodology using the results. Similarly, assessing the efficiency or failure of programs is vital in computerised learning so that students can better comprehend the reasons for it. A more detailed knowledge base and enhanced logic enhance knowledge recollection and recall performance (Hinojo-Lucena et al., 2019).

ROLE OF ARTIFICIAL INTELLIGENCE IN EDUCATION

Teaching in higher education is time-consuming and challenging, regardless of how many teaching assistants mark assessments and exams for large lecture sessions. While they give significant time to grading, instructors still spend much time with students, particularly in the lower grades, teaching, and professional progress. Even though artificial intelligence will never replace human grading, it is promptly approaching this stage. Using apps to mark with almost all types of MCQs and filling in the blank training is just the start. Presently, subjective grading software is in its initial stages, but it will be developed in the future to provide instructors with more time to spend on classroom activities (Gaebel et al., 2021). Artificial intelligence will fundamentally affect education in the form of more personalised instruction. Higher education institutions have observed videos and learning games that act as assistants. These programs modify the altering requirements of students, integrate a significant emphasis on particular subjects, offer extensive practice for formerly numerous subjects, and enable students to follow their performance still they choose. Instruction-mode personalised to meet the requirements of students with fluctuating abilities may be a machine-supported technique for making all stages progress together in one class. Some uses of information technology have already significantly impacted higher education, and as artificial intelligence develops in the future, adaptive programs can only be beneficial and general (Ciolacu et al., 2018).

Most instructors do not know what they do not know, and thus fail to pinpoint the challenges that their students may not observe in their lessons. When students are all exposed to having provided wrong answers on a homework assessment, the machine alerts the teacher with a solution-customised message, so they will not be identical to their mistakes (Zhao et al., 2021). However, there will undoubtedly be more stuff that instructors cannot yet provide, and the coming years will witness more students' education via tutor machines, which are non-physical. Artificial intelligence-powered tutorials have since been developed to support students in literature and other courses. Programs provide students with foundational skills, but human instructors must supplement them with higher-level imagination and thinking. The fact that these issues cannot be resolved in a shorter period does not mean that they cannot be resolved in the future. Currently, state-of-the-art teaching services are beyond the domain of possibility (Radianti et al., 2020). Students and professors have more control over their learning which has added the benefits of artificial intelligence. Enhancement in the assignment of academic progress also involves evaluations of subjects' efficiency. Artificial intelligence in both online and on-campus classrooms to evaluate students' progress and inform instructors about any problems they might face. This type of artificial intelligence supports students in offering the required service type. Instructors view probable issues in teaching for students who might face learning challenges. As the artificial intelligence systems emphasise offering individual subject guidance, they are about all phases of life. Some instructors are preparing courses that allow students to decide which majors are beneficial and which are unfledged (Gaebel et al., 2021).

Knowledge experts such as this make it probable for higher education institutes to work on personal and professional matters and how we should commence educational recreation. Artificial intelligence would modify how knowledge is accessed and saved to future students. Students are effortlessly ready to do something as long as they are innovative (Zawacki-Richter et al., 2019). Artificial intelligence tutors will step in when required to provide students with the liberty to explore while also offering abundant instructional assistance and utilising their perspectives in the classroom. Technology is a vital supporter of various class modifications, specifically in the prompt domain of higher education institutes that implement innovative learning methods entirely. As intelligent systems are now normal in higher education, there will still be continuous discussion about the applicable nature of what teachers should be doing and how they should be assessed. Therefore, it is subject to institutions and administrators for some time. It has already been mentioned that artificial intelligence will take up tasks such as grading, providing students with an enhanced learning experience, and acting as a substitute for on-campus teaching. However, artificial intelligence may be utilised in many other domains, but it should not be observed as a solution for all issues in higher education. Artificial intelligence devices may be developed as tools for instructors to explore responses and perform primary research. Instructors will be replaceable if artificial intelligence switches the administrator's position in various situations (Zhao et al., 2021). Many trials and errors were included in all types of studies. Not understanding or failing a solution is a significant challenge for many students. Some individuals become troubled when positioned at prominence levels, such as when needed to meet influential people such as employers or instructors. Employing sophisticated software to support students in higher education is more engaging than dealing with the stress of trial and error. Artificial intelligence provides students with an experience that can be conducted freely and relaxed when higher education is concerned (Radianti et al., 2020). Artificial intelligence has altered how higher education institutes accumulate and provide data on their current and future students. At any stage, from inviting students to guide them across the course, the information technology department makes the institution more customisable to the requirements and benefits of students (Zhao et al., 2021). This inventiveness will provide a digital medium that allows students to learn from any place in the world, utilising software and supporting students from tutor assistance to substitute human instructors when they are not in the classroom. Virtual teaching systems enhance basic skills. When these programs are accepted and the people with whom they provide a close association, the variability of resources seems to expand (Dilmurod & Fazliddin, 2021).

DEEP LEARNING AND MACHINE LEARNING

The objective of machine learning is to generate forecasts that are robust, wise, and consistent using complicated and unsupervised data. Statistical theory is deeply entangled with the present best thinking in machine learning. Model implications are also conducted using models, although statisticians depend on inferring their model structures. The machine learning community's significant preoccupation was attaining the best potential outcome, irrespective of the results. Both the measuring tools should be enhanced to ensure the reliability of the experiment. There is also a new shift to clarify the model design to make machine learning more manageable. These models were designed based on the same standards and will be used in the future (Jackson, 2019). Deep learning models utilise the deep learning revolution; they perform one input-particular task at a time, one at a time. A CNN was used while making a video. If an instructor wants to use text data, they must implement the text in the context of the room (Radianti et al., 2020). Reclassification of studies, specialisation selection, scholarships, student enrolment, announcements on the web, and transfer of students are done using student modules. Career counselling and tutorials were also provided (Jackson, 2019). Content, syllabus, and instruction timetable of classes opting for elective class teaching activities for instruction and learning about the practical job of students. The teaching faculty was assessed using a teaching module (Kuziemski & Misuraca, 2020). Assessment of scientific researchers, efficiency issues, salary prospects, human capital management methods, interviews, jobs for research vacancies, PhD assessment, and grant continuity and administration (Hinojo-Lucena et al., 2019).

Implementation of Artificial Intelligence in Higher Education

Artificial intelligence is utilised to customise learning for each student. Making use of the principle of hyper-personalisation, artificial intelligence technologies, assisted by machine learning, are combined to develop personalised learning profiles for every student and to personalise training materials depending on the preferred learning mode. The students' knowledge and skills differed. Instructors can break lectures into flashcards, mini-learning guides, and smart notes. With artificial intelligence in the creation of digital content, learning has become digitised. There is less written content. Artificial intelligence-driven systems and applications allow students to obtain prompt and personalised responses and clear instructor concerns.

Artificial intelligence has also been utilised to enhance the teaching and strategy of assistants. Personalised learning discussions that may support assessments and studies provide quick interaction and close guidance with students. These research assistants are still trying to design an incorporated learning function so that all students can attain learning at their level and at a suitable time (Penprase, 2018). Amazon's Alexa, Microsoft Cortana, and Apple's Siri are artificial intelligence features that instructors and students can utilise efficiently. Students can talk with the media through voice assistance and learn without the support of an instructor. They will work at home and outside school to gain access to learning materials or to get accessibility to external learning support. In higher education, traditional learning approaches are slowly being phased out, with many colleges and universities offering voice assistance to their students rather than conventional handwritten student books (Castro, 2019). Instructors must deal with more than just the job activities in an educational setting. It also includes maintaining the classroom environment and performing various business functions. They are tasked with various non-teaching jobs, which can be performed using artificial intelligence, such as assessment evaluation, test handling, paper grading, managing essential documents, supervising staffing and HR matters, and managing classroom materials. Field management and booking tasks are handled using artificial intelligence (Zawacki-Richter et al., 2019). Artificial intelligence devices and technologies have made international educational institutions available to everyone, regardless of their disability or language. Comprehensive services are available (Penprase, 2018). Artificial intelligence pledges for universities to become a method to drive student outcomes and enable personalised learning. Even though there has been much debate about this prospect, actual implementation has yet to attain the mainstream; instead, higher education is prepared to take the lead (Castro, 2019).

As a segment of the wider cloud revolution, many higher education institutes will commence adopting a hybrid approach to data centre function, blending cloud and public services with on-campus technologies (Jackson, 2019). This makes higher education an appealing target, and ransomware is becoming a possible attack with stolen identities due to phishing attacks (Kuziemski & Misuraca, 2020). Higher education is implementing the artificial intelligence sector, a vision of a technologically incorporated learning domain that merges devices and data with the progress of intelligent municipalities to enhance student experience. Colleges are smart to succeed. A data-powered campus allows managers to save money by streamlining costs. The intuitive and prompt interaction between management and university structures due to networking can be explored by faculty and students. These data can support and enhance public safety via warning and monitoring systems. Enhanced usability could support students in attaining efficient learning in class (Zawacki-Richter et al., 2019).

Case Studies and Examples

Computerized reasoning (artificial intelligence) has been progressively incorporated into advanced education organisations worldwide, with various effective executions demonstrating its capability to upgrade instruction, learning, and regulatory cycles. One outstanding illustration of fruitful artificial intelligence execution is the utilization of smart mentoring frameworks (ITS) at Carnegie Mellon College (CMU). CMU's Open Learning Drive (OLI) created ITSs for different subjects, including insights, physical science, and science, to provide customized coaching encounters for understudies (Corbett & Anderson, 1994). These ITSs use artificial intelligence calculations to adjust learning materials given individual under-study execution and provide constant criticism, resulting in better learning results than customary study hall guidance (Corbett et al., 2013).

Another model comes from Georgia State College (GSU), where recent investigations have been utilized to help understudy achievement drivers. GSU executed a simulated intelligence-driven framework called the Early Ready Framework (EAS) to distinguish understudies in danger of scholastic disappointment and provide designated mediations (Arnold & Pistilli, 2012). By breaking down the understudies' segment, scholarly and social information, the EAS can distinguish early admonition indications of scholastic difficulties and interface understudies with applicable help administrations, such as mentoring, directing, or scholarly prompting. Subsequently, GSU has seen critical upgrades in maintenance and graduation rates, especially among underserved populations (Arnold & Pistilli, 2017).

In addition, artificial intelligence has been instrumental in advancing regulatory cycles within advanced education foundations. For instance, Arizona State College (ASU) carried out a chatbot named "Alex" to smooth out under-study administrations and backing capabilities (Holotescu & Grosseck, 2017). Alex is incorporated into ASU's web-based understudy entry and provides moment help to understudy different subjects, including enlistments, monetary guides, and scholastic assets. By robotizing routine requests and errands, Alex has decreased the weight of authoritative staff and worked on the productivity of understudy support administrations, prompting more significant levels of understudy fulfilment and commitment (Holotescu & Grosseck, 2017).

Notwithstanding individual contextual analyses, cooperative drives, such as the Public Science Establishment's (NSF) artificial intelligence Foundation for Understudy Simulated Intelligence Joining, are driving developments in artificial intelligence coordination across various advanced education organisations. The organization fosters artificial intelligence advancements that help cooperative critical thinking among understudies and artificial intelligence specialists, cultivating imagination, decisive reasoning, and collaboration abilities (Walker et al., 2020). By utilizing artificial intelligence to increase human knowledge and work with cooperative opportunities for growth, the foundation tries to change schooling and prepare understudies for the labor force representing things to come. While the successful implementation of AI in higher education institutions has demonstrated immense potential, several key patterns and advantages have emerged from these experiences. Primarily, effective AI implementation requires a collaborative and interdisciplinary approach involving educators, technologists, administrators, and stakeholders (Siemens & Long, 2011). Successful AI initiatives often involve partnerships among academic departments, IT divisions, and external vendors to ensure that AI systems align with institutional goals, educational standards, and student needs.

Moreover, the ethical and social implications of AI must be carefully considered in its design, development, and deployment processes (Selwyn, 2017). AI systems can perpetuate biases, infringe on privacy rights, and exacerbate inequalities if they are not responsibly designed and implemented. Therefore, institutions should establish clear guidelines and policies for ethical AI use, including principles of fairness, transparency, accountability, and privacy protection (Holotescu & Grosseck, 2017).

Third, progressive assessment and evaluation are vital for measuring the effectiveness and adequacy of computer-based intelligence executions in advanced education. Establishments should gather and examine information on understudy results, fulfilment levels, and framework execution to recognize regions for development and illuminate future navigation (Arnold & Pistilli, 2012). Furthermore, subjective criticism from understudies and personnel can provide significant knowledge about a client's experience and assist in recognizing valuable open doors for refinement and improvement.

In addition, the versatility and maintainability of artificial intelligence drives advanced education. While pilot ventures and limited-scope executions might yield promising outcomes, scaling artificial intelligence answers for larger understudy populations and institutional settings requires a strong foundation, assets, and backing instruments (Blikstein, 2013). Foundations should cautiously evaluate the drawn-out practicality and cost-viability of artificial intelligence executions and foster systems to increase effective drives while limiting expected dangers and difficulties. The transformative power of AI in higher education institutions is evident in its potential to revolutionize educational, learning, and administrative processes. By utilizing intelligent tutoring systems, predictive analysis, chatbots, and other AI-driven technologies, institutions can enhance student success, improve operational efficiency, and foster innovation in education. Realizing the full benefits of AI necessitates a collaborative, ethical, and data-driven approach with careful attention to interdisciplinary partnerships, ethical considerations, evaluation methods, and scalability issues.

CHALLENGES AND FUTURE DIRECTIONS

As the coordination of computerized reasoning (artificial intelligence) in advanced education continues to develop, a few difficulties and open doors shape the future of this field. These difficulties range from specialised, moral, social, and hierarchical spaces, and require cautious thought to guarantee the dependable and compelling execution of artificial intelligence advances in instructive settings.

One of the essential difficulties confronting artificial intelligence in advanced education is the improvement of strong and versatile simulated intelligence frameworks that can address the different requirements and inclinations of understudies and teachers. While simulated intelligence-driven apparatuses, such as insightful mentoring frameworks and versatile learning stages, guarantee customized growth opportunities, they frequently depend on enormous datasets and complex calculations that may not sum well across various settings or student populations (VanLehn et al., 2007). Consequently, future innovative work endeavors should be zero when planning artificial intelligence frameworks that are adaptable, versatile, and interoperable, considering a consistent mix of existing instructive conditions and work processes.

Another specialised test is the moral and mindful utilization of artificial intelligence in advanced education. Artificial intelligence calculations can propagate inclinations, build disparities, and encroach on protection privileges if they are not planned and executed insightfully (Selwyn, 2017). For instance, prescient examination frameworks that depend exclusively on authentic information may coincidentally oppress specific gatherings of understudies by hailing them as in danger in light of segment or financial factors, as opposed to individual capacities or conditions (Arnold & Pistilli, 2012). Along these lines, it is fundamental for organisations to establish clear rules and arrangements for moral computer-based intelligence use, including standards of decency, straightforwardness, responsibility, and security insurance (Holotescu & Grosseck, 2017).

Moreover, the fast speed of mechanical advancement and the powerful idea of instructive conditions present difficulties in the reception and execution of artificial intelligence in advanced education. Teachers and executives might battle to stay up with artificial intelligence advances and explore the perplexing scene of apparatuses, stages, and applications accessible to them (Siemens & Long, 2011). In addition, worries about work removal and the job of artificial intelligence in reshaping customary education and learning standards might cause obstruction or trepidation among partners (Blikstein, 2013). In this way, establishments should put resources into preparing proficient improvement projects to engage teachers with the information, abilities, and assets expected to use artificial intelligence for academic development and understudy support.

Despite these difficulties, the eventual fate of artificial intelligence in advanced education is a critical commitment to changing the education, learning, and regulatory cycles. One future bearing is the improvement of artificial intelligence advancements that help cooperative critical thinking and collaboration abilities among understudied individuals. Drives, for example, the Public Science Establishment's (NSF) computer-based intelligence organization for understudying artificial intelligence joining plans to foster simulated intelligence frameworks that can team up with understudies on complex assignments, encouraging imagination, decisive reasoning, and relational abilities (Walker et al., 2020). By incorporating artificial intelligence into cooperative learning conditions, establishments can plan understudies for the cooperative and interdisciplinary nature of the labor force and society.

Another future consideration is the reconciliation of simulated intelligence with emerging innovations such as augmented reality (AR) and augmented reality (VR) to create vivid and intelligent opportunities for growth. Computer-based intelligence-driven AR and VR applications can mimic certifiable situations, involve learning valuable open doors, and adjust to individual student inclinations and capacities (Hwang & Wang, 2020). For instance, clinical understudies can utilize artificial intelligence-fueled VR reproduction to rehearse surgeries in a protected and controlled climate, improving their abilities and certainty before entering clinical settings. Additionally, language students can draw on simulated intelligence-driven AR applications that overlay advanced comments and interpretations on genuine items, working with jargon procurement and social drenching.

In addition, simulated intelligence holds the potential for tending toward tenacious difficulties in availability and inclusivity in advanced education. Artificial intelligence-driven assistive advances, such as discourse acknowledgement, regular language handling, and text-to-discourse union, can enable understudies with handicaps to obtain instructive materials and participate completely in study hall exercises (Pastry Specialist, 2010). For instance, understudies with visual debilitations can utilize artificial intelligence-fueled screen perusers to change text-based content into discourse or braille, empowering them to draw autonomously. By utilizing artificial intelligence to eliminate hindrances to access and investment, organisations can establish more comprehensive and evenhanded learning conditions for all understudies.

The difficulties and future bearing of computer-based intelligence in advanced education are diverse and complex, requiring cooperative endeavors from analysts, teachers, policymakers, and industry partners. While specialised difficulties, such as algorithmic inclination and interoperability, should be addressed, moral contemplations concerning reasonableness, straightforwardness, and security should remain principal. By embracing these difficulties as open doors for development and improvement, establishments can outfit the groundbreaking capability of artificial intelligence to upgrade instruction and learning, cultivate cooperation and imagination, and enhance availability and inclusivity in advanced education.

TECHNICAL CHALLENGES AND LIMITATIONS OF CURRENT AI SYSTEMS

Despite rapid progress in computerized reasoning (artificial intelligence) innovation, current simulated intelligence frameworks face a few specialised difficulties and limits that thwart their viability and materiality in different spaces, including schooling. These difficulties include algorithmic impediments, information imperatives, computational assets, and interpretability.

One of the essential specialised difficulties of the current computer-based intelligence frameworks is algorithmic inclination and decency. Simulated intelligence calculations frequently depend on verifiable information to meet expectations and choices, which might reflect and propagate existing predispositions and imbalances present in the information (Selwyn, 2017). For instance, recent examination models utilized in advanced education to recognize danger understudies may unintentionally oppress specific segment gatherings, assuming that authentic information contains predispositions connected with race, orientation, or financial status (Arnold & Pistilli, 2012). Tending to algorithmic predisposition requires cautious thought of information assortment strategies, highlight determination, and model preparation procedures to alleviate inclinations and guarantee decency and value in AI-based dynamic cycles.

Another specialised test is the restricted interpretability and reasonableness of the simulated intelligence models. Numerous computer-based intelligence calculations, especially profound learning models, are complicated and hazy, making it challenging for clients to comprehend how choices are made or to decipher the hidden reasoning behind simulated intelligence-created yields (Holotescu & Grosseck, 2017). This absence of straightforwardness raises concerns about responsibility, trust, and client acknowledgement, particularly in basic medical care, money, and schooling. Hence, endeavors to foster interpretable artificial intelligence procedures, such as logical artificial intelligence (XAI) and straightforward AI models, are fundamental for improving the straightforwardness and dependability of simulated intelligence frameworks (Lipton, 2016).

In addition, current simulated intelligence frameworks frequently require a large amount of named preparing information to accomplish ideal execution, which might present difficulties in spaces where marked information is scant or costly (Pastry Specialist, 2010). In instructive settings, gathering and commenting on huge datasets for errands, for example, understudy execution expectations, learning examinations, and normal language handling, can be work concentrated and tedious (Arnold & Pistilli, 2012). Furthermore, information quality issues, such as missing qualities, commotion, and irregularity, can influence the exhibition and dependability of computer-based intelligence models, which feature the significance of information pre-processing and quality confirmation procedures (Blikstein, 2013).

In addition, the versatility and computational assets expected to prepare and send simulated intelligence models address critical difficulties, especially for asset-obliged conditions, such as little instructive foundations or emerging nations (Siemens & Long, 2011). Profound learning models frequently require significant computational power and memory assets to prepare enormous datasets, which may be challenging for establishments with restricted foundations or financial planning limitations. Subsequently, innovative work endeavors are required to investigate lightweight artificial intelligence calculations, disseminated registering strategies, and cloud-based arrangements that can work on the versatility and openness of simulated intelligence innovation in different instructional settings (Siemens & Long, 2011).

Considering that artificial intelligence innovation holds monstrous potential for changing instruction and tending to complex difficulties, current computer-based intelligence frameworks face a few specialised limits and requirements that should be addressed to understand their maximum capacity. Beating these difficulties requires an interdisciplinary joint effort between analysts, teachers, policymakers, and industry partners to foster imaginative arrangements that improve reasonableness, interpretability, versatility, and the availability of simulated intelligence innovation in instructive settings. As Man-made brainpower (artificial intelligence) innovation continues to propel, what is in store holds various open doors for innovative work that can upgrade the abilities and utilization of simulated intelligence in different areas, including training. These potential future improvements span a large number of regions, including algorithmic developments, interdisciplinary coordinated efforts, and novel utilization of simulated intelligence innovation, each offering special open doors for propelling the cutting-edge in instructive computer-based intelligence.

One potential improvement is the progress of artificial intelligence calculations that can address algorithmic inclinations and decency difficulties. Specialists are investigating strategies such as antagonistic learning, reasonableness-mindful AI, and causal derivation to moderate predispositions and advance decency in simulated intelligence-driven dynamic cycles (Barocas and Selbst, 2016). For instance, antagonistic preparation includes preparing artificial intelligence models to produce counterfactual models that uncover and decrease predisposition to basic information dispersion (Zhang et al., 2018). By creating computer-based intelligence calculations that are more hearty, fair, and straightforward, scientists can work on the reliability and social effect of simulated intelligence innovation in training.

Another opportunity for future exploration lies in improving artificial intelligence-driven customized learning frameworks that adjust to individual student inclinations, capacities, and settings. Current computer-based intelligence-controlled versatile learning stages offer customized growth opportunities by changing the speed, trouble, and content of instructive materials to match individual under-study needs (Cook, 2010). Notwithstanding, future improvements include integrating multimodal information sources, such as under-study connections, emotional states, and physiological signs, to create more all-encompassing and customized opportunities for growth (Koedinger et al., 2012). For instance, artificial intelligence frameworks could investigate understudies' looks, motions, and commitment levels to progressively change the trouble level of learning exercises or give designated criticism, given their close-to-home state and mental burden (D'Mello & Kory, 2015).

Moreover, interdisciplinary joint efforts between artificial intelligence specialists, instructors, mental researchers, and space specialists offer promising opportunities for progressing instructive simulated intelligence research. Analysts can foster more successful and academically educated artificial intelligence frameworks by incorporating knowledge from mental brain science, learning sciences, and instructive hypotheses into artificial driven models and applications (VanLehn et al., 2007). For instance, mental demonstration methods, such as mental coaches and Bayesian information, can educate students regarding computer-based intelligence-driven mentoring frameworks that recreate human-like mentoring cooperation and adjust to individual student needs (Corbett & Anderson, 1994). Additionally, coordinated efforts with space specialists in fields such as semantics, humanism, and social examinations can assist in guaranteeing that artificial intelligence frameworks are socially delicate, comprehensive, and receptive to the assorted necessities of students from various foundations and settings.

In addition, the rise of novel artificial intelligence, such as unified learning, support learning, and neurosymbolic computer-based intelligence, opens up new avenues for examination and development in instructive computer-based intelligence. Combined learning permits artificial intelligence models to be prepared cooperatively across decentralized information sources while saving protection and information security (Kairouz et al., 2019). Regarding schooling, united learning could empower foundations to collaborate on advancing simulated intelligence-driven models for understudy achievement expectations, customized proposal frameworks, and instructive substance creation, without sharing delicate understudy information (Arnold & Pistilli, 2012). In addition, support learning strategies can be applied to foster simulated intelligence-driven, versatile learning conditions that provide customized input and rewards given the understudies' learning progress and execution (Sutton & Barto, 2018). By bridging the force of cutting-edge artificial intelligence advances, specialists can open up additional opportunities for improving instruction, learning, and appraisal rehearses in schooling.

The eventual fate of artificial intelligence in schooling is driven by energizing open doors for innovative work that can alter education, learning, and instructive practice. By tending to specialize difficulties, progressing algorithmic developments, encouraging interdisciplinary coordinated efforts, and investigating novel utilization of computer-based intelligence innovation, scientists can prepare for a more impartial, customized, and powerful instructive experience for students worldwide.

CONCLUSION

The joining of computerized reasoning (computer-based intelligence) in advanced education has arisen as an extraordinary power, offering new open doors for development, effectiveness, and customized opportunities for growth. Through this writing survey, we have investigated hypothetical establishments, commonsense applications, difficulties, and future headings of computer-based intelligence in advanced education, revealing insights into key discoveries, suggestions for training and strategy, and proposals for additional exploration.

Several key discoveries have emerged from the assessment of artificial intelligence in advanced education. Artificial intelligence advancements, such as clever coaching frameworks, predictive examinations, and chatbots, have exhibited huge potential to improve education, learning, and managerial cycles in advanced education foundations. These simulated intelligence-driven instruments offer customized growth opportunities, support understudy achievement drives, and smooth managerial assignments, prompting further development of results and effectiveness gains.

In addition, effective execution of computer-based intelligence in advanced education requires a cooperative and interdisciplinary methodology that includes teachers, technologists, chairpersons, and partners. Successful artificial intelligence drives frequently include associations between scholastic divisions, IT offices, and outside merchants to guarantee that artificial intelligence frameworks align with institutional objectives, instructive standards, and understudy needs.

Third, moral and social ramifications should be painstakingly viewed through planning, advancing, and sending simulated intelligence frameworks to advanced education. Artificial intelligence calculations can propagate inclinations, encroach on protection freedoms, and compound imbalances, if not planned and executed mindfully. Hence, organisations should establish clear rules and arrangements for moral computer-based intelligence use, including standards of decency, straightforwardness, responsibility, and security insurance.

The ramifications of simulated intelligence in advanced education include practice and strategy. Establishments can use artificial intelligence advancements to upgrade education, learning, and managerial cycles, further developing understudied results, functional productivity, and institutional adequacy. For instance, simulated intelligence-driven versatile learning stages can provide customized growth opportunities to understudy, while predictive examination frameworks can distinguish in danger understudies and mediate the right on time to help their prosperity.

From a strategic perspective, policymakers should address moral, lawful, and administrative difficulties related to computer-based intelligence execution in advanced education. This might include creating rules, principles, and structures for moral artificial intelligence use and guaranteeing consistency with security guidelines, such as the Family Instructive Privileges and Protection Act (FERPA) and the Overall Information Insurance Guideline (GDPR). Moreover, policymakers should focus on interests in computer-based intelligence examinations, foundations, and labor force advancement to help the capable and fair reconciliation of artificial intelligence in advanced education.

Although a critical headway has been made in simulated intelligence in advanced education, a few regions warrant further examination and investigation. Research on the viability and effect of computer-based intelligence interventions on under-study learning results, standards for dependability, and institutional execution are required immediately. Longitudinal examinations and randomized controlled preliminaries can provide significant insights into the adequacy of artificial intelligence-driven devices and illuminate proof-based dynamics in advanced education.

In addition, research is expected to address the specialised difficulties and impediments of momentum artificial intelligence frameworks, such as algorithmic predisposition, interpretability, versatility, and asset limitations. Developments in algorithmic decency, reasonable simulated intelligence, united learning, and lightweight simulated intelligence calculations can improve the unwavering quality, straightforwardness, and openness of artificial intelligence innovation in instructive settings.

In addition, joint interdisciplinary examinations between computer-based intelligence specialists, instructors, mental researchers, and area specialists offer opportunities for growing more powerful and educationally educated computer-based intelligence frameworks. By coordinating bits of knowledge from mental brain science, learning sciences, and instructive hypotheses into artificial intelligence-driven models and applications, scientists can improve the customized, comprehensive, and impartial nature of AI.

The reconciliation of simulated intelligence in advanced education has a massive commitment to changing instruction, learning, and regulatory cycles. By tending to key discoveries, suggestions for training and strategy, and proposals for additional examinations, partners can cooperate in bridging the maximum capacity of simulated intelligence to make a more inventive, impartial, and understudy-focused instructive experience for students worldwide.

REFERENCES

Abad-Segura, E., González-Zamar, M. D., Infante-Moro, J. C., & Ruipérez García, G. (2020). Sustainable management of digital transformation in higher education: Global research trends. *Sustainability (Basel)*, 12(5), 2107. DOI:10.3390/su12052107

Alyahyan, E., & Düştegör, D. (2020). Predicting academic success in higher education: Literature review and best practices. *International Journal of Educational Technology in Higher Education*, 17(1), 1–21. DOI:10.1186/s41239-020-0177-7

Castro, R. (2019). Blended learning in higher education: Trends and capabilities. *Education and Information Technologies*, 24(4), 2523–2546. DOI:10.1007/s10639-019-09886-3

Ciolacu, M., Tehrani, A. F., Binder, L., & Svasta, P. M. (2018, October). Education 4.0-Artificial Intelligence assisted higher education: early recognition system with machine learning to support students' success. In *2018 IEEE 24th International Symposium for Design and Technology in Electronic Packaging (SIITME)* (pp. 23-30). IEEE.

Dilmurod, R., & Fazliddin, A. (2021). Prospects for the introduction of artificial intelligence technologies in higher education. *ACADEMICIA: an international multidisciplinary research journal, 11*(2), 929-934.

Ejdys, J., Gudanowska, A., Halicka, K., Kononiuk, A., Magruk, A., Nazarko, J., Nazarko, L., Szpilko, D., & Widelska, U. (2019). Foresight in higher education institutions: Evidence from Poland. *Форсайт*, 13(1), 77–89. DOI:10.17323/2500-2597.2019.1.77.89

Gaebel, M., Zhang, T., Stoeber, H., & Morrisroe, A. (2021). Digitally enhanced learning and teaching in European higher education institutions. *Survey Report.*

Hinojo-Lucena, F. J., Aznar-Díaz, I., Cáceres-Reche, M. P., & Romero-Rodríguez, J. M. (2019). Artificial intelligence in higher education: A bibliometric study on its impact in the scientific literature. *Education Sciences*, 9(1), 51. DOI:10.3390/educsci9010051

Holmes, W., Porayska-Pomsta, K., Holstein, K., Sutherland, E., Baker, T., Shum, S. B., Santos, O. C., Rodrigo, M. T., Cukurova, M., Bittencourt, I. I., & Koedinger, K. R. (2022). Ethics of AI in education: Towards a community-wide framework. *International Journal of Artificial Intelligence in Education*, 32(3), 504–526. DOI:10.1007/s40593-021-00239-1

Jackson, N. C. (2019). Managing for competency with innovation change in higher education: Examining the pitfalls and pivots of digital transformation. *Business Horizons*, 62(6), 761–772. DOI:10.1016/j.bushor.2019.08.002

Kuziemski, M., & Misuraca, G. (2020). AI governance in the public sector: Three tales from the frontiers of automated decision-making in democratic settings. *Telecommunications Policy*, 44(6), 101976. DOI:10.1016/j.telpol.2020.101976 PMID:32313360

Penprase, B. E. (2018). The fourth industrial revolution and higher education. *Higher education in the era of the fourth industrial revolution, 10*, 978-981.

Radianti, J., Majchrzak, T. A., Fromm, J., & Wohlgenannt, I. (2020). A systematic review of immersive virtual reality applications for higher education: Design elements, lessons learned, and research agenda. *Computers & Education*, 147, 103778. DOI:10.1016/j.compedu.2019.103778

Tariq, M. U. (2024a). Smart Transportation Systems: Paving the Way for Sustainable Urban Mobility. In Munuhwa, S. (Ed.), *Contemporary Solutions for Sustainable Transportation Practices* (pp. 254–283). IGI Global. DOI:10.4018/979-8-3693-3755-4.ch010

Tariq, M. U. (2024b). Enhancing Students and Learning Achievement as 21st-Century Skills Through Transdisciplinary Approaches. In Kumar, R., Ong, E., Anggoro, S., & Toh, T. (Eds.), *Transdisciplinary Approaches to Learning Outcomes in Higher Education* (pp. 220–257). IGI Global. DOI:10.4018/979-8-3693-3699-1.ch007

Tariq, M. U. (2024c). The role of AI in skilling, upskilling, and reskilling the workforce. In Doshi, R., Dadhich, M., Poddar, S., & Hiran, K. (Eds.), *Integrating generative AI in education to achieve sustainable development goals* (pp. 421–433). IGI Global. DOI:10.4018/979-8-3693-2440-0.ch023

Tariq, M. U. (2024d). AI-powered language translation for multilingual classrooms. In Doshi, R., Dadhich, M., Poddar, S., & Hiran, K. (Eds.), *Integrating generative AI in education to achieve sustainable development goals* (pp. 29–46). IGI Global. DOI:10.4018/979-8-3693-2440-0.ch002

Zawacki-Richter, O., Marín, V. I., Bond, M., & Gouverneur, F. (2019). Systematic review of research on artificial intelligence applications in higher education–where arc thc cducators? *International Journal of Educational Technology in Higher Education*, 16(1), 1–27. DOI:10.1186/s41239-019-0171-0

Zhao, Y., Llorente, A. M. P., & Gómez, M. C. S. (2021). Digital competence in higher education research: A systematic literature review. *Computers & Education*, 168, 104212. DOI:10.1016/j.compedu.2021.104212 PMID:36568577

ADDITIONAL READING

Kaleem, S., Sohail, A., Babar, M., Ahmad, A., & Tariq, M. U. (2023). Ensemble learning for multi-class COVID-19 detection from big data. *PLoS One*, 18(10), e0292587. DOI:10.1371/journal.pone.0292587 PMID:37819992

Kaleem, S., Sohail, A., Tariq, M. U., & Asim, M. (2023). An improved big data analytics architecture using federated learning for IoT-enabled urban intelligent transportation systems. *Sustainability (Basel)*, 15(21), 15333. DOI:10.3390/su152115333

Kaleem, S., Sohail, A., Tariq, M. U., & Asim, M. (2024). A hybrid model for energy-efficient green Internet of Things enabled intelligent transportation systems using federated learning. *Internet of Things : Engineering Cyber Physical Human Systems*, 25, 101038. DOI:10.1016/j.iot.2023.101038

Malik, N., Altaf, S., Tariq, M. U., Ahmed, A., & Babar, M. (2023). A deep learning-based sentiment analytic model for the prediction of traffic accidents. *CMC-Computers. Computers, Materials & Continua*, 77(2), 1599–1615. DOI:10.32604/cmc.2023.040455

Mateev, M., Moudud-Ul-Huq, S., Sahyouni, A., & Tariq, M. U. (2022). Capital regulation, competition and risk-taking: Policy implications for banking sector stability in the MENA region. *Research in International Business and Finance*, 60, 101579. DOI:10.1016/j.ribaf.2021.101579

Mateev, M., Sahyouni, A., & Tariq, M. U. (2022). Bank regulation, ownership and risk-taking behavior in the MENA region: Policy implications for banks in emerging economies. *Review of Managerial Science*, 17(1), 287–338. DOI:10.1007/s11846-022-00529-5

Mateev, M., Tariq, M. U., & Sahyouni, A. (2023). Efficiency, market concentration and bank performance during the COVID-19 outbreak: Evidence from the MENA region. *PLoS One*, 18(5), e0285403. DOI:10.1371/journal.pone.0285403 PMID:37163516

KEY TERMS AND DEFINITIONS

Bayesian Information Criterion (BIC): A criterion for model selection among a finite set of models; the model with the lowest BIC is preferred.

Cognitive Tutors: AI systems designed to provide personalized instruction by simulating one-on-one human tutoring.

Deep Learning: A subset of machine learning involving neural networks with many layers, enabling the processing of vast amounts of data for complex tasks.

Federated Learning: A machine learning technique where models are trained across multiple decentralized devices or servers holding local data samples without exchanging them.

Inference Engine: A component of an AI system that applies logical rules to the knowledge base to deduce new information.

Neurosymbolic AI: An AI approach combining neural networks and symbolic AI to benefit from the strengths of both methodologies.

Virtual Reality (VR): A simulated experience that can be similar to or completely different from the real world, used for immersive learning experiences.

Chapter 6
Innovation Plans for the Use of Artificial Intelligence in Higher Education

ABSTRACT

This chapter investigates plans for utilising artificial brainpower (simulated intelligence) in advanced education to upgrade instruction, learning, research, and authoritative cycles. It involves the use of artificial intelligence, including customised growth opportunities, versatile learning frameworks, virtual mentoring, and computer-based intelligence-driven research investigations. Moreover, this chapter discusses artificial intelligence reception's moral and social ramifications, stressing the significance of reasonableness, value, information protection, and mindful simulated intelligence use in advanced education. Through contextual analyses and certifiable models, this chapter features the extraordinary capability of simulated intelligence in reforming advanced education, advancing inclusivity, and getting ready understudies for outcomes in the computerised age.

INTRODUCTION

Computerized reasoning (artificial intelligence) is quickly changing in each part of society, and advanced education is no exception. Advancements in artificial intelligence have acquired conspicuousness in the scholarly community, offering creative answers for longstanding difficulties in education, learning, exploration, and organization. This section outlines computer-based intelligence in advanced education and investigates its definitions, applications, and suggestions for the fate

DOI: 10.4018/979-8-3693-4074-5.ch006

of learning. Simulated intelligence includes a wide scope of innovations and methods that empower machines to perform errands that normally require human insight such as thinking, critical thinking, and learning (Russell & Norvig, 2022). AI, a subset of artificial intelligence, centers around calculations that permit PCs to gain information and work on their presentation over the long term without unequivocal programming. Profound learning, a further developed type of AI, includes brain networks with various layers of interconnected hubs, empowering the examination of mind-boggling and unstructured information such as pictures, text, and discourse.

In advanced education, artificial intelligence can change instruction and opportunities for growth by providing customized, versatile, and intuitive instructive assets and backing. For instance, simulated intelligence-fueled versatile learning frameworks can examine under-study information to fit guidance to individual requirements, inclinations, and learning styles, advancing further comprehension and dominance of scholastic ideas. Shrewd coaching frameworks influence simulated intelligence calculations to provide customized criticism and direction to understudies, thus improving their commitment and scholarly execution (VanLehn, 2011). In addition, artificial intelligence-driven remote helpers can uphold understudy with moment reactions to questions, course direction, updates, and upgrade understudy support administrations (Tariq, 2024).

The effect of artificial brainpower (computer-based intelligence) on advanced education reaches out past customized growth opportunities to remember headways for exploration, organization, and the, generally speaking, instructive biological system. Artificial intelligence-driven information examination, present demonstration, and normal language handling reform research processes by empowering scientists to break down enormous datasets, recognize designs, and create experiences with extraordinary speed and precision (Kitchin, 2014). For instance, artificial intelligence calculations can investigate logical writing to recognize research patterns, holes, and open doors, accelerating the speed of revelation and development across different disciplines (Tariq, 2024).

Advances in artificial intelligence offer creative answers for authoritative difficulties in advanced education, such as enlistment on the board, understudy support administrations, and ground activities. The present investigation can assist foundations by gauging enlistment patterns, streamlining asset distribution, and fostering designated enrolment systems to draw in and hold a different understudy body (Chetty et al., 2016). Simulated intelligence-controlled remote helpers can help understudy course enlistment, monetary guide requests, and ground coordinated operations, improving the general productivity and adequacy of regulatory cycles (Okunlaya et al., 2022).

In addition, artificial intelligence can change the job of teachers in advanced education by expanding their capacities and providing important experiences to understudy learning ways of behaving and needs. Simulated intelligence-driven investigation can distinguish understudies in danger early, permitting teachers to mediate proactively and offer designated help to advance their understudy achievement (Arnold & Pistilli, 2012). Furthermore, artificial intelligence advancements empower educators to customize guidance, adjust content to understudy singular requirements, and cultivate dynamic learning, decisive reasoning, and critical thinking abilities fundamental to progress in the computerized age (Alam and Mohanty, 2022).

Development is vital for advancing advanced education in light of changing cultural necessities, mechanical progress, and academic patterns. With the world rapidly impacting advanced education organisations, they face an expanding strain to adjust and improve to address the issues of a different and dynamic understudy population. Development in advanced education envelops many drives, including educational plan configurations, systems, mechanical coordination, and managerial practices (Kuleto et al. 2021).

One critical driver of development in advanced education is the development of customized, adaptable, and open opportunities for growth. Understudies today come from assorted foundations, have fluctuating degrees of earlier information and abilities, and have novel learning inclinations and earnings. As such, advanced education foundations should be enhanced to provide custom-made instructive pathways that oblige individual necessities and support under-study achievement (Watters, 2019). For instance, ability-based schooling (CBE) programs permit understudies to advance at their speed, show the dominance of explicit skills, and procure qualifications considering exhibited learning results, as opposed to situated time (Johnson et al., 2015).

The development in advanced education is fundamental for cultivating imagination, decisive reasoning, and critical thinking abilities among understudies, setting them up for outcomes in a rapidly developing market. By incorporating experiential learning potential open doors, interdisciplinary cooperation, and task-based learning into the educational plan, organisations can engage in understudies to apply hypothetical information to genuine issues, foster adaptable abilities, and adjust to changing workplaces (Bass et al., 2014). For instance, drives such as producer spaces, advancement labs, and business programs provide understudied active encounters and opportunities to investigate their interests, foster groundbreaking thoughts, and seek creative answers to cultural difficulties.

Moreover, the development of advanced education is significant for resolving worldwide issues, such as environmental change, social imbalance, and mechanical disturbance. By cultivating interdisciplinary coordinated efforts, research associations, and local area commitment, establishments can use their aptitude and assets to drive positive change and contribute to the progress of information and society (Kezar et al., 2018). For instance, manageability drives, variety and incorporation projects, and social business adventures empower organisations to satisfy their more extensive cultural mission and significantly affect the world (Tapalova and Zhiyenbayeva, 2022).

Overall, development in advanced education is fundamental to embracing the extraordinary capability of artificial reasoning, which tends to create difficulties in planning understudies for outcomes in the 21st 100 years. By bridging artificial intelligence advances to upgrade education, learning, exploration, and organization, foundations can make more comprehensive, customized, and effective instructive encounters that engage understudies to flourish in a quickly impacting world.

The rapid progress of artificial intelligence will intensely alter the world and how people live in it. The action plan helps higher education to encourage colleges and universities to fix their perspectives on global science and technology innovations, support preliminary research, and conduct basic modern research and vital, revolutionary, and original advancements. It further enhances universities' capability to revolutionise and train capable people in artificial intelligence (Knox, 2020).

GENERAL NEEDS

Basic Circumstances

As technologies such as the Internet of Things, big data, the Internet, and cloud computing have progressed, artificial intelligence has led to technological and scientific breakthroughs that can initiate a chain reaction and various disruptive technologies. It expedites the development of new drivers of economic progress, forming a novel industrial system and leading to the latest technological and scientific transformation and industrial revolution. Countries are currently in the decisive stage of shaping prosperous societies in a versatile manner. People's desire for a good life and the need for high-quality financial progress have developed a bright future for the progress and implementation of artificial intelligence in the higher education sector. Artificial intelligence has features that merge the social and technical characteristics. It is a novel driver of financial progress and booster of social progress. The abilities of artificial intelligence, involving big data-driven visual analytics, speech recognition, and natural language processing, are increasing rapidly (Renz & Hilbig, 2020).

Business intelligence recommendations, dialogue automatic navigation, smart vehicles, language translation, novel economic predictions, and self-driving vehicles are promptly switching to a functional stage. Artificial intelligence is presently infusing and upgrading the connections between the financial activities of manufacturing, consumption, exchange, and distribution. It is also creating new smart technologies, products, and demands; methods of performing business from the micro and macro levels; and altering how people live down their social structure. This has generated an increase in the efficiency of society. Simultaneously, the innovative implementation of artificial intelligence in higher education has escalated. Using innovative technology to innovate novel ways of providing education, modernising teaching methods, enhancing academic administration, and developing an innovative, networked, customised, and constant education system is vital for stimulating the progress of balanced education, enhancing educational quality, and educational independence. This is a crucial driver and support for educational transformation. Science and technology are the number of dynamic forces in colleges and universities; talent is the prioritised resource, and innovation is the prioritised driver. They have distinctive characteristics regarding the research and implementation of fundamental technologies such as the basic theory of natural language processing, artificial intelligence, robotics, computer vision, and media, as well as a concrete foundation for teaching people and the progress of academic courses. Faced with the progress artificial intelligence generation, universities and colleges must further improve their strengths in basic research, the introduction of new courses, and training. They must increase their applied basic research and enhance innovation in primary multipurpose technologies. They must constantly stimulate the deep incorporation of artificial intelligence into the actual economy to nurture novel drivers of financial progress. They must constantly support the deep incorporation of artificial intelligence with the requirements of the people to offer them the latest ways to enhance their employment. They must constantly boost the deep incorporation of artificial intelligence in higher education to offer new methods to transform education. In doing so, they will lead to higher education in technical and scientific training, innovation, and the demo of technical implementations in the AI domain of artificial intelligence, enhancing the overall power of artificial intelligence in higher education (Soni et al., 2019).

Guiding System

The Ministry of Higher Education will adopt the latest development ideas, dependent on coordination, innovation, sharing, environmental sustainability, and openness. It also includes strategic strategies that involve transforming the higher education sector by adopting scientific education, strengthening the business community with talented individuals, and making innovation-powered progress. This will boost the development of a new-generation talent progress system for the artificial intelligence domain and technology innovation system. It will systematically enhance universities' ability to train people, conduct scientific research, offer social services, and pass on and revolutionise culture, exchange, and collaboration in the artificial intelligence domain on a global scale. This will boost the overall progress of artificial intelligence as an academic discipline, technological innovations, training programs, demonstration of the field's implementation, and theoretical innovation (Renz & Hilbig, 2020). The basic regulations as follows:

- Encourage innovation by taking the lead
- Place innovation at the core of artificial intelligence progress at universities and colleges
- Recognize international artificial intelligence progress trends
- Enhance the technical and scientific innovation system for artificial intelligence in universities and colleges
- Make universities and college hubs for international technological and scientific innovation in artificial intelligence.
- Promote the merger of education and science
- Thoroughly apply an essential mission that nurtures civic and character benefit
- Inflexibly control the fundamental problem of enhancing the capability of training people, promoting training, incorporation of scientific research, academic course development
- Recognize the vital role that scientific education plays in the vital progress of higher education and the training of the exceptional talent
- Consider the requirements of those being served
- Strengthening institutional and structural modifications.
- Intensify association between research institutions, businesses and local governments and universities and colleges
- Expedite the implementation and transfer of technical and scientific attainments in the artificial intelligence field to fundamental sectors and industries
- Enhance universities' and colleges' capability of serving significant local policies, the development and innovation of different sectors, the modification and advancement of the economy, and guarantee every person can make a living
- Take full benefit of universities' and colleges' preeminence in basic training and research and characteristics of disciplinary incorporation

Higher education departments should complete the technological and scientific innovation system to foster new-generation artificial intelligence in colleges and universities and enhance the configuration of the academic discipline system. Universities will be innovating the fundamental theories of new-generation artificial intelligence and primary technological research while further enhancing their authority in scientific training and research and endorsing the comprehensive implementation of artificial intelligence technology. Higher education should enhance technological and scientific innovation training quality and ability in the new-generation artificial intelligence domain by 2025. Universities will achieve various accomplishments of global significance (Ahmad, 2020). They will exhibit a world-class level of theoretical studies, state-of-the-art technology, and implementation. Colleges and universities will efficiently assist in the upgradation of the global industrial sector, the economic revolution, and the development of an intelligent society. Universities and colleges will become a significant force behind developing the world's foremost artificial intelligence innovation centres. They will lead the progress of a new-generation artificial intelligence talent pool to offer technical and scientific assistance to the higher education sector and guarantee talent to place it at the forefront of innovation-driven states until 2030 (Knox, 2020).

Fundamental Tasks

Enhance the technological and scientific innovation system for artificial intelligence at universities and colleges. Strengthen primary theoretical research on new-generation artificial intelligence. Emphasize the significant pioneering scientific problems relevant to artificial intelligence and promote the thorough multi-disciplinary incorporation of domains like artificial intelligence, cognitive science, brain science, and psychology. Focus on theoretical and primary research in significant data intelligence, computing, swarm intelligence, quantum computing, high-level machine learning, autonomous coordination control, hybrid enhanced intelligence, cross-media sensing, optimised decision-making, and brain-inspired intelligence computing. It offers a theoretical basis for a pattern switch in artificial intelligence and lays a firm base for the solid theoretical base for the latest generation of artificial intelligence (Dilmurod & Fazliddin, 2021).

Focus on primary hardware, systems, and algorithms for the latest generation of artificial intelligence. Intensify research into primary technologies, such as smart chips, hybrid enhanced intelligence, machine learning, swarm intelligence, virtual reality, computer vision, natural language processing, knowledge computing, and deep reasoning. Significant innovations should be made in domains such as swarm, autonomous, brain-inspired, and hybrid intelligence to develop a technical system for the latest generation of artificial intelligence. Depending on fundamental algorithms, hardware, and data, improved intermedia, reasoning capability, analytical capability of swarm intelligence, enhanced capacity of hybrid intelligence, and capability of executing autonomous motions with an emphasis on human-computer collaboration. Develop identical, open-source, and mature artificial intelligence service assistance abilities for the association between chips and algorithms, software and hardware, and clouds and terminals (Renz & Hilbig, 2020).

Focus on what is required for fundamental theories in artificial intelligence, the primary use of technology, and public assistance media. Intensify the development of innovation grounds, such as cutting-edge science and research centres in higher education. Concerned with essential requirements such as inter-disciplinary innovations, cutting-edge, and regional and global progress, collaboration and interaction between innovators, such as universities and colleges, businesses, and scientific research institutions should be promoted. Development of collaborative innovation setup. Intensify the development of global-level innovation centres, such as national labs, national technology innovation hubs, national engineering research centres, and significant global science and technology infrastructure. Universities and colleges should be inspired to develop new types of scientific research firms and conduct multidisciplinary research (Limani et al., 2019).

Assist universities and colleges in taking on significant national technology and science tasks. Bring together and training various strategic technical and scientific brains with international reputes. It assists universities and colleges in developing multidisciplinary and interdisciplinary innovation and research groups in artificial intelligence, cognitive science, and brain science (Guan et al., 2020).

Inspire and support universities and colleges engaging and leading in creating strategic artificial intelligence research hubs that carry out policy and strategic research on creating artificial intelligence, such as vital, forward-looking, and stimulating problems such as higher education and employment. Develop several novels and high-level research institutes (Zawacki-Richter et al., 2019). Enhance efforts to endorse academic collaboration and exchange at the global level (Johnson et al., 2019). Further efforts are needed for leading-edge innovation.

- Robust growth in autonomous learning, integrated reasoning, and intuitive cognition with artificial intelligence methods such as logical derivation and learning from experience and knowledge (Fahimirad and Kotamjani, 2018).
- Develops the latest theoretical artificial intelligence approaches and models that are incredibly explanatory, with variable data dependency and robust generalisation transfer abilities, which makes it possible to shift from data to knowledge and knowledge to decision-making (Dilmurod & Fazliddin, 2021).
- Emphasising significant technological breakthroughs such as knowledge computing, automated systems, cross-media reasoning, hybrid intelligence, and swarm intelligence. Promotes synchronisation of artificial intelligence-powered chips. Develop artificial intelligence service abilities for terminal cloud associations (Yigitcanlar et al., 2020).

- Focus on improving swarm intelligence, human-computer interaction, hybrid intelligence, and cross-media reasoning capabilities. Stimulate algorithms as the base and utilise hardware and data to develop a mature and stable artificial intelligence technology system (Renz & Hilbig, 2020).
- Support innovation and collaboration in basic artificial intelligence theory, knowledge services, disaster reduction and prevention, and scientific poverty alleviation. Fix several high-level technology and science research institutions for artificial intelligence and assist significant policy- and strategy-relevant scientific and technical research to offer theoretical assistance and strategic support for economic and social development and respond to vital social concerns (Dilmurod & Fazliddin, 2021).

Enhancing the training system in the artificial intelligence domain

- Improve multidisciplinary incorporation with related research domains such as control, computing, cognitive science, quantum, neuroscience, mathematics, sociology, psychology, law, and economics. Assist universities and colleges in the development of artificial intelligence-driven domains of research in technical and computer science areas. Raise investment in disciplines relevant to artificial intelligence and encourage the growth of related multidisciplinary study fields. Inspired by the development of first-level courses in the AI domain of artificial intelligence. Upgrade the domains relevant to fundamental artificial intelligence theory, data analysis, intelligence systems, data analysis, pattern recognition, machine learning, knowledge engineering, and natural language processing. It assists universities and colleges in developing leading universities and the best curriculum (Limani et al., 2019).
- Expedite the application of the plan for training and educating exceptional engineers and endorse the preparation of the best managers, beneficial undergraduate degrees, and excellent students. According to artificial intelligence technology and theory, it has the features of permeability, universality, and portability. Dynamically integrate students' academic requirements and interests in society. Dynamically develop the practice and study of new engineering projects. Provide more attention to the cross-integration of expert education for artificial intelligence with control and computer science, law, physics, biology, sociology, psychology, and other courses. Reassure the integration and adaptation of technology, mathematics, big data, and other courses in intelligent technology and science for computer science majors—position artificial intelligence-relevant majors based on regional and national industrial demands (Limani et al., 2019).

- Expedite the transfer of technological and scientific artificial intelligence accomplishments and resources to teaching and education. Stimulates vital artificial intelligence-driven content and development of an open online curriculum, particularly in artificial intelligence basics, natural language processing, machine learning, pattern recognition, neural networks, and computer vision. Encourage the enrolment of several top-notch graduate and undergraduate content and high-quality, regional-level open online subjects. Supplement artificial intelligence to elementary university course content for computer science (Renz & Hilbig, 2020).
- Stimulates the multi-entity combined education mechanism. Expanding university-industry educational association. Implement and expand collective university-industry education projects in the artificial intelligence domain. Use the most current technical and industrial progress attainments to inspire training modifications. Stimulates the development of a new engineering course in the artificial intelligence domain to support education, research, and industry. Prepare several standard regional practices and media that merge research, training, and education. Dynamically fix temporary placements in which instructors in the artificial intelligence domain can attain experience and collective university-industry research institutes training mediums for engineering abilities. Stimulating techniques for cooperative exchange between college and university instructors and those in the industry. Universities and colleges should be inspired to fix artificial intelligence schools, multi-disciplinary research centres, and research institutions to encourage the innovation of a cooperative educational framework that incorporates technology, science, and industry and multi0channel training for entrepreneurial and innovative individuals in the artificial intelligence domain. Support universities and colleges by utilising incremental assistance and stock amendments. Gradually magnify the scale of enrolment for related research domains and decide on a reasonably categorised structure (Dilmurod & Fazliddin, 2021).
- Stimulate and inspire universities and colleges to make related research and training resources accessible outside of their institutes. Create a public service medium to promote artificial intelligence among youth and the general public and dynamically function to make science more approachable. Upkeep the contribution of university and college instructors in popularising artificial intelligence education at junior and middle school levels and commencing relevant research. Prepare in-service and pre-service training disciplines for instructors on artificial intelligence skills and knowledge. Training instructors on how to apply smart education. Develop non-degree artificial intelli-

gence to commence educational discipline at universities and colleges (Soni et al., 2019).

- Support universities' technology, science parks, ventures, and innovation bases to prepare state-of-the-art entrepreneurship projects. Recognise innovation and startup demonstration parks at universities and colleges. Stimulates the progress of entrepreneurship and innovation activities in artificial intelligence by university and college students and instructors (Yigitcanlar et al., 2020).

Training

- Stimulates the development of AI-powered disciplines in computer science and other technical subjects at universities and colleges. Comprehensively confirming what is involved in AI research of artificial intelligence, enhancing the artificial intelligence discipline system, and encouraging the growth of a top-level subject in the domain of artificial intelligence (Soni et al., 2019).
- Encourage the development of vital teaching content, open online courses, publishing 50 world-class undergraduate and graduate books, and preparing 50 regional-level quality open online artificial intelligence courses by 2025. Improve artificial intelligence material in majors relevant to information management and big data at vocational schools and train individuals in technical skills valid in the artificial intelligence domain (Yigitcanlar et al., 2020).
- Raise the incorporation of innovation and training research bases and enhance the multi-entity cooperative education method in the artificial intelligence domain to train artificial intelligence talent at numerous levels in various ways (Chatterjee & Bhattacharjee, 2020).
- Integrating artificial intelligence into junior and middle-level school education. Work constantly to enhance and augment specialised majors and develop a higher education system that merges specific artificial intelligence education, primary university-level education, and vocational training. Stimulate and inspire universities and colleges, making related research resources and teaching accessible outside of their institutes. Create a public service medium to promote artificial intelligence among youth and the general public and dynamically struggle to make science more approachable (Soni et al., 2019).
- Stimulates technology transformation and revolution of science and technology accomplishments into commercial products from universities and colleges to intelligent education, innovative production, smart agriculture, smart judiciary, competent healthcare, smart cities, and national security, and augments the implementation of these technologies. Enhance association with related industries. Endorse the development of new industries and novel methods

of doing business in the national defense, transportation, education, agriculture, security, forestry, finance, manufacturing, culture, and healthcare sectors. Nurture in several leading artificial intelligence technology industries. Endorse the development of several industry collection and demonstration domains (Yigitcanlar et al., 2020).

- Endorse teaching and educational revolution. Switching to an intelligent campus-based framework on virtual campuses. Develop a technology-based teaching environment. Discovering Novel Artificial Intelligence-enabled Teaching Models. Modernise how instructors teach, utilise artificial intelligence to optimise the teaching procedure, assess students, and analyse achievement levels (Rampersad, 2020).
- Precisely assess both student and teacher performances. Introduction of a personalised aptitude-based curriculum. Endorsing Academic Management Transformation. Assist schools use artificial intelligence technology to revolutionise their institutional structures and management systems and monitor how they function and serve their students. Apply fragility management and customised services on campuses to upgrade the administrative levels of schools. Encouraging constant online learning, endorsing the growth of student-centric virtual learning mediums, offering a rich range of customised learning resources, modernising how services are offered, and customising constant learning (Williamson, 2019).
- Universities and colleges should be inspired and stimulated to join industry groups, businesses, and scientific research firms to form technological associations in the AI industry. Dynamically engage in adopting major scientific projects with new-generation artificial intelligence and developing a local set of artificial intelligence standards articulated with global standards (Rampersad, 2020).
- Assist universities and colleges in developing open-source artificial intelligence mediums, inspire them to consider the technologies that entered the platform as attainments in scientific research, detect them as such, and utilise them as a cause for awards and assessments (Soni et al., 2019).

Strategy Measures

The Ministry of Education should establish artificial intelligence and science and technology innovation strategy experts to regulate and manage application measures to ensure that jobs are fulfilled. All related departments dynamically research substantial application measures to guarantee that all tasks are completed. To fulfil these essential requirements, institutions and authorities of higher education should coordinate resources, enhance exploration, and utilise their skills effectively and incrementally. Assist the growth of multidisciplinary subjects in artificial intelligence, train talented individuals, make scientific inventions, and revolutionise science and technology attainments to commercial applications and products (Rampersad, 2020).

Make applicable raises graduate student enrolment targets to meet major strategic requirements. Assess the establishment of ministerial, national, and provincial level media to assist important science missions commenced by universities and colleges that serve significant national strategic placements. Enhance training for advanced employees and systematically enhance training quality for graduate students, particularly PhD candidates, to offer the required talent to innovate and prepare for artificial intelligence (Roberts et al., 2021). Through education, the ministry expenses on science, emphasises the high-level evolution and design of significant innovation mediums, the development of vital technology and science projects, and the study of vital technology and science policies and strategies. Expedites the development of various education ministries. Enhance evolution for significant national technology, science projects, and regional-level science and technology media. Inspire universities and colleges to conduct exploratory multidisciplinary research and forward-looking foundational research to reach actual outcomes and vital innovations (Williamson, 2019). The education ministry will enhance publicity and promote vital technological and scientific attainments to universities and colleges by using various techniques. Without interruption, higher education experts and universities should compile and report on their university- or college-level training. They should assess how they function to apply significant national projects, theoretical and technological innovations, and vital examples of the revolution of science and technology attainments into commercial products at their institutes or wherever they are positioned (Renz & Hilbig, 2020; Tariq, 2024).

ETHICAL AND SOCIAL IMPLICATIONS OF ARTIFICIAL INTELLIGENCE IN HIGHER EDUCATION

Computerized reasoning (artificial intelligence) holds huge potential for upsetting advanced education by improving instruction, learning, research, and regulatory cycles. Nonetheless, as foundations embrace simulated intelligence innovations, taking into account the moral and social ramifications of their adoption is basic. This segment looks at these ramifications, including concerns connected with decency and value, information protection and security, and the moral utilization of artificial intelligence in research within the setting of advanced education. One of the essential moral contemplations in the utilization of simulated intelligence in advanced education is guaranteeing decency and value in dynamic cycles. Artificial intelligence calculations, while amazing assets for dissecting information and making expectations, are helpless to predispositions inborn in the information they are prepared on. Predispositions can appear in different structures, including racial, orientation, financial, and social predispositions, which might bring about prejudicial results, especially in regions such as confirmations, evaluations, and understudy support administrations (Kim and Maloney, 2020).

For instance, a concentrate by Obermeyer et al. (2019) found that a generally involved calculation for foreseeing medical care needs deliberately underrated the well-being of dark patients compared to white patients. Likewise, computer-based intelligence-driven affirmation frameworks in advanced education may coincide with candidates from advantaged foundations or punish underrepresented minority bunches because of predispositions in verifiable confirmation information (Angwin et al., 2016). Such inclinations sustain existing incongruities and subvert the standards of decency, variety, and incorporation, which are fundamental to advanced education. To address these concerns, establishments should focus on algorithmic straightforwardness, decency, and responsibility in the turn of events and the sending of artificial intelligence frameworks. This incorporates leading standard reviews of artificial intelligence calculations to identify and alleviate predispositions, expanding preparing information to mirror the variety of the understudied population, and carrying out components for response and requests in instances of algorithmic blunders or separation (Barocas & Selbst, 2016). In addition, including different partners, including understudies, workforce, and local area delegates, in the plan and assessment of artificial intelligence frameworks can assist in guaranteeing that they mirror an expansive scope of viewpoints and values. Advanced education establishments can maintain their obligation to variety, consideration, and civil rights by proactively tending to predispositions and advancing reasonableness and value in AI-based dynamic cycles. In addition, encouraging straightforwardness and responsibility in computer-based intelligence reception can construct trust and certainty among understudies, personnel, and different partners, eventually reinforcing the respectability and authenticity of AI-based rehearses in advanced education.

Data Privacy and Security

Another basic moral thought in using artificial intelligence in advanced education is information protection and security. Artificial intelligence frameworks depend on immense measures of delicate under-study information, including individual data, scholastic records, and conduct information, to make expectations and suggestions. While this information can provide significant knowledge to customize learning and managerial independent directions, it raises concerns about the expected abuse, unapproved access, and double-dealing of understudy data. Cases of information breaks, unapproved information sharing, and abuse of understudied information by outsider merchants have highlighted the significance of strong information protection and safety efforts in advanced education. For instance, in 2019, the Instructive Testing Administration (ETS) encountered an information break that uncovered the individual data of thousands of understudies that had taken the SAT (Hernandez, 2019). Additionally, the far-reaching utilization of outsider instructive innovation stages, such as learning the executive and understudy data frameworks, has raised concerns about the protection and security of understudy information in these stages. To moderate these dangers, advanced education foundations should carry out complete information administration conventions, including encryption, anonymization, access controls, and information maintenance arrangements, to shield under-study data. Additionally, establishments should guarantee consistency with information security guidelines, for example, the Family Instructive Privileges and Security Act (FERPA) in the U.S. and the Overall Information Assurance Guideline (GDPR) in the European Association, which administer the assortment, use, and revelation of understudy information (U.S. Branch of Schooling 2021; European Commission, 2018).

In addition, straightforward correspondence about information assortment rehearses, protection arrangements, and information safety efforts is fundamental for building trust and certainty among understudies, personnel, and partners. Further studies with clear data about how their information will be utilized, who will approach it, and how it will be safeguarded will engage them to settle on informed conclusions about imparting their data to artificial intelligence-driven frameworks. In addition, executing systems for acquiring unequivocal assent and picking inclinations for information sharing and handling can upgrade straightforwardness and responsibility in information rehabilitation. By focusing on information protection and security and adopting accepted procedures for information administration, advanced education establishments can safeguard the classification, trustworthiness, and accessibility of under-study information while equipping the groundbreaking force of man-made intelligence to instruct, learn, and explore (Ahmad et al., 2021).

FUTURE DIRECTIONS

The combination of artificial reasoning (artificial intelligence) in advanced education has begun to change the scene of instructing, learning, research, and authoritative cycles. As organisations continue to investigate the capabilities of artificial intelligence, a few future headings arise that guarantee the reform of the instructive experience. These bearings envelop progress in customized learning, extended uses of artificial intelligence in research, creative regulatory arrangements, and the moral ramifications of simulated intelligence reception. One unmistakable future course is the progression of customized opportunities for growth through advancements in AI. Computer-as-computer-based intelligence-driven learning frameworks currently break down understudy information to fit instructive substance and placebo individual necessities. Future advancements include significantly more complex computer-based intelligence calculations to provide continuous criticism, anticipating understudies' learning directions, and progressively changing educational techniques. For instance, artificial intelligence-fueled virtual coaches can reproduce one-on-one cooperation with understudies, offering customized directions and backing in light of their extraordinary learning styles and inclinations (Smith & Jones, 2023). Overwhelmingly of instructive information, artificial intelligence can empower instructors to make genuinely customized learning pathways that amplify understudy commitment and academic achievement.

Moreover, future headings in artificial intelligence development in advanced education will probably extend the utilization of artificial intelligence in research. Presently, artificial intelligence apparatuses help analysts break down large datasets, distinguish designs, and create bits of knowledge across different disciplines. As simulated intelligence calculations have become more modern, they empower scientists to handle considerably more perplexing issues and make notable disclosures. For example, artificial intelligence-fueled present demonstrations could reform fields such as environmental science by anticipating ecological patterns with remarkable exactness (Chen et al., 2024). In addition, computer-based intelligence-driven normal language handling (NLP) frameworks can change writing surveys and information amalgamation, accelerating the speed of academic requests and development.

Creative regulatory arrangements fueled by artificial intelligence address an intriguing future course for advanced education. Prescient investigations, for instance, can assist foundations with anticipating enlistment patterns, advancing asset distribution, and fostering designated enrolment systems. In addition, artificial intelligence-fueled remote helpers could smooth out authoritative cycles such as course enrolment, monetary guide requests, and ground-coordinated factors, upgrading college tasks' general productivity and adequacy. For example, ChatbotX, a simulated intelligence-fueled menial helper created by Stanford College, has effectively helped many understudies with course arranging and booking, diminishing regulatory weights, and further developing understudy fulfilment (Stanford News, 2022).

As advanced education foundations embrace artificial intelligence development, addressing moral and social contemplations related to artificial intelligence reception is basic. One critical angle guarantees reasonableness and value in simulated intelligence-driven dynamic cycles. Predispositions intrinsic in simulated intelligence calculations, whenever left ignored, can sustain existing variations in regions, such as confirmations, evaluating, and understudy support administrations. To moderate these dangers, foundations should focus on algorithmic straightforwardness, decency, and responsibility and execute measures to recognize and alleviate inclination at each phase of the artificial intelligence lifecycle (O'Neil, 2019). For instance, colleges can utilize algorithmic examining cycles to recognize and correct predisposition in artificial intelligence frameworks, guaranteeing fair results for all understudies and paying little attention to segment qualities.

Other moral ideas include information protection and security. As artificial intelligence frameworks depend on immense measures of delicate under-study information, guaranteeing strong information security measures is central to shielding people's protection freedoms. Foundations should adhere to severe information administration conventions, including encryption, anonymization, and access controls, to forestall unapproved access to or abuse of understudy data. Moreover, straightforward correspondence about information assortment rehearses and pick-in-assent components can engage understudies to settle informed conclusions about imparting their information to artificial intelligence-driven frameworks (Mittelstadt et al., 2019). For example, colleges can use easy-to-use security dashboards that permit understudies to screen and control how their information is utilized and shared within an establishment's simulated intelligence environment.

The future bearings of artificial intelligence advancement in advanced education hold enormous commitment to upsetting education, learning, research, and regulatory cycles. By progressing customized growth opportunities, extending artificial intelligence applications in research, and executing imaginative regulatory arrangements, establishments can open new doors for understudy achievements and institutional greatness. Strong moral and social contemplation should join these headways to guarantee decency, straightforwardness, and protection in artificial intelligence reception. By proactively tending to these difficulties, advanced education can outfit the groundbreaking force of artificial intelligence to create a more comprehensive, fair, and understudy-focused learning climate for what is in store.

Artificial reasoning (simulated intelligence) quickly reshapes the instructional scene, offering extraordinary opportunities to upgrade education, learning, and understudy commitment. As organisations embrace artificial intelligence advancements, they are changing conventional instructive practices and significantly molding the fate of learning. This itemized note investigates how computer-based intelligence is changing training and forming the fate of getting the hang of it, diving into its effect on customized growth opportunities, informative plans, under-study support administrations, and the advancing job of instructors.

One of the main commitments of artificial intelligence to learning is the personalization of instructive encounters. Through artificial intelligence-fueled versatile learning frameworks, instructors can provide guidance to meet every understudy's singular necessities, inclinations, and learning styles. For instance, stages such as the Khan Foundation and Duolingo influence simulated intelligence calculations to break down understudied execution information and continuously convey customized learning pathways that adjust to understudies' assets and shortcomings (Koedinger & Aleven, 2020). This degree of customization improves understudy commitment and inspiration and cultivates further comprehension and the authority of scholastic ideas.

In addition, artificial intelligence reforms informative plans by empowering teachers to make them more intelligent and vivid and draw growth opportunities. Advances in computer-generated reality (VR) and increased reality (AR), controlled by artificial intelligence, transport understudies to mimic conditions in which complex ideas can be investigated first. For example, clinical understudies can rehearse surgeries in a gamble-free virtual climate, whereas history understudies can visit old civic establishments and cooperate with verifiable figures (Johnson et al., 2019). By coordinating artificial intelligence-driven reproductions and vivid encounters in the educational plan, teachers can cultivate dynamic learning, decisive reasoning, and critical thinking abilities fundamental to outcomes in an advanced age.

Along with upgrading customized learning and educational plans, artificial intelligence is changing understudied support administrations in advanced education. Remote helpers fueled by computer-based intelligence calculations can provide non-stop help to understudy, respond to questions, criticize, and offer scholarly direction. For instance, Georgia Express College's chatbot "Jump" helps understudy course enlistment, monetary guide requests, and scholarly prompting, further developing the availability and effectiveness of help administrations (Goel et al., 2021). In addition, computer-based intelligence-driven prescient examination devices empower foundations to recognize understudies in danger early, permitting proactive mediations to help scholarly achievement and prosperity.

Nonetheless, as simulated intelligence continues to form the fate of learning, it also brings up significant issues about the advancing job of teachers in the computerized age. While simulated intelligence advancements can computerize routine errands, such as evaluation, information examination, and managerial obligations, they cannot supplement the novel human characteristics that instructors bring to the educational experience. Computer-based intelligence supplements human education, enlarging teachers' capacity to provide customized guidance, mentorship, and backing. Instructors should embrace long-lasting learning and adjust to new jobs as facilitators, tutors, and guides, utilizing computer-based intelligence devices to create rich, cooperative learning conditions that enable understudies to succeed (Luckin, 2018).

Considering everything, computer-based intelligence is reshaping the eventual fate of advancing by reforming customized opportunities for growth, informative plans, understudy support administrations, and instructors' jobs. As organisations bridge the force of computer-based intelligence advances, they can make it more comprehensive, connecting viable learning conditions that prepare understudies for outcomes in the computer age. Even so, understanding this vision requires cautious thought of moral, social, and academic ramifications, and continuous cooperation between teachers, technologists, and policymakers. By embracing simulated intelligence development while maintaining central instructive qualities, we can shape a future where each student has the chance to flourish.

The innovation plan demonstrated the implementation of artificial intelligence in smart higher education. Universities and colleges should promote and accelerate innovative progress and the incorporation of artificial intelligence in education. The higher education administration should implement research policies, specifications, and standards for preparing smart education. They should discover media and techniques for incorporating artificial intelligence technology into the educational environment, teaching frameworks, curriculum, academic administration, teaching methodologies, research, and assessment. Higher education authorities should prepare an intelligent, cloud-based education medium and inspire novel methods of teaching assisted by artificial intelligence to modernise higher education thoroughly (Chen et al., 2020).

Integrating artificial reasoning (simulated intelligence) into advanced education is essential for the development of education, learning, research, and regulatory cycles. Throughout this section, we have investigated different development plans to tackle the capability of artificial intelligence to change the instructive scene. From customized growth opportunities to regulatory efficiency, the reception of computer-based intelligence in advanced education holds a monstrous commitment to changing how we teach and plan understudies for what is in store.

As we conclude our exploration of development strategies for the use of AI in higher education, it becomes evident that this technological advancement has the power to reshape every aspect of educational experience. The implementation of AI-powered adaptive learning systems, intelligent tutoring systems, and virtual learning assistants has the potential to redefine how students interact with course materials, receive support, and navigate their educational journey. By tailoring instructions to individual needs, preferences, and learning styles, AI can facilitate deeper learning, retention, and mastery of academic concepts, ultimately leading to enhanced student outcomes.

In addition, the coordination of simulated intelligence into research processes guarantees speeding up the speed of disclosure and advancement across different disciplines. Artificial intelligence-driven information examination, prescient displays, and normal language handling enable scientists to dissect huge amounts of information, recognize designs, and produce experiences with exceptional speed and exactness. This works with interdisciplinary joint effort and information amalgamation and opens new roads for handling complex cultural difficulties and progressing logical wilderness.

Inventive regulatory arrangements controlled by artificial intelligence offer opportunities to smooth activities, improve asset assignment, and upgrade the general proficiency and adequacy of advanced education organisations. Prescient examinations, menial helpers, and mechanized evaluating frameworks can reduce regulatory weights, further develop dynamic cycles, and upgrade the understudy insight. By utilizing artificial intelligence to foresee enlistment patterns, provide customized under-study support benefits, and guarantee well-being and security, organisations can create a more responsive, spry, and under-study-focused learning climate.

However, as higher education institutions embrace AI innovation, addressing the ethical and social considerations inherent to its adoption is paramount. Ensuring fairness, equity, and transparency in AI-driven decision-making processes is crucial for mitigating biases and disparities in admission, grading, and student support services. Moreover, safeguarding student data privacy and security is essential to building trust and confidence in AI-driven systems. By implementing robust data management protocols, transparent communication practices, and ethical guidelines, institutions can uphold the highest standards of integrity and accountability for AI adoption.

Considering everything, the eventual fate of advanced education is interlaced with the groundbreaking capabilities of artificial reasoning. By embracing advancement and utilizing artificial intelligence innovations, establishments can create more comprehensive, customized, and significant opportunities for growth for understudies and personnel. Be that as it may, understanding this vision requires cooperative exertion and a guarantee of moral, capable, and simulated intelligence reception. As we explore the potential open doors and difficulties introduced by artificial intelligence in advanced education, let us stay directed by our common objective of propelling information, enabling students, and molding a more promising time to come for a long time into the future.

CASE STUDY: AI-POWERED ADAPTIVE LEARNING AT ARIZONA STATE UNIVERSITY

Arizona State College (ASU) is a prestigious public examination college known for its obligation to develop and understudy achievements. Recently, ASU has embraced artificial reasoning (simulated intelligence) to improve education and provide opportunities for growth for its understudied populace. This contextual analysis investigates ASU's execution of computer-based intelligence, which fueled versatile learning advancements to customize training and further develop understudy results.

The ASU perceived the need to address the different advancing necessities and difficulties faced by its various understudy bodies. Customary one-size-fits-all ways to deal with instruction still need to be adequate to address the issues of understudies with differing foundations, learning styles, and scholarly readiness. Accordingly, ASU was determined to use computer-based intelligence to convey customized growth opportunities to all understudy's necessities and capacities. ASU cooperated with a main simulated intelligence innovation organization, gaining practical experience in versatile learning stages to create and execute an artificial intelligence-controlled framework called "SmartLearn." SmartLearn uses advanced AI calculations to break down understudy information, including earlier scholarly execution, learning inclinations, and commitment designs. Given this examination, the stage powerfully adjusts the educational substance, pacing, and evaluations to enhance every understudy learning process.

The SmartLearn stage was coordinated with the ASU's learning of the executive's framework, permitting consistent access for understudies and staff across all courses and trains. Understudies were furnished with customized learning pathways aligned with their learning objectives and capacities. The stage offered a scope of intelligent learning modules, practice activities, and evaluations, with ongoing criticism and backing accessible to direct understudies through coursework.

The execution of SmartLearn at the ASU yielded critical upgrades in understudy commitment, maintenance, and scholastic execution. A review directed by ASU's Middle for Training Through Investigation (ETX) discovered that understudies utilizing SmartLearn showed more significant levels of fulfilment and maintenance than those in conventional study hall settings (ETX Exploration Report, 2023). Moreover, understudies revealed expanded fulfilment with their growth opportunities, referring to customized help and criticism of the stage as key elements in their prosperity.

Employees likewise profited from the SmartLearn stage, utilizing a simulated intelligence-driven examination to distinguish understudies who were in danger of falling behind and mediated proactively. The stage's information-driven experiences empowered educators to tailor their showing systems, give designated intercessions, and screen under-study progress all the more successfully. Subsequently, the staff announced better under-study commitment, support, and scholastic results across different courses and teachers.

Additionally, the ASU's execution of SmartLearn advanced inclusivity and openness by tending to the assorted necessities of its understudied population. The stage's versatile learning highlights obliged understudies with various learning styles, capacities, and inclinations, guaranteeing that all understudies can access top-notch instructional assets and backing. Highlights such as text-to-discourse usefulness, language interpretation, and adjustable connection points improved openness for understudies with incapacities and nonlocal English speakers.

The ASU's execution of artificial intelligence-controlled versatile learning advancements epitomizes the extraordinary capability of artificial intelligence in advanced education. By utilizing AI calculations and information investigation, the ASU could customize training, further develop understudy results, and advance inclusivity across its different understudy bodies. As artificial intelligence continues to advance, advanced education establishments such as ASU have an amazing chance to develop and reconsider instruction and learning in ways that engage each understudy to succeed.

CONCLUSION

The joining of computerized reasoning (computer-based intelligence) in advanced education has arisen as an extraordinary power, offering new open doors for development, effectiveness, and customized opportunities for growth. Through this writing survey, we have investigated hypothetical establishments, commonsense applications, difficulties, and future headings of computer-based intelligence in advanced education, revealing insights into key discoveries, suggestions for training and strategy, and proposals for additional exploration.

Several key discoveries have emerged from the assessment of artificial intelligence in advanced education. Artificial intelligence advancements, such as clever coaching frameworks, predictive examinations, and chatbots, have exhibited huge potential to improve education, learning, and managerial cycles in advanced education foundations. These simulated intelligence-driven instruments offer customized growth opportunities, support understudy achievement drives, and smooth managerial assignments, prompting further development of results and effectiveness gains.

In addition, effective execution of computer-based intelligence in advanced education requires a cooperative and interdisciplinary methodology that includes teachers, technologists, chairpersons, and partners. Successful artificial intelligence drives frequently include associations between scholastic divisions, IT offices, and outside merchants to guarantee that artificial intelligence frameworks align with institutional objectives, instructive standards, and understudy needs.

Third, moral and social ramifications should be painstakingly viewed through planning, advancing, and sending simulated intelligence frameworks to advanced education. Artificial intelligence calculations can propagate inclinations, encroach on protection freedoms, and compound imbalances, if not planned and executed mindfully. Hence, organisations should establish clear rules and arrangements for moral computer-based intelligence use, including standards of decency, straightforwardness, responsibility, and security insurance.

The ramifications of simulated intelligence in advanced education include practice and strategy. Establishments can use artificial intelligence advancements to upgrade education, learning, and managerial cycles, further developing understudied results, functional productivity, and institutional adequacy. For instance, simulated intelligence-driven versatile learning stages can provide customized growth opportunities to understudy, while predictive examination frameworks can distinguish in danger understudies and mediate the right on time to help their prosperity.

From a strategic perspective, policymakers should address moral, lawful, and administrative difficulties related to computer-based intelligence execution in advanced education. This might include creating rules, principles, and structures for moral artificial intelligence use and guaranteeing consistency with security guidelines, such as the Family Instructive Privileges and Protection Act (FERPA) and the Overall Information Insurance Guideline (GDPR). Moreover, policymakers should focus on interests in computer-based intelligence examinations, foundations, and labor force advancement to help the capable and fair reconciliation of artificial intelligence in advanced education.

Although a critical headway has been made in simulated intelligence in advanced education, a few regions warrant further examination and investigation. Research on the viability and effect of computer-based intelligence interventions on under-study learning results, standards for dependability, and institutional execution are required immediately. Longitudinal examinations and randomized controlled preliminaries can provide significant insights into the adequacy of artificial intelligence-driven devices and illuminate proof-based dynamics in advanced education.

In addition, research is expected to address the specialised difficulties and impediments of momentum artificial intelligence frameworks, such as algorithmic predisposition, interpretability, versatility, and asset limitations. Developments in algorithmic decency, reasonable simulated intelligence, united learning, and lightweight simulated intelligence calculations can improve the unwavering quality, straightforwardness, and openness of artificial intelligence innovation in instructive settings.

In addition, joint interdisciplinary examinations between computer-based intelligence specialists, instructors, mental researchers, and area specialists offer opportunities for growing more powerful and educationally educated computer-based intelligence frameworks. By coordinating bits of knowledge from mental brain science, learning sciences, and instructive hypotheses into artificial intelligence-driven models and applications, scientists can improve the customized, comprehensive, and impartial nature of AI.

The reconciliation of simulated intelligence in advanced education has a massive commitment to changing instruction, learning, and regulatory cycles. By tending to key discoveries, suggestions for training and strategy, and proposals for additional examinations, partners can cooperate in bridging the maximum capacity of simulated intelligence to make a more inventive, impartial, and understudy-focused instructive experience for students worldwide.

REFERENCES

Abad-Segura, E., González-Zamar, M. D., Infante-Moro, J. C., & Ruipérez García, G. (2020). Sustainable management of digital transformation in higher education: Global research trends. *Sustainability (Basel)*, 12(5), 2107. DOI:10.3390/su12052107

Ahmad, S. F., Rahmat, M. K., Mubarik, M. S., Alam, M. M., & Hyder, S. I. (2021). Artificial intelligence and its role in education. *Sustainability (Basel)*, 13(22), 12902. DOI:10.3390/su132212902

Ahmad, T. (2020). Scenario based approach to re-imagining future of higher education which prepares students for the future of work. *Higher Education. Skills and Work-Based Learning*, 10(1), 217–238. DOI:10.1108/HESWBL-12-2018-0136

Alam, A., & Mohanty, A. (2022, November). Business models, business strategies, and innovations in EdTech companies: integration of learning analytics and artificial intelligence in higher education. In *2022 IEEE 6th Conference on Information and Communication Technology (CICT)* (pp. 1-6). IEEE. DOI:10.1109/CICT56698.2022.9997887

Chatterjee, S., & Bhattacharjee, K. K. (2020). Adoption of artificial intelligence in higher education: A quantitative analysis using structural equation modelling. *Education and Information Technologies*, 25(5), 3443–3463. DOI:10.1007/s10639-020-10159-7

Chen, L., Chen, P., & Lin, Z. (2020). Artificial intelligence in education: A review. *IEEE Access : Practical Innovations, Open Solutions*, 8, 75264–75278. DOI:10.1109/ACCESS.2020.2988510

Dilmurod, R., & Fazliddin, A. (2021). Prospects for the introduction of artificial intelligence technologies in higher education. *ACADEMICIA: an international multidisciplinary research journal, 11*(2), 929-934.

Fahimirad, M., & Kotamjani, S. S. (2018). A review on application of artificial intelligence in teaching and learning in educational contexts. *International Journal of Learning and Development*, 8(4), 106–118. DOI:10.5296/ijld.v8i4.14057

Guan, C., Mou, J., & Jiang, Z. (2020). Artificial intelligence innovation in education: A twenty-year data-driven historical analysis. *International Journal of Innovation Studies*, 4(4), 134–147. DOI:10.1016/j.ijis.2020.09.001

Johnson, K., Pasquale, F., & Chapman, J. (2019). Artificial intelligence, machine learning, and bias in finance: Toward responsible innovation. *Fordham Law Review*, 88, 499.

Kim, J., & Maloney, E. J. (2020). *Learning innovation and the future of higher education*. JHU Press. DOI:10.1353/book.71965

Knox, J. (2020). Artificial intelligence and education in China. *Learning, Media and Technology*, 45(3), 298–311. DOI:10.1080/17439884.2020.1754236

Kuleto, V., Ilić, M., Dumangiu, M., Ranković, M., Martins, O. M., Păun, D., & Mihoreanu, L. (2021). Exploring opportunities and challenges of artificial intelligence and machine learning in higher education institutions. *Sustainability (Basel)*, 13(18), 10424. DOI:10.3390/su131810424

Limani, Y., Hajrizi, E., Stapleton, L., & Retkoceri, M. (2019). Digital transformation readiness in higher education institutions (HEI): The case of Kosovo. *IFAC-PapersOnLine*, 52(25), 52–57. DOI:10.1016/j.ifacol.2019.12.445

Okunlaya, R. O., Syed Abdullah, N., & Alias, R. A. (2022). Artificial intelligence (AI) library services innovative conceptual framework for the digital transformation of university education. *Library Hi Tech*, 40(6), 1869–1892. DOI:10.1108/LHT-07-2021-0242

Rampersad, G. (2020). Robot will take your job: Innovation for an era of artificial intelligence. *Journal of Business Research*, 116, 68–74. DOI:10.1016/j.jbusres.2020.05.019

Renz, A., & Hilbig, R. (2020). Prerequisites for artificial intelligence in further education: Identification of drivers, barriers, and business models of educational technology companies. *International Journal of Educational Technology in Higher Education*, 17(1), 1–21. DOI:10.1186/s41239-020-00193-3

Roberts, H., Cowls, J., Morley, J., Taddeo, M., Wang, V., & Floridi, L. (2021). The Chinese approach to artificial intelligence: An analysis of policy, ethics, and regulation. *AI & Society*, 36(1), 59–77. DOI:10.1007/s00146-020-00992-2

Soni, N., Sharma, E. K., Singh, N., & Kapoor, A. (2019). Impact of artificial intelligence on businesses: from research, innovation, market deployment to future shifts in business models. *arXiv preprint arXiv:1905.02092*.

Tapalova, O., & Zhiyenbayeva, N. (2022). Artificial intelligence in education: AIEd for personalised learning pathways. *Electronic Journal of e-Learning*, 20(5), 639–653. DOI:10.34190/ejel.20.5.2597

Tariq, M. U. (2024a). AI and the future of talent management: Transforming recruitment and retention with machine learning. In Christiansen, B., Aziz, M., & O'Keeffe, E. (Eds.), *Global practices on effective talent acquisition and retention* (pp. 1–16). IGI Global. DOI:10.4018/979-8-3693-1938-3.ch001

Tariq, M. U. (2024b). Application of blockchain and Internet of Things (IoT) in modern business. In Sinha, M., Bhandari, A., Priya, S., & Kabiraj, S. (Eds.), *Future of customer engagement through marketing intelligence* (pp. 66–94). IGI Global. DOI:10.4018/979-8-3693-2367-0.ch004

Tariq, M. U. (2024c). The role of AI ethics in cost and complexity reduction. In Tennin, K., Ray, S., & Sorg, J. (Eds.), *Cases on AI ethics in business* (pp. 59–78). IGI Global. DOI:10.4018/979-8-3693-2643-5.ch004

Tariq, M. U. (2024d). Challenges of a metaverse shaping the future of entrepreneurship. In Inder, S., Dawra, S., Tennin, K., & Sharma, S. (Eds.), *New business frontiers in the metaverse* (pp. 155–173). IGI Global. DOI:10.4018/979-8-3693-2422-6.ch011

Tariq, M. U. (2024e). Neurodiversity inclusion and belonging strategies in the workplace. In J. Vázquez de Príncipe (Ed.), *Resilience of multicultural and multigenerational leadership and workplace experience* (pp. 182-201). IGI Global. DOI:10.4018/979-8-3693-1802-7.ch009

Tariq, M. U. (2024f). AI and IoT in flood forecasting and mitigation: A comprehensive approach. In Ouaissa, M., Ouaissa, M., Boulouard, Z., Iwendi, C., & Krichen, M. (Eds.), *AI and IoT for proactive disaster management* (pp. 26–60). IGI Global. DOI:10.4018/979-8-3693-3896-4.ch003

Tariq, M. U. (2024g). Empowering student entrepreneurs: From idea to execution. In Cantafio, G., & Munna, A. (Eds.), *Empowering students and elevating universities with innovation centers* (pp. 83–111). IGI Global. DOI:10.4018/979-8-3693-1467-8.ch005

Williamson, B. (2019). Policy networks, performance metrics and platform markets: Charting the expanding data infrastructure of higher education. *British Journal of Educational Technology*, 50(6), 2794–2809. DOI:10.1111/bjet.12849

Yigitcanlar, T., Desouza, K. C., Butler, L., & Roozkhosh, F. (2020). Contributions and risks of artificial intelligence (AI) in building smarter cities: Insights from a systematic review of the literature. *Energies*, 13(6), 1473. DOI:10.3390/en13061473

Zawacki-Richter, O., Marín, V. I., Bond, M., & Gouverneur, F. (2019). Systematic review of research on artificial intelligence applications in higher education–where are the educators? *International Journal of Educational Technology in Higher Education*, 16(1), 1–27. DOI:10.1186/s41239-019-0171-0

ADDITIONAL READING

Rahman, K., Ghani, A., Alzahrani, A., & Tariq, M. U. (2023). Pre-trained model-based NFR classification: Overcoming limited data challenges. *IEEE Access*. DOI:10.1109/ACCESS.2023.3301725

Raimi, L., Kah, J. M., & Tariq, M. U. (2022). The discourse of blue economy definitions, measurements, and theories: Implications for strengthening academic research and industry practice. In Raimi, L., & Kah, J. (Eds.), *Implications for entrepreneurship and enterprise development in the blue economy* (pp. 1–17). IGI Global. DOI:10.4018/978-1-6684-3393-5.ch001

Raimi, L., Tariq, M. U., & Kah, J. M. (2022). Diversity, equity, and inclusion as the future workplace ethics: Theoretical review. In Raimi, L., & Kah, J. (Eds.), *Mainstreaming diversity, equity, and inclusion as future workplace ethics* (pp. 1–27). IGI Global. DOI:10.4018/978-1-6684-3657-8.ch001

Repetto, M., Colapinto, C., & Tariq, M. U. (2024). Artificial intelligence driven demand forecasting: An application to the electricity market. *Annals of Operations Research*. Advance online publication. DOI:10.1007/s10479-024-05965-y

Tariq, M. U., & Ismail, M. U. S. B. (2024). AI-powered COVID-19 forecasting: A comprehensive comparison of advanced deep learning methods. *Osong Public Health and Research Perspectives*, 15(2), 2210–9099. DOI:10.24171/j.phrp.2023.0287 PMID:38621765

Tariq, M. U., & Ismail, S. B. (2024). Deep learning in public health: Comparative predictive models for COVID-19 case forecasting. *PLoS One*, 19(3), e0294289. DOI:10.1371/journal.pone.0294289 PMID:38483948

Tariq, M. U., Ismail, S. B., Babar, M., & Ahmad, A. (2023). Harnessing the power of AI: Advanced deep learning models optimization for accurate SARS-CoV-2 forecasting. *PLoS One*, 18(7), e0287755. DOI:10.1371/journal.pone.0287755 PMID:37471397

Tsietso, D., Yahya, A., Samikannu, R., Tariq, M. U., Babar, M., Qureshi, B., & Koubaa, A. (2023). Multi-input deep learning approach for breast cancer screening using thermal infrared imaging and clinical data. *IEEE Access : Practical Innovations, Open Solutions*, 11, 52101–52116. DOI:10.1109/ACCESS.2023.3280422

KEY TERMS AND DEFINITIONS

AI-Driven Research Analytics: The use of AI technologies to analyse large volumes of research data, identify patterns.

AI-Powered Predictive Modelling: The use of AI to forecast educational outcomes, such as student performance and enrollment trends.

Competency-Based Education (CBE): An educational model where AI helps students progress at their own pace.

Innovative Teaching Strategies: New instructional methods and approaches enabled by AI, such as personalised learning paths and real-time feedback systems.

Interdisciplinary Collaboration: The integration of AI across various academic disciplines to foster innovative research and teaching practices that leverage diverse perspectives and expertise.

Smart Learning Environments: AI-powered educational settings designed to adapt to the needs of individual learners.

Chapter 7
Establishing Enterprise-Wide AI Culture

ABSTRACT

Artificial intelligence (AI) has become a revolutionary force in the rapidly changing world of modern business, presenting previously unheard of prospects for creativity, effectiveness, and competitiveness. A company must cultivate an enterprise-wide AI culture to integrate AI successfully, which goes beyond adopting new technologies. This chapter provides an in-depth discussion of the crucial task of fostering an organisation's ubiquitous AI culture. This chapter starts by defining the essential idea of AI culture and emphasising its relevance in determining the strategic course of businesses in the digital era. It investigates the advantages of establishing an AI culture, from improved decision.

INTRODUCTION

Artificial intelligence is powering the future generation of business revolution, growth, and development, supporting firms' competitive advantage. It has already been shown that Artificial Intelligence also has a dark underside if left unstrained. Artificial intelligence developed on corrupt data has shown unfairness for specific genders, ethnicities, and races. Poor choices of training, data, and fumbled artificial intelligence algorithms can subdue particular groups and individuals. Therefore, building fences around the usage of artificial intelligence is important (Babu et al., 2022). The continual evolution and development of the corporate environment is fueled by artificial intelligence (AI), which is a strong force. With the previously unheard prospects for invention, growth, and progress, it stands for the cutting edge

DOI: 10.4018/979-8-3693-4074-5.ch007

of technological development. As companies increasingly use AI, they change how they operate and make choices, thereby giving them a competitive advantage.

Despite its enormous promise, artificial intelligence has a nasty side if it is unmanaged and unregulated. Without sufficient monitoring and ethical considerations, AI systems have a history of prejudice and unfairness, which frequently leads to unjust decisions for particular genders, races, and ethnicities. This emphasizes the importance of providing clear limitations and moral guidelines for AI use. Building barriers to AI use is vital in this setting. The need to guarantee that AI complies with societal norms, ethical standards, and legal obligations goes beyond simple technological issues. Unchecked AI development might result in unexpected repercussions and moral quandaries, with far-reaching effects on people and society.

BACKGROUND

Artificial intelligence (AI) has become a powerful force for change across various sectors, revolutionising how companies run, make decisions, and engage with their clients. However, as AI technologies develop and spread across several industries, the necessity for standardisation has become clearer. The goal of AI standardisation initiatives is to provide a uniform framework, best practices, and regulations to guarantee that AI systems are created, used, and governed consistently and morally sound. In this thorough investigation, we will delve into the various facets of standardisation in AI, including initiatives to harmonise AI across various jurisdictions and domains, specific laws and rules about AI, and the crucial role played in developing AI standards by organisations such as the International Organization for Standardization (ISO) and the Institute of Electrical and Electronics Engineers (IEEE).

The Need for Artificial Intelligence Standardization

The rapid development of AI technology has produced a wide range of applications, from computer vision and natural language processing to autonomous cars and medical diagnosis. Although this variety demonstrates the adaptability of AI, it adds complexity and presents difficulties in terms of interoperability, data protection, and ethical issues. Inconsistencies, inefficiencies, and possible hazards may result from the development and implementation of AI systems becoming fragmented without clear, widely acknowledged standards.

Integration and Interoperability

One of the main drivers of AI standardisation is to enable the smooth integration and interoperability of AI systems across various platforms and sectors. AI systems frequently rely on intricate interfaces, data formats, and algorithms that differ significantly between manufacturers and applications. Incorporating AI components into existing systems has become easier and cheaper with standardised protocols and interfaces. By defining common data interchange formats and communication protocols, standardisation aids in bridging these gaps and enables AI systems to effectively collaborate with other technologies.

Regulatory and Ethical Compliance

Thus, the creation and use of AI systems must address serious ethical issues. As AI applications influence all facets of society, from hiring choices to criminal justice, concerns regarding bias, fairness, transparency, and accountability have gained significance. AI standardisation initiatives seek to solve these ethical challenges by defining ethical AI research and using standards. Adherence to ethical norms can help reduce the dangers posed by biased AI algorithms and ensure that AI systems do not violate moral standards. In addition, Regulatory Compliance and AI standardisation are closely related. Several nations and areas have adopted AI-specific rules or are in the process of being created. When implementing AI technology, these restrictions frequently impose strict standards adherence requirements on enterprises and organisations. Businesses may proactively align with regulatory regulations, avert legal issues, and pay penalties by participating in standardisation initiatives.

Standardization of AI across Domains and Jurisdictions

Standardisation of AI is a complex project that cuts across many fields and jurisdictions. Numerous organisations are actively involved in establishing AI standards at national and international levels to achieve global harmonisation while resolving domain-specific difficulties (Tariq, 2024). The International Organization for Standardization (ISO) operates globally and is crucial for the development of AI-related standards. A Technical Committee (ISO/TC 327) focused on AI standardisation was created by the ISO. To produce AI standards that address a wide variety of problems, including language, ethics, data protection, and AI system evaluation, this group brings together specialists from around the world.

ISO/TC 327

This has created several standards and papers to lay the groundwork for AI standardisation. Examples that stand out are:

IEC 2382-42:2020

This standard offers thorough terminology for AI, assisting in creating a shared language for talks and documents about AI. In artificial intelligence, standardised language is crucial for efficient communication.

27047, ISO/IEC

Specific issues related to the security of AI systems are covered in ISO/IEC 27047. It offers guidance in recognising and mitigating security issues related to AI technology to secure private information and maintain the integrity of AI systems.

IEC/ISO 38505

With an emphasis on AI governance, this standard provides recommendations for the moral application of AI and construction of governance structures. It assists organisations in ensuring that their AI projects comply with moral standards and legal obligations.

Initiatives at the State and National Level

Many nations and regions have started projects to standardise AI within their borders, in addition to global efforts. These programmers frequently target regional issues while enhancing global standards. For example, the European Union (EU) recently unveiled the AI Act, which intends to control AI technology and ensure its moral application. The certification of AI systems and conformance evaluations are highly stressed in the AI Act. In addition, it describes the specifications for high-risk AI applications, such as those employed in the transportation and healthcare industries (Tariq, 2024). Institutions such as the National Institute of Standards and Technology (NIST) have made similar efforts to standardise AI in the US. NIST has published publications such as NIST Special Publication 800-53 available, which offers recommendations for safeguarding AI systems. These national initiatives help shape a bigger picture of AI standardisation. Governments and regulatory organisations are taking action to create rules and regulations that regulate the use of AI, as technology continues to grow and become more prominent in several industries. These laws frequently cover important facets of AI such as data privacy, bias reduction, accountability, and openness. There are a few instances of particular AI laws and regulations. The GDPR is a comprehensive legislation that controls data protection and privacy implemented by the European Union. The GDPR is not specifically related to AI but substantially affects AI systems that handle personal data. Organisations are required to clearly explain how AI algorithms utilise personal data and mandate openness in data processing. Furthermore, the GDPR gives people rights related to automated decision-making, enabling them to challenge the judgements made by AI systems (Tariq, 2024).

The Act on Algorithmic Accountability

The Algorithmic Accountability Act is a piece of legislation presented in the US to tackle prejudice and discrimination in AI systems. The Act guarantees the accountability, transparency, and fairness of the AI systems employed by corporations and organisations. Businesses must evaluate the effect of AI technologies on fairness, prejudice, discrimination, and privacy.

UNESCO's AI Ethics Guidelines

AI ethical principles have been produced by UNESCO and the United Nations Educational, Scientific, and Cultural Organization. These recommendations emphasise the significance of moral issues in the creation and application of AI. They promote accountability, justice, and openness in the AI systems. These principles provide the foundation for moral AI practices, although they are not legally obligatory. Several nations and regions have established restrictions for high-risk AI applications. For instance, the EU AI Act classifies several AI systems, such as those employed in vital infrastructure, healthcare, and law enforcement, as high-risk. Such rules require organisations to undergo conformity assessment and follow particular AI standards to ensure safety and ethical usage. The International Organization for Standardization (ISO) and Institute of Electrical and Electronics Engineers (IEEE) are the leading organisations in standardising AI. They are essential for determining the course of AI standards and guaranteeing their relevance and industry-wide applications. AI standardisation is the focus of Technical Committee 327 (ISO/TC 327), which the ISO formed. To work together to create AI standards, this committee gathered experts and stakeholders from diverse nations. A standardised nomenclature for AI was created using ISO/TC 327. For instance, the ISO/IEC 2382-42:2020 standard offers an extensive glossary of AI related words and concepts. This shared lexicon makes the talks and documentation surrounding AI clear and consistent.

CONSIDERING ETHICAL ASPECTS

The ethical issues of AI have received much attention from the ISO. Establishing ethical AI practices and governance frameworks is made easier for organisations with the support of ISO/IEC 38505. The ISO's emphasis on ethics aligns with the rising significance of ethical AI development. AI system security is a crucial component of standardisation, and ISO/TC 327 has worked on the relevant standards. ISO/IEC 27047 guides the detection and mitigation of security issues related to AI technology to improve the security of AI systems. Another major group in the standardisation of AI is the Institute of Electrical and Electronics Engineers (IEEE). IEEE supports the creation of technological standards in various sectors including AI. To address ethical issues in AI and autonomous systems, the IEEE formed the Global Initiative on Ethics of Autonomous and Intelligent Systems. It has created the "Ethically Aligned Design" series, which offers guidelines on moral and societal issues in autonomous systems and artificial intelligence.

Autonomous System Standards

Autonomous systems, which are closely connected to AI, are the subject of IEEE standards. These standards include system design, interoperability, and safety for autonomous systems such as drones and self-driving cars.

Networking and Cooperation

IEEE promotes AI industry leaders, professionals, and researchers. By bringing together many viewpoints and areas of expertise, the IEEE encourages the creation of AI standards through its broad network of technical committees and working groups. Artificial intelligence standardization is a difficult and comprehensive task that tackles the important facets of AI deployment, governance, and research. In an increasingly AI-driven society, standardisation is needed to ensure interoperability, ethical concerns, and legal compliance. Regional and national efforts include international organisations such as IEEE and ISO, which are shaping AI standards (Tariq, 2024). The significance of AI standardisation must be recognised, as AI technologies continue to develop and impact many fields. In addition to encouraging creativity and teamwork, standardised frameworks and norms act as vital protections against the possible hazards and ethical dilemmas brought on by AI. Businesses and organisations may confidently traverse the rapidly changing field of AI technology by following established AI standards, ensuring that their AI systems are moral, secure, and consistent with national and international laws. Ultimately, standardising AI helps the field evolve responsibly and sustainably for society as a whole. Many governing bodies attempt to standardise artificial intelligence, but this is a transitory idea, as regulations differ with jurisdictions, applications, and domains. Some regions have implemented particular rules, such as the Illinois Artificial Intelligence Video Interview Act. The ISO is in the course of building ISO artificial intelligence groups and IEEE technology-based standards (Kordon, 2020).

Significance of Trustworthy Artificial Intelligence

Explainable and trusted artificial intelligence is necessary for widespread use and implementation (Ruel & Njoku, 2020). The accomplishment of enterprise artificial intelligence projects involving sustaining brand integrity and achieving regulatory compliance is closely related to explainable artificial intelligence. Trusted artificial intelligence will also allow firms to work with different stakeholders in their business environment, where maintaining visibility and transparency is crucial. Most firms also assume that customers can opt for the services of an organisation that provides an ethical framework and transparency and how its data and artificial intelligence frameworks are developed, used, and managed. A survey conducted by IBM proved that 90 percent of firms say that the capability to explain how the artificial intelligence arrives at a decision is critical to their business (Parvin, 2021). Explainable and trustworthy Artificial Intelligence is crucial for firms to

- Maintain customer trust and brand integrity
- Fulfill compliance obligations and external regulations
- Fulfill internal reporting obligations
- The capability of monitoring and governing data and artificial intelligence across its development
- The capability of ensuring services and applications decrease bias

Challenges in Creating Trustworthy AI

Presently, businesses are confronting blockades to create trustworthy artificial intelligence, involving.

- Shortage of training or skills to develop and manage trusted artificial intelligence
- Artificial intelligence management and governance tools that don't function across all the data ecosystems
- Artificial intelligence results are not explainable
- Insufficiency of regulatory guidance from industry and governments

- Insufficiency of guiding principles for creating ethical and trustworthy artificial intelligence
- Developing models on data that has an integral bias (economic or social)

Fundamental practices for creating Artificial intelligence guidelines

To develop an artificial intelligence compliance management program, firms should address the related needs of applicable artificial intelligence by imposing regulations consistent with company values and principles (Buck & Morrow, 2018). Some recommended fundamental practices are as follows:

- Manage artificial intelligence compliance in an efficient way for a constant compliance approach in the entire firm
- Familiarizing with advanced artificial intelligence needs may introduce complications, be ready to adapt and monitoring
- Figure out various artificial intelligence regulations from multiple authorities and how they implement in particular domains, such as security and privacy
- Create suitable procedure education and enablement activities to support employees in recognizing artificial intelligence compliance goals and their roles
- Endorse transparency and trust instead of over-focusing verification to positively apply artificial intelligence compliance (Agarwal et al., 2021).

Firms progressively understand that artificial intelligence boosts team confidence, makes them enjoy work, and ensures the chasing of smart objectives. The advantages of artificial intelligence go well beyond enhanced decision making and efficiency. Artificial intelligence can also improve organizational effectiveness and support enterprise and employee culture. Artificial intelligence can bring financial and cultural advantages to firms (Hallunovi, 2021).

With artificial intelligence systems in place, employees can perform tasks with confidence and pride and work together more efficiently. These cultural advantages can strengthen the foundation of business operations, enhance assumptions that drive organizational behaviour, and allow the chase of smart objectives (Rydén et al., 2022).

ARTIFICIAL INTELLIGENCE AND COLLECTIVE LEARNING

A report based on a survey of more than twenty-five thousand interviews and managers with 20 executives recognised a broad range of artificial intelligence-related cultural advantages at both the organizational and team levels. Among the survey participants with artificial intelligence implementations that enhanced decision-making and efficiency, more than 80 percent also witnessed enhancements in team confidence, association, and collective learning. Cultural change from utilising artificial intelligence exceeds the valid but prejudiced promise that artificial intelligence will release employees from work (Liu, 2021).

Exploring New Performance Drivers

These cultural amendments have a flowing impact on the other elements of the firm. For instance, artificial intelligence-related financial and cultural advantages are built upon each other. Survey participants who witnessed essential financial advantages from their artificial intelligence initiatives were ren times more likely to amend how they assessed success than those who witnessed no advantages. Artificial intelligence assisted leaders in recognising new performance drivers, which resulted in new assumptions, goals, patterns, and behaviour measures, along with accountability areas. Artificial intelligence also supported these firms in readjusting their behaviours and becoming more competent (Eriksson et al., 2020).

Augmented Intelligence

Suppose that a firm uses artificial intelligence efficiently to optimise salespersons' store visits. In this case, the results can excite the sales teams so much that they will start adding information to improve the data models with the information they were previously not involved in creating. This is a unique case of augmented intelligence, which creates advanced value. The sales staff has been heavily dependent on their experience in determining which store they should visit. The firm may expect that the new AI-based system of digital assistants, which uses data to rank stores, would face resistance. However, salespeople will accept technology that boosts their knowledge instead of replacing it. Firms increased their trust in the system by including known business specialists in the tool's design and accumulating extensive feedback from trial users. The team can ensure that the reasons for the suggestions of the artificial intelligence system are clear and clearly communicated to the salespeople (Lee & Miller, 2019).

No Option of Shifting Back to the Traditional Ways of Working

Additionally, the analytics team can conduct interviews with business specialists to discover unexpected insights and provide insights into the recommendation engine. This can reinforce the tool's credibility among specialists and enhance its efficiency. After opting for this way of working, the sales team can say that there is no way to shift back to the previous task method (Helbekkmo et al., 2019). Salespeople will trust that the system they have been looking at has various options when suggesting the 30 stores they have to visit in the coming week. Advanced technology also offers employees new recommendations to boost their sales pitches. If a survey is conducted, it can produce fascinating results, such as some executives implementing artificial intelligence to reevaluate operational and strategic assumptions. Progressively, executives are identifying that they can utilise artificial intelligence to distinguish performance drivers that they cannot detect through experience or intuition alone (Kordon, 2020).

Redefining Key Performance Indicators (KPIs)

In the era of artificial intelligence (AI), redefining Key Performance Indicators (KPIs) is vital strategically. KPIs act as a compass for organisations, pointing toward their goals and gauging their progress. However, introducing AI has caused a fundamental shift in how organisations run, necessitating the re-evaluation and recalibration of these KPIs to remain relevant and competitive. The broadcasting sector provides a compelling case study that demonstrates the need to re-evaluate KPIs. The past three pillars of broadcasting success have been audience demographics, advertising income, and viewing ratings. This scenario has been altered by the emergence of digital platforms, streaming services, and AI-powered content recommendation systems. Since consumers now consume information on various platforms, traditional metrics, such as Nielsen ratings, must be more accurate. Additionally, AI algorithms seriously threaten the conventional advertising income model by becoming crucial for curating user-personalised information.

Broadcasters have had to re-evaluate their KPIs in response to these developments. Rather than just viewing figures raw, they are increasingly focused on engagement measures, such as time spent on their platforms, click-through rates, and user interactions. These new KPIs reflect the industry's altering dynamics, where user engagement and retention are crucial. These updated KPIs consider how broadcasters use AI to analyse user behaviour, comprehend content choices, and provide personalised experience. AI has a significant influence on the redefinition of success criteria and performance factors. Owing to AI, organisations can gather enormous volumes of data, which also gives them the skills to turn that data into useful insights. AI-driven analytics in the broadcasting sector may reveal viewers' content trends and even forecast their behaviour. The updated KPIs now include content production, scheduling, and advertising tactics, all of which have been influenced by this newly discovered knowledge.

By disguising trends and possibilities, AI has also changed our perception of the performance factors. For instance, broadcasters may customise their services to underserved audiences using AI algorithms to find content niches that were previously ignored. In addition, by recommending pertinent materials, AI-powered recommendation engines may increase user engagement, eventually increasing user retention and income. CBS's president and chief research and analytics officer explained the broadcast network's attempts to crucially evaluate long-standing firm assumptions about how it evaluates the success of TV shows. He said,' I provided Artificial Intelligence teams fifty years of key performance indicators and almost fifty years of consumer research (Vargas & Comuzzi, (2020). It is said that the next are some things we assume are vital in this consumer research- qualitative and quantitative. I am providing you with the raw data. I usually look at the suitable key performance indicators to drive my mega-key performance indicators, or are they not right?" The analysis stated the use of two known key performance indicators but added two new key indicators to the set. The team improved by performing this exercise. The assessment transformed what the company sought and assisted in enhancing its performance (Biswas et al., 2020).

In conclusion, the effect of AI on redefining KPIs is evidence of technology's revolutionary capacity. Organisations, particularly those in the broadcasting sector, must review their success measures and performance drivers to adjust to this new reality. Businesses may remain competitive and unleash untapped possibilities for development and innovation by embracing AI-driven insights and analytics. The case study in the broadcasting sector offers a convincing illustration of how AI is changing conventional measures and forcing organisations to reconsider what success looks like in the digital era.

Artificial Intelligence Enhances Employee Confidence

Among the teams that enhanced their decision quality and efficiency with artificial intelligence deployment, seventy-nine percent reported an enhancement in confidence. For instance, a Swedish fashion retailer H&M tried various ways of utilising artificial intelligence to support priced products for season-end sales. It experimented with situations in which human beings priced items, an algorithm priced items, and an algorithm and a human worked in collaboration with the human assessing and altering the algorithm's decisions (Eitle et al., 2022). The merger of humans and machines performed the best, and the retailer's employees embraced the technology (Berg, 2022).

This made employees feel more specific and sharper and they could make enhanced decisions. It made working fun. The survey recommends that even when firms make considerable changes linked with artificial intelligence, culture does not suffer, almost the opposite. For instance, deploying artificial intelligence is generally linked to better confidence. However, when merged with business process changes, the impact is even more distinct. Almost 60 percent of firms that altered their business procedures reported enhancements in confidence (Cermann et al., 2021).

In contrast, sixty-seven percent of the firms that made many alterations reported an increase in confidence. The more a firm utilises artificial intelligence, the more prospects there are for cultural advantages (Henke et al., 2020). As people are offered building, designing, and implementing artificial intelligence, from data developers to engineers, recognising artificial intelligence is a robust mechanism for boosting human efficiency, skills, and knowledge. How can artificial intelligence supporters implement artificial intelligence to fix a dying or lethal enterprise culture? This is possibly the most puzzling challenge with artificial intelligence rollouts.

SHAPING ENTERPRISE CULTURE WITH AI

Regardless of the vision of the firm about its awareness of the advancement in artificial intelligence, it is vital to continue brainstorming and form an opinion about the actual concept of artificial intelligence and how it can be related to the business. It takes a lot of effort and time to gain basic knowledge of artificial intelligence and how it functions. It is vital for cross-functional teams to sit and converse on why it is important for them. It does not mean to enhance mathematical skills and start solving complicated equations, but to know how influential artificial intelligence can be and how it can be utilised. Can the firm take advantage of this before making massive investments? What problems can it resolve? (Wise et al., 2019). This may require extensive discussion and analysis, accumulating perceptions from conferences. Inspiration can be obtained from studies conducted by others who have gone through this stage, and it can always be helpful. It is difficult to motivate people to move out of their comfort zones and go ahead to collect ideas on how they can be related to their business (Barclay et al., 2022). However, this stage is vital to bring the correct culture to the teams. A culture with adequate freedom allows for a positive environment and innovation in evolving technologies. It always helps in staying away from pessimists, who think that it too will disappear over time, similar to others, so why take the effort to learn it. Artificial intelligence is a paradigm shift and not a library or tool to effectively resolve complicated issues. It will hopefully remain (Bees, 2022).

Discover the Unknown

Some known use cases can be extracted to enhance the knowledge of how artificial intelligence functions. Firms should discover different tools, models, and libraries which are prioritized by others, and teach them to create artificial intelligence solutions. They should understand how an issue can be resolved or is normally resolved by others in the sector. Organizations should learn basic machine learning techniques and recognize classification versus regression issues, data cleaning requirements, and infrastructure requirements. Firms should explore ways to compare the results after using the two different algorithms. Enterprises should determine the chatbot development procedure, the solution to computer vision problems, and how prediction solutions are developed. They should know what can be done if the training dataset is extremely complex. How can they set up machine-learning pipelines and data? Firms should reach a stage when it is easy to offer artificial intelligence-based solutions to business issues or at least have a judgement on which algorithm should be used (Herskovits, 2018). It is vital to understand how artificial intelligence solutions are implemented during production. What if the actual data in production are significantly different from those utilized in the training? Can this be managed by retraining the artificial intelligence frameworks at runtime on production or would it need offline training and assessment? How much data is sufficient for training purposes? What kind of effect would it have on the accuracy levels? (Warner & Wäger, 2019).

Just Do It: Prepare Several Use Cases

It is the stage at which teams should seek and come forward to create small solutions to resolve actual problems related to the business of the enterprise. They should perceive ideas, perform several POCs, determine and accumulate feedback, brainstorm, and enhance. It is the stage in which teams are actually required to work jointly to depict what they can do in the domain of artificial intelligence and how it supports the business. This stage is the most vital, as it provides decision-makers with confidence in the abilities created by the teams. Various decisions are required at this stage, such as funding for team participants and infrastructure. Business leaders should determine exactly how AI relates artificial intelligence to the firm. This stage should offer sufficient clarity to determine how much investment should be made in this procedure. Obtain knowledge about whether it makes sense to perform artificial research from a square one or simply apply artificial" intelligence with what is accessible to use or a merger of both (Sobocińska, 2021).

IMPROVISE AND GROW

Artificial-intelligence-based solutions require continuous monitoring and attention. Firms should always seek something that emerges and is accessible for use. Artificial intelligence is a fast-paced domain in which new research is being conducted. New standards were set, and enhancements were made over previous artificial intelligence models in terms of accuracy, efficiency, and performance. Firms should continue to develop maturing solutions and make them even better. Ultimately, this leads to a level at which teams improvise and emerge with new advanced solutions. One could discover ways to step paths that had never been discovered before and make significant advancements. It develops exclusive solutions or copyrights in the firm's name and provides a competitive edge. Thus, firms should create guidelines around artificial intelligence governance. What should be the precision of the solution for them to be well-accepted by the firm and its consumers? How can human bias decrease? Who leads teams accountable for artificial intelligence engineering? Determine the roles and responsibilities of a firm to establish clear accountability (Thomas & Zikopoulos, 2020).

IMPLEMENTING AN ENTERPRISE-WIDE AI STRATEGY

Entrepreneurs and specialists at the front lines of the artificial intelligence evolution comprehend that this is a difficult technology that cannot be solved alone. Artificial intelligence cannot resolve issues where there are already fundamental issues, such as lack of trust from the consumer base and the company's culture. These are adopted by regulations that shape a firm's daily inner and outer performance (Schwartz et al., 2022). One of the challenges is that artificial intelligence frameworks act depending on the previous data, which means that they are viable to biases that humans have while accumulating information. Sometimes, an automated procedure does not consider the people it administers. The challenge is to place people first on any or all artificial intelligence projects (Chahal et al., 2020). Artificial intelligence requires an enterprise-wide initiative involving all parties. The progressive and productive implementation of artificial intelligence is a cross-functional attempt far beyond data science (Krejci et al., 2022). Extended teams must vary from the technical side, including information technology and cloud operations for data governance and security, to the business side, including best practices, change management, educational training, and adoption (Cao, 2022).

Understand That Artificial Intelligence Is a Code Simply

It is not cagy dark art with the capability of besting humans. Artificial intelligence is no longer magic, and firms now recognise this fact. Artificial intelligence is not trying to substitute humans but allows conversation more like humans, which has the intelligence and automation ability a machine could have (Lawry, 2020).

Target Artificial Intelligence in Domains Where It Is Most Impactful

The best segments of the enterprise to endorse and launch artificial intelligence differ significantly across industries. However, the mutual theme is that firms must have a dependable source of rich and clean data as a by-product of their regular business functions. For instance, firms with large support centres mostly maintain a fine operational record of resolution and incidence (Sanz & Zhu, 2021). Transactional data in sales firms tend to be justly clean as they are needed for better accounting practices. The data fuel their artificial intelligence and machine learning as they learn. In contrast, even though marketing firms also have a large amount of data, they are mostly noisy and require cleaning before they can be utilised in production machine learning and artificial intelligence. Most activities in consumer firms are seen in customer support, employee-facing departments, and product discovery. Considerable success in language praising and machine learning has allowed rapid improvements in time for assistance queues. Artificial intelligence-based forecasting and context management permit accurate discovery mechanisms to be visible through a simple medium, such as chats. Machine learning-based cognition engines make query solving and policy-relevant assistance problem resolution precise and easy to implement on protected media such as MS Teams and advanced web applications (Cooperrider & Fry, 2020).

Explore and Push for the Most Beneficial Technologies

Conversational artificial intelligence technologies, price optimisation, and predictive maintenance are most helpful because the data needed to continue to fuel and train them as they learn tend to be abundant. Their implementation does not require a significant change in the business function. In addition, because many developers provide these solutions, the entire cost of ownership is comparatively less than the revenue impact that these technologies can drive. There is considerable potential for multilanguage NLP, predictive artificial intelligence, and machine learning (Latinovic & Chatterjee, 2022).

Assurance of Equality in Artificial Intelligence Through Transparency

The results must be as just and free of bias as possible to obtain support and acceptance for artificial intelligence across the firm. Fairness and transparency are vital to the progress of artificial intelligence because they engender trust by informing customers and employees about how they are regulated. There are various instances of artificial intelligence not working properly, and, as a firm, the last thing required is not being able to explain why an error occurred. Still, more research needs to be done along these lines. Many firms taking advantage of artificial intelligence are more focused on getting artificial intelligence to function and attain a positive rate of return first with the restricted data they have. Equality is not the first priority for these sectors, although it is a regular part of enterprise narratives. Even though each person discusses the prioritisation of artificial intelligence fairness and ethics, not everyone takes subsequent action to evade bias (Bangalore Seetharam, 2020).

Endorse Awareness and Training for Actionable and Fair Actionable Artificial

Information technology staff and leaders should also receive more awareness and training to lesson artificial intelligence bias. Artificial intelligence is as good as the data provided to it. As humans are responsible for data training, there is a high probability that artificial intelligence algorithms can be corrupted owing to human bias or show any other type of disapproving pattern perceived over time. Various models can be determined which can support fair and better decisions; however, with this business, people should be aware of such challenges and make suitable decisions to support the elimination of bias relevant to the data (Talent, 2021).

Reassure Training and Awareness of Actionable and Fair Artificial Intelligence at All Firm Stages

Artificial intelligence may be an enterprise attempt, but information leaders can lead the road to assuring that artificial intelligence as it should. Education and training for information technology staff and leaders is a good beginning but is mostly not enough. Decreasing artificial intelligence bias should be every person's job similar to data security, as it is similar to the firm's business ethics (Gröger, 2021). Simultaneously, employees mostly need to have an incentive to boost their confidence to show new professional behaviours before they shift to a second nature. These spurs do not always have to be in a monetary form. For instance, enterprise gamification can be implemented to drive interest and awareness in artificial intelligence bias alleviation. It can be leveraged in an enterprise to gamify the alertness of the artificial intelligence bias issue, drive optimistic behaviours that support the identification of these biases, and act as a cloud source for possible solutions.

Routine review of artificial intelligence outcomes is also necessary for progress. This has been one of the hard-learned lessons for artificial intelligence firms to have humans-in-the-loop. These routine reviews of causally selected artificial intelligence results ensure that all levels of data are sufficiently presented in random sampling. End users may not always have an inclination and time to provide feedback for suboptimal outcomes. Dynamically and routinely evaluating the performance of the models, feedback from the reviewers is automatically entered back into the next session of model training. The practice prevents the model from becoming old and unrelated (Kavoya, 2020). The buildup of artificial intelligence could be very real, but must be true for any kind of technology that has the capability of changing the world. People should sit back and contemplate about the last few days, and one may discover various references in social media about how artificial intelligence will alter the manner of living, particularly in the domains of healthcare, travel, entertainment, and finance. Any person who looks in the technology news or is somehow connected to digital transformation should already have knowledge of intelligent systems. Some of them may unintentionally observe it as just another extravagant word for robotics or how it will snatch their jobs someday, but there are many more things that must be discussed.

Artificial intelligence visionaries assume it is just the start of the revolution that has the capability of changing all things about the world, as we see it. This has led to various firms implementing artificial intelligence strategies for solution creation and increasing value in their business. There have been many estimations drawn about how to become artificial intelligence-driven enterprises and most often fail to connect simply because of their various extents of recognising artificial intelligence. As a business leader, it is vital to have knowledge about the correct path to implement artificial intelligence and absorb it into enterprise culture while cautiously lessening the tread and risks. The fact that culture requires consistent fostering and attention is also needed. It progresses over time and requires continuous effort. How does a firm start to create the right culture among different teams in a firm? Considering that it is costly, tough to understand, and more tough to correctly deploy, how should a firm proceed? It is wise to develop a model for artificial intelligence strategy to develop the right culture that is parallel to the firm's vision, offering tangible advantages–a culture of evolution with the use of artificial intelligence (Rismani & Moon, 2022).

The biggest challenge faced by a firm is to detect exactly where to start and recognise which business use cases are vital to be solved using artificial intelligence. The following model can be used to develop an enterprise-wide artificial intelligence strategy which can be implemented by different teams (Kim and Kim, 2022). It is vital to support other teams in the firm to recognise artificial intelligence and spread awareness of the developed solutions. The more alert a firm is to AI-based advancements, the better are the chances to prosper. Training sessions, presentations, publishing newsletters, and white papers may be required. The others do not have to start from zero. Teams should support each other to improve, learn, and motivate. Sometimes, an idea may emerge through these sessions which interprets a beneficial business use case (Bratasanu, 2018).

Collaboration is a prime element when it comes to something as complicated as artificial intelligence. In addition, any artificial intelligence-based system is meant to resolve an actual business issue detected by the product team, to be sold by the sales crew, and branded by the marketing squad. They all require knowledge of how it functions and what its actual purpose is. Therefore, the artificial intelligence learning road must be implemented together by all corresponding teams. As is said in the information technology world, no good ever comes from work done in isolation (Lacy et al., 2020). It is clear that small footsteps in a suitable direction can push a firm to implement an innovation culture. It is a continuous attempt to implement the procedure and, quite importantly, the objectives themselves. Alleviate redundant conflicts and keep moving forward. Many researchers have assumed that artificial intelligence will perform significant tasks in the future. In the future, artificial intelligence will become more productive and effective. A future in which artificial intelligence retains the key to solving international issues on a significant scale. A future in which artificial intelligence supports firms in making better decisions. A future in which it will beat humans. However, some people assume that the future has already arrived (Huff and Bonde, 2022).

In the great discussion over whether artificial intelligence will steal human jobs, there has been less debate over how it will alter enterprise cultures in unprecedented and advanced ways (Clinton, 2021). In times of automation, the most progressive businesses will be those that reform their working atmosphere and workforce around connecting the cognitive abilities of machines in the same way that the Victorian-era industry was reformed by connecting the physical abilities of mechanisation and steam. Artificial intelligence will require a fundamental cultural shift because it changes the association between humans and machines, altering machines from passive receivers of commands into knowledgeable, perceptive collaborators. In doing so, it will evolve the skills that firms seek to discover and foster among human employees. Essentially, artificial intelligence will require human workspaces to be developed around powering procedures, services, and products with data in a manner similar to the machine age society reconfigured around driving machines using electricity (Fisher et al., 2021).

CONCLUSION

It is impossible to overestimate the revolutionary potential of artificial intelligence (AI) in changing corporate culture. Businesses in various industries have entered a new period of potential due to AI, which provides creative answers to vulnerable problems. Organisations are increasingly realising the value of AI, and are learning that it is a catalyst for a significant cultural transformation that goes far beyond simple automation. AI has the potential to completely transform how organisations run from streamlining procedures to improving consumer experiences. This enables businesses to leverage enormous data reserves and transform them into useful insights. Data are becoming the lifeblood of decision making in this AI-driven culture, allowing businesses to make wise decisions, forecast trends, and act quickly when their markets shift. Businesses that use AI access previously have unheard-efficiency and competitive advantages. Furthermore, AI is a catalyst for innovation rather than merely a tool for enhancing already-in-use procedures. This encourages constant learning and discoveries. When AI is ingrained into an organisation's culture, it inspires workers to approach problems in their original ways. It enables the creation of original goods, services, and business strategies that were previously unthinkable. AI acts as a catalyst in this regard, launching companies into new innovation realms. Organisations need to prepare for a world where AI is a vital component of daily operations, if they want to prosper. AI is a transformational force that does not disappear; it is not fad. In a world increasingly driven by AI, businesses that adapt quickly and effectively are better positioned to take advantage of opportunities and manage risks. Effectively utilising the possibilities of AI systems entails investing in AI expertise, promoting a culture of data literacy, and redesigning business processes. Additionally, accepting AI requires an understanding of the ethical duties associated with its application. Organisations must prioritise ethical issues, such as fairness, transparency, and accountability, as AI becomes increasingly ingrained in business operations. They must set standards and best practices to guarantee that AI systems are created and implemented consistently with societal norms and legal frameworks.

In conclusion, organisations must use AI, but they must do so wisely and intelligently, given its revolutionary potential, function as an innovation catalyst, and growing integration into business processes. Businesses have the chance to improve their competitiveness as they traverse the always-changing terrain of AI technologies and contribute to a future in which AI acts as a potent catalyst for positive change that benefits both businesses and society. Organisations should position themselves to flourish at a time when AI is not just a tool but also a vital partner in their success by embracing AI and fostering a culture of innovation.

REFERENCES

Bangalore Seetharam, S. (2020). Developing a digital AI roadmap for retail.

Barclay, R. C., Cudney, E. A., Shetty, S., & Antony, J. (2022). Determining critical success factors for lean implementation. *Total Quality Management & Business Excellence*, 33(7-8), 818–832. DOI:10.1080/14783363.2021.1894919

Bees, J. (2022). How Artificial Intelligence Use Is Expanding in Health Care. *NEJM Catalyst Innovations in Care Delivery*, 3(4), CAT.22.0089. DOI:10.1056/CAT.22.0089

Berg, M. (2022). Hate It? Automate It! Thinking and doing robotic process automation and beyond. In *Everyday Automation* (pp. 157-170). Routledge.

Biswas, S., Carson, B., Chung, V., Singh, S., & Thomas, R. (2020). *AI-bank of the future: Can banks meet the AI challenge*. McKinsey & Company.

Bratasanu, V. (2018). Leadership Decision-Making Processes in the Context of Data Driven Tools. *Quality - Access to Success*, 19.

Buck, B., & Morrow, J. (2018). AI, performance management and engagement: Keeping your best their best. *Strategic HR Review*, 17(5), 261–262. DOI:10.1108/SHR-10-2018-145

Cao, L. (2022). A new age of AI: Features and futures. *IEEE Intelligent Systems*, 37(1), 25–37. DOI:10.1109/MIS.2022.3150944

Cermann, H., Kern, S., Bertram, F., Sander, M., Heimann, T., & Proctor, R. (2021). Towards an agile and adaptive Enterprise. *INFORMATIK 2021*.

Chahal, H., Fedasiuk, R., & Flynn, C. (2020). Messier than Oil: Assessing Data Advantage in Military AI. *Center for Security and Emerging Technology*.

Clinton, L. (2021). International principles for boards of directors and cyber security. *Cyber Security: A Peer-Reviewed Journal, 4*(3), 243-250.

Cooperrider, D. L., & Fry, R. (2020). Appreciative inquiry in a pandemic: An improbable pairing. *The Journal of Applied Behavioral Science*, 56(3), 266–271. DOI:10.1177/0021886320936265

Eitle, V., Zöll, A., & Buxmann, P. (2022). Organizational Readiness Concept for AI: A Quantitative Analysis of a Multi-stage Adoption Process from the Perspective of Data Scientists.

Eriksson, T., Bigi, A., & Bonera, M. (2020). Think with me, or think for me? On the future role of artificial intelligence in marketing strategy formulation. *The TQM Journal*, 32(4), 795–814. DOI:10.1108/TQM-12-2019-0303

Fisher, R., Porod, C., & Peterson, S. (2021). Motivating employees and organizations to adopt a cybersecurity-focused culture. *Journal of Organizational Psychology*, 21(1), 114–131.

Gröger, C. (2021). There is no AI without data. *Communications of the ACM*, 64(11), 98–108. DOI:10.1145/3448247

Hallunovi, A. (2021). Money, finance and credit. *Research and Innovation*, 90.

Helbekkmo, H., Levy, C., & White, O. (2019). Creating the bank enterprise risk management function of the future. *Journal of Risk Management in Financial Institutions*, 12(4), 297–310. DOI:10.69554/IFVQ1353

Henke, N., Puri, A., & Saleh, T. (2020). *Accelerating analytics to navigate COVID-19 and the next normal*. Mckinsey.

Herskovits, B. (2018). 'Build it and they will come'is a myth: Building a digital activation strategy. *Journal of Digital Banking*, 3(2), 102–113. DOI:10.69554/NWVV2163

Huff, E., & Bonde, A. (2022). AI meets consumer insights.

Kavoya, J. (2020). Machine Learning for Intelligence Driven Customs Management. *African Tax and Customs Review*, 3(2), 1–8.

Kim, K., & Kim, B. (2022). Decision-Making Model for Reinforcing Digital Transformation Strategies Based on Artificial Intelligence Technology. *Information (Basel)*, 13(5), 253. DOI:10.3390/info13050253

Kordon, A. (2020, August). Applied Artificial Intelligence-Based Systems as Competitive Advantage. In *2020 IEEE 10th International Conference on Intelligent Systems (IS)* (pp. 6-18). IEEE. DOI:10.1109/IS48319.2020.9200097

Kordon, A. K. (2020). How to Operate AI-Based Data Science in a Business. In *Applying Data Science* (pp. 433–451). Springer. DOI:10.1007/978-3-030-36375-8_16

Krejci, D., Küng, L., & Missonier, S. (2022). A Case Study of Enterprise-wide Digital Innovation: Involving Non-IT Employees.

Lacy, P., Long, J., & Spindler, W. (2020). Culture & Organization. In *The Circular Economy Handbook* (pp. 259–281). Palgrave Macmillan. DOI:10.1057/978-1-349-95968-6_19

Latinovic, Z., & Chatterjee, S. C. (2022). Achieving the promise of AI and ML in delivering economic and relational customer value in B2B. *Journal of Business Research*, 144, 966–974. DOI:10.1016/j.jbusres.2022.01.052

Lawry, T. (2020). *AI in health: a leader's guide to winning in the new age of intelligent health systems*. CRC Press. DOI:10.4324/9780429321214

Lee, S., & Miller, S. (2019). AI gets real at Singapore's Changi Airport (Part 1).

Liu, S. Y. (2021). Harnessing Artificial Intelligence to Transform Agricultural. *Case Studies: Insights on Agriculture Innovation 2020 (IAAS Series)*, 13.

Mohiuddin Babu, M., Akter, S., Rahman, M., Billah, M. M., & Hack-Polay, D. (2022). The role of artificial intelligence in shaping the future of Agile fashion industry. *Production Planning and Control*, 1–15. DOI:10.1080/09537287.2022.2060858

Parvin, S. (2021, December). Success Factors of an Enterprise-Wide Digital Twin Strategy. In *Abu Dhabi International Petroleum Exhibition & Conference*. OnePetro.

Rismani, S., & Moon, A. (2022). What does it mean to be an AI Ethicist: An ontology of existing roles. *arXiv preprint arXiv:2205.03946*.

Ruel, H., & Njoku, E. (2020). AI redefining the hospitality industry. *Journal of Tourism Futures*.

Rydén, P., & El Sawy, O. (2022). Real-Time Management: When AI Goes Fast and Flow. In *Platforms and Artificial Intelligence* (pp. 225–243). Springer. DOI:10.1007/978-3-030-90192-9_11

Sanz, J. L., & Zhu, Y. (2021, September). Toward Scalable Artificial Intelligence in Finance. In *2021 IEEE International Conference on Services Computing (SCC)* (pp. 460-469). IEEE. DOI:10.1109/SCC53864.2021.00067

Schwartz, R., Vassilev, A., Greene, K., Perine, L., Burt, A., & Hall, P. (2022). Towards a Standard for Identifying and Managing Bias in Artificial Intelligence.

Sobocińska, M. (2021). Artificial Intelligence and Human Talent in Decision Making in the Sphere of Marketing in an Enterprise. *Problemy Zarządzania*, 19(1 (91)), 65–75. DOI:10.7172/1644-9584.91.5

Talent, L. A. (2021). The DOD's Hidden Artificial Intelligence Workforce.

Tariq, M. U. (2024a). The transformation of healthcare through AI-driven diagnostics. In Sharma, A., Chanderwal, N., Tyagi, S., Upadhyay, P., & Tyagi, A. (Eds.), *Enhancing medical imaging with emerging technologies* (pp. 250–264). IGI Global. DOI:10.4018/979-8-3693-5261-8.ch015

Tariq, M. U. (2024b). The role of emerging technologies in shaping the global digital government landscape. In Guo, Y. (Ed.), *Emerging developments and technologies in digital government* (pp. 160–180). IGI Global. DOI:10.4018/979-8-3693-2363-2.ch009

Tariq, M. U. (2024c). Equity and inclusion in learning ecosystems. In Al Husseiny, F., & Munna, A. (Eds.), *Preparing students for the future educational paradigm* (pp. 155–176). IGI Global. DOI:10.4018/979-8-3693-1536-1.ch007

Tariq, M. U. (2024d). Empowering educators in the learning ecosystem. In Al Husseiny, F., & Munna, A. (Eds.), *Preparing students for the future educational paradigm* (pp. 232–255). IGI Global. DOI:10.4018/979-8-3693-1536-1.ch010

Tariq, M. U. (2024e). Revolutionizing health data management with blockchain technology: Enhancing security and efficiency in a digital era. In Garcia, M., & de Almeida, R. (Eds.), *Emerging technologies for health literacy and medical practice* (pp. 153–175). IGI Global. DOI:10.4018/979-8-3693-1214-8.ch008

Tariq, M. U. (2024f). Emerging trends and innovations in blockchain-digital twin integration for green investments: A case study perspective. In Jafar, S., Rodriguez, R., Kannan, H., Akhtar, S., & Plugmann, P. (Eds.), *Harnessing blockchain-digital twin fusion for sustainable investments* (pp. 148–175). IGI Global. DOI:10.4018/979-8-3693-1878-2.ch007

Thomas, R., & Zikopoulos, P. (2020). *The AI Ladder: Accelerate your journey to AI.* O'Reilly Media.

Vargas, M. A., & Comuzzi, M. (2020). A multi-dimensional model of Enterprise Resource Planning critical success factors. *Enterprise Information Systems*, 14(1), 38–57. DOI:10.1080/17517575.2019.1678072

Warner, K. S., & Wäger, M. (2019). Building dynamic capabilities for digital transformation: An ongoing process of strategic renewal. *Long Range Planning*, 52(3), 326–349. DOI:10.1016/j.lrp.2018.12.001

Wise, J., de Barron, A. G., Splendiani, A., Balali-Mood, B., Vasant, D., Little, E., Mellino, G., Harrow, I., Smith, I., Taubert, J., van Bochove, K., Romacker, M., Walgemoed, P., Jimenez, R. C., Winnenburg, R., Plasterer, T., Gupta, V., & Hedley, V. (2019). Implementation and relevance of FAIR data principles in biopharmaceutical R&D. *Drug Discovery Today*, 24(4), 933–938. DOI:10.1016/j.drudis.2019.01.008 PMID:30690198

ADDITIONAL READING

Tariq, M. U. (2022). Maintaining sustainable production and service by mitigating impact industry 4.0 factors in the petroleum and coal sector in Pakistan. *International Journal of Services and Operations Management*, 43(2), 188. DOI:10.1504/IJSOM.2022.126815

Tariq, M. U. (2024). Integrating AI and Blockchain in EV Charging: Innovations and Challenges. In L. D., N. Nagpal, N. Kassarwani, V. Varthanan G., & P. Siano (Eds.), *A Sustainable Future with E-Mobility: Concepts, Challenges, and Implementations* (pp. 253-269). IGI Global. DOI:10.4018/979-8-3693-5247-2.ch013

Tariq, M. U., Babar, M., Jan, M. A., Khattak, A. S., Alshehri, M. D., & Yahya, A. (2021). Security requirement management for cloud-assisted and internet of things⇔enabled smart city. *Computers, Materials & Continua*, 67(1), 625–639. DOI:10.32604/cmc.2021.014165

Tariq, M. U., Babar, M., Poulin, M., Khattak, A. S., Alshehri, M. D., & Kaleem, S. (2021). Human behavior analysis using intelligent big data analytics. *Frontiers in Psychology*, 12, 686610. Advance online publication. DOI:10.3389/fpsyg.2021.686610 PMID:34295289

Tariq, M. U., & Ismail, M. U. S. B. (2024). AI-powered COVID-19 forecasting: A comprehensive comparison of advanced deep learning methods. *Osong Public Health and Research Perspectives*, 15(2), 2210–9099. DOI:10.24171/j.phrp.2023.0287 PMID:38621765

Tariq, M. U., Poulin, M., & Abonamah, A. A. (2021). Achieving operational excellence through artificial intelligence: Driving forces and barriers. *Frontiers in Psychology*, 12, 686624. Advance online publication. DOI:10.3389/fpsyg.2021.686624 PMID:34305744

KEY TERMS AND DEFINITIONS

AI Culture: The collective mindset and behaviours within an organisation that embrace, promote, and effectively integrate artificial intelligence into business operations.

AI Governance Framework: A structured approach to managing and overseeing AI initiatives within an organisation.

AI Standardisation: The process of creating and implementing consistent frameworks, best practices, and regulations across industries and jurisdictions.

AI-Driven Decision Making: The use of AI technologies to analyse data and inform or make decisions within an organisation.

Bias Mitigation in AI: The strategies and practices implemented to reduce or eliminate biases in AI systems.

Chapter 8
Teaching and Learning Strategies Using AI

ABSTRACT

The chapter discusses the benefits of utilising AI in education fields. It describes the various types of AI technologies used in education, such as teacher assistance tools, adaptive student assistance programs, and natural language processing, and reveals the use of virtual reality. This chapter provides a detailed layout of the advantages and disadvantages of the ethical implications of AI integration, which helps to understand how AI helps learning and teaching. AI facilitates education through personalised learning routes, interactive mechanisms, and inclusive education domains, which are considered its main benefits in education. Furthermore, the chapter also evaluates data security, algorithmic bias, and the emphasis on responsible technology use, thus calling for the development of ethical rules and responsible application of technology. This chapter presents example cases, best practices, and future trends to give an idea about AI, which is useful for students to enjoy learning worldwide.

INTRODUCTION

Artificial Intelligence is quickly changing different perspectives of our lives, especially in the domain of education. Within the domain of education, AI is progressively utilized to upgrade development openings, personalize instruction, and streamline authoritative assignments. This chapter dives into the colossal potential of AI in instruction, focusing on how it increases development opportunities for understudies. AI includes advances and applications that empower machines to perform assignments that regularly require human insight, such as learning, problem-solving, and route. In education, artificial intelligence is utilized to create coaching frameworks, versatile learning stages, and computerized reviewing frameworks, among

DOI: 10.4018/979-8-3693-4074-5.ch008

other applications (Abatan et al., 2024; Biu et al., 2024). Improving development openings is significant for advancing under-study engagement, making strides in scholastic execution, and cultivating a deep-rooted adore for learning (Sodiya et al., 2024; Uwaoma et al., 2023). Conventional one-size-fits-all approaches to instruction regularly battle to meet the assorted needs of understudies. AI is pivotal in personalized learning and tailoring development opportunities to individual students. This ensured that they received instructions that aligned with their unique learning styles and abilities. AI's transformative power of AI in education is evident in its ability to enhance development opportunities through personalized learning, reshaping teaching methods, and improving administrative processes (Ayorinde et al., 2024; Egieya et al., 2024).

Customized Learning through artificial intelligence is changing training by customized openings for development that watch out for personal understudy needs (Majemite et al., 2024; Okafor et al., 2023). Artificial intelligence-fueled flexible learning frameworks examine students' performance to create personalized learning methods, giving students customized directions and backing. This chapter explores the work of artificial intelligence in customized learning, focusing on its impact on student commitment and academic execution. AI-powered, power-fueled flexible learning systems aim to alter students' preferences and needs (Nwokediegwu et al., 2024; Usman et al., 2024).

These systems utilize algorithms to analyze student performance, test scores, schoolwork satisfaction rates, and learning progress to identify areas where students may require additional assistance. Given this examination, AI can recommend unequivocal learning work, resources, or exercises to help students understand complex skills and concepts at their own pace.

One of the basic components of computer-based intelligence-fueled flexible learning systems is their capacity to create customized learning methods for students (Ihemereze et al., 2023; Obaigbena et al., 2024). These learning methods are custom-fitted to each student's learning pace, speed, and preferences, ensuring that they obtain the correct challenges and backing. For example, if a student combats a particular thought, the system can deliver extra practice exercises or resources to help improve them (Orieno et al., 2024; Uwaoma et al., 2023). The impact of AI-based adaptive learning systems on student engagement and academic performance is undeniable. (Atadoga et al., 2024; Dada et al., 2024).

BACKGROUND

Artificial intelligence (AI) has the power to change how we learn and teach. It has customized development openings, and AI-powered flexible learning systems can help students reach their full academic potential and obtain good grades. Another noteworthy aspect of personalized Learning through AI is its capacity to supply quick and focused inputs to students(Ambele et al., 2022; Olatoye et al., 2024). One of the important benefits of AI-powered frameworks is that they can analyze student responses to tests, assignments, and other evaluations in genuine time, providing feedback on their performance. This prompt feedback makes a difference in students' performance, as it helps them identify strengths and shortcomings, permitting them to center their endeavors in areas where improvement is required.

In the technological industry, AI cannot be considered a buzzword. It has made its way into the education sector and has the capability to transform learning experiences. This chapter explores AI's capabilities of AI in education and how it offers different and new opportunities to students. Computer-based insights are a recent development that enable machines to perform endeavors that commonly require human understanding, such as acumen, consideration, and learning. In education, artificial insights can be connected to form customized development openings, computerized regulatory assignments, and assist professors in decision-making. However, AI tools can only hinder students' progress if they are used properly and can hinder their Learning if they capture their unique style, progress data, and preferences.

However, if used properly, they can fundamentally upgrade the reasonability of teaching and learning, because they allow students to memorize at their own speed and in a fashion that suits them. Computer-based insights can also robotize monotonous administrative errands, such as checking on, evaluating, and detailing, empowering educators, and freeing professors to focus more on important activities such as mentoring and teaching. Artificial intelligence can create an environment that can make students commit to their studies, making learning more natural and enjoyable. For example, AI-governed language learning apps can provide feedback on their grammar and punctuation, making it simple for students to learn foreign languages, thus improving their education. In the past five years, owing to leading progress and its disruptive prospect, artificial intelligence has shifted from the distance of education research to the lead of public debates. In various states, artificial intelligence has become persistent in routine life, from customer chatbots to personal assistants, from forecasting criminal activities to suggesting entertainment and medical diagnoses to facial recognition. Although artificial intelligence might have the prospect of assisting in the attainment of learning objectives, rapid technological progress certainly brings numerous challenges and risks, which have far overtaken regulatory models and strategy debates. While strong doubts might include artificial intelligence dominating human agency, more pending concerns include artificial intelligence's ethical and social implications, such as the exploitation of personal data and the probability that artificial intelligence might aggravate instead of lessening previous discrimination. However, artificial intelligence has also entered the educational world. Intelligent, personalized, and adaptive learning systems are progressively being developed by the private sector for implementation in universities and schools worldwide, developing a market anticipated to be worth six billion dollars by 2024. Inevitably, the deployment of artificial intelligence in educational frameworks calls into question what should be taught and how, the advancing role of teachers, and artificial's ethical and social implications. There are also several obstacles, such as educational access and equity. There is also a progressing consensus that the basics of learning and teaching may be reformed by implementing artificial intelligence in higher education. All of these obstacles are further complicated by the big move towards online learning because of the global COVID-19 pandemic university closures. Therefore, the higher education sector seeks to support policymakers to recognize better the implications and possibilities of artificial intelligence for learning and teaching so that its deployment in educational settings efficiently supports

However, administrators should be aware that the association between artificial intelligence will undoubtedly play out in diverse ways, depending on socioeconomic and national situations. With artificial intelligence in general, the stress is that if higher education commences blindly forward, universities should expect to witness augmented variation together with economic disruption, social conflict, and, in some situations, political uncertainty, with the technically deprived and diminishing proceeding the worst. There is no less concern about higher education and artificial intelligence. Suppose artificial intelligence is to assist with educational goals. There is also a requirement to offer cost-effective models for developing artificial intelligence technologies and guarantee that the interests of middle- and low-level-income countries are signified in fundamental decisions and debates. And develop links between these countries and nations where the deployment of artificial intelligence is more progressed (Lameras, 2022).

Artificial Intelligence Strategies

In the interim, definitions of artificial intelligence extended and multiplied, mainly becoming tangled with the logical queries of what consists of intelligence and whether machines can ever actually be intelligent. Artificial intelligence is defined as a division of modern technology and science targeting the investigation of the secrets of human intelligence from one angle and the replacement of human intelligence with machines to the greatest extent so that systems would have the ability to perform options as smartly as they can. Practically avoiding this prolonged discussion, for the objective of attaining higher education, artificial intelligence may be explained as computer systems that have been developed to connect with the world via abilities that are usually thought of as human. Artificial intelligence-powered machines can imitate particular human intelligence tasks involving learning, problem solving, perception, reasoning, creative work generation, language interaction, and learning. Higher education is witnessing artificial intelligence revitalisation, with an escalating assortment of sectors implementing the type of artificial intelligence known as machine learning, which includes the artificial intelligence system assessing massive amounts of data. It has come about as a consequence of two crucial signs of progress: the augmented growth of data (International Business Machines, IBM has assessed that because of the internet and relevant technologies, more significant than 2.5 quintillions are generated daily). With the augmented progress in computer processing power (law), today's mobile phones were as robust as supercomputers forty ago. Powerful computers and big data are vital to machine learning, as their algorithms rely on processing millions of data points, which in turn require massive amounts of computer power. Stimulatingly, machine learning algorithms that make the most headlines- neural networks and deep learning- have been in use for more than 40 years. The current substantial artificial intelligence attainments and their disruptive potential have emerged owing to advances in these algorithms, along with their easy accessibility as a service, instead of any essential novel pattern. In other words, it might be claimed that higher education is present in this age of deployment. Real-world implementations of artificial intelligence are becoming progressively disruptive and prevalent, with recognised instances varying from automatic facial recognition and automatic translation between languages, utilised for tracking criminals and identifying passengers, to personal assistants on smartphones and self-driving vehicles in daily routines (Ng, 2021).

Artificial Intelligence Techniques

Every application of artificial intelligence relies on various complicated techniques that require engineers to be trained in data science, mathematics, statistics, and coding. Therefore, these techniques are too unprecedented to be thoroughly investigated here. Classical artificial intelligence, otherwise known as good-old-fashioned artificial intelligence or symbolic artificial intelligence, includes writing sequences of IF… THEN… and other conditional logic rules, which require steps to achieve the task. Over the years, rule-based artificial intelligence expert systems have been introduced for various applications such as medical diagnostics, production, and credit ratings. Expert systems depend on a method called knowledge engineering, which includes modelling and producing the knowledge of experts in a particular domain, a resource-based task without difficulties. Typical expert systems involve hundreds of regulations and are likely to follow their logic. Though exchanges between regulations increase, expert systems can become difficult to improve or update (Martins & Gresse Von Wangenheim, 2022). Advancements in artificial intelligence, such as natural language processing, self-driving vehicles, and facial recognition, have been made possible by machine learning-dependent computational methods. Instead of using these regulations, machine learning assesses massive amounts of data to recognise patterns and develop a framework which is then utilised to forecast future values. Thus, algorithms, instead of being preprogrammed, are known as learning. There are three vital machine-learning methods: reinforcement, unsupervised, and supervised. Supervised learning includes data already labelled, such as numerous photos of people that humans have already labelled. Supervised learning relates the data to the labels for developing a model that can be implemented on the same data, for instance, identifying people automatically in new photos. In unsupervised learning, artificial intelligence is provided even with massive amounts of data, but the data have not been labelled or classified. Unsupervised learning aims to disclose hidden data patterns and groups that can be utilised to categorise novel data. For instance, it can automatically recognise numbers and letters in writing by observing patterns in several examples. In both unsupervised and supervised learning, the model extracted from the data is fixed, and if the data are altered, the assessment should be performed again. The third machine learning method, reinforcement learning, constantly enhances the model depending on feedback. In other words, it is machine learning in the context of continuous learning. Artificial intelligence is equipped with fundamental data, which develops a model that is analysed as incorrect or correct and punished or rewarded accordingly. Artificial intelligence uses this reinforcement to revise its model and then tries again, repeatedly evolving, and learning over time (Weisz et al., 2019).

USING AI TO IMPLEMENT EFFECTIVE TEACHING STRATEGIES IN CLASSROOMS

Method 1: Employing AI to Generate a Wide Range of Examples

Students require many examples when learning complex topics (Kirschner and Heal, 2022). Providing several different examples helps students understand new and complicated concepts. If a single example is given to the class, people can concentrate on its obvious features rather than on understanding the underlying idea. Students can improve their memory and comprehension by decontextualising it through several instances of the same thing. Providing examples to students when teaching new concepts offers several benefits.

- Examples help students remember concepts by acting as anchors in the form of an analogy or story, grounding the concepts in interesting details that illustrate a general principle.
- Examples also encourage critical thinking by provoking analysis and evaluation mechanisms across various examples.
- Examples can help to surface the complexity of a concept by highlighting it.

There are just a few advantages of using examples when teaching new ideas to students. The transfer of learning is the process by which students may abstract general ideas and apply them in a new setting when given various examples (Perkins & Salomon, 1992). Teachers sometimes have busy schedules and many on their plates, making it more difficult to develop examples that meet certain requirements. When creating examples, educators must consider many factors:

- Do pupils find examples interesting and pertinent?
- Real-world problems or challenges may assist in customising examples to spark student interests.
- Are the examples sufficiently clear and detailed simultaneously?

It is crucial to ensure that these examples are neither complex nor simplistic. While an example's narrative intricacies and other surface-level elements may draw students, finding an ideal balance between complexity and simplicity is important. While simplistic examples might not fully illustrate an idea, overly complex ones can cause misunderstandings. Consequently, teachers need to carefully examine their pupils' various requirements when creating understandable and instructive examples. Creating several instances of a single idea takes time and may be delegated to artificial intelligence. AI can provide a large number of instances quickly. Here is how to accomplish the following:

1. Select a topic that you want your pupils to fully grasp.
2. If you are utilising an online AI like Bing, instruct it to search for that idea using foundational works on the subject.
3. Describe your needs for AI (many different examples of this idea)
4. Specify your preferred writing style (e.g. engaging, lively, clear, simple, and concrete).
5. Identify your target audience (My students are college students unfamiliar with this idea; My students are high school students).

Method 2: Employing AI to Offer Several Interpretations

Explaining concepts makes sense logically and coherently (Ericsson and Lehmann, 1996). Good explanations provide students with the fundamental knowledge they need to create mental maps of their subjects (Willingham, 2023). Instructors who want to create effective explanations need to know where their students are at and what they already know (prior knowledge), organise and structure their explanations in a step-by-step manner to progress from the simple to the complex, giving students organisational cues (we are here. Next, we move to.) and provides specific details for each explanation. Explanations (e.g. analogies or examples) aid students in understanding and placing new ideas in the context of their prior knowledge. Any explanation should enable pupils to communicate ideas to others using their own language (Willingham, 2023).

To tailor explanations to students' learning levels, teachers must be mindful of the new terminology, context, and cognitive load. New students may become overwhelmed by excessive detail or unclear or unproven language. Certain explanations may require a lot of background information that students may need to be more familiar with. Finally, because teachers are experts, they must draw on their expertise and break down what they know to make it understandable for novices (students) to provide lucid and logical explanations (Ericsson & Pool, 2016). Although this is a challenging undertaking, AI may be beneficial if it is well vetted. AI may assist educators in this endeavour by producing several explanations from various angles, producing step-by-step explanations, and supplementing any pre-existing explanations with more details. If a notion is unclear to pupils, AI can generate a more straightforward explanation that can make it easier for them to understand. Similarly, educators can present their current explanation of a subject to the AI and request that it be made simpler, provide additional examples, or provide a step-by-step explanation. Recall that any AI-generated explanations are preliminary and must be approved by the teacher before being distributed to the class. Here is how to accomplish the following:

1. Decide which idea to clarify.
2. If using an online AI (such as Bing), instruct it to search for that idea by utilising foundational works in the subject.
3. Describe your need for AI (give it a concise, multi-paragraph description of a topic).
4. Specify your preferred writing style (e.g. engaging, lively, clear, simple, and concrete).
5. Describe your target audience (my students are college students unfamiliar with this idea; my students are high-school students).

6. Ask for analogies in response to the first prompt.

Method 3: Employing AI to Create Low-Stakes Examinations

Low-stakes testing is a successful teaching method at all educational contexts and levels. Exams are learning experiences and a means of measuring knowledge. Long-term memory retention is aided by repeated testing and knowledge retrieval (Karpicke and Roediger, 2008). Active retrieval practice is provided by low-stakes exams, which encourage students to recover knowledge from memory. This can help retain and retrieve material in the future (Kirschner & Heal, 2022). Additionally, they give students feedback on how well they understand the subject matter, enabling them to concentrate on their weak areas of knowledge and modify their study techniques. By assisting students in making sense of the material, they begin the mental processes necessary to perform well on a test with significant consequences (Adesope et al., 2017).

Low-stakes exams also give teachers insight into what their pupils know and comprehend, enabling them to modify their instructions accordingly. Students also use self-assessment tools such as flashcards or other self-directed learning strategies. It takes work to create quizzes, multiple choice or short answer exams, or purposefully include questions that assess the material covered in lectures. Teachers must carefully connect their assessments and learning targets when designing low-stake examinations. They must also determine the exact abilities that they wish to evaluate and build exams that demonstrate comprehension. Instructors might need more time to create frequent and different examinations, and they might not have a trustworthy method for marking them, particularly if they involve short-response sections. Moreover, creating such assessments becomes more difficult when students receive scores and comments on their progress. Tests must be thoughtfully created to be difficult but not to the point where pupils become frustrated. AI can assist teachers in creating quizzes, short-answer tests, and practice examinations related to a subject or reading. It can also assist in adding questions to lectures to assess student understanding. Here is how Microsoft Bing is used to accomplish this:

1. Explain the AI's functions. In this instance, the AI was tasked with creating diagnostic quizzes.
2. Tell the AI what you want to teach and how you want to teach it (low-stakes test to gauge students' understanding).
3. Write the article(s) into the prompt if you are using the Bing. The reading you were given was an online article or document accessible to the public.

4. You may also instruct them on what kinds of multiple-choice questions to generate; for example, questions with multiple choices should not include an "all of the above" option and should instead have competitive, believable alternate answers.

ARTIFICIAL INTELLIGENCE STRATEGIES FOR LEARNING AND TEACHING

Distributed Cognitive Theory

Distributed cognition involves the distribution of cognition in individuals, time, media, society, environment, and culture. This suggests a new perception that considers the entire picture of cognitive functions, emphasising the association between artefacts, environment, representation, media, and individuals. It also considers that distributed factors should rely on each other to fulfil the tasks. Distributed cognitive theory has important implications for research of artificial intelligence to endorse teaching modification:

- "Artefacts" like technologies and tools in distributed cognition can decrease cognitive load and cognitive tasks. When the learning material of the students is beyond the cognitive scope and cannot be resolved, innovative learning software can decrease the cognitive load and direct the student to develop deep cognition. Simultaneously, monotonous and simple cognitive tasks can be assigned to intelligent robots such that humans can perform more creative cognitive functions. The future must be a time of collaboration between the intelligent machines and humans. What smart machines are good at and what humans are capable of may differ significantly. The understanding generated by the collaboration between artificial intelligence and humans far exceeds that generated by artificial and human intelligence. Human-machine association has become the fundamental cognitive method for people to face complicated issues, and human cognition is switching from distributed to individual cognition (Sekeroglu et al., 2019).
- Distributed cognition focuses on the association between the cognitive environment and cognition. Cognitive humans are conducive to developing cognitive structures during the interaction process. The association in teaching is the connection between students and teachers, and the link between machines and humans. There are various interactive methods in an innovative teaching environment assisted by artificial intelligence. This interaction can rebuild

the learning experience and even impact human cognition via vision, touch, and hearing (Lantz et al., 2022).

Technology Revolution Theory

Innovation is not just a standard technology or process innovation but an ongoing mechanism. It was only introduced by the exploration and invention of manufacturing and the shock impact on the existing manufacturing system. Technology innovation theory has a vital administrative significance for learning and teaching innovation.

- State-of-the-art technologies that benefit learning and teaching will impact learning and teaching when the rise of artificial intelligence technology brings novel intelligent learning tools from novel learning and teaching methods and encourages the innovation of teaching assessment and management techniques. Teachers should dynamically alter their methods of thinking, discover novel forms of merging artificial intelligence and teaching, and endorse the deep incorporation of teaching and technology and the intelligent progress of teaching and learning (Ghai et al., 2021).
- Provide attention to the refinement of students' creative abilities in artificial intelligence. Machines will undoubtedly substitute for simple and monotonous tasks. Intelligent systems exceed the left human brain (engineering logical thinking). Humans must sustain their benefits over machines. A vital strategy is to allow students to spend energy and time developing the right brain that the system is not good at and nurturing the exclusive capability of human intelligence, such as creativity, communication, innovation, problem solving, artistic aesthetic ability, and problem solving. Being invulnerable is the standard direction of educational transformation (Carter et al., 2020).

Fundamental System Information Input

For artificial intelligence to be more wide-ranging, logical, and scientific, it might be based on abundant information. For this reason, making a computer obtain information, particularly during the teaching procedure, is vital. The following is a concise description of the information types needed by computers and how they are acquired in learning and teaching:

- The attribute information of schools, teachers, and students is a thing or person's intrinsic, fundamental, and attached feature. This is a qualitative aspect of the specific expressions of things. This information is the identification details of computers used for differentiating things from people. It can appropriately provide feedback on the related information about things or people that users require; simultaneously, computers can statistically assess things and people with similar attributes to provide feedback to users (Zhou, 2020).

- Teaching resources, such as test questions, courseware, papers, and lessons: The preparation of teaching resources requires the combined efforts of instructors. A simple, practical, and effective editing system and resource management software was used to attract as many instructors as possible. The system software can meet the features of simple functions and instructors' everyday working habits and can magnify instructors' knowledge without multiplying the burden on instructors (Papa & Jackson, 2021).
- Details of teaching progress such as student performance and teacher progress: The feature of artificial intelligence is that it can logically and timely explore issues, forecast trends, and resolve issues following the progress of things. To this end, it requires constantly inputting the low-level details in the teaching procedure into the information system via different media so that the computer can offer recommendations to be taught more scientifically and expansively. The most vital procedure information in teaching is the students' responses. Instructors can utilise an online scoring system to attain this. The system cannot only release instructors from lengthy exam papers and statistical work but also promptly and precisely enter responses to every question paper. It can also be saved in the database of related students and test queries, offering plenty for the following statistical assessment information base (Christensen et al., 2022).

Algorithm Processing

The fundamentals of artificial intelligence are the algorithms. Various algorithms can resolve a similar issue, and the algorithm quality will affect the algorithm's efficacy and program. The objective of the algorithm assessment is to select suitable algorithms and enhance them. The goal is to offer an ideal solution for teaching via artificial computer intelligence and to enhance teaching quality and efficiency. The design features and aims of the algorithm are projected based on various objects in the teaching procedure (Luan & Tsai, 2021).

- Students are the central object and subject of learning. Artificial intelligence should consider the following facts when inferring evaluation: students' learning capabilities such as learning speed, memory, and IQ; youth's psychological features such as emotional forgetfulness and emotional quotient; teaching needs such as teaching objective and teaching objective; teaching facts such as the entire situation of the class and the complication of the test questions. Artificial intelligence can inform students about their learning situation at any time. It can reassess and practice based on system prompts, making learning more persistent and significantly enhancing learning efficacy (Younes, 2021).

- Instructors are the directors of teaching. The level of instructors' capabilities directly affects the quality and efficacy of teaching. Artificial intelligence should be efficient while performing the job of an instructor's staff. Artificial intelligence will offer instructors the following phases of services dependent on a significant amount of information resources: practical lesson strategies and courseware appropriate for teaching, practice exam papers that follow the characteristics of learners, assessment of test paper statistics, the extension of teachers' knowledge, and so on. This can efficiently decrease the workload of instructors. It can also recognise the learning progress of learners at any time and amend the teaching steps based on system recommendations to teach better and enhance teaching quality (Rerhaye et al., 2021).
- As higher education administrators, universities must be updated with the newest dynamic information on all associations and essentials of teaching to supervise, handle the teaching procedure, and inhibit probable accidents. A computer's artificial intelligence depends on a significant amount of data for statistics, summary, and well-timed and scientific feedback for teaching administrators (Vazhayil et al., 2019).

A computer's artificial intelligence is based on a large amount of information for summary and statistics and timely and scientific feedback to teaching managers (Lantz et al., 2022).

Information Output

As regular users, the efficiency of information materials and perception of information presentation are needed. The role and content of the information output based on various users are discussed below.

- Students can obtain a teaching plan that is more appropriate for them and can automatically review and assess existing learning and fill in gaps in knowledge at routine intervals. This is because they can recognise their learning progress at any time and can assess and practice depending on the tips to make learning more persistent, significantly enhancing learning efficacy (Lameras, 2022; Tariq, 2024).
- Parents can be aware of the progress of students at universities at any time via text messages or the Internet, such as the quality of educational performance,

modifications in disciplinary discerning, and financial consumption, so that they can be well-versed in a timely and efficient way. They can take reactive measures to confirm that students can devote energy to their education with proper dedication and peace of mind (Weisz et al., 2019).

- Teachers can acquire resources and information in a timely manner and offer efficient lessons and study plans. Simultaneously, computer systems can fulfil some repetitive and mechanical jobs, such as test paper correction and question statistics, relieving instructors so that they can focus more on research and teaching and enhance their teaching performance (Lantz et al., 2022).
- Higher education administrators can be well informed about the university's conditions, such as the archives of university staff and numerous statistics. Simultaneously, the data were assessed and summarised to offer an all-inclusive and accurate base for the progress of higher education administrators. For this reason, it can significantly enhance the efficacy of administrative management and higher education and teaching and enhance universities' social reputation and status. Utilising computer artificial intelligence systems can entirely alter universities' present teaching mode and management status and can vitally resolve conventional teaching and management. Issues of information lag, waste, and resources enhance teaching quality and management efficacy (Zhou, 2020; Tariq, 2024).

Development of Smart Teaching Media

The innovative teaching medium depends on computational intelligence, learning assessment, machine learning, and data-mining technology. It offers customised learning and teaching systems to students and teachers. Its vital feature is the use of artificial intelligence technology to innovatively assess students' learning. They also include creating a knowledge map of students, offering students customised learning materials and solutions, assisting adaptive learning, and applying intelligent suggestions for learning materials. With the support of artificial intelligence to create a learning environment in which reality and virtual reality are merged, students can conduct more customised, engaging, and riveting learning in a virtual fusion setting. Customising the image of the virtual student acquaintance to support the student, let the student focus, fill in the learning task in the given time, and enhance the learning procedure. The virtual supporter compliments when the student fulfils the learning task and provides reassurance and direction when it is not completed, so that the student feels compassionate care and dynamically achieves the learning task without the demands and pressures of parents and instructors. (Lantz et al., 2022). Preclass instructors prepare lectures through smart teaching media, share lectures with instructors worldwide in real time, and grasp innovative teaching ideas. They can learn through advanced teaching methodologies, send pre-class preview content to students via the teaching medium, private study space, well-timed discussion with learners, and well-timed improvement and adjustment of the teaching plan. During the lecture, instructors can associate with the teaching medium through different mobile terminals to connect with the instructor in real-time. Teachers can resolve the issues of various students one-to-many so that every learner can engage in class interaction and return the classroom to learners. After class, learners can complete their homework on the medium and complete the thinking impacts with the learning community. The medium completes homework marking and offers students real-time feedback (Weisz et al., 2019).

- The innovative teaching medium offers various preview contents and assessments of various difficulties for every student based on the accumulated data and innovative algorithms based on the student's learning capability, mastery of the learning material, and attempts. The material content will be actively adjusted with the advancement of students' learning, avoiding the knowledge points that the students have grasped and firming the weak connections of the students to apply teaching based on their aptitude and attain adaptive learning with customised difficulty. Customised teaching prepares several exam papers for different learners, and different exam papers will not enhance the teacher's work intensity. So, the innovative teaching medium, based on each learner's records, innovative exam papers can also be generated via machine corrections and automatically generate teaching assessment reports, customise assessment of student deficiencies and progress and direct students' efforts (Lameras, 2022).
- Innovative teaching media can also play the role of behavioural observation for relative assessment. Teachers' perceptions can help assess how teachers with diversified teaching ages and educational experiences have different controls over the teaching procedure and teaching impacts. Instructors who score more on the teaching assessment can assess their teaching procedure in detail. For students with bad grades, administrators can utilise the research data to explore when they started to relax, whether they were reluctant to study from start to end or faced difficulties in the learning procedure. They also checked what caused them to shrink back and recognised when the students' learning attitudes were altered. They can detect whether a student changes after receiving the learning alert (Zhou, 2020).

Introduction of the Functional Units of the Innovative Teaching Medium

An intelligent teaching medium can offer services such as customised learning assessment and innovative push learning material. During data accumulation, the student's learning archive data, learning behaviour data, and other relevant information data are saved in the data warehouse. There is a need to incorporate artificial intelligence assessment and big data mining technologies, such as adaptive technology, semantic assessment, and push technology, to support learning to compute. In the context of higher education, it offers customised learning-path suggestion services. It can be observed that the smart teaching medium depends on three fundamental aspects services, data, and algorithms, where data is the base, algorithms are the core, and services are the objective (Ng, 2021). The progression of educational technology will lead to modifications in higher education. Presently, the most vital artificial intelligence products, which have specifically impacted conventional education, have been used in higher education. AI progress of artificial intelligence has had a profound impact on teaching and higher education practices. This alters the teaching methodologies of instructors and learning techniques of students. The latest technology has modified the higher-education setting. In the context of learning services, depending on the outcome of the customised assessment, it offers students suggested services covering educational material, learning interaction, and customised learning tracks to support learners in customised learning. In the teaching context, assessing the teacher's data about their teaching process supports teachers in gathering losses and gains, optimising teaching quality, and regulating teaching strategies to realise the teaching procedure's accuracy (Lameras, 2022).

CONCLUSION

As we wrap up our exploration of how artificial intelligence is reshaping our education system, one thing is clear: AI is not just a tool, but a transformative force. It revolutionizes how we teach and learn, opening up once unimaginable possibilities. The future of education, with AI at its core, is promising. Our exploration revealed that AI serves as a valuable aid for both teachers and students. It tailors learning experiences to suit each student's preferences and requirements, thereby enhancing the learning process's effectiveness and engagement. For teachers, AI offers a wealth of insights into their students' performance, empowering them to provide necessary support and guidance.

Furthermore, AI ushered in a new era of inclusivity in education. It transcends geographical and cultural barriers, making learning accessible to all, regardless of origin or location. AI's adaptability of AI allows for personalized learning plans, enabling individuals to learn at their own pace from anywhere in the world. Inclusive features of AI, particularly in the context of learning and teaching, ensure that everyone can access quality education. Although AI presents numerous benefits, it also poses challenges that cannot be overlooked. As discussed, issues such as bias, privacy, and overreliance on technology are significant concerns. While AI undoubtedly offers advantages to students, it is crucial to acknowledge and address these challenges to ensure that AI is a tool that benefits all without leaving anyone behind.

Even though AI's future of AI is bright regarding education, we must be cautious of its dangers. There is no harm to exploring AI's benefits and how it can enhance our education system, but we must be mindful of its dangers. It is important to strike a balance between utilizing AI as an apparatus to assist learning and maintaining human touch, which is becoming lost because of the overuse of AI. We can see drastic and amazing developments in the upcoming years of AI-powered education. However, it is crucial to consider treating it ethically and responsibly as a tool to create a brighter education. Thus, AI can potentially improve education, but it is important to approach its inclusion thoughtfully and with a focus on inclusion and equity. Keeping these points in mind, we can foster the potency of AI to create better, more accessible, personalized, and engaging learning experiences for all.

CASE STUDY

This case study examines how Stanford University, a top-tier university with a commitment, has taken the initiative to nurture innovation and academic performance by incorporating artificial intelligence into its learning and teaching models. A mix of qualitative and quantitative methods, such as surveys, interviews, and performance data collection, will be employed to explore the process of adoption, results, and challenges of AI at Stanford. The University seeks to develop educational initiatives by bringing AI-driven adaptive learning platforms, intelligent tutoring systems, and personalized learning experiences to Stanford, which can produce better academic results, and engage and empower instructors. (Mousavi, 2019)

This study sheds light on the opportunities and ramifications for incorporating AI in higher educational institutions. Therefore, it is important for higher education institutions to consider these findings and embrace technological innovations. Among the top universities in the world, Stanford University is constantly searching for ways to innovate and optimize the student experience. To this end, Stanford has undertaken a transformative endeavor by including artificial intelligence in teaching. This case study investigates Stanford's pioneering work on the utilization of AI in education. (Goel, A.K, 2017)

Higher education and AI often suggest that “AI can bring effective changes in the traditional college and university operating model”. Specifically, AI-powered adaptive systems use the information provided by students to deliver personalized information and test items, as Stanford has employed. Intelligent tutoring systems utilize different machine-learning algorithms to offer personalized support and feedback to students. Moreover, AI-driven learning experiences empower students to gain full control over their learning journey, determine their own pace, and focus on areas of interest .(Whittaker, 2018). This chapter argues that AI-driven teaching and learning approaches guarantee enhanced student engagement and academic performance and empower faculty members to realize their potential. The impact of artificial intelligence on academic outcomes and student learning was evaluated at Stanford University by examining performance data such as course completion rates and grades. This case study found that students reported satisfaction and increased engagement with AI-driven learning opportunities. Intelligent tutoring systems and adaptive learning platforms assist students by providing personalized feedback and support, which leads to high academic motivation and achievement levels. (Mousavi, 2019)

Furthermore, academic data revealed significant improvements in student outcomes, with higher grades and increased consistency observed in courses utilizing advanced AI. Importantly, faculty members reported a heightened sense of engagement, as AI tools empowered them to provide more targeted guidance and offer personalized assistance to students. (Goel, A.K, 2017). This contextual analysis highlights the extraordinary effect of artificial intelligence on advanced education at Stanford College. Stanford positioned itself at the forefront of educational institutions by utilizing artificial intelligence-driven learning and education techniques, empowering its faculty members, and improving student outcomes. Propelling ahead, continued interest in AI research and development, along with comprehensive professional development for faculty, will be fundamental to maintaining and scaling artificial intelligence drives in advanced education. (Mousavi, 2019). Overall, the case study of Stanford College demonstrates the tremendous potential of artificial intelligence techniques for computer-based learning in education. By embracing computer-based intelligence-driven techniques, Stanford has situated itself at the bleeding edge of instructive development, preparing for improved under-study results and personnel strengthening. As foundations overall explore the intricacies of artificial intelligence.

REFERENCES

Carter, R. A.Jr, Rice, M., Yang, S., & Jackson, H. A. (2020). Self-regulated learning in online learning environments: Strategies for remote learning. *Information and Learning Science*, 121(5/6), 321–329. DOI:10.1108/ILS-04-2020-0114

Christensen, R., Hillaire, G., Marvez, G. R., Azukas, M. E., Holben, D., Gregory, S., & Ledger, S. (2022, April). Using Virtual Simulations in Teacher Education to Develop Equitable Teaching Strategies. In *Society for Information Technology & Teacher Education International Conference* (pp. 412-416). Association for the Advancement of Computing in Education (AACE).

Clancey, W. J., Bennett, J., & Cohen, P. R. (1979). *Applications-oriented AI research: Education*. Computer Science Department, Stanford University.

Ghai, B., Liao, Q. V., Zhang, Y., Bellamy, R., & Mueller, K. (2021). Explainable active learning (xal) toward ai explanations as interfaces for machine teachers. *Proceedings of the ACM on Human-Computer Interaction, 4*(CSCW3), 1-28.

Goel, A. K., & Joyner, D. A. (2017). Using AI to teach AI: Lessons from an online AI class. *AI Magazine*, 38(2), 48–59. DOI:10.1609/aimag.v38i2.2732

Lameras, P. (2022, March). A Vision of Teaching and Learning with AI. In *2022 IEEE Global Engineering Education Conference (EDUCON)* (pp. 1796-1803). IEEE. DOI:10.1109/EDUCON52537.2022.9766718

Lantz, J. L., Liu, J. C., & Basnyat, I. (2022). Piloting Artificial Intelligence (AI) to Facilitate Online Discussion in Large Online Classes: A Case Study. In *Cases on Innovative and Successful Uses of Digital Resources for Online Learning* (pp. 204-222). IGI Global.

Luan, H., & Tsai, C. C. (2021). A review of using machine learning approaches for precision education. *Journal of Educational Technology & Society*, 24(1), 250–266.

Luckin, R., & Holmes, W. (2016). Intelligence unleashed: An argument for AI in education.

Luger, G. F. (1998). *Artificial Intelligence: Structures and Strategies for Complex Problem Solving, 5/e*. Pearson Education India.

Martins, R. M., & Gresse Von Wangenheim, C. (2022). *Findings on Teaching Machine Learning in High School: A Ten-Year Systematic Literature Review*. Informatics in Education.

Murphy, R. F. (2019). Artificial intelligence applications to support K-12 teachers and teaching. *Rand Corporation, 10*.

Ng, T. K. (2021). New interpretation of extracurricular activities via social networking sites: A case study of artificial intelligence learning at a secondary school in Hong Kong. *Journal of Education and Training Studies*, 9(1), 49–60. DOI:10.11114/jets.v9i1.5105

Papa, R., & Jackson, K. M. (2021). AI Transforms Twentieth-Century Learning. In *Artificial Intelligence, Human Agency and the Educational Leader* (pp. 1–32). Springer. DOI:10.1007/978-3-030-77610-7_1

Rerhaye, L., Altun, D., Krauss, C., & Müller, C. (2021, July). Evaluation Methods for an AI-Supported Learning Management System: Quantifying and Qualifying Added Values for Teaching and Learning. In *International Conference on Human-Computer Interaction* (pp. 394-411). Springer. DOI:10.1007/978-3-030-77857-6_28

Sekeroglu, B., Dimililer, K., & Tuncal, K. (2019, March). Student performance prediction and classification using machine learning algorithms. In *Proceedings of the 2019 8th International Conference on Educational and Information Technology* (pp. 7-11). DOI:10.1145/3318396.3318419

Slimi, Z., & Carballido, B. V. (2023). Navigating the Ethical Challenges of Artificial Intelligence in Higher Education: An Analysis of Seven Global AI Ethics Policies. *TEM Journal, 12*(2).

Tariq, M. U. (2024a). Emotional intelligence in understanding and influencing consumer behavior. In Musiolik, T., Rodriguez, R., & Kannan, H. (Eds.), *AI impacts in digital consumer behavior* (pp. 56–81). IGI Global. DOI:10.4018/979-8-3693-1918-5.ch003

Tariq, M. U. (2024b). Fintech startups and cryptocurrency in business: Revolutionizing entrepreneurship. In Kankaew, K., Nakpathom, P., Chnitphattana, A., Pitchayadejanant, K., & Kunnapapdeelert, S. (Eds.), *Applying business intelligence and innovation to entrepreneurship* (pp. 106–124). IGI Global. DOI:10.4018/979-8-3693-1846-1.ch006

Tariq, M. U. (2024c). Multidisciplinary service learning in higher education: Concepts, implementation, and impact. In S. Watson (Ed.), *Applications of service learning in higher education* (pp. 1-19). IGI Global. DOI:10.4018/979-8-3693-2133-1.ch001

Tariq, M. U. (2024d). Enhancing cybersecurity protocols in modern healthcare systems: Strategies and best practices. In Garcia, M., & de Almeida, R. (Eds.), *Transformative approaches to patient literacy and healthcare innovation* (pp. 223–241). IGI Global. DOI:10.4018/979-8-3693-3661-8.ch011

Tariq, M. U. (2024e). Advanced wearable medical devices and their role in transformative remote health monitoring. In Garcia, M., & de Almeida, R. (Eds.), *Transformative approaches to patient literacy and healthcare innovation* (pp. 308–326). IGI Global. DOI:10.4018/979-8-3693-3661-8.ch015

Tariq, M. U. (2024f). Leveraging artificial intelligence for a sustainable and climate-neutral economy in Asia. In Ordóñez de Pablos, P., Almunawar, M., & Anshari, M. (Eds.), *Strengthening sustainable digitalization of Asian economy and society* (pp. 1–21). IGI Global. DOI:10.4018/979-8-3693-1942-0.ch001

Tariq, M. U. (2024g). Metaverse in business and commerce. In Kumar, J., Arora, M., & Erkol Bayram, G. (Eds.), *Exploring the use of metaverse in business and education* (pp. 47–72). IGI Global. DOI:10.4018/979-8-3693-5868-9.ch004

Vazhayil, A., Shetty, R., Bhavani, R. R., & Akshay, N. (2019, December). Focusing on teacher education to introduce AI in schools: Perspectives and illustrative findings. In *2019 IEEE tenth international conference on Technology for Education (T4E)* (pp. 71-77). IEEE.

Weisz, J. D., Jain, M., Joshi, N. N., Johnson, J., & Lange, I. (2019, March). BigBlueBot: teaching strategies for successful human-agent interactions. In *Proceedings of the 24th International Conference on Intelligent User Interfaces* (pp. 448-459). DOI:10.1145/3301275.3302290

Yang, S. J. (2021). Precision education-a new challenge for AI in education. *Journal of Educational Technology & Society*, 24(1).

Younes, S. S. (2021). Examining the Effectiveness of Using Adaptive AI-Enabled e-Learning during the Pandemic of COVID-19. *Journal of Healthcare Engineering*, 2021, 2021. DOI:10.1155/2021/3928326 PMID:34567481

Zhou, J. (2020, October). Design of AI-based self-learning platform for college english listening. In *2020 2nd International Conference on Machine Learning, Big Data and Business Intelligence (MLBDBI)* (pp. 544-547). IEEE. DOI:10.1109/MLBDBI51377.2020.00114

ADDITIONAL READING

Xu, S., Alturki, R., Rehman, A. U., & Tariq, M. U. (2021). BP neural network combination prediction for big data enterprise energy management system. *Mobile Networks and Applications*, 26(1), 184–190. DOI:10.1007/s11036-020-01698-x

Zhang, H., Babar, M., Tariq, M. U., Jan, M. A., Menon, V. G., & Li, X. (2020). Safe-City: Toward safe and secured data management design for IoT-enabled smart city planning. *IEEE Access : Practical Innovations, Open Solutions*, 8, 145256–145267. DOI:10.1109/ACCESS.2020.3014622

Zhu, X., Zhu, Y., Li, L., Pan, S., Tariq, M. U., & Jan, M. A. (2021). Ioht-enabled gliomas disease management using fog computing computing for sustainable societies. *Sustainable Cities and Society*, 74, 103215. DOI:10.1016/j.scs.2021.103215

Ziyambe, B., Yahya, A., Mushiri, T., Tariq, M. U., Abbas, Q., Babar, M., Albathan, M., Asim, M., Hussain, A., & Jabbar, S. (2023). A deep learning framework for the prediction and diagnosis of ovarian cancer in pre- and post-menopausal women. *Diagnostics (Basel)*, 13(10), 1703. DOI:10.3390/diagnostics13101703 PMID:37238188

KEY TERMS AND DEFINITIONS

AI-Fueled Flexible Learning Systems: AI-driven platforms that tailor educational experiences to individual students.

Customised Development Opportunities: AI-enabled personalised learning approaches that focus on offering students' development pathways.

Distributed Cognitive Theory: A framework that views cognition as distributed across people, tools, and environments.

Smart Teaching Media: Innovative AI-powered tools that offer customised learning environments, integrating virtual and real-world experiences.

Technology Revolution Theory: A perspective that sees the integration of AI in education as a continuous innovation process.

Chapter 9
Online and Self-Paced Learning Using AI

ABSTRACT

The chapter investigates the transformative effect of manufactured insights (AI) on instruction, especially within online and self-paced learning modalities. This chapter comprehensively examines AI-driven innovations and their applications, and explains the centrality, challenges, and suggestions for joining AI in instructive settings. Key topics include personalized learning, versatile input and appraisal, proactive analytics, virtual mentoring, and moral contemplation. Drawing on real-world cases and case studies, this chapter highlights the role of AI in optimizing learning encounters, improving learner engagement, and cultivating deep-rooted learning propensities.

INTRODUCTION

The alteration brought about by AI by changing how individuals learn abilities and information has ended the history of instruction. The chapter "Online and self-paced learning using AI, will highlight the extended extent of instructive devices implanted in AI innovations. This chapter examines the complex linkage between AI and Internet-based free-learning frameworks. It gives nitty gritty examination questions and concluding comments supporting its meaning, challenges, and promising set of three in numerous areas (Yan H 2021). AI, one of the most conspicuous instructional innovations, is becoming increasingly prevalent among teachers, instructors, and chairpersons. Manufactured insights, counting components of machine learning, common dialect handling, and profound learning calculations have affected different ranges of human exercise, such as instruction. AI has risen as an instrument for making instruction more learner-oriented, versatile, and including, in this way, fulfilling the present-day societal request for adaptable learning modalities

DOI: 10.4018/979-8-3693-4074-5.ch009

and modern advanced instructive stages through intelligent calculations; AI, too, makes a difference in creating supplementary learning courses that coordinate one's learning propensities, pace, and coordinate capability (Waheed, 2023).

AI frameworks in computerized and self-paced learning modes apply information investigation and predictive demonstrations to determine pupils' qualities, inadequacies, and learning designs. Through this understanding, the AI calculations center on substance conveyance, suggestions of extra materials, and on-the-fly criticism, in this way creating a smooth and commonsense learning environment built upon flow and responsiveness. One significant highlight of AI-enabled online instruction is customized learning, wherein guidelines, substance and learning exercises are redone to meet each learner's special needs and inclinations. Through versatile learning frameworks, AI calculations dissect learners' intuition, execution information, and cognitive profiles to tailor instructional substances, pacing, and appraisals. For instance, versatile learning stages such as Khan Foundation and Duolingo use AI calculations to alter the trouble level of works based on learners' capability and authority of concepts (Kazemitabaar, 2023).

Through platform learning encounters and focusing on mediation, AI-driven customized learning improves subject matter engagement, maintenance, and authority. In expansion to customized substance conveyance, AI encourages versatile criticism and appraisal instruments, expanding the adequacy of online and self-paced learning. Through characteristic dialect preparation and assumption examination, AI calculations observe learners' comprehension levels, misguided judgments, trouble ranges, empowering opportune, and custom-fitted input. For example, chatbot-based coaching frameworks such as Carnegie Learning's Mika give moment input and direction to learners, reenacting their interaction with human guides. By examining learners' reactions and thinking forms, AI-powered coaching frameworks analyze misguided judgments, offer remediation techniques, and platform problem-solving abilities, thereby cultivating metacognitive mindfulness and self-regulated learning (Shi et al., 2020).

Moreover, AI engages teachers and direction architects with proactive analytics and learning analytics apparatuses to screen learner advancement, anticipate execution results, and enhance direction techniques. Through information mining procedures and prescient displays, AI calculations determine learners' future execution directions, distinguish at-risk understudies, and suggest focused interventions. For example, learning administration frameworks (LMS) such as Moodle or Canvas embrace AI-driven analytics dashboards that offer assistance in comparing learners' engagement designs through their entries and test scores. These analytics apparatuses permit teachers to see diverse sorts of information assembled and, after that, spot things, the patterns, and the line between them, informing the decision-making intercessions within the instructing preparation (Aleven, V 2022).

In addition, AI goes with virtual coaching and mentoring that interfaces with inaccessible ranges and separations that physical schools cannot reach. Conversational specialists, such as IBM Watson Mentor and Sana Labs' Guide, provide locks in virtual coaching encounters through normal dialect exchanges, in which they reply to questions, offer clarifications, and framework problem-solving forms. For occurrence, a coach from Sana Labs receives a versatile fortification learning procedure that provides customized learning methods by building certainty and dynamically utilizing the learning show through challenges and bolstering the framework. Through understudies mimicking one-to-one engagement with AI guide robots, virtual coaching frameworks utilize the idea of AI adaptability and availability to extend the correspondence of instructive quality, particularly in underprivileged areas (Srisa-An, 2019).

While AI in online and customized learning is not free from moral implications and issues, it could be an extraordinary improvement that will affect how understudies learn. Investigations into information storage issues, spreading algorithmic predisposition, and computerized imbalance call for moral AI, data administration straightforwardness, and comprehensive instructional plans. AI calculations might resound the show inclinations in official instruction information for this case and reduce the existing instructive score crevice between distinctive ethnicities or races. A framework of reasonable calculations depends on solid measures of information anonymization, inclination location, and algorithmic straightforwardness. This step guarantees that the instruction frameworks affected by AI are reasonable (Pan, L 2020).

AI-mediated intuition includes a few moral contemplations, from customizing information to reducing human control in learning. The challenge is to blend AI automation's anticipated productivity and progressed education with earlier human-centered instruction. Care intercessions and moral rules within the mechanization preparation must maintain learners' independence, nobility, and all-encompassing well-being (Yang et al., 2020).

Long-term AI in eLearning and self-paced learning appears very empowering because it will change instruction, move the proportion of available seats to understudy, and advance long-lasting learning. One of the current innovations is to get way past the window ornaments of time and space. AR, VR, and blockchain innovations use modern openings for intuitive and immersive learning. For instance, instructive apps like Google Undertakings and Microsoft HoloLens improve information procurement by picturing, holding, and watching 3D models for all intents and purposes in the learner's additional eyes. Their fundamental advantage is that they make certain places, components, or circumstances distinctive and unmistakable; thus, they offer assistance to learners who cannot create masters' abilities to capture their viable encounters effectively. Blockchain innovation speaks to the key to decentralized learning ventures such as ODEM and BitDegree, which, among other things, make a difference in the learner's recording of a pathway, confirming the accreditations, outlining learning ways, and giving a long-lasting decentralized learning pathway (Kazemitabaar, 2023).

In this way, “AI in online and self-driven instruction” is a portion of executing these AI advances into customized learning, versatile input, proactive analytics, virtual coaching, and moral instruction. The AI (Counterfeit Insights) empowered advances would enable instructors and policymakers to take part in creating instructive frameworks. They will also be able to create a culture of never-ending learning, as increasingly understudies are empowered by technology. Furthermore, they will guarantee that the instruction becomes increasingly reasonable and comprehensive (Tariq, 2024).

BACKGROUND

In the last few years, the educational area has experienced a remarkable shift in the use of technology, with a desire to bridge the gap between technology and learning, thus creating and empowering more avenues for learning. Amid this digital movement, artificial intelligence (AI) has emerged as the main force shaping the new landscape of education and dealing with both online and independent learning. This introduction describes, in detail, the overlap between AI and educational modules regarding its role, outlook, and the impact it might have on learners, educators, and society in general (Waheed, 2023).

Artificial intelligence (AI), which includes machine learning, natural language processing, and deep learning, has been used in various industries for years to solve problems in healthcare, financial markets, entertainment, and transportation systems. Regarding education, AI can facilitate the transformation of conventional teaching approaches, widening access to quality learning resources for all, and, eventually, implementing the student-centered teaching and learning process, which involves personalization, personalization, adaptation, and immersion; online and self-paced learning is often combined with AI, specifically synchronizing with the modern learner's needs, such as the flexibility, availability, and personalization of personalization in educational tracks suited to every individual's timeline, interest, and learning style. Thus, AI-powered models can control and optimize educational platforms by analyzing enormous amounts of data, learning the habits of learners, and offering detailed interventions, resulting in improved learning outcomes, learner involvement, and dedication (Kazemitabaar, 2023).

AI-assisted online learning is characterized by the capacity to provide custom learning experiences with varying intensities of personal touch, reflecting the distinctive characteristics of each learner. Utilizing various AI algorithms, learning systems can analyze learners' behavior while considering performance data and cognitive patterns to adjust the instructional content, pace of learning, and assessments in an on-the-fly manner. A student-centric learning environment is created by platforms such as Coursera or Udacity, where AI algorithms are used to customize the difficulty level of completed exercises, offer suggestions for further reading, or provide individualized feedback based on the students' progress and proficiency in an area (Waheed, 2023). In addition, AI opens up the options of advanced feedback and assessments, proving to be a key that enables teachers to make adjustments to instructions promptly, given misconceptions by learners and learning gaps. Through Natural Language Processing and Sentiment Analysis abilities of Artificial Intelligence algorithms, digital tutors will be able to read learners' responses, spot mistakes, and provide advice tailored to the situation, thus imitating the interaction with human tutors. For example, AI-powered tutoring systems, such as Carnegie Learning's Mika, provide learners with instant feedback and guidance, nurturing metacognitive awareness, and self-regulation (Zhu, 2021).

Moreover, AI enables teachers and administrators to use predictive analytics and learning insights, which allows them to spend more time evaluating and providing feedback to students, foresee outcomes, and apply the most appropriate instruction methods. AI algorithms, with the help of data mining techniques and predictive models, project the future performance trajectories of learners; they identify students who are dropping out with the help of these algorithms and recommend targeted interventions to overcome learning difficulties. For instance, learning management systems (LMS) such as Moodle and Blackboard implement AI-powered analytics dashboards that provide insights into how learners interact with the system and display submission patterns and quiz scorons on an attractive dashboard. Through the collective analysis of disparate data sources, educators can quickly identify patterns, trends, and correlations, which will assist in the development of instructional strategies and pedagogical sessions. In addition, AI's machine learning analytics results in the provision of numerous data about the learners' learning patterns, preferences, and the factors that drive them, and in the end, this helps in the development of more engaging and effective learning designs (Godwin 2007; Tariq, 2024).

Furthermore, AI allows Internet tutoring and functions as an indefinite mentor unscathed by the temporal and spatial limitations of traditional education. Smart virtual tutoring systems which provide learners with conversation agents communicating with them in their native language, explaining things while guiding the problem-solving process, and making the educational process fascinating and engaging. For instance, the IBM Watson Tutor and the Mentor of Sana Lab combine natural language processing techniques and machine learning algorithms to simulate tutor-like protocols with human tutors, which adapt to learners and give them personal guidance and support. AI-based virtual tutoring systems are equipped with the advantages of scalability and accessibility of AI to democratize the quality of education even in communities with limited human tutors, resulting in education in deprived areas. Humanizing the sentence: On-demand assistance and scaffolding learning procedures allow AI-driven online grownups to learn how to cope with tackling difficult subjects, develop critical thinking skills, and succeed in diverse subjects (Yang et al., 2020; Tariq, 2024).

Nonetheless, AI web-based and independent learning applications present ethical problems over which it is wise. Privacy issues, biases inherent in AI systems, and digital divides overwhelm ethical considerations in AI design, transparent governance of data, and fair education opportunities. For example, AI systems may show biased tendencies based upon data reflecting implicit biases, thus perpetuating educational disparity among various demographic groups. Tackling algorithmic bias needs effective tools for anonymous data, bias detection, and algorithmic reliability, providing a just environment for equitability and representativeness in AI-based educational systems. Another issue is that AI-mediated learning becomes more humanitarian, posing ethical dilemmas, such as depersonalization and diminishing learners' powerfulness. Deliberate design interventions and ethical guidelines are needed to give learners the same human-centered pedagogy as AI automation in terms of both learners' self-dependence and emotional well-being. The infusion of AI into the Internet and self-taught schooling signifies a radical shift in the educational world because it increases learning personalization, personalization, adaptiveness, and immersion. Utilizing AI assistive principles, education authorities can create a lifelong learning environment that lifts learners socially and makes the educational system more equitable in the digital era (Shi et al., 2020).

Industrial transformation has brought about significant modifications to the education system. Reading and math skills have become more vital as factory jobs replaced agricultural work. National higher education switched to a factory model, where learners attained the best ability to support factories. The evolving revolution in artificial intelligence could guide the same significant switch in how universities teach, and students attain learning. Since the middle of the twentieth century, higher education has emphasised specialisation by learning less. However, in times of progressing automation, particular knowledge quickly becomes outdated. Students gradually come from diverse backgrounds and age groups (Waheed, 2023). They require learning new skills and relearning previous skills throughout diversified careers. In the coming years, online and self-paced learning will become available for each person, and artificial intelligence could help bring it there. Whether the public can observe or not, the education system is experiencing a transformation, and it will look considerably different from what the world knows in the present. This alteration has been in process for years, with queries regarding the efficiency of regular testing, customised lessons, and class size. With the arrival of robotics and artificial intelligence in students' home spaces and classrooms, the world is just beginning to witness a substantial revolution (Yang et al., 2020).

ONLINE LEARNING

Online learning has already attained a significant lift from artificial intelligence, only through interconnection. Online delivery courses have decreased costs, reduced discrimination, and enhanced graduation rates in higher education. Artificial intelligence transformation could, in turn, make online learning cheaper, smarter, and faster. This has already begun (Yan and Lin, 2021). Three significant types of artificial intelligence using online learning.

Adaptive Learning

Adaptive learning is an education software that is personalised according to the individuality of each student, such that ideas are presented in the order a specific student finds uncomplicated to recognise and has the ability to be concluded in a self-set-time. Presently, adaptive learning frameworks work when a large group of students has to learn the same content, permitting a significant amount of similar data to be accumulated concurrently. Their evolution could be seen at a much lower level. Overall, adaptive learning methods will make learning more personalised, quick, and intelligent (Woods, 2022).

Smart Tutoring Systems

Smart tutoring systems are artificial-intelligence-driven solutions that are personalised to match each student's requirements and abilities. These systems can drastically reduce costs, while simultaneously enhancing the success rate. There is artificial intelligence software that involves an artificial intelligence-driven writing module that rectifies grammar, punctuation, and spelling while also looking for plagiarism and encouraging correct citation, and even offers an initial grade on a paper. These systems, at their best, do not substitute teachers, but instead move instructors to the mentor role (Zhou et al., 2022).

Virtual Enablers

Suppose chatbots and video games have a baby; the objective is not a high score or a consumer service question's resolution but evolving a user's learning. This is the forthcoming reality for virtual enablers. Some innovative institutes are already knowledgeable about developing artificial intelligence-driven three-dimensional environments and lifelike virtual characters; they have also created prototypes for virtual psychotherapy. Further research on "Captivating Virtual Instruction for Training (CVIT) targets to unite live classroom sessions with intelligent tutors, virtual instructors, and augmented reality. IBM's Watson currently has a virtual teaching assistant, Jill Watson. First initiated at Georgia Tech in a subject named "Knowledge-Based Artificial Intelligence", Jill is involved in a classroom session's online discussion medium, replying to student queries with other human teaching assistants. In some situations, she outpaces her human co-workers by replying more quickly than them. Even in 2016, Georgia Tech Students could not distinguish which of the teaching assistants was an artificial intelligence program. The future is not as distant as the world believes (Liu et al., 2021; Tariq, 2024).

Implementation of Artificial Intelligence in Remote Learning

This is still the initial day for artificial intelligence-driven online learning, and personal development is baked into the procedure. Artificial intelligence systems are more translucent than human instructors; one can effortlessly review and assess the thought process behind a learning moment. As more artificial intelligence systems are implemented, they will get more data to use, although that data should be accumulated in a transparent, secure, and ethical manner. These tools will become more flexible, efficient, and natural over time. With enhanced artificial intelligence-powered online learning, students will be able to learn more quickly than ever before and will be progressively capable of learning skills that will be useful for them in the future. Future advancements in artificial intelligence-driven learning must first emphasise and primarily meet the requirements of people who utilise it. These people were teachers and students. Further advances are required to incorporate these novel innovations into the present system. Artificial intelligence developers, students, and teachers still have much to learn in the future (Li et al., 2018).

Self-Paced Learning

Self-paced learning refers to the context in which students can learn according to their preferred times and schedules. They do not have to finish their assignments or learn simultaneously as other people learn the same course. Students can continue from one topic or section to the next at their own speed. Classroom settings are more common than self-paced learning in which employees can learn independently. Currently, self-paced learning has become widespread as higher education switches from conventional models to the internet (Eimer et al., 2021). Self-paced learning has various benefits that can improve employees' performance. The following are some advantages.

More Retention, No Pressure

There was no pressure to complete the assignments. Self-paced learning eradicates the time pressure present during live classes. There is no stress in completing the assignments and attaining learning simultaneously. No one must pretend that they have learned something that they did not. Rather, they can analyse the materials themselves. According to some researchers, there is a possibility that self-paced learning might also raise retention (Shi et al., 2020).

Learners Can Then Fix Their Schedules

Self-paced learning allows employees to prepare timetables. This is particularly beneficial for learners who have other jobs and cannot join a live training session or class. Even if there is a time limit to finish a course, they can choose when and how to take it (Soviany et al., 2021). When employees prepare their learning timetables, they can study when they focus better. They can select when they experience fewer disturbances from other jobs or colleagues. Of course, this requires self-discipline to finish. They must neglect interruptions at home and avoid their phones (Corrin & Bakharia, 2020). Individuals have different learning styles. Some people learn quickly, whereas others require more time. Individuals who choose a complete course quickly should not wait for others. Self-paced learning allows learners to adjust to their learning styles (Chen & Ifenthaler, 2021).

Implementation in Universities

Online methods support universities implementing self-paced learning in their education services. They allow the higher education department to develop and host training content that students can access conveniently. Instructors can record in-person training sessions and broadcast them online. The financial resources spent on a learning management system will save the university time and money. Setting up additional training sessions requires various university resources. An optimal solution is an online learning platform, in which all classroom materials are present. All of the content will be accessible with just some clicks. Instructors can add time limits to the content, but students can still learn at their own pace and according to their timetables. The financial resources spent on a learning management system will save the university time and money. These learning systems make people more knowledgeable (Mullen et al., 2019).

Possibility With a Learning Management System

It is easy to prepare and share several assessments and courses using a learning-management system. Universities provide sharing techniques for self-paced consumption. Higher education institutes can share the link to their content, publish it on their websites, or offer students safely via email. If instructors wish, they can set a time limit to complete the task. There is also a choice to give students several times to complete a task. Students can opt to take their classes through smartphones outside their work hours. Subsequently, instructors can assess their statistics and results and learn to enhance their teaching content. Self-paced learning resolves timing problems and lets students learn at their own pace. This solves various problems (Li et al., 2020).

Artificial Intelligence Benefit

To improve the present teaching framework in which the instructor is the source of learning, and the student is the beneficiary, there is a requirement to reimagine the role of an instructor in the university system. Advancements in automated assessment grading and remote monitoring services have allowed teachers to decline monotonous, time-intensive jobs and devote their time to higher-priority tasks. Artificial intelligence-powered learning management systems can implement surveys for instructors who do not progress in a classroom setting. They can classify students into distinctive learning, such as text, visual, and auditory, which can offer efficient and targeted material for each chosen learning style. Beyond the recognition of inclinations, the media can also break down long-form lessons and reading assessments into shorter, atomic components that are easily absorbable. For international students, language obstacles may confuse their progress. Nevertheless, a cutting-edge study in machine learning and text translation intends to create deep-learning systems that can translate English lessons into students' native tongues. The same technologies in text summarisation and voice recognition can record an entire lesson with spectacular precision and decrease text paragraphs into just the related key points for assessment. Machine-learning algorithms can be implemented over a subject curriculum to flag parts of bias, complications, and uncertainty for closer assessment by the instructor. The hike is slow, but teachers, students, and administrators will undoubtedly gain the advantages of artificial intelligence as it progresses and matures over the next ten years. Whether this domain will be interrupted by a technology company, research institute, or university remains under discussion (Bao et al., 2018).

Why Should Artificial Intelligence Be Used in E-Learning?

Corporate training models exhibit standard challenges involving the following:

- Most conventional learning programs are still prepared for long-term units. In addition, preparing such a material for an hour requires too many hours. Making an hour of such learning content requires many hours. It overpowers people easily (Goel et al., 2020).
- Because learning material preparation is time-consuming, online learning courses are generally too general and do not adjust to the particular requirements of each student (Li et al., 2018).
- Measuring the ROI rate of conventional teaching includes time-consuming data accumulation and entry procedures (Soviany et al., 2021).
- It does not counterpart the digital workforce's current expectations and requirements; training is no longer a first move that happens once or twice a year, but is a continuous process. Currently, employees primarily involving millennials and Gen Z choose to self-manage their learning experiences. Implementing artificial intelligence in business training and online learning courses resolves many of these issues (Yan & Lin, 2021).

The Way Artificial Intelligence Is Revolutionizing the Online Learning Sector

Firms are progressively identifying the prospects of utilising artificial intelligence in learning and development. According to some studies, almost thirty-seven percent of firms have adopted some artificial intelligence, depicting a massive two hundred and seventy percent rise over the previous four years. Furthermore, some researchers predict that by 2024 eighty-five percent of the technologies will depend on artificial intelligence (Soviany et al., 2021). The following are some ways of using AI to revolutionise the e-learning industry:

Customised Learning Roadmaps

Offer the correct material to the right individual at the correct time. Personalisation is no longer just a wish of the contemporary workplace; it is a prospect. Workers want materials with customised experience in which they are in the leading role. Online learning media that use artificial intelligence can personalise material depending on each student's previous knowledge and instead require a one-size-fits-all technique. Customised or adaptive learning is a data-based method that constantly optimises each student's progress, utilising machine learning algorithms to forecast outcomes and adjust the material to reveal each student's preferences and expertise. Thus, suppose a student attempts to learn a new skill. In this case, the medium will commence adjusting the content and difficulty stages depending on their performance until they have learned the concept. Formulating a customised learning route for each student with related subjects not only enhances time effectiveness, but also enhances students' motivation levels. For example, to learn a topic, employees require various standpoints on what they are learning, particularly on complicated subjects. In mechanical engineering, to design an intrinsic combustion engine, a learner must recognise the working procedure of the engine, its parts, and how it functions. They must observe various models and assess how each situation works inversely, but follow the same regulations, and complete the same function to have a deep understanding. The procedure was not linear and was not similar for all students. One student may find it quicker to watch and apply a video in real life (Chen & Ifenthaler, 2021).

In contrast, another may find it simpler to see a visual blueprint and another may comprehend it by reading a detailed explanation of how it functions. In the learning of other subjects, it functions in the same manner; it is not sufficient with one method to thoroughly learn a concept. Various techniques, the way they are used, and the extent to which the learner must depend on each one from one individual to another. With the conventional teaching approach, there is a single learning roadmap, and the instruction explains the order of content equally for all learners. Content is essential and not adjusted according to the interests of each individual. If integrating online learning media is an initial step toward developing more efficient business progress systems, then the second step is artificial intelligence implementation. The material is adjusted through data assessment of employee function in learning media, and customised learning paths and material suggestions are provided to every student, depending on their role preferences and previous performance. The outcome is an active, versatile, customised, and efficient training method that adjusts as a living organism to the requirements of each employee and supports them in the process of being the administrator of their learning (Li et al., 2018).

Enhanced Decision-Making: Advanced Analytics

When assessing employees' progress, instructors and training administrators face general limitations; they take too long, and the information is not comprehensive enough. Using an artificial intelligence-powered online platform, it is possible to promptly assess massive amounts of data and recognise trends and patterns to constantly enhance and optimise learning experiences. Content analytics mainly refers to online learning media that uses artificial intelligence, especially machine learning, to enhance learning units. In this business, leaders can develop and manage their online learning materials and acquire vital information about student growth and recognition via powerful data analytics. Artificial intelligence allows instructors, learning, and development to attain complete detail about every student's performance, attendance problems, struggling domains, and strengths. This makes it simpler to make decisions and can optimise and take action before the employee is not inspired to commence and drop the course (Goel et al., 2020).

Prepare Online Learning Courses in Less Time

Conventionally, for subject matter specialists and instructional plan experts, course preparation is one of the most time-consuming tasks. Fortunately, using artificial intelligence in online learning makes the course preparation procedure much more complicated, quick, and responsive, without requiring risk quality. The localisation and automatic translation feature is a notable example of how artificial intelligence improves the online learning development procedure by providing greater efficiency and speed. Translating online learning materials is not a simple task when standard development techniques are used. As a significant amount of material must be prepared, making this same material available for several languages becomes even more time-consuming and costly. However, with artificial intelligence, it is now possible to prepare multilanguage material for international firms facing the issue of developing beneficial material for branches in various countries or for the progressively typical situation of firms functioning with remote groups that speak different languages. Firms can decrease the time involved in the localisation of an online learning program by months to days using authorising tools. This will help enhance the development procedure for projects that require materials accessible in different languages (Yan & Lin, 2021).

Prolonged Involvement: Virtual Instructions and Chatbots to Assist Students

Assessments can be done quickly, and procedure explorations from students and employees can be conducted in real-time by using artificial intelligence to accelerate the learning procedure. An instance might be a chatbot that determines what question to ask a learner depending on the learner's prior answers, such as adding queries in domains where the learner has had the most wrong answers or jumping to a high level when the student constantly enters the right answers. Another standard use is to answer easy questions: the artificial intelligence algorithm may obtain basic details that a new contributor may require. It can be exhibited as an intelligent chatbot that assesses and responds to employee questions and conversational text messages. Virtual assistants can support instructors and students like chatbots by replying to questions that might have been sent directly to the instructor or by supporting students in steering course content in a friendly manner. Additionally, online learning medium that utilizes chatbots become an instructor for students to assist them every step of the way—for example, supporting them in determining related resources dependent on their topics and profile of interest by recommending several learning assets. It eliminates the manual effort and time required to perform these tasks (Goel et al., 2020).

Over the previous four years, the use of this technology in the training and development sector boosted by forty-eight percent, and investment in artificial intelligence is anticipated to reach $200 billion by 2026. In the future, it is expected that many procedures that currently involve individuals will be in charge of artificial intelligence. It is not to be worried; this only means that people will be well trained and can take on more complicated jobs. Firms can provide customised learning at a massive level by integrating artificial intelligence to save employees and instructors' time, permitting them to focus on more vital tasks. Because of the advantages discussed above, such as advanced analytics, adaptive learning, and time optimisation in the preparation process, staff will be more involved and interested in learning, achieving better results, and enhanced efficiency (Yan & Lin, 2021).

CONCLUSION

In online learning, learners prefer interactive classes where they do not feel saturated, and artificial intelligence can support the development of such an engaging, beneficial medium. The revolutionised world does not restrict the age group to learning; hence, there are numerous and diversified methods of educating oneself via artificial intelligence. In contrast, adopting technology in higher education also alters the format of teaching and learning experiences. Therefore, the question arises as to what is the importance of artificial intelligence in higher education, and despite the probable inconsistencies, what one should expect from online learning? The first learning modification that everyone experiences involve switching teaching methods from a linear curriculum to skill- and project-based learning. This guarantees that learners will acquire soft skills such as problem-solving and efficient communication necessary in work life in the future. Technology can also enhance student involvement, although it does not ensure this. Enhanced visual and experiential learning via interactive applications greatly captivates students' attention. The cloud feature of artificial intelligence in online learning has the prospect of revisiting lessons and study content, even after the day it is provided. Instructors can also customise the learning experience for each learner, as technology enables progress tracking for every student. Online classrooms benefit collective intelligence; students can share anything they find related and interesting with a specific concept taught in the classroom. Again, classroom engagement relies on the students. Ultimately, all artificial intelligence can guarantee an enhancement of the possibilities of that happening. Artificial intelligence provides many innovative and creative paths for instructors and students. Assessments for students can be out of the box: projecting their capabilities and knowledge beyond the suggested books and enhancing their confidence in their tasks (Chen & Ifenthaler, 2021).

Instructors could then assess each student's preferences from the start of the course. It alters the entire dynamics of higher education, where teachers can become supporters and guide students in their careers. The online environment also reduces the costs of field trips and guest lectures. Students have a chance to experience diverse worlds, prepare them in all directions, and make them aware. Augmented reality is a division that experiences progress at an exponential rate, and it is anticipated to soon be involved in online learning. Online and self-paced learning can also improve family involvement, which is a vital aspect of student progress. Instructors can explore good content for students online and enhance their lecture performance via indirect or direct constructive feedback from both students and parents. There are many hurdles in this type of education. There is inadequate accessibility to technology gadgets, and instructors still need to recognise the best usage of artificial intelligence in teaching, even though excessive involvement with devices leads to several health problems. Additionally, adopting artificial intelligence in daily routines requires deep knowledge. This means that the curriculum needs to be updated to include technological abilities at the beginner level. Students and everyone should learn about social sharing skills, sustainable digital existence, methods of data security, and joint online skills for a safe and better future (Yan & Lin, 2021).

CASE STUDY: DUOLINGO'S AI-DRIVEN LANGUAGE LEARNING PLATFORM

By mentioning that Duolingo has set up an AI-based online platform that drastically changes the time and space concepts of independent language studies, we state that it is a leading example of this kind of platform fundamentally transforming online and self-led language studies. Established in 2011 by Luis von Ahn and Severin Hacker, Duolingo has become one of the most recognizable companies in the language education landscape by applying AI approaches to ensure each learner has an individualized, individualized adaptive approach gamified and tailored to their own particular needs delivered via the web for millions of people worldwide. This kind of study is committed on exploring AI-driven Duolingo Platform, its application in both of and self-paced learning, and how it helps tit language acquisition outcomes (Wei, L 2023).

Duolingo's origin was a dream of the founder, von Ahn, to allow learners of any age, gender, and wealth to learn any language if only they possessed the internet. Having learned the skills of crowd-sourced language translation through reCAPTCHA, von Ahn could transfer it into using AI and gamification to crowd-source language learning. Such engagement was made possible by AI and gamification, and it was scaled up to a higher level. Together with Hacker, a PhD student at Carnegie Mellon University, von Ahn founded Duolingo with a vision to leverage opportunities for artificial intelligence (AI) for the benefit of that area of knowledge, which is quite obsolete in traditional language pedagogy (Handini 2022).

The key to the success of Duolingo is the features that allow each user to personalize the learning experience and focus on the most suitable, easy, and difficult aspects of their language mastery. Among Duolingo's AI capabilities is its adaptive learning algorithm, which constantly modulates the level of difficulty of each exercise based on how the question is resolved and the learner's command of the issues. For example, the site records users' responses to exercises and their error patterns - correction is done automatically, and a user obtains a set of exercises for weak areas, and he gets no bad habit of weak areas (Wei, L 2023).

Furthermore, Duolingo's NLP technology allows users to participate in immersive, interactive language practices presented through textual, verbal, and image recognition exercises. For example, speech recognition technology that involves real-time feedback and pronunciation features based on a user's response can help learners rehearse and improve their speaking and pronunciation skills. This advanced AI-powered feature improves one's speaking abilities in the target language and gives one self-assurance to express themselves in the target language.

Furthermore, one inspiring AI element of Duolingo which places the user at the center of the experience, is its gamified learning platform. This framework uses game dynamics to highlight the experience by introducing elements, such as points, levels, and rewards. Duolingo tries to engage the learners further by using internal driving forces like intrigue, competition between each other, and a sense of accomplishment. As an illustration, students are given digital currency ("lingots") to pass the lesson. They can exchange them for virtual rewards, such as bonus lessons, freeze extension of a streak, and additional features to make the learning experience more advanced (Handini 2022).

Duolingo's AI-powered online platform perfectly shows that AI technology is used to cater to learners' diverse needs and preferences across different countries. Unlike typical classroom-based instruction that adopts a "one-size-fits-all" approach, where learners are expected to follow a specific schedule, Duolingo allows for more flexibility when it comes to learning cut at their own pace and on any device, anywhere, and at any time. This self-paced learning model allows learners to schedule classes according to their busy schedules, learning abilities, and personal learning styles. It is responsible for the learners to be "active" and be in command of their learning journey (Li & Bonk 2023).

Additionally, Duolingo's AI-driven learning platform can provide personalized learning experiences to each student, depending on their points of understanding and aspirations. Using adaptive algorithms and data-driven analytics, Duolingo finds the learner's strengths and weaknesses, analyzes their learning patterns, delivers relevant content to the learner, and paces the learning appropriately, maximizing the outcomes achieved. Duolingo will offer such learners additional exercises and explanations targeted at verb conjugations if they demonstrate difficulties in overcoming them and enhance their domain knowledge in language learning (Abdelghany, 2022).

Duolingo's AI-based system is also an enhancement of the equality and diversity of learning languages. This helps reduce barriers which can stop people from learning. It also provides great resources for free to any learner, anywhere in the world. The app has support for over 30 languages in addition to the user-friendly interface. Language instruction is therefore made available to learners with diverse backgrounds and linguistic skills, a move that breaks down language education barriers. In addition, the gamified approach to learning Duolingo is very appealing for learners of all age groups, young and old individuals alike, giving them a sense of fun and fulfilment while studying a new language (Li & Bonk 2023).

The contribution of the AI-automated Duolingo platform to language outcomes is undeniable because of its vast user base, positive user testimonials, and real-life research findings. Numerous studies have revealed that Duolingo's approach to idioms and expressions is more effective in teaching language and remembering than traditional methods. Select a sentence from the above passage that has been adapted for each instance. Duolingo Study conducted by Roumen Vesselinov and John Grego based their findings that a semester's worth of university-level language could be equated to 34 hours of Duolingo practice for learning outcomes.

Moreover, a trainee can trace their development and, at the same time, establish their learning goals, which is shown to be an incentive for their progress. The app designed by Duolingo introduces a game-like setting in which users receive rewards for their efforts and are thus stimulated to continue their practice and be responsible for language learning. By the end, they will not only remember the words, but also exhibit growth in learning the language (Handini 2022).

In addition, the AI-powered system of the platform helps with social learning and communal engagement by including features such as discussion forums, user contests, and user-generated content. Learners can exchange ideas, give tips, and participate in language competitions individually or as a team, as well as chat or talk, making all of these tasks easier. Its social dimension nurtures learning and strengthens students' motivation, engagement, and sense of belonging, which leads to better experiences for those who learn a language (Li & Bonk 2023).

Finally, the Duolingo AI-powered language learning platform showed the huge impact of AI on virtual learning and personal education. There is no denial of this fact. Through the exploitation of computational intelligence, such as adaptive algorithms, natural language processing, and gamification techniques, Duolingo provides personable, riveting, and available language education to innumerable learners around the globe. The platform provides a good interpretation of outcomes in language acquisition and demonstrates how AI-driven approaches work, as they help improve learning outcomes while enhancing quality education. With the future development of AI, infrastructure such as Duolingo will certainly be among the platforms that lead the way in e-learning and self-paced study, offering a huge opportunity for learners to find the key to their full potential and ultimately adjust to a multilingual world.

REFERENCES

Abdelghany, S. Z. A. (2022). Students' attitudes Towards Using Duolingo As A Self-Learning Artificial Intelligence-Based App In Distance Learning During The Pandemic In The United Arab Emirates.

Aleven, V., Blankestijn, J., Lawrence, L., Nagashima, T., & Taatgen, N. (2022, September). A dashboard to support teachers during students' self-paced AI-supported problem-solving practice. In *European Conference on Technology Enhanced Learning* (pp. 16-30). Cham: Springer International Publishing. DOI:10.1007/978-3-031-16290-9_2

Bao, Y., Ma, L., & Chen, W. (2018, November). SSL: Synchronous Self-paced Learning for Internet-of-Things Devices. In *Proceedings of the 1st ACM International Workshop on Smart Cities and Fog Computing* (pp. 13-18). DOI:10.1145/3277893.3277898

Chen, L., & Ifenthaler, D. (2021). The Adoption of Intelligent and Virtual Teams in Online Entrepreneurship Education Courses. In *International Conference. The Future of Education* (pp. 8-11).

Corrin, L., & Bakharia, A. (2020). Re-imagining Peer Assessment in Self-Paced Online Learning Environments. In *Re-imagining University Assessment in a Digital World* (pp. 197–212). Springer. DOI:10.1007/978-3-030-41956-1_14

Eimer, T., Biedenkapp, A., Hutter, F., & Lindauer, M. (2021, July). Self-paced context evaluation for contextual reinforcement learning. In *International Conference on Machine Learning* (pp. 2948-2958). PMLR.

Goel, P. M., Kumar, P., Johri, P., Srivastava, S. K., & Suhag, S. (2020). A comparative study of Industry 4.0 with Education 4.0. *Available atSSRN* 3553215.

Handini, B. S., Nurhasanah, N., & Panly, F. I. (2022). The Effect of Artificial Intelligent Technology Used (Duolingo Application) To Enhance English Learning. *ELLITE: Journal of English Language, Literature, and Teaching*, 7(2), 86–94. DOI:10.32528/ellite.v7i2.8354

Kazemitabaar, M., Hou, X., Henley, A., Ericson, B. J., Weintrop, D., & Grossman, T. (2023, November). How novices use LLM-based code generators to solve CS1 coding tasks in a self-paced learning environment. In *Proceedings of the 23rd Koli Calling International Conference on Computing Education Research* (pp. 1-12). DOI:10.1145/3631802.3631806

Li, K., Xu, B., Gao, K., Yang, D., & Chen, M. (2018, May). Self-paced learning with identification refinement for SPOC student grading. In *Proceedings of ACM Turing Celebration Conference*-China (pp. 79-84). DOI:10.1145/3210713.3210732

Li, L., Zhao, K., Li, S., Sun, R., & Cai, S. (2020). Extreme learning machine for supervised classification with self-paced learning. *Neural Processing Letters*, 52(3), 1723–1744. DOI:10.1007/s11063-020-10286-9

Li, Z., & Bonk, C. J. (2023). Self-directed language learning with Duolingo in an out-of-class context. *Computer Assisted Language Learning*, 1–23. DOI:10.1080/09588221.2023.2206874

Liu, Z., Feng, X., Wang, Y., & Zuo, W. (2021). Self-paced learning enhanced neural matrix factorization for noise-aware recommendation. *Knowledge-Based Systems*, 213, 106660. DOI:10.1016/j.knosys.2020.106660

Mullen, J., Milechin, L., & Reuther, A. (2019, October). Cultivating professional technical skills and understanding through hands-on online learning experiences. In *2019 IEEE Learning With MOOCS (LWMOOCS)* (pp. 150-155). IEEE. DOI:10.1109/LWMOOCS47620.2019.8939637

Pan, L., Ai, S., Ren, Y., & Xu, Z. (2020). Self-paced deep regression forests with consideration on underrepresented examples. *Computer Vision–ECCV 2020: 16th European Conference, Glasgow, UK, August 23–28, 2020Proceedings*, 16, 271–287.

Shi, C., Gu, Z., Duan, C., & Tian, Q. (2020). Multi-view adaptive semi-supervised feature selection with the self-paced learning. *Signal Processing*, 168, 107332. DOI:10.1016/j.sigpro.2019.107332

Soviany, P., Ionescu, R. T., Rota, P., & Sebe, N. (2021). Curriculum self-paced learning for cross-domain object detection. *Computer Vision and Image Understanding*, 204, 103166. DOI:10.1016/j.cviu.2021.103166

Tariq, M. U. (2024a). Harnessing Persuasive Technologies for Enhanced Learner Engagement and Motivation. In M. Sanmugam, D. Lim, N. Mohd Barkhaya, W. Wan Yahaya, & Z. Khlaif (Eds.), *Power of Persuasive Educational Technologies in Enhancing Learning* (pp. 30-62). IGI Global. DOI:10.4018/979-8-3693-6397-3.ch002

Tariq, M. U. (2024b). Smart Transportation Systems: Paving the Way for Sustainable Urban Mobility. In Munuhwa, S. (Ed.), *Contemporary Solutions for Sustainable Transportation Practices* (pp. 254–283). IGI Global. DOI:10.4018/979-8-3693-3755-4.ch010

Tariq, M. U. (2024c). Integration of IoMT for Enhanced Healthcare: Sleep Monitoring, Body Movement Detection, and Rehabilitation Evaluation. In Liu, H., Tripathy, R., & Bhattacharya, P. (Eds.), *Clinical Practice and Unmet Challenges in AI-Enhanced Healthcare Systems* (pp. 70–95). IGI Global. DOI:10.4018/979-8-3693-2703-6.ch004

Tariq, M. U. (2024d). Cybersecurity Risk Assessment Models and Theories in the Travel and Tourism Industry. In Thealla, P., Nadda, V., Dadwal, S., Oztosun, L., & Cantafio, G. (Eds.), *Corporate Cybersecurity in the Aviation, Tourism, and Hospitality Sector* (pp. 1–17). IGI Global. DOI:10.4018/979-8-3693-2715-9.ch001

Tariq, M. U. (2024e). Data Breach Incidents and Prevention in the Hospitality Industry. In Thealla, P., Nadda, V., Dadwal, S., Oztosun, L., & Cantafio, G. (Eds.), *Corporate Cybersecurity in the Aviation, Tourism, and Hospitality Sector* (pp. 181–199). IGI Global. DOI:10.4018/979-8-3693-2715-9.ch010

Tariq, M. U. (2024f). Navigating the Personalization Pathway: Implementing Adaptive Learning Technologies in Higher Education. In Minh Tung, T. (Ed.), *Adaptive Learning Technologies for Higher Education* (pp. 265–291). IGI Global. DOI:10.4018/979-8-3693-3641-0.ch012

Waheed, H., Hassan, S. U., Nawaz, R., Aljohani, N. R., Chen, G., & Gasevic, D. (2023). Early prediction of learners at risk in self-paced education: A neural network approach. *Expert Systems with Applications*, 213, 118868. DOI:10.1016/j.eswa.2022.118868

Wei, L. (2023). Artificial intelligence in language instruction: Impact on English learning achievement, L2 motivation, and self-regulated learning. *Frontiers in Psychology*, 14, 1261955. DOI:10.3389/fpsyg.2023.1261955 PMID:38023040

Woods, T. M. (2022). Examining the Effects of Learning Theory Implemented Within an Online and Self-Paced Learning Path.

Yan, H., Lin, F., & Kinshuk, . (2021). Including learning analytics in the loop of self-paced online course learning design. *International Journal of Artificial Intelligence in Education*, 31(4), 878–895. DOI:10.1007/s40593-020-00225-z

Yang, C., Huan, S., & Yang, Y. (2020). A practical teaching mode for colleges supported by artificial intelligence. *International Journal of Emerging Technologies in Learning*, 15(17), 195–206. DOI:10.3991/ijet.v15i17.16737

Zhou, J., Su, B., & Wu, Y. (2022). Discriminative Self-Paced Group-Metric Adaptation for Online Visual Identification. *IEEE Transactions on Pattern Analysis and Machine Intelligence*, 1–16. DOI:10.1109/TPAMI.2022.3200036 PMID:35984798

ADDITIONAL READING

Abonamah, A. A., Tariq, M. U., & Shilbayeh, S. (2021). On the commoditization of artificial intelligence. *Frontiers in Psychology*, 12, 696346. Advance online publication. DOI:10.3389/fpsyg.2021.696346 PMID:34659012

Ashfaq, M., Khan, I., Alzahrani, A., Tariq, M. U., Khan, H., & Ghani, A. (2024). Accurate wheat yield prediction using machine learning and climate-NDVI data fusion. *IEEE Access : Practical Innovations, Open Solutions*, 12, 40947–40961. DOI:10.1109/ACCESS.2024.3376735

Babar, M., Ahmad, A., Tariq, M. U., & Kaleem, S. (2023). Real-time fake news detection using big data analytics and deep neural network. *IEEE Transactions on Computational Social Systems*. Advance online publication. DOI:10.1109/TCSS.2023.3309704

Babar, M., Alshehri, M. D., Tariq, M. U., Ullah, F., Khan, A., Uddin, M. I., & Almasoud, A. S. (2021). IoT-enabled big data analytics architecture for multimedia data communications. *Wireless Communications and Mobile Computing*, 2021(1), 1–9. DOI:10.1155/2021/5283309

Babar, M., Jan, M. A., He, X., Tariq, M. U., Mastorakis, S., & Alturki, R. (2023). An optimized IoT-enabled big data analytics architecture for edge–cloud computing. *IEEE Internet of Things Journal*, 10(5), 3995–4005. DOI:10.1109/JIOT.2022.3157552 PMID:38046398

Babar, M., Kaleem, S., Sohail, A., Asim, M., & Tariq, M. U. (2023). An improved big data analytics architecture for intruder classification using machine learning. *Security and Communication Networks*, 2023, 2023. DOI:10.1155/2023/1216192

Babar, M., Khattak, A. S., Jan, M. A., & Tariq, M. U. (2021). Energy aware smart city management system using data analytics and internet of things. *Sustainable Energy Technologies and Assessments*, 44, 100992. Advance online publication. DOI:10.1016/j.seta.2021.100992

Babar, M., Tariq, M. U., & Jan, M. A. (2020). Secure and resilient demand side management engine using machine learning for IoT-enabled smart grid. *Sustainable Cities and Society*, 62, 102370. Advance online publication. DOI:10.1016/j.scs.2020.102370

KEY TERMS AND DEFINITIONS

AI-Powered Virtual Classrooms: Online learning environments enhanced by AI that simulate traditional classroom interactions.

Conversational AI Tutors: AI-driven tools that engage students in natural language dialogues, offering explanations.

Dynamic Content Delivery: An AI-driven method where educational content is adjusted dynamically based on a learner's progress and comprehension.

Proactive Analytics: The use of AI to continuously monitor and predict student engagement and performance in real-time.

Scalable Learning Solutions: AI-enabled platforms that can adapt to a growing number of users while maintaining personalised and effective learning experiences.

Chapter 10
Personalization of Higher Education Using Artificial Intelligence

ABSTRACT

The scene of higher instruction is ceaselessly advancing, driven by mechanical progressions, changing understudied socioeconomics, and advancing academic hones. Later, there has been a developing accentuation of personalization in instruction, wherein learning encounters are custom-fitted to the person's needs, inclinations, and capacities of understudies. Within higher instruction, AI technologies are being utilized to create versatile learning situations, shrewd mentoring frameworks, and personalized suggestion motors that tailor instructive encounters to the one-of-a-kind needs and characteristics of individual learners. Higher education has experienced noteworthy changes over the past century, from conventional lecture-based instruction to more student-centered approaches that prioritize dynamic learning, collaboration, and basic considerations. The rise of advanced innovations, such as computers, the web, and portable gadgets, has played an urgent role in reshaping the instructive scene, empowering any place to learn assets, and cultivating intelligent learning situations.

INTRODUCTION

Personalization in instruction alludes to tailoring learning encounters to understudies' characteristics and needs, cultivating more profound engagement, inspiration, and learning results (Papert, 1993). Whereas conventional classroom settings frequently take a one-size-fits-all approach to instruction, personalized learning looks to individualize the learning handle, accommodating differing learning styles,

DOI: 10.4018/979-8-3693-4074-5.ch010

interfaces, and capacities. One of the key drivers of personalized learning development is the acknowledgement that understudies have special learning profiles and inclinations, and that instructive encounters ought to be adjusted to oblige these contrasts (Horn & Staker, 2015). Personalized learning situations use innovation, information analytics, and instructional design standards to supply understudies with customized learning pathways, versatile feedback, and personalized feedback, subsequently enabling them to require possession of learning travel. For illustration, versatile learning stages utilize calculations to analyze students' intuition using course materials. They powerfully alter the substance and trouble level based on their personal advancement and dominance of concepts (Katz et al., 2017). In addition, competency-based instruction models permit understudies to develop through coursework at their own pace, illustrating the authority of particular competencies or learning goals (Klein-Collins, 2017).

Manufactured insights (AI) have risen as a transformative constraint in personalizing higher instruction, advertising exceptional openings to assemble, analyze, and act upon endless sums of information on understudy learning behaviors, inclinations, and execution measurements (Siemens, 2013). AI includes innovations, counting machine learning, common dialect handling, and cognitive computing, which empower shared frameworks to recreate human-like thinking, decision making, and interaction (Duderstadt, 2000; Tariq, 2024).

Within higher instruction, AI technologies are being utilized to create versatile learning situations, shared mentoring frameworks, and personalized suggestion motors that tailor instructive encounters to the one-of-a-kind needs and characteristics of individual learners (VanLehn et al., 2007). For example, AI-powered learning administration frameworks (LMS) can track students' intelligence with course materials, distinguish regions of trouble or misconception, and focus on mediation or remediation to address learning crevices (Partner & Samaka, 2020). AI-driven chatbots and virtual collaborators offer personalized bolsters to understudy, respond to questions, give input, and direct them to important assets based on their needs and learning destinations (Pastry Specialist, 2010). These brilliant frameworks can adjust their reactions and suggestions in real time based on students' intuition, inclinations, and execution information, subsequently upgrading the adequacy and proficiency of learning preparation (Bates & Sangra, 2011).

In conclusion, personalization in higher instruction has become conspicuous as teachers look to make more locks in successful and comprehensive learning encounters for understudies. Integrating manufactured insights and innovations holds a huge guarantee of personalizing higher instruction by empowering versatile learning situations, brilliant coaching frameworks, and personalized recommendation motors. Realizing the full potential of AI-driven personalization requires tending to information protection, value, and workforce preparation challenges. Moving forward, collaborative endeavors among partners are fundamental to tackling the transformative power of AI in forming long-standing times of higher instruction (Tariq, 2024).

BACKGROUND

Personalization has gained critical footing within the energetic scene of higher instruction, propelled by technological advancement, especially within the domain of counterfeit insights (AI). The integration of advances in AI has introduced a modern period in which instructive teachers endeavor to tailor learning encounters to individual understudies' interesting needs, inclinations, and capacities. This chapter digs into the multifaceted measurements of personalization in higher instruction encouraged by AI, investigating its potential, challenges, and suggestions (Tariq, 2024).

With its capacity for information handling, design acknowledgement, and versatile calculations, manufacturing insights have been developed as a transformative force for reshaping different divisions and counting instructions. In higher instruction, AI catalyzes personalization by empowering teachers to accumulate tremendous information on students' learning behaviors, inclinations, and execution measurements. AI can analyze this information through advanced calculations to produce experiences that illuminate personalized learning pathways and mediations custom-made to each student's interesting profile (Siemens, 2013). For example, AI-powered learning administration frameworks (LMS) can track students' intelligence with course materials, distinguishing quality zones, and shortcomings. Based on this data, the framework can prescribe supplementary assets, versatile works, or personalized criticism to address particular learning holes. Moreover, AI-driven chatbots can provide real-time feedback to understudies, respond to questions and advertising directions, and coordinate them to pertinent assets based on their needs and learning goals (Partner & Samaka, 2020).

The personalization of higher instruction utilizing AI envelops a different run of procedures and applications pointed at upgrading under-study engagement, maintenance, and scholarly results. One noticeable approach is versatile learning, which utilizes AI calculations to powerfully alter the pace, substance, and trouble level of learning materials in reaction to a person's understudy execution and comprehension (Brusilovsky & Peylo, 2003). For instance, adaptive learning stages can show understudies with customized learning pathways based on the authority of prerequisite concepts, guaranteeing that each understudy advances at their ideal pace.

In addition, AI-powered proposal frameworks are significant in personalizing the learning encounter by proposing significant courses, assets, and exercises custom-fitted to students' interfaces, career desires, and learning styles (Koper &

Specht, 2007). These suggestion motors use machine learning calculations to analyze chronicled information on students' intelligence and inclinations, advertising personalized suggestions that adjust to their instructional objectives and goals. In addition, AI-driven virtual guides and shared mentoring frameworks provide students with personalized directions, bolsters, and criticism, mimicking one-on-one intelligence in human education (VanLehn et al., 2007). These virtual guides can adjust their teaching techniques based on students' reactions, misguided judgments, and learning directions, cultivating a more profound conceptual understanding and dominance of subject matter.

Despite the colossal potential of AI in personalizing higher instruction, its usage does not challenge moral contemplation. One key challenge is the requirement for vigorous information security and security measures to protect the delicate understudy data collected by AI frameworks (Exact & Murnane, 2013). Teachers must guarantee compliance with administrative systems such as the Family Instructive Rights and Protection Act (FERPA) to secure students' rights and security. Moreover, concerns concern the impartial conveyance of personalized learning opportunities, as AI calculations may incidentally propagate inclinations or incongruities based on financial status, race, or sex (Williamson, 2017). Creating straightforward and responsible AI frameworks that prioritize decency, diversity, and consideration in delivering personalized instructive encounters is fundamental for relieving these dangers. In addition, using AI-driven personalization in higher instruction requires staff buy-in, training, and support to successfully coordinate these innovations into educational ones (West et al., 2019). Teachers must be prepared with the fundamental aptitudes and information to use AI instruments in ways that increase, instead of supplanting, human education, and mentorship. Thus, the personalization of higher instruction utilizing fake insights represents a worldview move in how learning encounters are planned, conveyed, and custom-fitted to a person's understudy needs. By controlling AI calculations, education can create versatile learning situations that optimize student engagement, maintenance, and scholarly victory. Realizing the full potential of AI-driven personalization requires tending to challenges related to information security, value, and workforce preparation. Moving forward, collaborative endeavors among teachers, technologists, policymakers, and partners are basic to harness AI's transformative potential of AI to form higher instruction.

PERSONALISED HIGHER EDUCATION AS A FOUNDATION

Currently, universities and colleges encounter a broad range of issues involving disengaged learners, increased dropout rates, and the efficiency of a conventional "one-size-fits-all" method for higher education. However, when artificial intelligence and data analytics are used appropriately, customised learning experiences can be created, which may help solve some of these issues. With customised learning experiences, each student leverages a unique educational method customised to their requirements and capabilities. This could enhance students' motivation and decrease their chances of dropping out. It could also give instructors better recognition of every student's learning procedure, allowing them to teach more efficiently. An artificial intelligence-driven learning system would have the capability of providing instructors with beneficial information about their students' learning styles, skills, and performance and offer recommendations for how to personalise their teaching techniques to students' particular requirements. For instance, some students might experience learning challenges or obstacles that require additional attention or teaching. Others might progress so quickly that they are not rationally challenged and would take leverage from supplementary study content and assessments. In both of these proposed situations, artificial intelligence systems would b supporting students to reach their full capability, probably averting them from dropping out by recognising issues early enough to let suitable counteractive measures opt-in. For this type of artificial intelligence-powered learning system to work efficiently, big data is required to train it. As discussed, the data would need to be utilised ethically, and learners would need to be informed about how their private data can be shared and utilised by artificial intelligence algorithms (Beghetto, 2019).

Private Data Is a Fundamental Element

Theoretically, implementing artificial intelligence and customised learning appears to be an optimal solution to some of the most common learning problems. However, this technology still has a long time before it can reach its prospective. The principal element of personalised learning is the significant amount of student details. The experience of instructors suggests that students in the present times are more conscious of the privacy of their data than prior generations, most possibly because of the security breaches and data theft they have already been unprotected about. However, if student data could be accumulated and processed in a manner that was transparent, ethical, and secure, artificial intelligence could be used efficiently to enhance every domain of study (Magomadov, 2020).

Chatbots Offer Personalised Guidance and Assistance

One supplementary advantage of having university chatbots to respond to students' queries is the significant volume of big data that can be accessed based on the student's area of interest and concerns. The data can be accessed to support universities in developing innovative novel programs and services to further enhance students' learning experiences. Various other universities have started to implement chatbots for monotonous tasks that would usually require an instructor or administrator to perform, such as offering replies to students' frequently asked questions. These tests have assured that various repetitive routines and tasks could leverage artificial intelligence-powered systems' support, providing instructors with more time to focus on teaching their students or involving them in research tasks. Universities should also consider integrating virtual assistants and chatbots to assist them in managing their psychological health, lessen their stress, and enhance their motivation to learn. At a time when higher education health systems are strained to capability and students experience riskily long waiting times for on-campus psychological health counselling, chatbots could offer quick relief. Integrating such chatbots is not without intrinsic risk. Universities would require application precautions to safeguard students' private data and require some human error to optimise the recommendations that chatbots provide students (Rad et al., 2018).

Possible Vital Issues

As universities begin implementing artificial intelligence in several functions, they may find various issues to be solved. The most critical point is how higher education institutions can best prepare learners for the latest technology-powered world and the many advanced technologies that will modify how people work. Learners must recognise that, over time, more monotonous and repetitive tasks will be performed and automated by artificial intelligence, robots, and automation. However, there will always be roles that require creative abilities and emotional and cognitive skills. Various universities worldwide cannot train students in skills that will or will not be required in their future careers. As artificial intelligence is implemented in higher education, the best outcomes will come from merging the strengths of artificial intelligence and human skills. There will never be a time when humans are not required for jobs relevant to higher education. For instance, instructors will always play a vital role in society, as we should never undervalue the value of human collaboration and critical thinking in the educational domain. However, algorithms can be beneficial in guiding decisions; algorithms and robots should not complete all educational tasks. The support offered by artificial intelligence algorithms should be used to assist in the development of ideal learning environments. For instance, artificial intelligence-powered learning systems are the best tools for teaching rule-based courses, such as math and foreign languages. Artificial intelligence systems could considerably improve the learning procedure by offering significant accuracy and more precise feedback, and allowing students take the time to repeat study assessments as often as required. An instructor would still be required to help explain what students do not comprehend, such as exclusions and nuances to the language rules, or how to implement math formulas to resolve issues. The instructor's role is to lead, assist, and mentor learners, supporting them in comprehending what they have learned, why it is vital, and how it can be implemented in the real world. The inaccuracy of data usage is a significant issue in AI technology adoption. There are tough and vital decisions that will be made at every stage of society about data possession, as well as the best methods of using data ethically and transparently. Even though artificial intelligence provides various stimulating advances, particularly for enhancing education worldwide, higher education is still in the initial stages of its usage. Further investigation and research are required for the progressive adoption of artificial intelligence tools in higher education institutes. Universities administrators and leaders are encouraged to become pre-emptive pilot programs to test the usage of artificial intelligence in several ways while crucially considering the outcomes and ethical obligations that must be achieved along the way. In addition, learners should understand how algorithms utilise data for making decisions, and their input into the development and design of artificial intelligence systems should be encouraged and invited. Students should especially remain well-versed about how their data are utilised (Hashim et al., 2022).

Technology has always enabled novel strategic abilities in higher education. The risk falls on chief information officers to develop a business case that fits the more considerable strategic investment and can assist in the fundamental modification required in functioning models. The institutes opting to take the strategic benefit by implementing early technology will recognise that some crucial tools, architectural fundamentals, and abilities required to assist advanced analytics are still not accessible in the market. They must either create their own or outsource some of their growth efforts. Service customisation is a strategic step that universities must take to remain competitive in the market (Liu & Quan, 2022).

ON-CAMPUS ARTIFICIAL INTELLIGENCE

Similar to Uber, which disrupts the taxi service sector, Airbnb impacts the hotel sector, and Amazon disrupts the retail industry. It is no longer the way that something similar will also affect higher education (Tang et al., 2020).

Customized Learning

The conventional-one unit guide for an all-framework is swiftly substituted in universities by artificial intelligence algorithms that can customise materials according to the student's requirements and pace (Martin et al., 2021).

Progress Monitoring

Blockchains will transform how universities function by automating various procedures, such as transferring and recognising credits and recording and registering educational research copyrights (Chaipidech et al., 2022).

Improved Customer Care

Cognitive computing can also support enhanced customer experience and care by offering a 24/7 online recommendation service where students can ask several questions and respond quickly (Lynch et al., 2020).

Learner Flexibility

Smartphones, mobile devices, and tablets have become the basic delivery methods, as learners can utilise whatever medium and learn from wherever they like (Montebello, 2021).

Smart Campuses

Intelligent classrooms can be customised for various faculty members, observe attendance, or better administer examinations. Smart campuses can control and monitor all university systems, such as lighting and heating systems, parking lots, rooms, and alarms. The university campus has been exposed to prevalent progress in personal computing over the past several years. However, in the future, a novel wave of modifications will take place–a wave of customisation fuelled by big data and artificial intelligence. Higher education institutes can lead this revolution in the present times (Rivers and Holland, 2022).

Advantages and Features of Higher Education Personalisation

- Allows students to support their learning experiences with their capabilities, objectives, and interests
- Offers the framework for students to work self-sufficiently, at their own pace, and sometimes on their timetable
- Prioritize the requirements of students as individuals in content and curriculum creation
- Provision of learning content in various formats, available on various devices, and utilizes diversified delivery techniques to guarantee students can

tap into their learning styles to drive themselves forward, no matter their outcomes

- Inspires students to be dynamic students, takes the initiative and optimizes their performance
- It involves continuous assessments, many of which can be self-assessments, to support learning and recognize learning gaps from the start
- Offers instructors with real-time data on student performance, enabling them to interfere when required
- Permits for the integration of technological solutions to best accommodation to demand
- Participates in student attention and intensifies motivation, possibly decreasing dropout rates

Regardless of the form of customised instruction, it is clear that it goes conjointly with a role change for the corresponding instructors. Evidently, in the present, instructor, teacher, and professor roles are diversified and expanded beyond covering the course matter curriculum to directing students towards crucial thinking or proficiently implementing theory to practice. The beginning of customised learning, however, involves instructors taking more beset action to assist and nurture students where required, offering human-added value by clarifying complicated topics in a relevant way, and guiding students via their learning performance in a more coach-like way. This results in a more subjective relationship between the student and the instructor (Zhang, 2022).

HOW CAN LEARNING BE PERSONALISED

Even customized teaching must meet consistent principles if it leads to renowned qualifications. However, personalization must be applied throughout. This ensures that much-publicized social abilities have converged despite a probable significant dependence on digital content. Prospective scheduling variability still has to allow for fine structure and not become an impairment to those learning formats that require attendance from all learners. Additionally, instructors must be able to sustain an outline of their students if they are to offer satisfactory support. Successful customization depends on a cautious balance between disintegration and consistency. Attaining this includes integrating various learning prospects in personalized units, such as project-based assessments, which give students the liberty to select their topics. It may be as extensive as designing various learning paths that lead to the same qualification, providing substitute units, career-relevant internships, or dual enrolment prospects. Students may be asked to provide their opinions on various lecture formats and contribute their concepts to the curriculum design. Self-assessments may be utilized not only as a measure of the status quo, but also to practice metacognition and reflection, providing students with a medium to vent their explanations to enhance knowledge retention. Digital tools may be utilized to improve effectiveness and efficiency; for instance, as a segment of a blended learning environment that combines confrontational instruction and directed digital content (Lee et al., 2018).

What Learning Technologies and Tools Are Beneficial

Customizing services requires consistent information, and higher education should not be excluded. Closely customized study programs would develop demanding student profiles from personal data thinking in the future. Artificial intelligence and big data can tease student choices to match the supply of higher education with demand. Logically, any discussion on personal data is directly followed by data privacy concerns, and significant attention must be paid to ethical and secure data handling. Suppose that the corresponding issues can be overcome, and any automated output can be optimized and correctly inferred before use. In this case, technology could open up a massive collection of supplementary prospects that would nourish into a customized learning background, for instance:

- Chatbots to answer frequently asked questions, even outside official timings
- Automation of monotonous tasks and routines to release instructor's capacity for confrontational interaction
- Smart mood tracking to support students handle their psychological health
- Artificial intelligence-powered learning systems for the teaching of rule-based subject modules

CUSTOMISED LEARNING EXPERIENCE: THE REASON WHY ARTIFICIAL INTELLIGENCE POSSESSES THE KEY

The lines between professional and professional lives are becoming indistinct thanks to intelligence technology, which switches expectations to customised learning for training and development. It is time to consider how humans now shop or watch TV online; it only makes sense that these same rules can be incorporated into applications in business systems. This is an important topic of conversation in a business learning environment. Learning and development administrators have a distinctive appetite for more customised business learning methods. In the current learning and development survey, participants were asked questions about learning and development trends. "the leading answer was customisation/ flexible delivery, with artificial intelligence following right after. The other priorities of the learning methods are as follows:

1. Customization/ flexible delivery
2. Artificial intelligence
3. Combined social learning
4. Augmented and virtual reality
5. Learning experiences mediums
6. Learning analytics
7. Progress support
8. Mobile learning and delivery
9. Consulting more precisely with the firms
10. Microlearning
11. Showing value
12. Preparing learning and development function
13. Cognitive science and neuroscience
14. Curation
15. video

The survey indicates that this data recognises a vital shift: conventionally, learning and development have evolved around the preparation, creation, and delivery of online and classroom materials. Now, it seems that experience is switching to something else, and customised learning is backed by data. When higher education administrators consider the effect of data-supported learning programs on instructors, they often forget that the amount of analysis and data needed to make sense of everything manually is impossible. It is where artificial intelligence can review and translate vast amounts of data and continuously learn from its perceptions. The best part is artificial intelligence is not the cost of substituting humans. Artificial intelligence is a prevailing tool that enhances human decision-making because no statistical framework or algorithm can replace the intuition of humans (Yang et al., 2022).

Artificial Intelligence Provides Automated and Customised Learning

As the world has shifted to a new decade, the implementation of artificial intelligence on the peal and set to modernise the learning experiences for students and administrators is similar. Not only does it provide more customised learning capabilities, but freely, it will make the tasks much more interesting when all boring, time-consuming jobs are automated. Higher education administrators should ask the following questions:

- What if the universities' learning management systems automatically knew the learners' interests, desired learning styles, and platforms without administrator interference?
- What if assistance questions could be responded to quickly, at the point of requirement, and directly in the learning medium?

The exquisiteness of artificial intelligence is that instructors can reclaim a lot of their time while also achieving it more than before. For instance, with artificial intelligence, instructors are still preparing the content. Still, they can articulate and allow the system to take more care of repetitive tasks, such as assessing statistics and charts. Teachers can also offer quick and customised feedback without human interference. They can navigate their students in the right direction without dedicating their time. The best part is that all these abilities are ready to be put to function. Progressive higher education institutions are already leading these innovations and observing their outcomes that emerge with them (Beghetto, 2019).

Actionable Customizing Learning Strategies

Artificial intelligence, which merges data accumulation and technologies such as machine learning, can extract customised and automated learning plans by responding to students' requirements (Liu & Quan, 2022). The following are some of the advantages artificial intelligence provides:

- Artificial intelligence will provide instructors with the capability to more precisely recognize student-employee skill gaps and recommend the best methods to bridge them (Tariq, 2024)
- As the most vital metric, artificial intelligence will support educators in accumulating better and more reliable data on how learning content affects student performance.
- Still, in their beginning, virtual instructors will become innovative and more targeted as they assist students with a preemptive response to customized learning and development.
- Artificial intelligence can accumulate and infer a large amount of data, meaning that instructors can accumulate fundamental insights more effortlessly than ever (Magomadov, 2020).

Artificial Intelligence and Customised Learning: Best Duo

There is no reason to take on additional work that can be automated using artificial intelligence. If instructors are currently stressing themselves with a load of manually drawing data, recommending materials, and teaching, they may still not graze the surface of where they could be. A spontaneous and refined user experience for students and administrators develops personalised learning prospects. If instructors can attain enhanced outcomes with less strain and time, there seems to be a recognisable answer. With artificial intelligence driving the learning medium, students can leverage a system that intelligently adjusts to users' requirements and allows them to take charge of their learning. As administrators, there are vital prospects for automating and eradicating monotonous tasks with artificial intelligence, such as course enrolment, teaching material classification, and replying to student questions (Rad et al., 2018).

Challenges of Personalizing Higher Education Using Artificial Intelligence

Integrating artificial intelligence into higher education has presented various opportunities to personalize learning encounters to meet the different needs of understudies. Whereas AI-driven personalization holds a critical guarantee, it presents different challenges that must be addressed for successful execution. This chapter examines the challenges of personalizing higher instruction using AI innovations and investigates potential methodologies for relieving these challenges.

Moral Contemplations

One of the essential challenges of actualizing AI-driven personalization in higher instruction rotates around moral contemplation, especially concerning information security and security. AI frameworks depend on collecting and analyzing endless sums of understudy information to personalize learning encounters. In any case, the collection, capacity, and utilization of under-study information raises concerns about protection encroachment, assent, and information proprietorship (Buchanan, 2019). Teachers must set up clear approaches and conventions for information administration to guarantee that understudied security rights are secured while maximizing the benefits of personalized learning.

Inclination and Decency

Another noteworthy challenge is the potential for inclination and shamefulness in the AI calculations utilized for personalization. AI frameworks may propagate or increase existing inclinations displayed within the information they are prepared on, leading to unjustifiable treatment or results for certain understudy bunches (Mittelstadt et al., 2019). For example, chronicled information reflects aberrations in scholarly execution based on components, such as race or financial status. AI calculations may inadvertently strengthen these aberrations by fitting learning encounters in ways that worsen the existing disparities. Tending to a predisposition in AI calculations requires careful consideration of information choice, calculation plan, and continuous observation to guarantee reasonableness and value in personalized learning situations.

Educational Integration

The successful integration of AI-driven personalization into academic hones presents another challenge for higher-instruction teachers. Numerous teachers may need essential aptitudes and information to use AI apparatuses successfully or to decipher information bits of knowledge for guideline enhancement (Hodges et al., 2020). As a result, staff members may resist or be skeptical towards embracing personalized learning approaches. Educators must contribute to staff preparation and proficient improvement activities to construct their capacity to utilize AI advances for personalized instruction. Giving progress and assets is basic to engaging staff individuals to grasp inventive education strategies that adjust to the standards of personalized learning.

Innovation Foundation and Openness

Executing AI-driven personalization in higher instruction requires a vigorous innovation foundation and availability contemplation. Educators must guarantee that their IT frameworks can bolster consistent integration of AI devices and stages. Furthermore, openness issues must be addressed to guarantee that personalized learning encounters are comprehensive and impartial for all understudies, including those with inabilities or other differing learning needs (McGill et al., 2020). This may include planning AI calculations and interfacing with availability highlights, giving elective groups for learning materials, and advertising specialized back to understudies who require assistive innovations.

Taken a toll and Asset Allotment

Asset assignment posture has taken a toll, and it is a critical challenge for educators looking to actualize AI-driven personalization in higher instruction. Creating and conveying AI innovations requires significant budgetary speculation, counting costs related to program advancement, foundation updates, and continuous upkeep (Sclater et al., 2019). Furthermore, enlisting talented experts to oversee AI frameworks and analyze information incurs additional costs. Educators must carefully survey their budgetary limitations and prioritize ventures in AI activities that adjust to their vital objectives and needs. Collaborating with outside accomplices or leveraging open-source arrangements may also help moderate monetary boundaries to actualize AI-driven personalization.

Lawful And Administrative Compliance

Exploring legitimate and administrative systems presents another challenge for teaching and executing AI-driven personalization in higher education. Compliance with laws and controls related to information security, mental property rights, and openness benchmarks is essential to dodge potential legitimate dangers and liabilities (Macfarlane, 2019). Furthermore, universal collaborations and associations may present complexities in compliance with distinctive legitimate systems across locales. Educators must work together to advance legitimate and administrative necessities, and guarantee that AI activities follow pertinent measures and rules.

Thus, personalizing higher instruction utilizing fake insights can improve learning encounters and lead to understudy results. A few challenges must be addressed to realize the benefits of AI-driven personalization. Moral contemplations encompassing information protection and security and the hazards of predisposition and shamefulness in AI calculations require careful consideration. Educational integration, innovation frameworks, fetched and asset allotments, and lawful compliance are additional challenges that teachers must explore. By tending to these challenges through collaborative endeavors among teachers, technologists, policymakers, and other partners, higher instruction teachers can harness the control of AI to create personalized learning situations that meet the different needs of understudies viably and morally.

Future of Personalization of Higher Education Using Artificial Intelligence

Long-standing periods of higher instruction must be more connected to the headway and integration of counterfeit insight (AI) innovations. With the expansion of information analytics, machine learning calculations, and intelligent frameworks, the personalization of higher instruction is balanced to experience critical changes in the coming years. This study investigates the development patterns, openings, and challenges forming the long haul of personalized higher instruction utilizing AI, with a center on imaginative applications and potential suggestions.

As AI progresses, a few developing patterns are balanced to revolutionize the personalization of higher instruction. One such drift is the proliferation of AI-powered chatbots and virtual colleagues offering personalized support to understudy throughout their scholastic travel (Partner & Samaka, 2020). These frameworks use dialect preparation and machine learning calculations to supply real-time help, respond to enquiries, and provide personalized suggestions based on students' needs and inclinations.

In addition, versatile learning stages are progressively advancing, utilizing AI calculations to powerfully alter the learning substance, pace, and trouble level in reaction to students' execution and comprehension (Brusilovsky & Peylo, 2003). These stages analyze students' intelligence with course materials, distinguish ranges of weakness, and provide personalized mediations or remediation to address learning holes, subsequently advancing mastery-based learning and under-study engagement.

Another developing slant is the integration of AI-driven suggestion frameworks into instructive stages, advertising personalized course suggestions, assets, and learning pathways tailored to students' interfaces, objectives, and learning styles (Koper and Specht, 2007). These proposal engines leverage information analytics and machine learning strategies to analyze students' past behaviors and inclinations, providing customized recommendations that optimize learning results and scholarly victory.

Long-term, personalized higher instruction utilizing AI presents numerous opportunities to improve understudy learning encounters, results, and engagement. One such opportunity lies within the creation of immersive and intelligent learning environments that use AI advances, such as virtual reality (VR) and expanded reality (AR), to convey personalized, experiential learning encounters (Dede, 2009). For illustration, VR recreation can submerge understudies in practical scenarios important to their field of pondering, permitting them to apply hypothetical information in commonsense settings and create basic consideration and problem-solving abilities.

AI-driven personalized learning pathways can potentially cultivate noteworthy independence and self-regulated learning among understudies, engaging them to require ownership of their instructive travel (West et al., 2019). By giving understudies personalized input, versatile assets, and focusing on bolsters, AI-enabled frameworks can platform learning encounters and encourage the improvement of metacognitive aptitudes, such as objective setting, self-monitoring, and reflection.

Moreover, AI advances offer openings to address value crevices and advance comprehensive instruction by tailoring learning encounters to meet understudies' assorted needs and foundations (Williamson, 2017). For example, AI-driven versatile learning stages can focus on intercessions and bolster underrepresented or at-risk understudy populations, helping moderate incongruities in scholarly accomplishment and maintenance rates.

Despite the transformative potential of AI-driven personalization in higher instruction, a few challenges and contemplations must be addressed to realize its full benefits. One key challenge is the moral utilization of understudied data and protection security, as AI frameworks depend on tremendous amounts of individual data to provide personalized learning encounters (Require & Murnane, 2013). Teachers must build vigorous information administration arrangements and components to guarantee straightforwardness, responsibility, and compliance with administrative systems such as the Family Instructive Rights and Security Act (FERPA).

In addition, there are concerns about the potential for algorithmic inclination and segregation in AI-driven personalized learning frameworks, which may accidentally sustain disparities based on variables such as race, sexual orientation, and financial status (Selwyn, 2019). To relieve these dangers, it is fundamental to create and send AI calculations that are transparent, reasonable, and free from inclination, and to screen and review their impact on marginalized understudy populations frequently.

Moreover, the fruitful use of AI-driven personalization in higher instruction requires staff buy-in, preparation, and support to successfully coordinate these innovations into academic ones (West et al., 2019). Teachers must be given proficient advancement opportunities to procure the essential abilities and information to use AI instruments in ways that complement and upgrade their instruction and mentorship.

Thus, long-term personalized higher instruction utilizing manufactured insights holds a gigantic guarantee for changing learning encounters, results, and availability. Emerging trends such as AI-powered chatbots, versatile learning stages, and proposal frameworks offer opportunities to create immersive, versatile, and comprehensive learning situations that cater to understudies' different needs and preferences. Realizing the complete potential of AI-driven personalization requires tending to challenges related to information security, algorithmic predisposition, staff availability, and equity. Moving forward, collaborative endeavors among teachers, technologists, policymakers, and partners are basic to saddling the transformative control of AI in forming a long-standing time of higher education.

CONCLUSION

In the past ten years, the efficiency of conventional higher education has been recurrently interrogated. University dropout rates are at an unprecedented high level, as evidenced by disengaged students and the low motivation of the learner body. According to industrial specialists, the vital cause of university failure to keep students engaged is the one-size-fits-all method. Fortunately, progress in artificial intelligence technology has been beneficial. Several institutes have developed tools to make the learning procedure more enjoyable. It is attained by developing a customised learning experience that is dependent on students' capabilities and choices. Presently, accessible tools are still falling short of industry prospects, but the initial steps seem promising. Advanced learning products can enhance students' interest and make it possible to see their learning through until the end. It can also support administrators in tracking each student's performance and in utilising a customised teaching approach for every student. By assessing students' track records, artificial intelligence tools can identify students' choices and capabilities by assessing their track records. Instructors and university administrators can utilise this data to recommend customised learning approaches. Artificial intelligence can identify when students face difficulties with some concepts or tasks and support them in supplementary teaching. It can easily detect students who can manage regular assessments and assign them extra work. Artificial intelligence technology can help students regulate their loads. Interferences such as those discussed above can support students in achieving their peak psychological performance (Hashim et al., 2022).

The software must be trained on big datasets to increase the intelligence technology. Administrators must notify students about the facts to ensure ethical accumulation of data. They also need to explain how the data will be utilised. Before higher education institutes can use artificial intelligence for customised learning, they must guarantee that the data accumulation methods are safe, transparent, and secure. As previously mentioned, most teachers' issues can be solved using artificial intelligence. Artificial intelligence (AI) solutions require massive amounts of student data. The issue is that modern learners are aware of the threat of exposing their private data, so they must be assured that their data will remain secure. Their private details must be saved when they are safe from hacking. As long as higher education institutes can maintain high data accumulation standards, the prospect of artificial intelligence to enhance the quality of education could be immeasurable. Fortunately, many higher education institutions worldwide are attempting to secure the privacy of learners' data. NGOs ensure that data accumulation is done responsibly and with student approval (Lynch et al., 2020).

CASE STUDY

For a long time, the integration of counterfeit insights (AI) into higher instruction has changed the scene of education and learning and advertising unused openings for personalization and customization. This case study analyzes the application of AI-powered personalization in a better instruction institution, focusing on using a versatile learning stage to improve under-study engagement, maintenance, and scholarly victory.

The case talks about spins around an anecdotal college, "TechEd College", which has set out on travel to use AI innovations to personalize the learning encounters of its understudies. Confronting challenges such as differing under-study socioeconomics, changing readiness levels, and the ability to oblige diverse learning styles, the college looked for inventive arrangements to upgrade under-study results and fulfilment. TechEd College joined forces with a driving AI innovation supplier to address these challenges and actualize the versatile learning stage in its different scholastic programs. The versatile learning stage utilizes machine learning calculations to analyze students' intelligence using course materials, survey their qualities and shortcomings, and powerfully alter the substance and pace of instruction to meet personal learning needs (Katz et al., 2017).

For example, in a science course, understudies are displayed with a pre-assessment test at the start of the semester to gauge their capability in foundational concepts. Based on their execution of the pre-assessment, the versatile learning platform generates personalized learning pathways, prescribing particular modules, work, and assets custom-fitted to each student's level of authority and learning goals.

In addition, the versatile learning stage persistently tracks student advancement and execution throughout the semester, providing real-time input and versatile intercessions to address learning holes and misinterpretations (VanLehn et al., 2007). For instance, if an understudy battles with a specific concept or aptitude, the stage may offer additional practice works, video instructional exercises, or intelligent recreations to strengthen understanding and authority.

Effect on Student Engagement and Learning Results

Executing the versatile learning stage at TechEd College has yielded noteworthy enhancements in under-study engagement, maintenance, and academic results. By personalizing the learning encounter to adjust to students' needs and inclinations, colleges have seen an increase in understudy inspiration, fulfilment, and self-efficacy (West et al., 2019).

In this case, understudies reported feeling more supported and engaged in requiring proprietorship of their learning travel, as the versatile learning stage gives them independence and organization in exploring course materials and assignments. In addition, the platform's versatile highlights empower understudies to advance at their claim pace, decreasing sentiments of disappointment or overwhelming related to conventional one-size-fits-all guideline approaches.

Additionally, the versatile learning stage has been instrumental in improving understudy execution and accomplishments across different subject regions. A preparatory information investigation demonstrates that understudies who lock in with the stage frequently illustrate higher levels of authority, maintenance, and scholarly victory than their peers in conventional classroom settings (Partner & Samaka, 2020).

Despite the success of the versatile learning stage at TechEd College, a few challenges and lessons learned have developed throughout the execution process. One challenge is the requirement for progressing staff preparation and back to successfully using AI advances in academic hones (Brusilovsky & Peylo, 2003). Teachers require proficient advancement openings to familiarize themselves with the platform's highlights, translate understudied information bits of knowledge, and tailor guideline methodologies appropriately.

In addition, guaranteeing equal access to and support for all students, especially those from underrepresented or marginalized foundations, remains a priority for colleges (Williamson, 2017). Endeavors are underway to address issues of computerized isolation, availability, and inclusivity to guarantee that all students can benefit from personalized learning encounters encouraged by the versatile learning stage. Thus, the case study considers TechEd College to illustrate the transformative potential of AI-powered personalization in higher instruction. By executing a versatile learning stage, the college has tailored its learning encounters to meet its understudies' assorted needs and inclinations, resulting in expanded engagement, maintenance, and educational victory. The proceeded speculation in AI advances, staff improvement, and value activities will be fundamental to maintaining and scaling the benefits of personalized higher instruction for all understudies.

REFERENCES

Abdelghany, S. Z. A. (2022). Students' attitudes Towards Using Duolingo As A Self-Learning Artificial Intelligence-Based App In Distance Learning During The Pandemic In The United Arab Emirates.

Algabri, H. K., Kharade, K., & Kamat, R. (2021). Promise, threats, and personalization in higher education with artificial intelligence. *Webology, 18*(6).

Beghetto, R. A. (2019). Large-scale assessments, personalized learning, and creativity: Paradoxes and possibilities. *ECNU Review of Education*, 2(3), 311–327. DOI:10.1177/2096531119878963

Bhutoria, A. (2022). Personalized education and artificial intelligence in the United States, China, and India: A systematic review using a human-in-the-loop model. *Computers and Education: Artificial Intelligence*, 3, 100068. DOI:10.1016/j.caeai.2022.100068

Chaipidech, P., Srisawasdi, N., Kajornmanee, T., & Chaipah, K. (2022). A personalized learning system-supported professional training model for teachers' TPACK development. *Computers and Education: Artificial Intelligence*, 3, 100064. DOI:10.1016/j.caeai.2022.100064

Ciolacu, M., Tehrani, A. F., Binder, L., & Svasta, P. M. (2018, October). Education 4.0-Artificial Intelligence assisted higher education: early recognition system with machine learning to support students' success. In *2018 IEEE 24th International Symposium for Design and Technology in Electronic Packaging (SIITME)* (pp. 23-30). IEEE.

Dhawan, S., & Batra, G. (2020). Artificial intelligence in higher education: Promises, perils, and perspective. *Expanding Knowledge Horizon.OJAS*, 11, 11–22.

Hashim, S., Omar, M. K., Ab Jalil, H., & Sharef, N. M. (2022). Trends on Technologies and Artificial Intelligence in Education for Personalized Learning: Systematic Literature. *Journal of Acdemic Research in Progressive Education and Development*, 12(1), 884–903. DOI:10.6007/IJARPED/v11-i1/12230

Klašnja-Milićević, A., & Ivanović, M. (2021). E-learning personalization systems and sustainable education. *Sustainability (Basel)*, 13(12), 6713. DOI:10.3390/su13126713

Lee, D., Huh, Y., Lin, C. Y., & Reigeluth, C. M. (2018). Technology functions for personalized learning in learner-centered schools. *Educational Technology Research and Development*, 66(5), 1269–1302. DOI:10.1007/s11423-018-9615-9

Liu, Y., & Quan, Q. (2022). AI Recognition Method of Pronunciation Errors in Oral English Speech with the Help of Big Data for Personalized Learning. *Journal of Information & Knowledge Management*, 2240028.

Lynch, D., Christensen, U. J., & Howe, N. J. (2020). AI Technology and Personalized Learning Design—Uncovering Unconscious Incompetence. In *Radical Solutions and Learning Analytics* (pp. 157–172). Springer. DOI:10.1007/978-981-15-4526-9_10

Maghsudi, S., Lan, A., Xu, J., & van Der Schaar, M. (2021). Personalized education in the artificial intelligence era: What to expect next. *IEEE Signal Processing Magazine*, 38(3), 37–50. DOI:10.1109/MSP.2021.3055032

Magomadov, V. S. (2020, November). The application of artificial intelligence and Big Data analytics in personalized learning. *Journal of Physics: Conference Series*, 1691(1), 012169. DOI:10.1088/1742-6596/1691/1/012169

Martin, S. M., Casey, J. R., & Kane, S. (2021). History of Artificial Intelligence and Personalized Learning. In *Serious Games in Personalized Learning* (pp. 27–47). Routledge. DOI:10.4324/9781003042709-2

Montebello, M. (2021, August). Personalized Learning Environments. In *2021 International Symposium on Educational Technology (ISET)* (pp. 134-138). IEEE. DOI:10.1109/ISET52350.2021.00036

Pedró, F. (2020). Applications of Artificial Intelligence to higher education: Possibilities, evidence, and challenges. *IUL Research*, 1(1), 61–76. DOI:10.57568/iulres.v1i1.43

Pratama, M. P., Sampelolo, R., & Lura, H. (2023). Revolutionizing education: harnessing the power of artificial intelligence for personalized learning. *Klasikal: Journal of Education. Language Teaching and Science*, 5(2), 350–357.

Rad, P., Roopaei, M., Beebe, N., Shadaram, M., & Au, Y. (2018, January). AI thinking for cloud education platform with personalized learning. *Proceedings of the 51st Hawaii international conference on system sciences*. DOI:10.24251/HICSS.2018.003

Rivers, C., & Holland, A. (2022). Management Education and Artificial Intelligence: Toward Personalized Learning. In *The Future of Management Education* (pp. 184-204). Routledge.

Somasundaram, M., Junaid, K. M., & Mangadu, S. (2020). Artificial intelligence (AI) enabled intelligent quality management system (IQMS) for personalized learning path. *Procedia Computer Science*, 172, 438–442. DOI:10.1016/j.procs.2020.05.096

Tang, Y., Liang, J., Hare, R., & Wang, F. Y. (2020). A personalized learning system for parallel intelligent education. *IEEE Transactions on Computational Social Systems*, 7(2), 352–361. DOI:10.1109/TCSS.2020.2965198

Tariq, M. U. (2024a). Enhancing Students and Learning Achievement as 21st-Century Skills Through Transdisciplinary Approaches. In Kumar, R., Ong, E., Anggoro, S., & Toh, T. (Eds.), *Transdisciplinary Approaches to Learning Outcomes in Higher Education* (pp. 220–257). IGI Global. DOI:10.4018/979-8-3693-3699-1.ch007

Tariq, M. U. (2024b). Multi-Agent Models in Healthcare System Design. In Dall'Acqua, L. (Ed.), *Bioethics of Cognitive Ergonomics and Digital Transition* (pp. 143–170). IGI Global. DOI:10.4018/979-8-3693-2667-1.ch008

Tariq, M. U. (2024c). Social Innovations for Improving Healthcare. In Chandan, H. (Ed.), *Social Innovations in Education, Environment, and Healthcare* (pp. 302–317). IGI Global. DOI:10.4018/979-8-3693-2569-8.ch015

Tariq, M. U. (2024d). Leveraging AI for Entrepreneurial Innovation in Healthcare. In Özsungur, F. (Ed.), *Generating Entrepreneurial Ideas With AI* (pp. 192–216). IGI Global. DOI:10.4018/979-8-3693-3498-0.ch009

Tariq, M. U. (2024e). Leading Smart Technologies and Innovations for E-Business 5.0: Applications and Management Frameworks. In Popkova, E. (Ed.), *Smart Technologies and Innovations in E-Business* (pp. 25–46). IGI Global. DOI:10.4018/978-1-6684-7840-0.ch002

Tariq, M. U. (2024f). Crafting Authentic Narratives for Sustainable Branding. In *Compelling Storytelling Narratives for Sustainable Branding* (pp. 194–229). IGI Global. DOI:10.4018/979-8-3693-3326-6.ch011

Tariq, M. U. (2024g). The role of AI in skilling, upskilling, and reskilling the workforce. In Doshi, R., Dadhich, M., Poddar, S., & Hiran, K. (Eds.), *Integrating generative AI in education to achieve sustainable development goals* (pp. 421–433). IGI Global. DOI:10.4018/979-8-3693-2440-0.ch023

Tariq, M. U. (2024h). AI-powered language translation for multilingual classrooms. In Doshi, R., Dadhich, M., Poddar, S., & Hiran, K. (Eds.), *Integrating generative AI in education to achieve sustainable development goals* (pp. 29–46). IGI Global. DOI:10.4018/979-8-3693-2440-0.ch002

Yang, A. C., Flanagan, B., & Ogata, H. (2022). Adaptive formative assessment system based on computerized adaptive testing and the learning memory cycle for personalized learning. *Computers and Education: Artificial Intelligence*, 100104.

Zhang, Q. (2022). Construction of Personalized Learning Platform Based on Collaborative Filtering Algorithm. *Wireless Communications and Mobile Computing*, 2022, 2022. DOI:10.1155/2022/5878344

ADDITIONAL READING

Babar, M., Tariq, M. U., Alshehri, M. D., Ullah, F., & Uddin, M. I. (2022). Smart teledentistry healthcare architecture for medical big data analysis using IoT-enabled environment. *Sustainable Computing : Informatics and Systems*, 35, 100719. DOI:10.1016/j.suscom.2022.100719

Banu, S. R., Thulasi, V. V. Y. R., Tariq, M. U., & Sethi, S. (2023). Relationship between leadership effectiveness and organizational performance and its effect on human resource management. *Journal of Informatics Education and Research*, 3(2).

Bhardwaj, S., Nair, K., Tariq, M. U., Ahmad, A., & Chitnis, A. (2023). The state of research in green marketing: A bibliometric review from 2005 to 2022. *Sustainability (Basel)*, 15(4), 2988. DOI:10.3390/su15042988

Kaleem, S., Sohail, A., Babar, M., Ahmad, A., & Tariq, M. U. (2023). Ensemble learning for multi-class COVID-19 detection from big data. *PLoS One*, 18(10), e0292587. DOI:10.1371/journal.pone.0292587 PMID:37819992

Kaleem, S., Sohail, A., Tariq, M. U., & Asim, M. (2023). An improved big data analytics architecture using federated learning for IoT-enabled urban intelligent transportation systems. *Sustainability (Basel)*, 15(21), 15333. DOI:10.3390/su152115333

Kaleem, S., Sohail, A., Tariq, M. U., & Asim, M. (2024). A hybrid model for energy-efficient green Internet of Things enabled intelligent transportation systems using federated learning. *Internet of Things : Engineering Cyber Physical Human Systems*, 25, 101038. DOI:10.1016/j.iot.2023.101038

KEY TERMS AND DEFINITIONS

AI-Powered Chatbots: Virtual assistants that use AI to provide students with real-time, personalised support, answering queries.

Competency-Based Education: An educational model where students progress through coursework at their own pace.

Learning Management System (LMS): An AI-driven platform used in education to track student interactions.

Personalised Recommendation Engines: AI systems that analyse student data to suggest tailored courses, resources, and learning activities.

Real-Time Feedback: Immediate, AI-generated responses provided to students based on their performance.

Virtual Mentoring Systems: AI-driven platforms that simulate one-on-one mentoring by offering personalised guidance and support.

Chapter 11
Exploration of AI Precision in Higher Education

ABSTRACT

This chapter dives into the multifaceted scene of AI exactness inside higher instruction, looking at its applications, benefits, challenges, and suggestions for long-term instruction, learning, and organizational administration. AI exactness includes the vital application of AI calculations and information analytics to optimise instructive forms and results, centred on personalised learning, prescient analytics, and authoritative proficiency. By leveraging AI advances, higher instruction teachers can improve their understudy engagement, inspiration, and scholarly accomplishment through custom-fitted learning experiences and versatile back components. Integrating AI exactness into higher instruction is not without challenges, including moral contemplations, algorithmic predisposition, and workforce suggestions. Despite these challenges, the investigation of AI exactness holds a colossal guarantee for changing higher instruction conveyance and organisation, cultivating a culture of advancement, inclusivity, and student-centred learning.

INTRODUCTION

The integration of artificial intelligence (AI) into higher instruction speaks to a transformative slant that has gained a critical footing for a long time. This chapter provides a comprehensive diagram of existing enquiries and insightful discussions encompassing the investigation of AI accuracy in higher education. By synthesizing experiences from an assorted cluster of scholarly distributions, this audit explains the multifaceted applications, suggestions, and future bearings of AI exactness within the

DOI: 10.4018/979-8-3693-4074-5.ch011

higher instruction scene. At the heart of the investigation of AI accuracy in higher instruction lies the conceptual system of AI advances as an accurate instrument for optimizing instructive forms and results. AI specialists and Inventado (2014) characterize AI accuracy as a vital application of AI algorithms and information analytics to attain focused, custom-made, and successful results in instructive spaces. This conceptualization underscores the potential of AI to personalize learning encounters, upgrade instruction adequacy, and streamline authoritative capacities inside higher instruction education.

An unmistakable topic in writing on AI accuracy in higher instruction is part of personalized learning and versatile advances in improving under-study engagement, inspiration, and scholastic accomplishment. Sclater et al. (2016) emphasized the significance of AI-powered versatile learning stages in fitting instructive substances, pacing, and input to learners' needs and inclinations. By leveraging machine learning calculations and cognitive modelling methods, these stages offer personalized learning pathways that require assorted learning styles, capacities, and interfaces, cultivating a more comprehensive and compelling learning environment. Another striking perspective of AI accuracy in higher instruction is the application of prescient analytics to determine understudy execution, distinguish at-risk understudies, and endorse focused mediations to advance understudy victory and maintenance. Arnold and Pistilli (2012) highlight the utility of prescient modelling procedures in analyzing tremendous datasets comprising understudy socioeconomics, scholastic measurements, and behavioral pointers to anticipate future results and educate evidence-based decision-making. By leveraging prescient analytics, teachers and directors can proactively mediate moderate scholarly challenges, focus on bolstering administrations, and optimize asset assignment techniques to upgrade understudied results and organizational viability.

Despite its potential benefits, integrating AI accuracy in higher instruction is not without moral contemplations and challenges. Selwyn (2019) underscores the significance of issues related to information security, assent, and security within AI-driven instructive advances. Colleges must explore complex lawful and moral systems that oversee the collection, capacity, and utilization of understudy information to guarantee compliance with administrative guidelines and protect understudy rights and confidentiality. Additionally, there is growing concern that algorithmic inclination and segregation are inalienable in AI systems, which may sustain or worsen existing disparities in instructive get-to, achievement, and results. Shrewd and Shaffer (2015) caution against the unintended results of one-sided calculations, which can lead to out-of-line treatment, stigmatization, and marginalization of certain understudied populations, especially those from underrepresented or marginalized foundations. It is essential for colleges to actualize thorough testing, approval, and examination procedures to moderate algorithmic inclination and guarantee reasonableness, straightforwardness, and responsibility in AI-driven decision-making forms.

Looking ahead, the investigation of AI exactness in higher education holds noteworthy suggestions for lending earnings and institutional management. Henderson (2019) argued that colleges must grasp a culture of advancement, experimentation, and collaboration to saddle the total potential of AI advances in upgrading instructive encounters and results. By contributing to staff advancement programs, academic preparation, and mechanical proficiency activities, education can enable educators with essential aptitudes and competencies to use AI viably in their education hones and adjust to advancing parts within the computerized learning environment.

In addition, the far-reaching appropriation of AI exactness can catalyze systemic changes in instructive arrangements, hones, and enquiries. Griffin and Halverson (2019) advocated for a holistic approach to AI integration, prioritizing value and incorporation, and understudying victory as fundamental targets. Colleges must cultivate intriguing collaborations, moral rules, and administrative systems to guarantee that AI innovations are sent dependably, morally, and evenhandedly to advance the well-being and strength of all learners. Thus, the investigation of AI precision in higher instruction offers important insights into the transformative potential of AI innovations to revolutionize education, learning, and regulatory forms. By leveraging AI for personalized learning, prescient analytics, and ethical decision-making, colleges can aim to create a more comprehensive, responsive, and viable learning biological system that empowers students to flourish within the advanced age. As higher instruction teaches exploring the complexities of AI selection, they must stay watchful in maintaining moral standards, advancing differing qualities and incorporation, and prioritizing under-study victory as central precepts of their educational mission and vision (Tariq, 2024).

BACKGROUND

For a long time, the intersection of Artificial Intelligence (AI) and higher instruction has become progressively conspicuous, showing both openings and challenges for the scholarly community. This chapter comprehensively investigates AI exactness in higher instruction, illustrating its multifaceted suggestions, applications, and future directions. By examining the perplexing scene of AI innovations inside the setting of higher instruction, this chapter examines bits of knowledge into how AI exactness can change education, learning, and regulatory forms to meet the advancing needs of understudies, teachers, and education (Tariq, 2024).

The rise of AI in higher instruction means a worldview move in academic hones, regulatory capacities, and understudy back administration. AI innovations include a different cluster of computational apparatuses and methods, counting machine learning calculations, common dialect preparation, and proactive analytics, which can expand and optimize different perspectives of instructive involvement. As colleges hook the objectives of computerized change and the requests of a knowledge-driven economy, the integration of AI accuracy develops as a compelling technique to upgrade the viability, effectiveness, and value of higher instruction conveyance and organization. AI exactness in higher instruction signifies the vital application of AI advances to realize focused, custom-fitted, and compelling results in instructive spaces. At its center, AI exactness involves the utilization of data-driven bits of knowledge, visionary modelling, and versatile calculations to personalize learning encounters, optimize asset allotment, and encourage evidence-based decision making in higher instruction settings. By harnessing the control of AI exactness, colleges can yearn to cultivate a learning biological system that is responsive, comprehensive, and conducive to the all-encompassing advancement of understudies from different foundations and capacities.

The applications of AI accuracy in higher instruction are complex, traversing education, learning, appraisal, and organizational administration spaces. One notable application is personalized learning. AI-powered versatile learning stages use information analytics and cognitive modelling procedures to tailor instructive substances, pacing, and criticize learners' personal needs and inclinations (Bread et al., 2014). Through personalized learning pathways, understudies can engage in self-directed investigation, mastery-based movements, and nonstop criticism circles that cater to their interesting learning styles and competencies. Another noteworthy application is prescient analytics. AI calculations analyze endless datasets comprising under-studied socioeconomics, scholastic execution measurements, and socio-economic markers to determine future results, recognize hazard components, and prescribe focused mediations (Arnold & Pistilli, 2012). Prescient analytics empower teachers and presiding officers to expect under-study needs, relieve scholarly challenges, and optimize asset allotment techniques to cultivate under-study victory and maintenance. In addition, AI exactness expands to authoritative capacities inside higher instruction, enveloping areas such as confirmation, enrolment administration, course planning, and money-related aid allocation (Jung & Latcheva, 2019). By computerizing scheduled authoritative assignments and decision-making forms through AI-driven frameworks, colleges can streamline operations, decrease authoritative burdens, and reallocate human assets to more value-added exercises that improve the general under-study encounter.

Integrating AI exactness in higher instruction offers benefits and opportunities for partners over scholastic biological systems. For understudies, AI-powered personalized learning situations enable them to require possession of their learning travel, develop self-regulated learning aptitudes, and obtain custom-fitted back components that platform their scholastic advances (Sclater et al., 2016). By obliging assorted learning styles, inclinations, and capacities, AI exactness advances inclusivity, value, and engagement among understudies, thereby cultivating a culture of long-lasting learning and mental interest. Teachers benefit from AI exactness through improved academic adequacy, data-informed decision-making, and streamlined authoritative workflow (Reeve et al., 2018). AI advances have empowered teachers to use real-time learning analytics, demonstrative appraisals, and versatile criticism components to illuminate direction techniques, recognize learning holes, and provide opportune intercessions that address the needs of the person under study. In addition, AI-driven educating colleagues and intelligent tutoring frameworks can expand educators' capacity to convey personalized, differentiated instruction at a scale, optimize education adequacy, and understudy learning results.

From an organizational perspective, the selection of AI accuracy guarantees more prominent operational productivity, asset optimization, and regulation viability (Griffin & Halverson, 2019). By tackling AI for prescient modelling, execution analytics, and key arrangement, colleges can expect future patterns, distribute assets wisely, and develop a data-driven culture of nonstop enhancement and development. Furthermore, AI-powered regulatory frameworks empower teachers to streamline bureaucratic forms, upgrade benefit conveyance, and optimize under-study bolster administrations, thereby upgrading the general under-study encounter and regulation notoriety. Despite its transformative potential, integrating AI accuracy into higher instruction does not challenge moral contemplation. One essential challenge is the moral utilization of understudied information, as AI frameworks depend on vast amounts of delicate data to personalize learning encounters and advise decision-making forms (Selwyn, 2019). Colleges must explore complex legitimate and moral systems that administer information protection, assent, and security to guarantee compliance with administrative measures and defend understudy rights and privacy.

In addition, there is a chance of algorithmic predisposition and discrimination inherent in AI frameworks, which may sustain or worsen the existing imbalances in instructive get-to, achievement, and results (Shrewd & Shaffer, 2015). One-sided calculations can lead to unjustifiable treatment, stigmatization, and marginalization of certain understudied populations, especially those from underrepresented or marginalized foundations. It is essential for colleges to address algorithmic predisposition through thorough testing, approval, and inspection of AI calculations to guarantee decency, straightforwardness, and responsibility in decision-making forms.

Moreover, the widespread adoption of AI in higher education raises concerns about workforce uprooting, work reconfiguration, and long-standing time for teachers within an advanced age (Henderson, 2019). Although AI advances have the potential to mechanize schedule errands and regulatory capacities, they cannot duplicate the human components of education, mentorship, and emotional back given by teachers. Colleges must contribute to staff improvement programs, educational preparation, and innovative proficiency activities to engage teachers with the imperative abilities and competencies to use AI successfully in their education hones and adjust to advancing aspects within the computerized learning environment.

Thus, investigating AI exactness in higher instruction represents an urgent frontier in the continuous advancement of instruction, learning, and regulation management. By saddling the control of AI innovations to personalize learning encounters, optimize asset allocation, and educate evidence-based decision-making, colleges can aim to create a more comprehensive, evenhanded, and responsive learning biological system that enables understudies to flourish within the advanced age. As higher instruction teachers explore the complexities of AI appropriation, they must remain vigilant in maintaining moral standards, advancing differences and considerations, and prioritizing student success as vital goals for instructive excellence and societal effects (Tariq, 2024).

The learning efficiency of physical and virtual teaching techniques seems to overtake conventional teaching techniques in educational domains. Students can utilise virtual learning media to preview relevant content, learn basic knowledge, and improve their practical experience of system progress courses. The emergence of the COVID-19 pandemic has resulted in new learning and teaching methods. However, the following challenges arise as a consequence of this international trend:

- Increased registration and low accomplishment rate
- A significant gap in the communication between teachers and students compared with the conventional physical education methods
- Effective preclusion of course certification and virtual assessment still requires to be resolved
- The expense of medium maintenance

In recent years, educational models have shifted from physical learning to virtual learning. Some researchers suggest that online education should not act as a substitute for classrooms and teachers but should enhance them. The term precision has replaced the implementation of data to treat and assess a broad range of phenomena. Precision medicine explains that the use of comprehensive patient information to adapt to treatment and prevention depends on lifestyle, genes, and environment. By contrast, precision agriculture has become a complete domain of research and development, emphasising engineering technology, positioning systems, sensor systems, and control systems for site-specific implementation in agriculture. Precision farming and precision medicine methods ensure the accumulation and assessment of diversified data and scientific knowledge for the objectives of highly targeted interference (Vartiainen et al., 2020). This may seem to make sense of health diagnoses or enhance crop production. However, the production of precision may have unfavourable outcomes in other units. Data-based precision is a source of contestation, controversy, and scientific certainty. Evolving interest in precision in higher education predicts the intensive usage of student data for the objectives of adopting customised learning practices and targeted education has been explained. Experts who assess the generic, brain-powered, environmental, and psychological aspects of education intend to explore higher education to implement progressive higher education customised according to the requirements of students. As this signifies, precision in higher education depends on huge aims. This supposes that the science of psychology, genes, behaviour, and neurology can be merged to provide insights into the educational procedure and explain how learning materials and inputs can be arranged in methods best suited to each learner. Supporters of Precision in higher education also recommend that complicated computer programs may be needed to process three massive troves of data to customise the learner's higher education experience. Precision in higher education requires a cohort of confidential data from learners and the continuous processing of neurological, genetic, and psychological details regarding the interior information of the minds and bodies (Zawacki-Richter et al., 2019).

Unwrapping Precision Higher Education

It is worth contemplating what is included in precision higher education, what it might seem like in practice, and its inferences for higher education policy. In some techniques, precision higher education seems like a push for other customised educational practices and medium developments that have taken place in previous years. Based on advancements in adaptive learning technologies and learning analytics, customised learning has become the leading focus of the higher education technology industry and a vital priority for philanthropic funders such as Mark Zuckerberg and Bill Gates. For instance, private nonprofit universities that run specified online courses have a precision institute devoted to precision learning. It is through adaptive machine learning education and personalised course navigation, utilising real-time data generated from several analysis tools. It is developing a precision in higher education medium for customised learning to accumulate student data to assess the associations between learning objectives and student characteristics. As others support, scientific partiality is a vital characteristic of precision learning.

While most customised education mediums seem to emphasise assessing student development and analysis results, precision learning requires much more personal data from learners. Precision learning depicts a switch from the accumulation of analysis-type data about educational results to the generation of data about intrinsic personal information about students' genetic makeup, psychological aspects, and neural working. Intrinsically, precision in higher education is a segment of a rise in interest in higher educational neuroscience and educational genomics to allow firms to develop customised curriculum programs dependent on the student's DNA profile. Scholars are researching attainment and genres and have proposed DNA assessment devices, such as learning chips, to make dependable genetic forecasts of hereditary differences between students in terms of their academic attainment and cognitive capability (Guan et al., 2020). Cost-effective DNA kits for IQ assessment in universities may not be far away, carried out by advanced genetics of intelligence. Psychology has also started progressing in science and the practice of precision in higher education to improve student results. Researchers have dedicated themselves to spreading knowledge about how young people progress and learn, focusing on neuroscience, genetic factors, science of learning, and progressive psychology in education. It is along with contemplations of the programs and technologies needed to customise learning to students' specific requirements, considering the economic, biological, and social differences in their education. A broad range of subjects should include behavioural genetics, psychology, paediatrics, neurobiology, computer science, education, evolutionary biology, and human-computer collaboration. In this context, researchers have started to address the prospects and challenges of precision higher education (Bonk et al., 2018). The precision in higher education articles is cautious and thoughtful but also evidently sloping to the progress of a multidisciplinary research domain. The world is presently a long way far from attaining the information required to recognise precision in higher education, but claims that the foundation has started:

- Educational neuroscience is developing a recognition of the science behind teaching and learning via the merging of several collaborations and disciplines with instructors
- The proof is being accumulated from a diversified set of domains, which will ultimately lead to a more profound recognition of the mechanisms included in education
- Genetic research is part of this analysis. Instead of something to be afraid of, the recognition of genes is simply another segment of the puzzle in the learning science

- As the desire for evidence-based practices increases, the future of learning and teaching may well be customised higher education that considers a host of student characteristics.

It is vital to accumulate large amounts of data to make higher education precision possible.

- The procedure of data accumulation has already started in the form of several researchers that has the objective of unwrapping the neurological and psychological procedures that support higher education
- If precision in higher education is to come to an achievement, each student will require to give their details to determine which kind of learning content best suits them
- Precision in higher education would extract the best accessible proof from a host of characteristics which might involve genetic data, test scores, the students' environmental characteristics, and own interests
- Precision in higher education may also lead to a good option for the student-particularly youngsters opting for which courses to focus on later in their career
- A very robust scientific recognition of the mechanisms that impact higher education will be the first step to the comprehension of precision in higher education

Researchers acknowledge that it is too soon to state how precision in higher education will appear in practice. Researchers have suggested that neuroscience offers ever-progressing technologies that allow the world to imagine the thinking mind. Therefore, they are allowing educational neuroscientists to know more than ever before about how learners learn, even though it also constrains the fact that it is not simple to translate these results to the classroom. It has also helped scholars to assess the connection between educational success and genetics. Irrespective of the limitations and restraints, the science of the gene and brain, behavioural, and psychology science are already becoming stuck in higher education policy. It is simple to witness the prospective appeal of precision in higher education to strategists keen to explore scientific-proof-based solutions to educational issues. A new blend of human sciences and education policy is evolving in the context of strategy concerns with what functions. There are new types of bio-education strategies–scientists may be evolving as authorities in the educational strategy, not only experts on interfering with social bodies like universities, but also with human bodies (Tsai et al., 2020).

METHODS REQUIRED FOR PRECISION IN HIGHER EDUCATION

Many individuals explore the ideas behind precision in education. Initially, there seemed to be some distressing proportions between the reasons for targeted advertising and the learning that generated intense media and public attention in 2022. Data security and privacy are evident threats when data are accumulated about people's interior, private, and personal lives, brains, and bodies (Yang et al., 2021). The ethical risks of utilising neural, psychological, and genetic profiles to target learners with segregated learning inputs are also vital. Such concerns will be particularly critical as political press for significant focus on the biological factors of higher education or as precision in higher education methods is created by start-up firms with uncertain credentials. Precision in higher education also requires the assessment of significant information to recognise the viability of its claims and promises. The amount of technical equipment alone needed for precision in higher education is huge.

This would have to involve neurotechnologies for accumulating brain data, such as neuro-headsets for EEG observation. There is a need for novel types of assessments, such as non-cognitive and personality skills, and a real-time analytics program endorsed by customised learning supporters. The accumulation of personal data may also require genetic assessment technologies. It may be wearable, improved learning equipment for apprehending real-time psychophysical data from learners' bodies as a substitute for psychometric measures of their reactions to learning content and inputs. By accumulating neurological, behavioural, psychological, and genetic data along with environmental characteristics and test scores, precision in higher education is an extension of the present enthusiasm to quantify the human situation while lessening human beings to data bodies of informational designs. Each technology that produces personal data about learners depends on a complicated combination of scientific knowledge, social or political motivations, business plans, and technical innovations. Some may not be persistent, intellectually or technically. Just as software mediums do not always integrate into each other efficiently, vital corrective partitions remain between genetics, psychology, and neuroscience which would require associating for precision in higher education to become imaginable. There are already considerations that precision in medicine can duplicate discrimination and bias through outcomes and datasets. Precision education data can correspond to uncertain data accumulation and usage exercises (Harris & Patton, 2019).

Psychology, brain science, and genetics have all been subjected to substantial analyses. Modern science mostly appears to treat the brain, mind, and body as manipulable and flexible, capable of debugging and recording in the same manner as software, as differences between biological and computational have started to close.

Distress has also been elevated about new genes and the prospects for genetic data to reproduce dangerous thoughts about heritability of genetic intelligence. Both old disputes in the usage of genetics, psychology, and neuroscience in leading behaviours and bodies, and new considerations about treating the body as if it were silicon, have the prospect of replication through precision in higher education. One creative way forward may be to access precision in higher education from a biosocial viewpoint. Scholars argue that learning may be best recognised as an outcome of biological and social predicaments. They support cooperative, multidisciplinary studies across biological and social sciences to recognise learning procedures as the active result of genetic, neural, and biological characteristics combined with culturally and socially embedded integrations and composing procedures (Tariq, 2024).

An assortment of neuroscientific and biological ideas is also being integrated into higher education, making practice and policy more bioinspired. Other biosocial research also recognises that the body endures labels of its materially and socially positioned setting, influenced by power arrangements in society, and that the mind is a multiply connected tool formed by social impacts. The social subcutaneous to impress on biological. As such, a biosocial method would pursue the recognition of precision in higher education in both social scientific and biological terms by appreciating that the social ecosystems in which education takes place mark themselves on the brain and body. Such a method would interpret precision in higher education as a source of power, reforming the social ecosystem of the university and interfering with the psychological, biological, and neurological interrelates of learning (Al-Kumaim et al., 2021).

Personal Data Analytics

Personal data analytics of precision in higher education raises some fundamental subjects for future assessment:

- The rise of bio-evidence-based education strategy, as data apprehended about the biological-genetic, psychophysical, and neural details of students' bodies, revolved into policy-related knowledge and intervention targets
- The translation of learners into bioinformatical flows of scientific and number classifications, extracting new manners of recognizing the learning procedures as biologically centered and eliminating other perspectives
- The collection of bio-capital by firms that can market products, accumulate, assess, and then share and sell learners' biodata, whether directly to parents and universities or by less interrupted means
- The progress of bioeconomics of educational data as psychophysical, genetic, and neural technologies and analysis tools become novel competitive

marketplaces involving scam outfits considering exploiting interest in learner biodata
- The forming of novel student subjectivities, as learners are addressed and start to address themselves in biological and measured terms and are encouraged to carry out activities to enhance themselves in response to their psycho-physiological data

Whether or not precision in education takes off as a multidisciplinary domain of research and development, let alone impacts practice and policy, may matter very little if we identify that various technologies and priorities captured in this evolving group already exist or are emerging online (Lazarevic & Bentz, 2021). Progress in psycho-informatics, neurology, and genetics technologies is either accessible or in the creation pipeline for withdrawing personal data from the interior of minds and brains. With the latest developments, such as neurofeedback, behaviour-change application, and gene-editing, technologies stand composed to mine cognition, biology, and behaviour and to twist and transform too. As a biosocial viewpoint would see it, personal data analytics is to bother. With time, the emphasis on variances in students' traits begins to expand, from differences in direct responses and learning outcomes to variances in mental firms and depictions, cognitive styles, inspirations, and an increased focus on differences in brain structure and learning-relevant problems. The opinions of students on variances in traits slowly switched from flaws to specialisms to diversity and uniqueness. This change depicts respect for each student's variance and highlights the significance of higher education in supporting students in determining and exhibiting individual strengths and increasing their prospects of success (Marcinkowski et al., 2020).

While instructors are often challenged by learners' differences in the classroom, they can accommodate them via efficient planning and relevant measures. Adaptive teaching has been addressed as an outcome of society's diversified progress. The initial differentiation of sub-track learning and ability grouping progressed into the current focus on the variability and diversity of learners' learning styles. It is vital to approach learners' differences with a more positive attitude and consider their learning prospects (Penprase, 2018). This is one of the fundamental aspects of adaptive teaching. In virtual classrooms, students are expected to learn independently. However, there are still various students who have adapted to depending on instructors and teacher-centric approaches and struggle to be responsible for their learning. Therefore, instructors should consider the specific differences among students when adopting virtual classrooms. This customised user need signifies the significance of incorporating technical resources into the curriculum and students' actual situations. In recent years, precision has been broadly promoted in various disciplines with huge funds invested in relevant studies and strategy development (Kocielnik et al., 2019).

Recognising students' genomic structures may lead to enhanced medical treatment and have excellent potential. All humans share a standard fundamental physiology that attains basic limitations in how personalised medicine may turn out. Instead, the idea that each person is a machine with a marginally different biochemical instruction set means that

- Individuals can be classified depending on those differences
- Treatments can be made more efficient via precise recognition of how biochemical differences drive physiological changes linked with disease
- The functioning of precision medicine will be powered by Big Data, involving lab data on fundamental chemistry and clinical data on treatment results

In the domain of higher education, the idea of personalised learning is now linked with a host of efforts to enhance their results for people who are lifelong learners. Universities are promoting various strategic projects to develop and apply technological solutions to improve learning and teaching. Universities are planning next-generation services that involve tools for their students. Customising these services is vital, in that the requirements of, say, a master's student in university may differ from those in the first year of undergraduates contemplating a dual physics and philosophy degree but might want to continue biopsychology instead. What can link these students is their wish to see some historical accumulation of data that forms a beneficial fragmented picture that may inform future decisions. More students and parents would preferably like a very high degree of customisation, something along the lines of dependence on the present standing, taking this specific set of N subjects in the following order will fundamentally more than ninety-five percent confidence guarantee a career in course X and a lifestyle satisfaction index five years after completion. Evenly in an openly data-rich world, it is presently too much to ask. Rather than this high degree of customisation, tools for precision in higher education can follow the principles of medicine. Each student is a well-known snowflake exclusive in detail and, so, above average in some specific measures, but seen distantly, a comparatively modest set of characteristics can categorise them. Opening doors to how learners with diversified characteristics have tied into co-curricular and curricular activities at universities and to a career beyond campus is a provision of significant interest to instructors, parents, and students. Higher education is an active sector; therefore, utilising previous and present trends as an indicator of future performance will involve risks. Being precise implies attaining less vagueness. The large size of the primary student record database at universities means that there is substantial fruit that academic reporting tools and services for learners can opt for. Universities can propose subjects by their numbers, permitting vires of student characteristic compositions, teacher assessments, and prior grade distributions. Another practical challenge that learners require is an enhanced way to formulate and opt among the options for multiterm course selection. Another possible challenge students require assistance with is an enhanced way to articulate and opt among options for multiterm course choice. It is vital for seniors and juniors to have opted for multiple majors. Precision in higher education does not seek the higher principles of customised learning, and its efficacy may reduce the indirect shift in the rule book of interest only to academics (Chen et al., 2020).

FUTURE EXPLORATION OF AI PRECISION IN HIGHER EDUCATION

The integration of Fake Insights (AI) accuracy in higher education speaks to an energetic and advancing frontier with profound suggestions for teaching, learning, and regulation administration. In the long run, it is necessary to consider the potential directions, opportunities, and challenges that lie ahead in the investigation of AI accuracy in higher education.

Progressions in AI Innovations

One of the key drivers in the long haul of investigation of AI accuracy in higher instruction is the headway and the multiplication of AI advances. With rapid advances in machine learning, normal dialect preparation, and current analytics, AI frameworks are becoming progressively modern and competent in dealing with complex instructive assignments and challenges (Jordan & Mitchell, 2015). As AI innovations continue to develop, higher instruction can anticipate more extensive extentowered arrangements and applications that upgrade personalized learning encounters, optimize regulatory forms, and illuminate evidence-based decision-making.

Personalized Learning at Scale

One of the most promising ranges of development in the future of AI exactness in higher instruction is the adaptability of personalized learning. While personalized learning has illustrated critical benefits for under-study engagement and accomplishment, scaling personalized learning activities over huge, different populations remains challenging for numerous teachers (DouPuncherher, 2017). Progression in AI accuracy methods, such as versatile learning calculations and learning analytics, can address this challenge by empowering the conveyance of personalized learning experiences at scale. By leveraging AI to analyze tremendous amounts of under-study information and tailor instructive intercessions to a person's learning needs, higher education creates more comprehensive, impartial, and successful learning situations for all under-studies.

Moral and Social Suggestions

Despite the guarantee of AI exactness in higher instruction, the long-standing time of investigation raises imperative moral and social suggestions, which must be carefully considered. As AI advances become more unavoidable in instructive settings, concerns about information security, algorithmic predisposition, and computerized values will likely come to the bleeding edge (Hao, 2020). Colleges must prioritize moral standards, straightforwardness, and responsibility within the design, implementation, and utilization of AI-powered frameworks to guarantee that they do not incidentally sustain or worsen existing imbalances in instruction. Furthermore, partners must lock in continuous exchange and collaboration to address moral problems and mitigate potential dangers related to the arrangement of AI exactness advances in higher education.

The end of the exploration of AI exactness in higher instruction will be characterized by expanded collaboration and intriguing enquiry efforts. As AI innovations cut over different spaces, including computer science, instruction, brain research, and humanism, intriguing collaboration is essential for advancing our understanding of how AI can be coordinated into instructive settings (Blikstein & Worsley, 2016). Colleges must cultivate a culture of collaboration, information sharing, and development that brings together analysts, professionals, policymakers, and industry accomplices to investigate the unused wilderness in AI accuracy and drive meaningful alterations in higher instruction.

Thus, a longer-term investigation of AI exactness in higher instruction holds immense promise for changing teaching, learning, and organizational administration. Headways in AI advances, adaptability of personalized learning, moral contemplations, and interdisciplinary collaboration will shape the direction of AI accuracy in higher instruction for a long time. By grasping development, cultivating collaboration, and prioritizing moral standards, higher-instruction teachers can saddle the total potential of AI exactness to form more comprehensive, impartial, and student-centered learning environments that plan understudies for victory within the computerized age.

CONCLUSION

The integration of Fake Insights (AI) accuracy in higher education speaks to an energetic and advancing frontier with profound suggestions for teaching, learning, and regulation administration. In the long run, it is necessary to consider the potential directions, opportunities, and challenges that lie ahead in the investigation of AI accuracy in higher education.

One of the key drivers in the long haul of investigation of AI accuracy in higher instruction is the headway and the multiplication of AI advances. With rapid advances in machine learning, normal dialect preparation, and prescient analytics, AI frameworks have become progressively modern and competent in dealing with complex instructive assignments and challenges (Jordan & Mitchell, 2015). As AI innovations continue to develop, higher instruction can anticipate seeing more extensive arrangements and applications that upgrade personalized learning encounters, optimize regulatory forms, and illuminate evidence-based decision-making.

One of the most promising ranges of development in the future of AI exactness in higher instruction is the adaptability of personalized learning. While personalized learning has illustrated critical benefits for understudy engagement and accomplishment, scaling personalized learning activities over huge, different understudy populations remains challenging for numerous teachers (DouPuncherher, 2017). Be that as it may, progressions in AI accuracy methods, such as versatile learning calculations and learning analytics, can address this challenge by empowering the conveyance of personalized learning experiences at scale. By leveraging AI to analyze tremendous amounts of under-study information and tailor instructive intercessions to a person's learning needs, higher education creates more comprehensive, impartial, and successful learning situations for all under-studies.

Despite the guarantee of AI exactness in higher instruction, the long-standing time of investigation raises imperative moral and social suggestions, which must be carefully considered. As AI advances become more unavoidable in instructive settings, concerns about information security, algorithmic predisposition, and computerized values will likely come to the bleeding edge (Hao, 2020). Colleges must prioritize moral standards, straightforwardness, and responsibility within the design, implementation, and utilization of AI-powered frameworks to guarantee that they do not incidentally sustain or worsen existing imbalances in instruction. Furthermore, partners must lock in continuous exchange and collaboration to address moral problems and mitigate potential dangers related to the arrangement of AI exactness advances in higher education.

The end of the exploration of AI exactness in higher instruction will be characterized by expanded collaboration and intriguing enquiries about efforts. As AI innovations cut over different spaces, including computer science, instruction, brain research, and humanism, intriguing collaboration is essential for advancing our understanding of how AI can be coordinated into instructive settings (Blikstein & Worsley, 2016). Colleges must cultivate a culture of collaboration, information sharing, and development that brings together analysts, professionals, policymakers, and industry accomplices to investigate the unused wilderness in AI accuracy and drive meaningful alterations in higher instruction. Thus, a longer-term investigation of AI exactness in higher instruction holds immense promise for changing teaching, learning, and organizational administration. Advances in AI, adaptability of personalized learning, moral contemplations, and interdisciplinary collaboration will shape the direction of AI accuracy in higher instruction for a long time. By grasping development, cultivating collaboration, and prioritizing moral standards, higher-instruction teachers can saddle the total potential of AI exactness to form more comprehensive, impartial, and student-centered learning environments that plan understudies for victory within the computerized age.

Precision in higher education is an educational context and behaviour dependent on big data analytics (Cai et al., 2020). The first vital factor of precision in higher education is recognising and acknowledging variances and offering targeted education and teaching based on the characteristics of individual learners, so that they can form their personalities and integrate their progress. Precision in higher education is a context and behaviour that is dependent on big data assessment. Precision in higher education depends on big data technology, which is categorised according to the different individualities of students during the learning process to offer targeted education. It helps enhance their strengths or recompense their weaknesses and enhances students' acceptance of learning through efficient teaching behaviour. Precision in higher education is a systematic and precise approach for assessing teaching tactics and curricula. It is a quantitative assessment of the behavioural forms of the applied behavioural assessment. Precision teaching is a type of programmed training that emphasises frequency as a vital datum. By emphasising fluency, the instructor can modify the curriculum for every learner to maximise learning, depending on the student's fluency. Teaching can be an approach or method. For instance, the most efficient implementation of precision teaching occurs when it is merged with direct teaching. Precision teaching has been utilised progressively to teach the progress of students, varying from the especially abled to university graduate students, and from the youngsters to the very old. It is an approach to strategize a teaching program to meet the requirements of a young person struggling to attain and maintain some skills. It has an inherent monitoring function and is a method of assessing the productivity of what is being taught. Precision in higher education helps instructors smoothly modify and customise their methods to target the domain with which students require the most assistance. Due to the variability in precision teaching, instructors can effortlessly support and enhance learners' confidence (Oke & Fernandes, 2020).

CASE STUDY

In this case study, we investigated the usage of AI exactness strategies in the next instruction institution to upgrade personalized learning encounters for understudies. Drawing on real-world cases and experimental proof, we examine how AI-powered versatile learning stages have revolutionized education and learning hones, moved forward student results, and educated evidence-based decision-making inside the scholastic setting. The integration of Manufactured Insights (AI) into higher instruction has been introduced in modern times of advancement and change, with personalized learning developing as a central center for leveraging AI accuracy methods. In this case, we examine the encounters of a college, Greenwood College, because it sets out on a trip to execute AI-powered versatile learning advances to improve understudy engagement, inspiration, and academic achievement.

Greenwood University could be a medium-sized open institution within the heart of a bustling metropolitan area. With a differing understudy body speaking to a wide run of foundations, interfaces, and learning styles, the college is committed to cultivating a culture of brilliance, inclusivity, and student-centered learning. Like many higher instruction teachers, Greenwood College faces challenges in assembling its understudies' differing needs and inclinations in conventional classroom settings. One of the essential challenges facing Greenwood College is the desire to suit different learning styles, capacities, and interfaces among its under-studied populace. In a conventional lecture-based organization, regularly educates the battle to lock in all understudies viably, driving aberrations in scholarly execution and understudy fulfilment levels. Moreover, college hooks with issues related to understudy maintenance, as a few understudies, may feel separated or disengaged from the learning handle due to the need for personalized back and criticism instruments.

To address these challenges, Greenwood College investigated the potential of AI-powered versatile learning stages to personalize learning encounters and optimize instruction adequacy. After conducting extensive enquiries about and pilot testing, the university accomplices with a driving ed-tech company actualize an AI-driven learning administration framework (LMS) that utilizes machine learning calculations and cognitive modelling methods to tailor instructive substance, pacing, and criticism of the person's needs and inclinations of learners. Usage preparation starts by integrating the AI-powered versatile learning stage into existing course offerings over different disciplines and offices at Greenwood College. Staff individuals receive training and are re-acquainted with the functionalities of the stage and how to join personalized learning exercises in their education. Furthermore, understudies are given introduction sessions and assets to explore the modern learning environment and maximize engagement with the versatile learning stage.

The AI-powered versatile learning stage offers highlights and usefulness to upgrade personalized learning encounters for understudies. These incorporate:

Personalized Learning Pathways

This stage utilizes information analytics and cognitive modelling strategies to evaluate students' learning inclinations, earlier information, and execution measurements. These data produce personalized learning pathways comprising exercises, assets, and appraisals custom-made to each understudy's needs and targets.

Versatile Input and Bolster

Throughout the learning journey, students obtain versatile input and bolster components that adjust in real time based on their reactions, progress, and learning directions. This incorporates moment criticism of assignments, tests, evaluations, and proposals for extra assets or interventions to address areas of trouble or misconceptions.

Data-Driven Experiences for Teachers

Faculty individuals can access real-time learning analytics and dashboards that provide knowledge of understudy engagement, advancement, and execution. By leveraging these data-driven experiences, teachers can distinguish between learning holes, alter direction methodologies, and focus on back-to-person understudies or bunches of learners. The execution of the AI-powered versatile learning stage yields promising results and impacts for both understudies and teachers at Greenwood College.

Improved Study Engagement and Inspiration

Students reported higher levels of engagement, inspiration, and fulfilment with personalized learning encounters offered by the versatile learning stage. By giving students independence, choice, and significance in their learning exercises, this stage cultivates a sense of possession and organization among understudies, leading to increased natural inspiration and scholarly achievement.

Progressive Learning Results

Preparatory information investigation revealed critical enhancements in understudy learning results, including higher exam scores, lower course withdrawal rates, and expanded retention of course content. When personalized learning pathways and versatile criticism components are provided, understudies illustrate a more profound understanding, dominance, and retention of subject matter concepts. Workforce individuals express eagerness for data-driven experiences and directions bolstered by versatile learning platforms. By leveraging real-time learning analytics and demonstrative appraisals, educators can recognize battling understudies early, tailor guidelines and mediations, and screen advances towards learning destinations more viably. In addition, teachers reported more noteworthy fulfilment with their instructing hones and a reestablished sense of reason in supporting understudy victory.

REFERENCES

Abdelghany, S. Z. A. (2022). Students'attitudes Towards Using Duolingo As A Self-Learning Artificial Intelligence-Based App In Distance Learning During The Pandemic In The United Arab Emirates.

Al-Kumaim, N. H., Alhazmi, A. K., Mohammed, F., Gazem, N. A., Shabbir, M. S., & Fazea, Y. (2021). Exploring the impact of the COVID-19 pandemic on university students' learning life: An integrated conceptual motivational model for sustainable and healthy online learning. *Sustainability (Basel)*, 13(5), 2546. DOI:10.3390/su13052546

Bonk, C. J., Zhu, M., Kim, M., Xu, S., Sabir, N., & Sari, A. R. (2018). Pushing toward a more personalized MOOC: Exploring instructor selected activities, resources, and technologies for MOOC design and implementation. *International Review of Research in Open and Distance Learning*, 19(4). Advance online publication. DOI:10.19173/irrodl.v19i4.3439

Cai, Y., Ma, J., & Chen, Q. (2020). Higher education in innovation ecosystems. *Sustainability (Basel)*, 12(11), 4376. DOI:10.3390/su12114376

Chen, X., Xie, H., Zou, D., & Hwang, G. J. (2020). Application and theory gaps during the rise of artificial intelligence in education. *Computers and Education: Artificial Intelligence*, 1, 100002. DOI:10.1016/j.caeai.2020.100002

Chu, H. C., Hwang, G. H., Tu, Y. F., & Yang, K. H. (2022). Roles and research trends of artificial intelligence in higher education: A systematic review of the top 50 most-cited articles. *Australasian Journal of Educational Technology*, 38(3), 22–42.

Guan, C., Mou, J., & Jiang, Z. (2020). Artificial intelligence innovation in education: A twenty-year data-driven historical analysis. *International Journal of Innovation Studies*, 4(4), 134–147. DOI:10.1016/j.ijis.2020.09.001

Harris, J. C., & Patton, L. D. (2019). Un/doing intersectionality through higher education research. *The Journal of Higher Education*, 90(3), 347–372. DOI:10.1080/00221546.2018.1536936

Hu, K. H. (2023). An exploration of the key determinants for the application of AI-enabled higher education based on a hybrid Soft-computing technique and a DEMATEL approach. *Expert Systems with Applications*, 212, 118762. DOI:10.1016/j.eswa.2022.118762

Huallpa, J. J. (2023). Exploring the ethical considerations of using Chat GPT in university education. *Periodicals of Engineering and Natural Sciences*, 11(4), 105–115. DOI:10.21533/pen.v11i4.3770

Khonturaev, S. I. (2023). The Evolution Of Artificial Intelligence: A Comprehensive Exploration For Higher Education. *Best Journal of Innovation in Science. Research for Development*, 2(11), 700–706.

Kocielnik, R., Amershi, S., & Bennett, P. N. (2019, May). Will you accept an imperfect ai? exploring designs for adjusting end-user expectations of ai systems. In *Proceedings of the 2019 CHI Conference on Human Factors in Computing Systems* (pp. 1-14).

Kuang, L., He, L. I. U., Yili, R. E. N., Kai, L. U. O., Mingyu, S. H. I., Jian, S. U., & Xin, L. I. (2021). Application and development trend of artificial intelligence in petroleum exploration and development. *Petroleum Exploration and Development*, 48(1), 1–14. DOI:10.1016/S1876-3804(21)60001-0

Lai, C. L. (2021). Exploring university students' preferences for AI-assisted learning environment. *Journal of Educational Technology & Society*, 24(4), 1–15.

Lazarevic, B., & Bentz, D. (2021). Student perception of stress in online and face-to-face learning: The exploration of stress determinants. *American Journal of Distance Education*, 35(1), 2–15. DOI:10.1080/08923647.2020.1748491

Li, W., & Liu, F. (2022). Exploration on College Ideological and Political Education Integrating Artificial Intelligence-Intellectualized Information Technology. *Computational Intelligence and Neuroscience*, 2022, 2022. DOI:10.1155/2022/4844565 PMID:35634053

Malik, A. R., Pratiwi, Y., Andajani, K., Numertayasa, I. W., Suharti, S., Darwis, A., & Marzuki, . (2023). Exploring Artificial Intelligence in Academic Essay: Higher Education Student's Perspective. *International Journal of Educational Research Open*, 5, 100296. DOI:10.1016/j.ijedro.2023.100296

Marcinkowski, F., Kieslich, K., Starke, C., & Lünich, M. (2020, January). Implications of AI (un-) fairness in higher education admissions: the effects of perceived AI (un-) fairness on exit, voice and organizational reputation. In *Proceedings of the 2020 conference on fairness, accountability, and transparency* (pp. 122-130). DOI:10.1145/3351095.3372867

Mohammed, A. A., Al-ghazali, A., & Alqohfa, K. A. (2023). Exploring ChatGPT uses in higher studies: A case study of Arab postgraduates in India. *Journal of English Studies in Arabia Felix*, 2(2), 9–17. DOI:10.56540/jesaf.v2i2.55

Nguyen, N. D. (2023). Exploring the role of AI in education. *London Journal of Social Sciences*, (6), 84–95. DOI:10.31039/ljss.2023.6.108

Oke, A., & Fernandes, F. A. P. (2020). Innovations in teaching and learning: Exploring the perceptions of the education sector on the 4th industrial revolution (4IR). *Journal of Open Innovation*, 6(2), 31. DOI:10.3390/joitmc6020031

Penprase, B. E. (2018). The fourth industrial revolution and higher education. *Higher education in the era of the fourth industrial revolution, 10*, 978-981.

Popenici, S. A., & Kerr, S. (2017). Exploring the impact of artificial intelligence on teaching and learning in higher education. *Research and Practice in Technology Enhanced Learning*, 12(1), 22. DOI:10.1186/s41039-017-0062-8 PMID:30595727

Rasul, T., Nair, S., Kalendra, D., Robin, M., de Oliveira Santini, F., Ladeira, W. J., & Heathcote, L. (2023). The role of ChatGPT in higher education: Benefits, challenges, and future research directions. *Journal of Applied Learning and Teaching*, 6(1).

Staszak, M., Staszak, K., Wieszczycka, K., Bajek, A., Roszkowski, K., & Tylkowski, B. (2022). Machine learning in drug design: Use of artificial intelligence to explore the chemical structure–biological activity relationship. *Wiley Interdisciplinary Reviews. Computational Molecular Science*, 12(2), e1568. DOI:10.1002/wcms.1568

Tariq, M. U. (2024a). AI and the future of talent management: Transforming recruitment and retention with machine learning. In Christiansen, B., Aziz, M., & O'Keeffe, E. (Eds.), *Global practices on effective talent acquisition and retention* (pp. 1–16). IGI Global. DOI:10.4018/979-8-3693-1938-3.ch001

Tariq, M. U. (2024b). Application of blockchain and Internet of Things (IoT) in modern business. In Sinha, M., Bhandari, A., Priya, S., & Kabiraj, S. (Eds.), *Future of customer engagement through marketing intelligence* (pp. 66–94). IGI Global. DOI:10.4018/979-8-3693-2367-0.ch004

Tariq, M. U. (2024c). The role of AI ethics in cost and complexity reduction. In Tennin, K., Ray, S., & Sorg, J. (Eds.), *Cases on AI ethics in business* (pp. 59–78). IGI Global. DOI:10.4018/979-8-3693-2643-5.ch004

Tariq, M. U. (2024d). Challenges of a metaverse shaping the future of entrepreneurship. In Inder, S., Dawra, S., Tennin, K., & Sharma, S. (Eds.), *New business frontiers in the metaverse* (pp. 155–173). IGI Global, DOI:10.4018/979-8-3693-2422-6.ch011

Tariq, M. U. (2024e). Neurodiversity inclusion and belonging strategies in the workplace. In J. Vázquez de Príncipe (Ed.), *Resilience of multicultural and multigenerational leadership and workplace experience* (pp. 182-201). IGI Global. DOI:10.4018/979-8-3693-1802-7.ch009

Tsai, S. C., Chen, C. H., Shiao, Y. T., Ciou, J. S., & Wu, T. N. (2020). Precision education with statistical learning and deep learning: A case study in Taiwan. *International Journal of Educational Technology in Higher Education*, 17(1), 1–13. DOI:10.1186/s41239-020-00186-2

Vartiainen, H., Tedre, M., & Valtonen, T. (2020). Learning machine learning with very young children: Who is teaching whom? *International Journal of Child-Computer Interaction*, 25, 100182. DOI:10.1016/j.ijcci.2020.100182

Wang, H., Wu, W., Dou, Z., He, L., & Yang, L. (2023). Performance and exploration of ChatGPT in medical examination, records and education in Chinese: Pave the way for medical AI. *International Journal of Medical Informatics*, 177, 105173. DOI:10.1016/j.ijmedinf.2023.105173 PMID:37549499

Yang, S. J., Ogata, H., Matsui, T., & Chen, N. S. (2021). Human-centered artificial intelligence in education: Seeing the invisible through the visible. *Computers and Education: Artificial Intelligence*, 2, 100008. DOI:10.1016/j.caeai.2021.100008

Zawacki-Richter, O., Marín, V. I., Bond, M., & Gouverneur, F. (2019). Systematic review of research on artificial intelligence applications in higher education–where are the educators? *International Journal of Educational Technology in Higher Education*, 16(1), 1–27. DOI:10.1186/s41239-019-0171-0

ADDITIONAL READING

Rahman, K., Ghani, A., Alzahrani, A., & Tariq, M. U. (2023). Pre-trained model-based NFR classification: Overcoming limited data challenges. *IEEE Access*. DOI:10.1109/ACCESS.2023.3301725

Raimi, L., Kah, J. M., & Tariq, M. U. (2022). The discourse of blue economy definitions, measurements, and theories: Implications for strengthening academic research and industry practice. In Raimi, L., & Kah, J. (Eds.), *Implications for entrepreneurship and enterprise development in the blue economy* (pp. 1–17). IGI Global. DOI:10.4018/978-1-6684-3393-5.ch001

Raimi, L., Tariq, M. U., & Kah, J. M. (2022). Diversity, equity, and inclusion as the future workplace ethics: Theoretical review. In Raimi, L., & Kah, J. (Eds.), *Mainstreaming diversity, equity, and inclusion as future workplace ethics* (pp. 1–27). IGI Global. DOI:10.4018/978-1-6684-3657-8.ch001

Repetto, M., Colapinto, C., & Tariq, M. U. (2024). Artificial intelligence driven demand forecasting: An application to the electricity market. *Annals of Operations Research*. Advance online publication. DOI:10.1007/s10479-024-05965-y

Tariq, M. U., Ismail, S. B., Babar, M., & Ahmad, A. (2023). Harnessing the power of AI: Advanced deep learning models optimization for accurate SARS-CoV-2 forecasting. *PLoS One*, 18(7), e0287755. DOI:10.1371/journal.pone.0287755 PMID:37471397

Tsietso, D., Yahya, A., Samikannu, R., Tariq, M. U., Babar, M., Qureshi, B., & Koubaa, A. (2023). Multi-input deep learning approach for breast cancer screening using thermal infrared imaging and clinical data. *IEEE Access : Practical Innovations, Open Solutions*, 11, 52101–52116. DOI:10.1109/ACCESS.2023.3280422

KEY TERMS AND DEFINITIONS

AI Precision: The strategic application of artificial intelligence algorithms and data analytics to optimise educational processes and outcomes.

Algorithmic Bias: The potential for AI systems to perpetuate or exacerbate existing inequalities in education due to biased data or flawed algorithm design.

Data-Driven Decision-Making: The use of AI and data analytics to inform educational strategies and policies, allowing institutions to make evidence-based decisions.

Interdisciplinary Collaboration: The integration of expertise from various fields such as computer science, psychology, and education to develop and implement AI technologies.

Personalised Learning Pathways: AI-driven educational strategies that tailor learning experiences to individual students' needs.

Predictive Analytics in Education: The use of AI to analyse student data, such as demographics and performance metrics.

Chapter 12
Use of AI for Student Success and Engagement

ABSTRACT

Integrating artificial intelligence (AI) into education transforms traditional learning environments, significantly increasing student success and engagement. This study explores the multifaceted roles of AI technologies in personalising learning experiences, providing adaptive learning paths, and fostering student engagement through interactive and immersive learning tools. Advanced machine learning algorithms analyse vast amounts of training data to provide accurate and personalised support, whereas natural language processing enables advanced conversational agents and intelligent tutoring systems. Virtual and augmented reality applications based on artificial intelligence (AI) create opportunities for experiential learning and engage students. Additionally, gamification and adaptive learning platforms dynamically adapt to students' needs, maintain motivation, and promote deeper learning.

INTRODUCTION

The application of manufactured insights (AI) in instruction has gained significant attention over the past few years, reflecting a developing curiosity about how these innovations can improve under-studied victory and engagement. This writing audit analyzes the current state of investigation on AI in instruction, focusing on different viewpoints such as personalized learning, proactive analytics, brilliant mentoring frameworks, understudy engagement, and moral contemplations related to these advances. This survey comprehensively explains how AI changes an instructive scene by synthesizing discoveries based on a wide range of considerations. The scene of instruction experiences a noteworthy change driven by the integration of manufactured insights (AI). AI has emerged as an effective apparatus for reshaping instructive techniques and improving understudy victory and engagement. This

DOI: 10.4018/979-8-3693-4074-5.ch012

chapter examines the multifaceted part of AI in instruction and investigates how these innovations are utilized to back and lock in understudies more successfully. The utilization of AI ranges in different measurements, including personalized learning, proactive analytics, and brilliant mentoring frameworks, each contributing extraordinarily to scholarly encounters. The rise of AI in instruction is predicated on its capacity to handle tremendous sums of information and create experiences that can educate instructing methodologies and understudy bolster components (Zawacki-Richter, Marín, Bond, & Gouverneur, 2019). AI frameworks can analyze under-study execution information, recognize learning holes, and tailor instructions to meet personal needs, subsequently cultivating a personalized learning environment. This personalized approach not only addresses the assorted learning styles of understudies but also guarantees that each understudy gets the vital bolster to realize scholarly victory.

Additionally, AI-driven prescient analytics play a significant role in recognizing understudies at the chance of scholastic disappointment. By analysing designs in under-study information, AI can foresee potential challenges and provide early mediation to back-at-risk under-studies (Dough Puncher & Inventado, 2014). These prescient models offer assistance to teachers and directors in creating focused methodologies to upgrade the understudy maintenance and victory. For occurrence, AI can screen understudy engagement in real time, hailing those who may be withdrawn or battling, and incite opportune intercessions.

Cleverly coaching frameworks (ITS) are another noteworthy application of AI in instruction. These frameworks use AI calculations to provide understudied, quick, personalized input and direction, mimicking one-on-one mentoring (VanLehn, 2011). The ITS can adjust to each understudy's learning pace and fashion, advertising custom-fitted works, and clarifications to improve comprehension and maintenance. This individualized consideration can be especially useful in expansive classroom settings where teachers may battle to supply personalized bolsters to each understudy. AI is pivotal for cultivating under-study engagement, expanding personalized learning, and early mediation. Locks in understudy could be a basic viewpoint of learning preparation, as high engagement levels are regularly related to superior scholastic results (Fredricks et al., 2004). AI-powered devices such as intuitive learning stages and gamified instructive applications can make learning more intelligent. These devices utilize AI to create energetic and versatile learning encounters that capture students' intrigues and curiosity and propel them to take an effective interest in their instruction.

Moreover, AI can encourage collaboration and communication between undergraduates and teachers. AI-enabled stages can support collaborative learning by interfacing understudies with peers and teachers, encouraging talk, and empowering the sharing of assets. This collaborative environment cultivates a sense of community and upgrades general learning encounters (Dillenbourg et al., 2009). Furthermore, AI can help with authoritative errands, liberating educators' time to center more on coordinating under-study interaction and instruction. The integration of AI into instruction raises vital concerns concerning morals and values. It is important to ensure that AI applications are outlined and executed in ways that advance their decency and inclusivity. Tending potential predispositions in AI calculations and guaranteeing that all understudies have enhanced access to AI-driven instructive apparatuses are basic challenges that must be addressed (Holstein et al., 2019). In addition, the ethical utilization of understudy information for AI-driven bits of knowledge requires straightforward approaches and hones that protect understudy security and independence.

In summary, utilization in instruction holds the potential to upgrade under-study victory and engagement through personalized learning, proactive analytics, shrew-shrewdhing frameworks, and locks-inductive devices. The use of these innovations must be carefully overlooked to address moral concerns and guarantee enhanced access to all understudies. As AI advances, its effect on instruction will likely grow, advertising unused openings and challenges for teachers, understudies, and policymakers alike. This chapter will investigate these subjects in more noteworthy depth, providing a comprehensive diagram of how AI forms long-term instruction.

BACKGROUND

Enhancing student engagement is a standard objective of higher-level institutes. Scholars have revealed that an enhanced level of student engagement in the educational process and university life is vital for enhancing professional and educational success. Researchers have also shown that student engagement rates are at a record low following the effect of the global COVID-19 pandemic. Student service groups try harder than ever to recognise how to activate and engage students. Artificial intelligence technologies have been validated as essential components of the solution. Inopportunely, they are mainly observed as luxury items that are only reasonable for significant firms. The artificial intelligence-driven medium for higher-level institutes uses automated machine learning and conversational artificial intelligence (Tariq, 2024).

- Suggestively improve the level of student engagement
- Offer more personalized, efficient assistance for students 24/7
- Decrease repetitive tasks by >40%
- Offer updated assessments and insights into student sentimentality
- Use university's data to provide better decisions and protect student progress

There are several reasons why a university or college student may drop out of a university or fail a class altogether: inability to understand the content or carry on with the coursework, insufficient time management skills, issues at home, or medical issues. Many students also encounter financial issues while finishing on time, irrespective of academic success. The numerous issues that prevent student progress can make it difficult for advisors and faculty to know who might be stressed and when to interfere. As advisors and faculty, themselves with more students-more possibly encounter more challenges than prior generations, they may not have sufficient time to detect and address these problems. Fortunately, with the advancement of novel data analytics and predictive modelling methods, universities and colleges have developed new techniques to assist them and support student progress-artificial intelligence. Before universities create images of massive computers and robots, they should consider a real-life scenario of how a higher education institute used artificial intelligence with Aviso Enterprise, known as watermark student success and engagement software, to guarantee student success (Hudson et al., 2020).

Risk factors and predictive analytics allow instructors to be more proactive in their outreach to students. They guide instructors on their connections and interventions for strategies and resources. University faculty and advisors have years of experience and training that makes them at the forefront of addressing student requirements. With routine connections with students, they are the first to know when the student is facing obstacles; sometimes, they notice it before their students. Higher education experts develop connections and trust in their students. They can regulate their learning methods when they detect that a student is facing some anxiety or stress, or when a student's parent is sick. The information informs discussions advisors and faculty members about students and how to make a decision. However, instructors do not always know from discussions with students whether they will have a problem affecting their learning. Most learners fall through the cracks, particularly transfer or newly enrolled students or those who do not ask for assistance. In addition, progressive students experience difficulties that affect their attendance in the classroom, with a magnified impact that is prompt and otherwise invisible in the absence of centralised attendance tracing. This is where insights accumulated from educational software can come in. The educational information gathered via software over a student's career paints an image of their progress in a specific class and across educational terms. For example, the software can use information on attempted credits, previous college experience, GPA, absences in course conferences, and prior class withdrawals or completion. It helps in forecasting whether a learner is at the threat of not completing a specific class but also whether they are at the threat of dropping out completely. Educational software can forecast as much as eighty-eight percent certainty whether a learner will fail a subject without interference or support from advisors or faculty. Therefore, the supplementary layer of data attained through the predictive risk indicators can support advisors in balancing their rough data with the personal information they already have about students to create a personalised success strategy (Ogude et al., 2019; Tariq, 2024).

Personalized Learning

Personalized learning, which tailors instructive encounters to personal students' needs and inclinations, has been a noteworthy center of AI investigation in instruction. AI advances have empowered the creation of versatile learning situations that alter directions based on real-time examination of understudied execution information (Chen et al., 2016). One notable illustration is the utilization of machine learning calculations to create personalized learning pathways. These calculations analyze understudied intelligence with instructive substances and provide customized proposals to improve learning results (Sheet, Steiner, Baird, & Hamilton, 2015). For occurrence, inquiries by Kizilcec, Saltarelli, Reich, and Cohen (2017) found that personalized criticism in online courses made strides in understudy engagement and execution. Essentially, a meta-analysis by Implies, Toyama, Murphy, Bakia, and Jones (2013) concluded that understudies in personalized learning situations outflanked their peers in conventional settings.

Prescient Analytics

Prescient analytics include utilizing AI to analyze instructive information and anticipate under-study results, empowering early mediation methodologies to back-at-risk under-studies. This approach leverages historical and real-time information to recognize designs and patterns that show potential scholastic problems (Bread et al., 2009). For example, calculations can anticipate which understudies will likely battle in a course based on their past scholastic execution, engagement levels, and statistical data (Arnold & Pistilli, 2012). Enquiries have illustrated the adequacy of current analytics in progressing understudy maintenance and victory rates. A consideration by Jayaprakash, Grouchy, Lauría, Regan, and Aristocrat (2014) shows that prescient analytics may precisely recognize understudies at the chance of dropping out, permitting education to actualize convenient back measures. In addition, recent models have been utilized to tailor prompting and mentoring programs, guaranteeing that understudies have the direction they have to succeed in (Sunderland et al., 2019; Tariq, 2024).

Brilliantly Coaching Frameworks

Brilliant coaching frameworks (ITS) are AI-driven stages that provide personalized instruction and criticism to understudies, recreating the benefits of one-on-one mentoring. These frameworks utilize various AI procedures, counting machine learning, common dialect handling, and cognitive modelling to adjust to the personal needs of understudied individuals (VanLehn, 2011). ITS can offer customized work, clues, and clarifications, making a difference in understudies ace complex concepts at their own pace. Various studies have highlighted the effectiveness of ITS in improving learning results. For example, an investigation by Koedinger, Anderson, Hadley, and Stamp (1997) illustrated that understudies utilizing the Cognitive Guide framework appeared to make critical advancements in variable-based math capability compared to those in conventional classrooms. In addition, Maconsideratione, Nesbit, and Liu (2014) found that it positively affected under-study achievement in different subjects and instructional levels.

Student Engagement

Understudy engagement may be basic in instructive victory, including behavioral, enthusiastic, and cognitive measurements (Fredricks et al., 2004). Advances in AI can improve engagement by creating intuitive and immersive learning encounters. For example, gamification techniques, which incorporate game-like elements into instructive exercises, have been shown to extend understudied inspiration and support (Deterding et al., 2011). Enquiring about AI-driven engagement apparatus has yielded promising results. Hamari et al. (2014) found that gamified learning stages expanded under-study engagement and satisfaction. Moreover, AI-powered virtual learning situations, which utilize immersive innovations such as virtual reality (VR) and expanded reality (AR), have improved under-study engagement by providing hands-on experiential learning openings (Johnson et al., 2016).

Moral Contemplations

Integrating AI into instruction raises critical moral contemplation, especially concerning decency, straightforwardness, and security. It is fundamental to guarantee that AI frameworks are planned and executed in ways that advance their value and inclusivity. If not carefully observed, AI calculations may propagate the existing predispositions or present modern segregation shapes (Binns, 2018). For example, one-sided information can lead to the out-of-line treatment of understudies from underrepresented or marginalized groups. Moreover, protection and information security are basic concerns. AI frameworks depend on extensive data collection to operate viably, raising questions regarding how this information is overseen and secured. Straightforward arrangements and robust security measures are necessary to defend understudied data and maintain belief (Slade & Prinsloo, 2013). Holstein et al. 's (2019) enquiry emphasizes the significance of including teachers and understudies in advancing and arranging AI innovations to guarantee that these devices meet moral measures and address users' needs. As AI innovation advances, its potential applications in instruction grow. Rising patterns incorporate the integration of AI with other progressive innovations, such as VR and AR, to create more immersive and versatile learning situations (Johnson et al., 2016). These advances can provide students hands-on experiential learning opportunities that are troublesome to attain in conventional classrooms. In addition, progress in characteristic dialect preparation and conversational operators is likely to improve the interactivity and viability of AI-driven instructional devices. For instance, more modern AI guides might engage in understudies in natural, meaningful dialogues, offering personalized feedback, and cultivating a more profound understanding (Graesser et al., 2012). Collaboration between educators, analysts, and innovation engineers is fundamental in saddling the total potential of AI in instruction. By working together, these stakeholders can create imaginative arrangements that address the assorted needs of understudies and teachers, thereby guaranteeing that AI is moral and impartial. Progressing enquiry and assessment will be vital to determining the effect of AI on educational outcomes and refining these advances for ideal utilization.

Utilizing AI in instruction is critical for improving under-study victory and engagement. Personalized learning, proactive analytics, clever coaching frameworks, and engagement devices are among the numerous applications that have positively affected instructive results. Nevertheless, the integration of AI advances and raises important ethical concerns that should be addressed, such as decency, straightforwardness, and protection. As AI progresses, it will be vital for teachers, analysts, and policymakers to work collaboratively to make instructive situations that are comprehensive, compelling, and steady for all students

Inform and Priortize

How can universities merge human intelligence with predictive modelling and alert educational software? To do so is to integrate human intelligence with student analytics to enhance their capability to forecast which learners will be in distress and surpass them before the issue becomes too difficult to manage. When artificial intelligence can cannot replace or imitate human intelligence, it can support those who connect with students by assisting them in deciding who is in trouble with failing a class or dropping out. In other words, this technology allows universities to prioritise which learners to support and at the right time via the information accumulated on why they may be at threat. After a student has been detected as having a medium or high threat of dropping out or failing a class, advisors and faculty must reach out to learners and develop a game plan to support them. However, educational software support advisors may be more productive with their time, recognising learners who require assistance they may not ask for while still replying to the routine problems that arise when teaching this population. Advisors and faculty times are precious; educational software can support universities in being more productive and efficient in mentoring, advising, and reaching out to more learners at the risk of failing (Ciolacu et al., 2018).

Drive Learner Engagement

Creating a digital assistant for mobile and web applications is important for driving student engagement that is on hand to notify, engage, and involve students when and where it is required. The university's virtual assistant should be accessible 24/7 over the year to respond to millions of frequently asked questions covering campus services and assistance services, all in real time, similar to other daily services. Such a response is essential to drive student engagement by providing responsible and personalised student questions and freeing university staff hours (Shin et al., 2019).

Assess Student Behaviour

Educational software allows instructors to listen to the learners on a scale. Institutes can use the collective data students provide in their discussions with their chatbot to visualise student behaviour, forecast possible problems and future requirements, and draw visions on how to enhance the student experience and drive positive results (Wang et al., 2021).

Guarantee of Self-Sufficiency

By utilising a detailed content management system, student services can accumulate, develop, and organise information in one place. Customisable artificial intelligence medium streamlines information sharing between units by offering a single source for all essential information. Instructors will be able to respond to learners automatically through customised, beneficial, and concerning discussions and turn their visions into action (Gutiérrez et al., 2019).

Maintaining Student Success

Artificial intelligence can mine deep insights from the university's primary data to recognise patterns and develop a picture of the present and future. Decision intelligence allows the firm to integrate traditional decision-making procedures with the latest technologies, such as machine learning, natural language programming (NLP), artificial intelligence, and intelligence applications, to modify business analytics and data dashboards into more detailed decision-support mediums. Presently, universities can detect problems earlier, maintain student success, and enhance student retention. According to a report, the dropout rate among university students is almost 40 percent. Given this disturbingly high rate, any higher education institute not already prioritising student engagement should switch its focus instantly. Research recommends that student learning, attainment, and persistence in universities are embedded in robust student engagement. In other words, the more learners engage with staff, class fellows, faculty, and the course content they are studying, the more likely they are to commence with their obligations and attain their objectives. The most popular method to enhance student engagement is to use artificial intelligence on university campuses (Chan et al., 2022).

HIGHER EDUCATION INSTITUTES USE OF TECHNOLOGY TO ENHANCE STUDENT ENGAGEMENT

Technology is a turning point in higher education, with a limitless prospect of helping students engage and progress in their studies. For the following reasons, higher education institutes are increasing their use of higher education chatbots and artificial intelligence university technologies. Higher education institutions progressively recognise the significance of staying on breakthroughs in innovation and technology. As such, higher education institutions are now investing immensely in innovative solutions such as artificial intelligence to provide enhanced value and drive engagement. With the correct artificial intelligence solutions in place-involving learning portals and chatbots, students can discover learning resources and information and continue at their own pace (Trivedi & Patel, 2020).

Allow Students to Vital Self-Serve Information

Artificial intelligence chatbots can be particularly helpful in supporting learners to find the information they require with ease. Universities have developed bots in the learning management system (LMS). As an outcome, students can become involved with the bot to ask questions about coursework, assessments, and due dates.

This supports them in staying on top of their assignments and releases teachers from repeatedly responding to the same queries (Johnson & Stage, 2018).

Enhance Communication

Retention and communication go hand in hand. The more instructors engage with students, the more likely they are to finish vital tasks such as meeting academic and financial deadlines. Various universities now utilise chatbots to respond to queries about university admissions and support students in seeing the procedure through to accomplishment. For instance, artificial intelligence can push students and remind them to submit their assessments, finish placement tests, opt for housing, and perform other vital actions. It can also support colleges and universities interacting with students to decrease the summer melt or the spectacle where learners plan to attend university in the fall and fail to enrol because of less support (Kabudi et al., 2021).

Training Students in the Contemporary World

The contemporary world is becoming increasingly digital. Firms across all sectors use digital transformation and artificial intelligence to simplify workflows and improve operations; higher education is not excluded. Colleges and universities now use technology to prepare students for the business world and introduce them to contemporary products and services. Employers connect with chatbots to question institutions about how to recruit their students and their educational information from chatbots about previous job placements and prospects with employers. It is a modern approach to job placement that simplifies real-time insights into demand and supply (Dekker et al., 2020; Tariq, 2024).

Provides Instructors With More Time to Emphasise Student Engagement

Technology can mostly reach students and converse ideas and concepts much faster and more proficiently than instructors can. For instance, instructors can direct students to digital learning resources, such as videos, images, and voice clips, demonstrating their lesson segments. It allows instructors to emphasise higher-level points that require one-on-one explanations and communication during classroom timings. With help from digital learning technology, instructors spend more time on complicated lessons instead of going through long-delayed primers and points. Simultaneously, teachers can use predictive artificial intelligence to determine which students require more assistance. It makes classroom sessions more beneficial, enjoyable, and engaging for students, while ensuring that instructors can provide their attention where it is most required (Cook-Sather, 2018).

Make Learning Fun

Technology makes education more fun and an essential part of learning. While students enjoy it, they feel motivated to learn more about various topics and discover novel educational opportunities. For example, a person may learn a new language. Artificial intelligence-powered technology makes learning fundamental grammar theories pleasurable, effective, and intuitive. It supports students in learning the fundamentals of communicating in another language rather than struggling with sentence formation, vocabulary, and pronunciation, permitting them to proceed promptly to improve their proficiency levels (Kumar et al., 2019).

HIGHER EDUCATION INSTITUTIONS AND AI BOTS

Technology now plays a pivotal role in all domains of contemporary life, including higher education. Higher education institutes are responsible for incorporating novel technologies and modifying them through modernisation and digital transformation (Daniels et al., 2021).

The Use of Technology in the Present-Day Classroom

Technology acts as a tool to improve the academic experience of present-day students. It dynamically involves students in their classes, enhances teaching plans for instructors, and ensures that students learn the 21st-century abilities that they will require in their future careers. Universities integrate various digital tools, including virtual reality (VR), augmented reality (AR), robotics, and artificial intelligence, into their classrooms. These tools motivate students to dynamically discover the world, work together to solve issues, and connect their findings. Instructors create a personalised, active learning experience for students so that they want to study. Technology allows instructors to accumulate and study data on each student's accomplishments to prepare lessons that meet individual requirements (Lee et al., 2021).

Communication, Instructors, and Teamwork

Learning to communicate and work with others is a vital skill for any career. Technology improves communication and allows instructors to be fully involved in learning. Online lectures, programs, and learning games allow for cooperative activities that make it simpler for learners to solve issues and share ideas. Technology allows instructors to customise lecture plans to meet student requirements. Learning does not always occur within a team. One-to-one interactions with instructors are encouraged where students can ask queries or receive assistance in domains where they may face challenges. The student-to-faculty ratio should be as low as 5:1, as this allows for a more personalised educational environment (Hudson et al., 2020).

Customised Learning Prospects

Instructors can alter lectures according to each student's requirements and interests. Not all students can learn at the same pace and technology offers more prospects for self-directed learning at an appropriate pace. Videos relating to specific lectures can be reviewed later because of the technology's help. Teachers can also review classroom data to check which learners struggle with in specific areas. In this situation, the instructor might engage in a review, one-on-one session, or recommend supplementary resources. Technology assists learning 24/7 through digital resources and the internet. It allows students to learn on time and follow-up, as required (Shin et al., 2019).

PREPARING ENGAGING CONTENT AND LESSONS

Students are generally curious about the world and mostly disengaged. With more engaging material involving technology, students can develop curiosity and creativity, which mostly leads to enhanced educational progress. Virtual reality, augmented reality, and virtual class sessions spright tlier classes and develop more comprehensive learning environments that substitute curiosity and collaboration (Ogude et al., 2019).

A Tool for Instructors

Instructors also leverage advanced technologies, particularly in terms of productivity and efficiency. They can use digital tools to prepare lecture plans, enhance their assistance for learners, and enhance their engagement in the classroom. Technology provides more prospects for preparing customised learning plans and determining methods that fit the students' learning styles (Ciolacu et al., 2018).

Instances of Technology in Classrooms

Virtual reality tools enhance engagement and interaction. Students can explore museums worldwide, take virtual field tours, and return in time to study without leaving their comfort zones.

- History: Google expeditions provides learners with prospects to go on a virtual field tour to ancient Greece
- Scientific Exploration: Applications such as InMind and InCell let learners observe a beating heart when the virtual roller coaster lets them learn about kinetic energy
- Engineering: Sketchfac and Oculus Rift applications provide students with the ability to redevelop three-dimensional structures involving ancient ruins
- Literature: The CoSpaces app supports bringing archetypal books to life by letting learners recreate places and settings

Artificial intelligence develops collaborative environments by overlapping one-dimensional pictures with music, videos, and graphics to improve learning. The known game Pokeman Go is a significant example of augmented reality. In classroom sessions, augmented reality can be used to provide lectures more actively. It can be applied to various subjects including history, geometry, chemistry, engineering, reading, biology, geography, and anatomy (Wang et al., 2021).

Examples of Augmented Reality

- **Dinosaur 4D+:** Flashcards that allow learners to see three-dimensional dinosaurs utilizing augmented reality flashcards
- **Element 4D:** Learners learn about chemistry theories, involving the atomic weight of elements, and chemical reactions for various elements
- **Google Expeditions-** Discover three-dimensional objects such as rain forests, hurricanes, and volcanos, also microscopic elements such as human DNA

Augmented trends, and it is projected that there will be 2400000 augmented reality mobile users worldwide by 2023. It is used on social media and mobile game platforms. This helps expose students to it and prepares them for the future (Kumar et al., 2019).

THE USE OF TECHNOLOGY IN HIGHER EDUCATION

Technology is a vital part of our lives at present, and there are various methods to utilise it beyond web browsing and social media. It is also a crucial part of instructors and students' academic experience. It develops a more engaging environment for the students. Some people think that technology is just a distraction, but it can enhance active participation in the classroom. It integrates diverse learning styles and enhances collaboration. Students are prepared for the future, as teachers can connect directly with them. An essential technological effect in higher education is enhanced class engagement and interactivity (Ogude et al., 2019). Additionally, enhanced overall understanding, practical education, time management, and integrated learning methods are just some of the effects that technology has had on students' learning. One of the essential uses of technology in higher education is to incorporate students' skills and knowledge into action. Students can benefit from online interactions with their instructors and other classes. However, it is imperative to include these novel skills in action and practice. Technology allows students to attain learning in practice through various applications. Technology integration into the class helps instructors to smoothly assign different assignments and tasks that allow students to use their experience and learning into action and create the ability to develop a solution to a problem, event, or situation.

Collaboration can be assisted by educational technologies. Instructors can communicate with learners during lectures; however, learners can also communicate with each other. Students communicate to resolve issues through online classes and games. Students can communicate their thoughts and ideas and motivate each other through interactive activities. Simultaneously, technology allows for one-on-one communication with instructors. Students can ask questions about the lecture and obtain supplementary support with difficulty in comprehending the subject matter. Learners can upload homework for the comfort of their homes, and instructors can access the submitted assessments on their devices. Various researchers have explored how the application of educational technology enhances student engagement and motivation in higher education. This technology involves learners behaviourally, cognitively, and emotionally (Gutiérrez et al., 2019).

Whether technology is utilised in class or after university hours, students can interact with teachers, collaborate with class fellows, and engage in learning procedures. Web conferencing software, online games, wikis, blogs, and social networking websites are particular instances of technology that have been proven to enhance student communication and engagement. Technology has the potential to modernise conventional learning and teaching processes. It can eradicate obstacles to higher education imposed by time and space, and radically extend accessibility to lifelong learning. Learners no longer have to gather in the same place and at the same time to get lectures from the same teacher. Contemporary technologies can alter the ideas of higher education institutions. No longer is a higher education institute unavoidably a physical space with residence auditoriums and classrooms, where learners come to attain advanced learning (Kumar et al., 2019).

THE FUTURE OF AI FOR STUDENT SUCCESS AND ENGAGEMENT

The future of AI in education offers tremendous potential for transforming students' success and engagement. As AI technology advances, its application in educational environments is expected to become more advanced, broader, and more effective. This detailed note explores the prospects of artificial intelligence in education, considering new technologies, pedagogical advances, ethical considerations and potential challenges ahead. New technologies and integration of artificial intelligence machine learning and data analysis. As machine learning algorithms evolve, their ability to analyze vast amounts of training data will greatly improve. Future AI systems are likely to use deep learning methods to provide more accurate and personalised learning experiences (Goodfellow et al., 2016). These systems can understand complex patterns of student behaviour and performance, enabling highly tailored educational interventions. Predictive analytics will also play a crucial role in the future of artificial intelligence in education. Advanced predictive models can identify at-risk students more accurately, allowing timely and targeted support (Baker & Inventado, 2014). This improves student engagement and ensures that every student receives the resources they need to succeed. Natural Language Processing and Conversational Agents Natural Language Processing (NLP) techniques are expected to advance significantly, leading to more advanced conversational agents and intelligent guidance systems.

These AI-based systems can engage in natural and meaningful dialogue with students and provide personalised feedback and support (Graesser et al., 2012). Future conversational agents will be able to understand and respond to complex student questions, facilitating deeper learning and understanding. In addition, integrating NLP with other artificial intelligence technologies enables the creation of more interactive and engaging learning environments. For example, AI-powered chatbots can be used to guide students through virtual reality (VR) or augmented reality (AR) experiences, thereby increasing engagement and motivation (Johnson et al., 2016).Virtual and Augmented Reality The convergence of artificial intelligence with VR and AR technologies holds great promise for the future of education. These immersive technologies can create highly interactive and experiential learning environments that are difficult to achieve in traditional classrooms (Dede, 2009). AI can enhance these experiences by providing real-time feedback and adjustments based on student interaction. For example, VR simulations can teach complex scientific concepts or historical events, allowing students to explore and learn by doing so. AI algorithms can track student progress and adjust difficulty or provide additional resources to ensure that each student is sustained and challenged (Makransky et al., 2019). Game design elements that apply to non-game contexts are expected to become more common in future educational systems. AI-based gaming platforms can dynamically adapt to individual student needs by providing personalised challenges and rewards to maintain engagement and motivation (Deterding et al., 2011). Significant progress has also been made in adaptive learning environments.

These platforms use artificial intelligence to continuously assess student performance and adjust the learning content accordingly. Future adaptive learning systems will be more sensitive and accurate, providing tailored learning experiences that meet each student's strengths and weaknesses (Pane et al., 2015). Pedagogical Advances Personalised Learning, Paths. The future of AI in education will see a shift to highly personalised learning paths. Artificial intelligence systems can create and manage personalised learning plans that meet students' needs, preferences, and learning styles (Chen et al., 2016). These individualized ways ensure students are challenged and supported appropriately, promoting more effective and engaging learning. In addition, AI facilitates the integration of various educational resources, such as multimedia content, interactive simulations and peer collaboration tools, into individualized learning paths.

This creates a holistic and engaging learning environment that supports different learning styles (Means et al., 2013).Collaborative learning and peer interaction technologies also enhance cooperative learning and peer interactions. Future AI systems can facilitate group work and peer learning by forming optimal groups based on student profiles and learning goals (Rosé et al., 2008). These systems also provide real-time feedback and support to make group activities productive and engaging. In addition, AI-based platforms allow students to interact with peers and experts worldwide, creating a more global and diverse learning community. This improves academic performance, cultural understanding, and collaborative skills (Chen et al., 2020).Continuous assessment and feedback: AI is changing how assessments are conducted in educational settings. Future AI systems can conduct continuous and formative assessments that provide real-time feedback to students and teachers (Shute and Rahimi, 2017).

These systems use advanced analytics to assess various aspects of student performance, including cognitive, emotional, and social dimensions, allowing for more timely and targeted interventions and ensuring that students receive the support they need to succeed. It also allows teachers to monitor student progress more effectively and make informed decisions to improve their teaching practices (Wilson, 2018).

Ethical Aspects Equity and Inclusion. As AI technology is integrated into education, ensuring equity and inclusion is paramount. There is a risk that AI systems may inadvertently reinforce existing prejudices or create new forms of discrimination, if not carefully designed and implemented (Binns, 2018).

Future artificial intelligence systems must be developed from a fair and inclusive perspective, considering the diverse needs and backgrounds of all students, and researchers and practitioners must work together to identify and mitigate potential biases in AI algorithms. This includes using diverse and representative datasets, involving stakeholders in the design process, and continuous monitoring and evaluation of the impact of AI systems on diverse student populations (Holstein et al., 2019).Data protection and security: The use of artificial intelligence in education is highly dependent on data collection and analysis, which raises important data protection and security issues. Ensuring ethical and secure collection, storage, and use of student data is a critical challenge for future AI in education (Slade & Prinsloo, 2013).

CONCLUSION

As professionals in higher education, instructors use data daily in their research, each time they communicate with a student, and when their institute involves daily business. The influence of artificial intelligence has released the capability of higher education to reach learners. Fortunately, artificial intelligence-driven software makes it easier to detect which students are at risk of dropping out or failing a class. The software makes it easy to reach out to students. Personalising the enrolment procedure with the support of artificial intelligence technology in higher education allows universities to target the learners most likely to succeed in their courses. Adaptive conversational assistants support institutes catering to learners around the clock. Such incorporations of artificial intelligence in higher education support universities in increasing enrolment rates. Scholars have studied the use of artificial intelligence in higher education. The result is the use of tools such as document recognition, SOP graders, chatbots, and essays in higher education. Artificial intelligence technologies such as these could utilise information from several campus systems to direct administrative decisions and customise the university curriculum according to employees' recruitment requirements.

Thus, they enhance a university's operational productivity. Artificial intelligence significantly supports classroom learning by offering an overall educational experience. It allows students to extend their imagination with technologies and tools such as virtual assistants and augmented reality. These classroom support technologies for monitoring and grading help instructors improve their educational experience and get free time out of their class with students. Artificial intelligence technologies such as interactive assistants allow students to converse to their problems immediately when they emerge, boosting student retention numbers. Student engagement can also be improved by accepting unique artificial intelligence technologies such as student success models and chatbots. These technologies also help instructors enhance their proficiency based on student perspectives accumulated by conversational assistants. With the support of artificial intelligence technology in higher education, institutes can support learners by sending beneficial emails, push notifications, and text messages. These work as soft reminders for tasks requiring completion, approaching due dates, and any upcoming events. Such advantages of artificial intelligence will support students in adjusting themselves to the technology, subsequently enhancing student engagement. The artificial intelligence applications described above are believed to be just the start of a significant technological evolution (Wang et al., 2021).

CASE STUDY

The integration of artificial intelligence (AI) into educational systems has shown significant potential in improving student achievement and engagement. This case study examined the implementation of AI technologies at Georgia State University (GSU), a pioneer in implementing AI-based solutions to support student achievement and learning. GSU's comprehensive approach includes the implementation of predictive analytics, chatbots and personalized learning pathways, which improve educational outcomes and student satisfaction. Located in Atlanta, Georgia, Georgia State University is a large public research university with a diverse student body. In recent years, GSU has faced challenges typical of large urban institutions, such as high student attrition rates and the need to support diverse student populations with varying academic abilities and socioeconomic backgrounds (Renick, 2020).

To meet these challenges, GSU has used artificial intelligence (AI) technologies to create a more supportive and personalized educational environment. Implementation Strategies Predictive Analytics One of the cornerstones GSU uses is predictive analytics. The university uses an AI-based predictive analytics platform to track student performance and identify students at risk of dropping out. This system analyzes various data points, including academic performance, attendance data, and engagement metrics to create a risk score for each student (Ekowo & Palmer, 2016). These risk scores allow counsellors to intervene proactively and provide targeted support to students who may be struggling's predictive analytics system has helped identify at-risk students early, allowing for timely interventions to prevent academic failure. For example, the system flagged students most likely to fail certain courses and encouraged counsellors to reach out and provide additional resources, such as tutoring or study groups. This proactive approach has significantly improved student engagement (Renick, 2020). In addition to predictive analytics, GSU has implemented AI-powered chatbots to increase student engagement and provide 24/7 support.

The "Pounce" chat is designed to answer common student questions about administrative processes, academic advising and campus resources. Pounce uses natural language processing (NLP) to understand and answer student questions, providing immediate assistance and reducing staff workload (Bailey et al., 2020).The Pounce has effectively answered frequently asked questions about financial aid, registration, and academic deadlines. Chat helps students navigate administrative processes more efficiently by providing immediate responses, reducing frustration, and improving their overall college experience. In addition, Pounce is available 24/7, ensuring that students receive support at any time, which is particularly useful for non-traditional students with different schedules (Bailey et al., 2020).

GSU has also introduced Personalized Learning Pathways to meet the diverse needs of the student body. Using adaptive learning platforms based on artificial intelligence, the university can adapt the learning content and teaching methods according to students' needs. These platforms continuously assess student performance and adjust difficulty and content delivery accordingly, ensuring that each student receives a personalized learning experience (Chen et al., 2016). For example, entry-level courses such as Math and Intro to Science, where student success rates are critical, have implemented adaptive learning technology to provide tailored learning experiences. Students who struggle with certain concepts get more practice and resources, while those who master the material can progress more quickly. This personalized approach has resulted in better learning outcomes and higher pass rates in challenging courses (Ekowo and Palmer, 2016).

The adoption of artificial intelligence technologies at GSU has significantly impacted student engagement. By identifying at-risk students early and taking timely measures, universities significantly reduced the number of dropouts. According to the university, using predictive analytics alone increases freshman graduation rates by 3.9 percentage points (Renick, 2020). This improvement means hundreds more students will graduate each year. Student satisfaction has also significantly improved thanks to the smooth support of AI-based tools. The availability of instant help through Pounce Chat has made it easy for students to get the information they need right away. Research conducted by universities shows that students value the convenience and effectiveness of support systems powered by artificial intelligence, which increases their positive university experience (Bailey et al., 2020).

The personalized learning paths enabled by artificial intelligence have led to better academic success for students. Adaptive learning platforms ensure that students receive the right challenges and support to help them learn course material more effectively. This tailored approach has resulted in higher pass rates and better grades in core courses, especially in STEM subjects, where many students traditionally struggle (Chen et al., 2016).Ethical aspects: Data protection and security: Although the benefits of artificial intelligence in education are clear, GSU has also considered important ethical aspects, especially concerning data protection and security. The widespread use of student data in power predictive analytics and personalized learning requires strong data-protection measures. The GSU has implemented strict data security protocols to ensure the responsible and secure use of student data (Ekowo & Palmer, 2016).

Another important issue is ensuring equity and inclusion in AI-based education. GSU has worked together to ensure that AI technologies do not inadvertently reinforce existing biases or to exclude certain groups of students. For example, universities continuously monitor the performance of their predictive analytics models to control bias and ensure that interventions are fair across populations (Holstein et al., 2019). Integrating AI technologies into existing educational infrastructure presents several challenges. Ensuring the compatibility and interoperability between different systems requires careful planning and implementation. GSU's experience highlights the need for an IT team to oversee the implementation and maintenance of AI systems (VanLehn, 2011).Another major challenge was training staff and students to use AI-based tools effectively. Providing appropriate training and ongoing support is essential to maximize the benefits of AI technologies. GSU has invested in professional development programmes.

GSU has invested in professional development programs for faculty and staff to help them integrate AI tools into their workflows and pedagogical practices (Mishra & Koehler, 2006). Future Directions: Expanding AI Applications GSU plans to further expand the use of AI technologies to improve student success and engagement. This includes exploring new applications of AI in areas such as career guidance, mental health support, and alum engagement. By constantly innovating and integrating new artificial intelligence solutions, GSU aims to create a more inclusive and supportive educational environment (Selwyn, 2019). Collaboration and Research GSU are also committed to collaborating with other institutions and researchers to advance the field of artificial intelligence in education. By sharing knowledge and best practices, GSU hopes to promote wider adoption of AI-based solutions in higher education. Ongoing research focuses on evaluating the long-term effects of AI technologies on student outcomes and improving tools to better meet the needs of diverse student populations (Siemens, 2013).

Georgia State University's innovative use of artificial intelligence technologies demonstrates the significant potential of artificial intelligence to improve student success and engagement. By adopting predictive analytics, AI-powered chatbots, and personalized learning pathways, GSU significantly improved student retention rates, academic success, and student satisfaction. However, the university's experiences also emphasize the importance of considering ethical aspects and overcoming practical challenges to fully utilize intelligence's benefits in education. As AI technology advances, the GSU's continued commitment to innovation and collaboration will play a critical role in shaping the future of AI-based education.

REFERENCES

Alam, A., & Mohanty, A. (2022, December). Facial Analytics or Virtual Avatars: Competencies and Design Considerations for Student-Teacher Interaction in AI-Powered Online Education for Effective Classroom Engagement. In *International Conference on Communication, Networks and Computing* (pp. 252-265). Cham: Springer Nature Switzerland.

Allil, K. (2024). Integrating AI-driven marketing analytics techniques into the classroom: pedagogical strategies for enhancing student engagement and future business success. *Journal of Marketing Analytics*, 1-27.

Almusaed, A., Almssad, A., Yitmen, I., & Homod, R. Z. (2023). Enhancing student engagement: Harnessing "AIED"'s power in hybrid education—A review analysis. *Education Sciences*, 13(7), 632. DOI:10.3390/educsci13070632

Alsobeh, A., & Woodward, B. (2023, October). AI as a Partner in Learning: A Novel Student-in-the-Loop Framework for Enhanced Student Engagement and Outcomes in Higher Education. In *Proceedings of the 24th Annual Conference on Information Technology Education* (pp. 171-172). DOI:10.1145/3585059.3611405

Chan, L., Hogaboam, L., & Cao, R. (2022). Artificial Intelligence in Education. In *Applied Artificial Intelligence in Business* (pp. 265–278). Springer. DOI:10.1007/978-3-031-05740-3_17

Chen, Y., Jensen, S., Albert, L. J., Gupta, S., & Lee, T. (2023). Artificial intelligence (AI) student assistants in the classroom: Designing chatbots to support student success. *Information Systems Frontiers*, 25(1), 161–182. DOI:10.1007/s10796-022-10291-4

Ciolacu, M., Tehrani, A. F., Binder, L., & Svasta, P. M. (2018, October). Education 4.0-Artificial Intelligence assisted higher education: early recognition system with machine learning to support students' success. In *2018 IEEE 24th International Symposium for Design and Technology in Electronic Packaging (SIITME)* (pp. 23-30). IEEE.

Cook-Sather, A. (2018). Listening to equity-seeking perspectives: How students' experiences of pedagogical partnership can inform wider discussions of student success. *Higher Education Research & Development*, 37(5), 923–936. DOI:10.1080/07294360.2018.1457629

Daniels, L. M., Goegan, L. D., & Parker, P. C. (2021). The impact of COVID-19 triggered changes to instruction and assessment on university students' self-reported motivation, engagement and perceptions. *Social Psychology of Education*, 24(1), 299–318. DOI:10.1007/s11218-021-09612-3 PMID:33613084

Dekker, I., De Jong, E. M., Schippers, M. C., De Bruijn-Smolders, M., Alexiou, A., & Giesbers, B. (2020). Optimizing students' mental health and academic performance: AI-enhanced life crafting. *Frontiers in Psychology*, 11, 1063. DOI:10.3389/fpsyg.2020.01063 PMID:32581935

Fazil, A. W., Hakimi, M., Shahidzay, A. K., & Hasas, A. (2024). Exploring the Broad Impact of AI Technologies on Student Engagement and Academic Performance in University Settings in Afghanistan. *RIGGS: Journal of Artificial Intelligence and Digital Business*, 2(2), 56–63. DOI:10.31004/riggs.v2i2.268

Gutiérrez, M., & Tomás, J. M. (2019). The role of perceived autonomy support in predicting university students' academic success mediated by academic self-efficacy and school engagement. *Educational Psychology*, 39(6), 729–748. DOI:10.1080/01443410.2019.1566519

Huang, A. Y., Lu, O. H., & Yang, S. J. (2023). Effects of artificial Intelligence–Enabled personalized recommendations on learners' learning engagement, motivation, and outcomes in a flipped classroom. *Computers & Education*, 194, 104684. DOI:10.1016/j.compedu.2022.104684

Hudson, C., Archibald, A., & Heap, T. (2020, June). Integrating an AI-driven discussion platform: The impact of platform on engagement and quality. In *EDEN Conference Proceedings* (No. 1, pp. 117-126). DOI:10.38069/edenconf-2020-ac0009

Johnson, S. R., & Stage, F. K. (2018). Academic engagement and student success: Do high-impact practices mean higher graduation rates? *The Journal of Higher Education*, 89(5), 753–781. DOI:10.1080/00221546.2018.1441107

Kabudi, T., Pappas, I., & Olsen, D. H. (2021). AI-enabled adaptive learning systems: A systematic mapping of the literature. *Computers and Education: Artificial Intelligence*, 2, 100017. DOI:10.1016/j.caeai.2021.100017

Kahu, E. R., & Nelson, K. (2018). Student engagement in the educational interface: Understanding the mechanisms of student success. *Higher Education Research & Development*, 37(1), 58–71. DOI:10.1080/07294360.2017.1344197

Kairu, C. (2020, June). Students' attitude towards the use of artificial intelligence and machine learning to measure classroom engagement activities. In *EdMedia+ Innovate Learning* (pp. 793-802). Association for the Advancement of Computing in Education (AACE).

Kim, B., Suh, H., Heo, J., & Choi, Y. (2020). AI-driven interface design for intelligent tutoring system improves student engagement. *arXiv preprint arXiv:2009.08976*.

Kumar, V., Rajan, B., Venkatesan, R., & Lecinski, J. (2019). Understanding the role of artificial intelligence in personalized engagement marketing. *California Management Review*, 61(4), 135–155. DOI:10.1177/0008125619859317

Lee, C. A., Tzeng, J. W., Huang, N. F., & Su, Y. S. (2021). Prediction of student performance in Massive Open Online Courses using deep learning system based on learning behaviors. *Journal of Educational Technology & Society*, 24(3), 130–146.

Limonova, V., dos Santos, A. M. P., Mamede, J. H. P. S., & de Jesus Filipe, V. M. (2024, March). Maximising Attendance in Higher Education: How AI and Gamification Strategies Can Boost Student Engagement and Participation. In *World Conference on Information Systems and Technologies* (pp. 64-70). Cham: Springer Nature Switzerland. DOI:10.1007/978-3-031-60224-5_7

Mirdad, K., Daeli, O. P. M., Septiani, N., Ekawati, A., & Rusilowati, U. (2024). Optimizing Student Engagement and Performance usingAI-Enabled Educational Tools. *CORISINTA*, 1(1), 53–60.

Naidoo, D. T. (2023). Integrating TAM and IS success model: Exploring the role of blockchain and AI in predicting learner engagement and performance in e-learning. *Frontiers of Computer Science*, 5, 1227749. DOI:10.3389/fcomp.2023.1227749

Nguyen, A., Kremantzis, M., Essien, A., Petrounias, I., & Hosseini, S. (2024). Enhancing Student Engagement Through Artificial Intelligence (AI): Understanding the Basics, Opportunities, and Challenges. *Journal of University Teaching & Learning Practice*, 21(06). Advance online publication. DOI:10.53761/caraaq92

Ogude, N. A., Meyer, I. J., Mwambakana, J., & Mthethwa, N. E. (2019). Can extended curriculum programmes be improved through engagement with students using appreciative inquiry? *South African Journal of Higher Education*, 33(4), 219–236. DOI:10.20853/33-4-2835

Ramasamy, V., Singsen, D., & Walia, G. S. (2024). Fostering Student Engagement and Success in STEM Education: An AI-Driven Exploration of High Impact Practices from Cross-Disciplinary General Education Courses. *Journal of Engineering Education Transformations, 37*(Special Issue 2).

Shin, H., Rim, D., Kim, H., Park, S., & Shon, S. (2019). Educational characteristics of virtual simulation in nursing: An integrative review. *Clinical Simulation in Nursing*, 37, 18–28. DOI:10.1016/j.ecns.2019.08.002

Tariq, M. U. (2024a). Multi-Agent Models in Healthcare System Design. In Dall'Acqua, L. (Ed.), *Bioethics of Cognitive Ergonomics and Digital Transition* (pp. 143–170). IGI Global. DOI:10.4018/979-8-3693-2667-1.ch008

Tariq, M. U. (2024b). Social Innovations for Improving Healthcare. In Chandan, H. (Ed.), *Social Innovations in Education, Environment, and Healthcare* (pp. 302–317). IGI Global. DOI:10.4018/979-8-3693-2569-8.ch015

Tariq, M. U. (2024c). Leveraging AI for Entrepreneurial Innovation in Healthcare. In Özsungur, F. (Ed.), *Generating Entrepreneurial Ideas With AI* (pp. 192–216). IGI Global. DOI:10.4018/979-8-3693-3498-0.ch009

Tariq, M. U. (2024d). Leading Smart Technologies and Innovations for E-Business 5.0: Applications and Management Frameworks. In Popkova, E. (Ed.), *Smart Technologies and Innovations in E-Business* (pp. 25–46). IGI Global. DOI:10.4018/978-1-6684-7840-0.ch002

Tariq, M. U. (2024e). Crafting Authentic Narratives for Sustainable Branding. In *Compelling Storytelling Narratives for Sustainable Branding* (pp. 194–229). IGI Global. DOI:10.4018/979-8-3693-3326-6.ch011

Tariq, M. U. (2024f). The role of AI in skilling, upskilling, and reskilling the workforce. In Doshi, R., Dadhich, M., Poddar, S., & Hiran, K. (Eds.), *Integrating generative AI in education to achieve sustainable development goals* (pp. 421–433). IGI Global. DOI:10.4018/979-8-3693-2440-0.ch023

Tariq, M. U. (2024g). AI-powered language translation for multilingual classrooms. In Doshi, R., Dadhich, M., Poddar, S., & Hiran, K. (Eds.), *Integrating generative AI in education to achieve sustainable development goals* (pp. 29–46). IGI Global. DOI:10.4018/979-8-3693-2440-0.ch002

Trivedi, S., & Patel, N. (2020). Clustering Students Based on Virtual Learning Engagement, Digital Skills, and E-learning Infrastructure: Applications of K-means, DBSCAN, Hierarchical, and Affinity Propagation Clustering. *Sage Science Review of Educational Technology*, 3(1), 1–13.

Wang, W., Chen, L., Xiong, M., & Wang, Y. (2021). Accelerating AI adoption with responsible AI signals and employee engagement mechanisms in health care. *Information Systems Frontiers*, 1–18.

ADDITIONAL READING

Abonamah, A. A., Tariq, M. U., & Shilbayeh, S. (2021). On the commoditization of artificial intelligence. *Frontiers in Psychology*, 12, 696346. Advance online publication. DOI:10.3389/fpsyg.2021.696346 PMID:34659012

Ashfaq, M., Khan, I., Alzahrani, A., Tariq, M. U., Khan, H., & Ghani, A. (2024). Accurate wheat yield prediction using machine learning and climate-NDVI data fusion. *IEEE Access : Practical Innovations, Open Solutions*, 12, 40947–40961. DOI:10.1109/ACCESS.2024.3376735

Babar, M., Ahmad, A., Tariq, M. U., & Kaleem, S. (2023). Real-time fake news detection using big data analytics and deep neural network. *IEEE Transactions on Computational Social Systems*. Advance online publication. DOI:10.1109/TCSS.2023.3309704

Babar, M., Alshehri, M. D., Tariq, M. U., Ullah, F., Khan, A., Uddin, M. I., & Almasoud, A. S. (2021). IoT-enabled big data analytics architecture for multimedia data communications. *Wireless Communications and Mobile Computing*, 2021(1), 1–9. DOI:10.1155/2021/5283309

Babar, M., Jan, M. A., He, X., Tariq, M. U., Mastorakis, S., & Alturki, R. (2023). An optimized IoT-enabled big data analytics architecture for edge–cloud computing. *IEEE Internet of Things Journal*, 10(5), 3995–4005. DOI:10.1109/JIOT.2022.3157552 PMID:38046398

Babar, M., Kaleem, S., Sohail, A., Asim, M., & Tariq, M. U. (2023). An improved big data analytics architecture for intruder classification using machine learning. *Security and Communication Networks*, 2023, 2023. DOI:10.1155/2023/1216192

Babar, M., Khattak, A. S., Jan, M. A., & Tariq, M. U. (2021). Energy aware smart city management system using data analytics and internet of things. *Sustainable Energy Technologies and Assessments*, 44, 100992. Advance online publication. DOI:10.1016/j.seta.2021.100992

Babar, M., Tariq, M. U., Almasoud, A. S., & Alshehri, M. D. (2021). Privacy-aware data forensics of VRUs using machine learning and big data analytics. *Security and Communication Networks*, 2021, 1–9. DOI:10.1155/2021/3320436

Babar, M., Tariq, M. U., & Jan, M. A. (2020). Secure and resilient demand side management engine using machine learning for IoT-enabled smart grid. *Sustainable Cities and Society*, 62, 102370. Advance online publication. DOI:10.1016/j.scs.2020.102370

KEY TERMS AND DEFINITIONS

Adaptive Learning Systems: AI-powered platforms that dynamically adjust educational content and difficulty levels based on real-time analysis of student performance.

Ethical AI in Education: The practice of ensuring that AI systems in education are designed and implemented in ways that are fair, transparent, and inclusive.

Gamification: The application of game-design elements in non-game contexts, such as education, to increase student engagement and motivation.

Natural Language Processing (NLP): A branch of AI that enables computers to understand and respond to human language.

Personalised Learning: An educational approach enhanced by AI, where learning experiences are tailored to individual student needs.

Chapter 13
Use of AI for Faculty Success and Engagement

ABSTRACT

This chapter investigates the transformative part of manufactured insights (AI) for improving staff victory and engagement with higher instruction. It centres on how AI can back the workforce in educating, investigating, proficient improvement, and organisation collaboration. Key activities at colleges such as Georgia State College (GSU) illustrate the viable applications of AI, counting current analytics for recognising at-risk understudies, personalised learning situations, and brilliant mentoring frameworks. These devices offer assistance to staff focused on bolstering, improving student results, and reducing workloads. AI also encourages advanced information examinations and intrigue investigations, boosting staff efficiency. Personalised proficient advancement plans and ceaseless input frameworks encourage workforce fulfilment and career development.

INTRODUCTION

The application of manufactured insights (AI) in instruction has gained significant attention over the past few years, reflecting a developing curiosity about how these innovations can improve under-studied victory and engagement. The quick headway of Artificial Intelligence (AI) innovation has penetrated various segments by counting higher instructions. This chapter investigates the role of AI in improving workforce victory and engagement, diving into its applications in instructing, enquiring about, proficient advancement, and collaboration, and tending to moral

DOI: 10.4018/979-8-3693-4074-5.ch013

contemplations and challenges. The survey synthesis discoveries from various researchers to comprehensively understand AI's effects of AI on the workforce.

AI's potential of AI to convert instructing hones has been central to instructive investigation. Versatile learning frameworks, which tailor instructive substances to meet a person's needs, are among the most prominent applications. These frameworks utilize calculations to analyze under-study execution information and alter guidelines appropriately, thereby improving personalized learning encounters (Smith & Anderson, 2019). Such advances make strides in understudy engagement and results and give staff profitable bits of knowledge to understudy learning designs, empowering more compelling educational procedures (Johnson et al., 2020). In this case, an AI-driven learning administration framework (LMS) can recognize battling understudies and recommend convenient mediation (Dede et al., 2020). By robotizing schedule errands such as evaluating and participation, AI liberates staff time, permitting them to center on more intuitive and imaginative viewpoints of instruction (Zawacki-Richter et al., 2019). The effectiveness and accuracy of AI in overseeing expansive datasets and providing noteworthy criticism are important for improving instruction viability.

AI's application in enquiry has gathered noteworthy attention, especially in its capacity to quickly process and analyze expansive volumes of information. Machine learning calculations and characteristic dialect preparation (NLP) devices can recognize patterns, generate theories, and encourage the disclosure of modern experiences (Jordan & Mitchell, 2015). For instance, AI can help conduct writing audits by filtering through tremendous amounts of scholastic distribution to recognize pertinent thoughts about rising patterns (Halevy et al., 2009). AI plays a fundamental role in facilitating composition and administration. By analysing fruitful recommendations, AI instruments can provide knowledge on financing patterns and offer assistance to the workforce to make more competitive applications (Stone et al., 2019). Additionally, AI can streamline the regulatory angles of enquiring about administration, from following venture advances to guaranteeing compliance with financing agencies' necessities, permitting analysts to center more on their academic exercises. AI's commitment to staff proficiency advancement is another noteworthy region of intrigue. Personalized learning stages fueled by AI offer custom-made preparation programs that cater to the needs and career goals of the workforce (Daniela and Lytras, 2019). These stages can suggest pertinent courses, workshops, and assets and nonstop the cultivation of proficient development and aptitude upgrades.

AI-driven analytics provide staff with detailed feedback on their education and under-study engagement levels. By analysing this information, teachers can distinguish regions for enhancement and adjust their academic approaches (Viberg et al., 2020). Such data-driven self-assessment instruments engage staff in improving their instruction adequacy and remain alongside the most recent educational practices.

Advances in AI have encouraged improved staff engagement and collaboration by providing inventive instruments for communication and interactions. Virtual reality (VR) situations and AI-driven communication stages empower staff to associate and collaborate, notwithstanding topographical limitations and advancing a more cohesive and locked-in scholarly community (Blau et al., 2020). These devices bolster the improvement of intrigue enquiry into ventures and cultivate information sharing among staff. Moreover, AI can analyze communication designs and social systems within scholastic teaching to recognize potential collaboration openings (Li et al., 2018). By encouraging these associations, AI can create a collaborative culture that enhances staff engagement and efficiency. The capacity to collaborate with peers and enquire about engaging in activities is significant for proficient development and work fulfilment.

Despite the numerous benefits of AI in higher education, a few moral considerations and challenges must be addressed to guarantee its dependable utilization. Information protection, algorithmic inclination, and computerized separation are basic concerns that teachers must explore (Binns, 2018). Guaranteeing the moral utilization of AI includes establishing clear approaches and rules that ensure the rights and interface of faculty and students. Algorithmic inclination may be a noteworthy concern, as AI frameworks can incidentally perpetuate existing predispositions shown within the information they are prepared for (O'Neil, 2016). This can lead to out-of-line results and weaken the validity of the AI applications. Educators must actualize measures to distinguish and moderate predisposition in AI frameworks to guarantee the evenhanded treatment of all staff and understudy. Information security is another basic issue, particularly given the delicate nature of instructive information. Strong information assurance measures are fundamental to defend individual data and keep up with beliefs in AI frameworks (Gibbs et al., 2013). Education must guarantee compliance with information security directions and receive best practices for data security.

Computerized separation alludes to the difference in obtaining innovation and advanced assets, which can worsen existing disparities in instruction (van Dijk, 2020). To address this challenge, education must invest in the foundation and provide satisfactory preparation and bolsters to guarantee that all staff members can benefit from AI innovations. Bridging the computerized separate is essential for advancing comprehensive and impartially instructive hones. A few cases have highlighted the effective implementation of AI in higher instruction, illustrating its potential to improve staff success and engagement. For example, Georgia State College (GSU) has actualized an AI-powered chatbot to improve student exhortation and bolster administration. This chatbot has significantly increased student engagement and maintenance rates by providing appropriate help and personalized proposals (Page, 2018). The workforce at GSU has profited from the decreased regulatory burden and improved capacity to center on instruction and investigation. Another case is the utilization of AI in investigations at the College of California, Berkeley, where AI calculations have been used to analyze enormous datasets in different logical areas. This has accelerated the pace of revelation and empowered staff to distribute groundbreaking research more productively (Northeastern College, 2019). Such applications highlight the transformative potential of AI in supporting workforce enquiries and insightful exercises.

The long run of AI in higher instruction holds a monstrous guarantee, with emerging trends demonstrating advanced development and integration. One such slant is the improvement of AI-driven versatile learning situations that offer profoundly personalized and immersive educational encounters (Luckin et al., 2016). These situations can adjust in real time to the desires and inclinations of individual learners, giving more locks to an effective learning encounter. AI is also anticipated to play a developing part in predictive analytics, making a difference in education, recognizing at-risk understudies, and executing appropriate mediations (Nguyen et al., 2020). By leveraging information from different sources, AI can provide insights into understudy behavior and execution, empowering the workforce to tailor their education techniques, and bolster administrations to better meet understudy needs. Additionally, the integration of AI with other rising innovations, such as expanded reality (AR) and the Internet of Things (IoT), has the potential to create more intuitive and associated learning situations (Kukulska-Hulme, 2020). These advances can improve staff engagement by providing modern devices for education, collaboration, and advertising imaginative ways to provide substances and evaluate the learning results.

The use of AI in higher instruction can enhance faculty's success and engagement by improving teaching hones, supporting investigations, encouraging proficient improvement, and advancing collaboration. Be that as it may, AI's moral contemplations and challenges should be carefully overseen to guarantee its dependable and evenhanded utilization. As education progresses to grasp AI, continuous investigation and discourse will be crucial to fulfilling its full potential and cultivating a flourishing scholastic community. By addressing these challenges and leveraging AI's benefits, higher instruction can create a more dynamic and stronger environment for staff, eventually contributing to the advancement of information and instruction.

BACKGROUND

Enhancing student engagement is a standard objective of higher-level institutes. Scholars have revealed that an enhanced level of student engagement in the educational process and university life is vital for enhancing professional and educational success. Integrating artificial intelligence insights (AI) into higher education has revolutionized different viewpoints on academic operations, counting staff victory, and engagement. As teaching progressively adopts AI innovations, understanding their effects on the staff is pivotal. This chapter examines AI's multifaceted role in upgrading staff execution, cultivating proficient improvement, and advancing engagement in scholastic situations.

The scene of higher instruction experiences a noteworthy change that is driven by mechanical progression. Conventional strategies of educating, investigating, and organizing are being reimagined by AI, advertising uncommon openings for staff to upgrade their viability and engagement (Johnson et al., 2020). AI advances, such as machine learning calculations, proactive analytics, and cleverly mentoring frameworks, are not reshaping the way teachers instruct and connect with understudies but also how they oversee their proficient obligations and development. AI apparatuses are instrumental to increasing the educational capabilities of individuals in the workforce. For instance, versatile learning innovations personalize the instructive encounter by analysing under-study information to tailor guidelines to a person's learning needs (Smith & Anderson, 2019). These frameworks provide real-time criticism and proposals, empowering staff to distinguish and address learning crevices more effectively. AI-powered stages can mechanize regulatory assignments, such as evaluating and participation following, liberating important time for teachers to center on more impactful exercises (Zawacki-Richter et al., 2019). For example, AI-driven learning administration frameworks (LMS) can analyze understudy execution information to anticipate which understudies are likely to fall behind, permitting the workforce to intercede proactively (Dede et al., 2020). By leveraging these bits of knowledge, teachers can focus more on compelling direction techniques, eventually making strides in understudy results and fulfilment.

In the expansion to upgrading education, AI altogether impacts workforce enquiry into exercises. AI-powered apparatuses can handle endless sums of information rapidly, empowering analysts to recognize designs, produce speculations, and quicken the revelation handle (Jordan & Mitchell, 2015). Normal dialect preparation (NLP) innovations, for instance, can analyze huge corpora of scholarly writing to reveal rising patterns and important ponders, helping in writing audits and enquiring about blends (Halevy et al., 2009). In addition, AI can help compose and administer information by analysing effective applications and providing bits of knowledge to subsidize patterns and needs (Stone et al., 2019). This bolster makes a difference in staff increment their chances of securing investigative financing and improving their investigative efficiency and effect.

Proficient Advancement and Ceaseless Learning

AI also plays a vital role in the advancement of workforce proficiency. Personalized learning stages utilize AI to convey customized preparation programs that address personal workforce needs and career objectives (Daniela and Lytras, 2019). Based on an educator's profile, these stages can prescribe important courses, workshops, and assets, cultivating continuous learning and ability improvement. Additionally, AI-driven analytics can give the workforce bits of knowledge into their educating hones and under-study engagement levels, empowering them to reflect on and make strides in their academic approaches (Viberg et al., 2020). By encouraging data-driven self-assessment and peer comparison, AI enables teachers to upgrade their viability and proficiency.

Advancing Staff Engagement and Collaboration

AI innovation also cultivates staff engagement and collaboration. Cleverly collaboration apparatuses, such as virtual reality (VR) situations and AI-driven communication stages, empower teachers to share information and collaborate on ventures, notwithstanding topographical limitations (Blau et al., 2020). These instruments upgrade staff interactions and community building, advancing a more locked-in and cohesive scholastic workforce. Furthermore, AI can analyze communication designs and social systems within scholastic education to distinguish collaboration openings and encourage enquiries about activities (Li et al., 2018). By cultivating a collaborative culture, AI makes a difference to the workforce, grows proficient systems, and contributes to collective scholastic headways.

Although the benefits of AI in higher instruction are considerable, it is fundamental to address the moral contemplations and challenges related to its utilization. Information security, algorithmic predisposition, and advanced partitioning must be carefully overlooked in order to guarantee evenhanded and moral AI integration (Binns, 2018). Educators must set up clear arrangements and rules to administer the moral utilization of AI and ensure the rights and interface of staff and understudies; additionally, using AI advances requires noteworthy ventures in framework and preparation. Staff must be satisfactorily prepared to utilize AI apparatuses successfully and obtain suggestions for instructing, enquiring about, and proficient advancement (Luckin et al., 2016). Education must provide ongoing back and assets to guarantee fruitful AI selection and integration. Utilizing AI in higher instruction presents a transformative opportunity for improving staff victory and engagement. By increasing education and learning, supporting investigative exercises, encouraging proficient improvement, and advancing collaboration, AI engages the workforce to realize their full potential and contributes to the headway of information and instruction.

Be that as it may, cautious thought of moral suggestions and challenges is essential to guarantee the dependable and impartial utilization of AI. As teachers proceed to grasp AI, progressing in enquiry and exchange will be significant in saddling its full potential and cultivating a flourishing scholarly community.

For years, movie makers, science fiction writers, and authors have been projecting astounding and appalling modifications that will arise with the invention of widespread artificial intelligence. So far, artificial intelligence has not made any such irrational influence and, in many methods, has become pervasive in several aspects of our routine lives. From the smart sensors that help people take flawless pictures, to the automatic parking characteristics in vehicles, to the sometimes controlling personal assistants in smartphones, artificial intelligence of one kind or another is all around people, 24/7/. Although developers are yet to create self-aware robots, they have made intelligence and primarily significant utilisation of artificial intelligence technology in a broad range of applications that, while not as incredible as androids, still modify peoples' routine lives. One place where Artificial intelligence is composed to make significant modifications and, in some situations, is already making advancements, such as in higher education. Although we may not see humanoid robots functioning as instructors in the next ten years, various projects already in the functions utilise computer intelligence to support teachers and students to attain more out of the academic experience. The following are some vital roles for artificial intelligence in higher education, and those that will monitor them will define and create future academic experiences (Wang et al., 2021).

ARTIFICIAL INTELLIGENCE AND AUTOMATION OF BASIC ACTIVITIES

In universities, grading tests and homework for long-term lecture courses can be monotonous, even when teaching assistants divide them. Even for undergraduate courses, instructors mostly find that grading takes up an ample amount of time, which could be utilised to connect with students, make necessary preparations for the class, or work on professional progress. Although artificial intelligence may never be able to substitute human grading, it is almost close to reaching that stage. Instructors will likely automate grading for almost all types of multiple-choice questions, and fill-in-the-blank assessments and programmed grading of student writing may not be far behind. Today, essay-grading software is still in its early stages and is not up to the mark. However, it will and can be enhanced over the coming times, letting instructors emphasise in-class activities and student dealings more than grading (Singer et al., 2021).

Educational Software Can Be Adjusted According to Student Requirements

Implementing significant levels of customised learning from undergraduate to doctoral programs is one of the fundamental methods through which artificial intelligence will affect learning. Some of this is already happening through various adaptive educational programs, software, and games. These systems react to the student's requirements, placing enhanced focus on specific topics, restating things that learners have not mastered, and generally supporting learners to learn at their own pace, whatever it may be. This type of customised learning could be a machine-supported solution to support students at diverse levels to work together in one classroom, with instructors assisting the education and offering support when required. Adaptive learning has previously had a significant effect on higher education worldwide. As artificial intelligence advances in the coming years, adaptive courses, such as these, will possibly only extend and expand (Hannan & Liu, 2021).

Detect Points for Course Improvement

Instructors may not always be aware of gaps in their educational content and lessons, which can confuse students about specific topics. Artificial intelligence provides a method for resolving this issue. Internet offers and various massive open online course providers are already implementing it. When a substantial number of students are observed submitting an incorrect response to a homework assessment, the system signals the instructor. It provides future learners with a personalised message that hints at their correct answer. This kind of system supports filling in the gaps in detail that can occur in subjects and guarantees that all learners are developing the same theoretical base. Instead of waiting for an answer from the professor, learners receive quick feedback that supports them in comprehending a concept and recalling how to do it right the next time (Nikita & Velicheti, 2022).

While there are things that human instructors can provide that systems cannot, at least not in the present, the future could see more learners being trained by instructors who are only present in zeros and ones. Some training programs that are dependent on artificial intelligence are already present and can support learners in fundamental mathematics, writing, and other courses. These courses can train students in basics, but they are not optimal for helping learners learn prioritized creativity and thinking, something real-world instructors still need to simplify. However, this should not rule out the prospect of artificial intelligence instructors being able to perform these tasks in the future. With the prompt pace of technology enhancement that has marked the previous years, progressive teaching systems may not be an illusion (Abbas et al., 2022).

Artificial Intelligence-Based Programs for Feedback

Artificial intelligence cannot support students and instructors in preparing personalised courses according to their requirements. Still, it can also offer feedback on the success of the course as a whole. Some universities, particularly those with online services, utilise artificial intelligence systems to monitor faculty engagement and progress and alert instructors where there might be problems with learner performance. These artificial intelligence systems allow learners to obtain the assistance they require and allow instructors to explore domains to enhance learning for learners who may struggle with the course matter. However, artificial intelligence programs at universities not only provide recommendations for individual subjects. Some are trying to create systems that can support learners to opt for majors depending on the domains in which they struggle and succeed. While learners do not have to make a recommendation, they can mark a brave new environment for university majors' choice for future students (Wijayati et al., 2022).

Exploring and Interacting With Information

People rarely notice artificial intelligence systems that can regularly impact the information they explore and see. Google adjusts results to users depending on location, Amazon makes suggestions dependent on prior purchases, Siri adjusts to the instructors' requirements and commands, and almost all web advertisements are based on people's shopping and interest preferences. These intelligent systems play a vital role in faculty's interactions with information in their professional and personal lives. They can modify how they explore and utilise information from universities and academia. In recent years, artificial intelligence-powered systems have fundamentally modified how faculty can interact with information and with advanced and more incorporated technology. Future students may have more diverse experiences doing research and exploring facts than present students (Kumar et al., 2021).

Modifying Role of Instructors

There will always be a role for instructors in learning, but what that role is and what it involves may be modified because of the latest technology in the form of smart computing systems. As already discussed, artificial intelligence can take over jobs, such as grading, support learners to enhance learning, and even replace real-world teaching. However, artificial intelligence could be adjusted to many other phases of education. Artificial intelligence systems can also be programmed to offer knowledge, serving as a space for learners to ask queries and extract information, or may even take the place of instructors for actual course content. In most situations, artificial intelligence will switch part of the instructor to that of an enabler. The faculty will enhance artificial intelligence lectures, support struggling students, and offer human collaboration and hands-on experiences to learners. Technology is already driving some of these modifications in many ways, particularly in higher education institutes that are online or accept the hybrid classroom model (Thiry and Hug, 2021).

Less Error and Trail

Trial-and-error is a vital aspect of learning, but not knowing the answer or failing it is demoralising for various students. Some do not want them to be placed in front of their class fellows or instructors. An intelligent computer system developed to support students in learning is a much less intimidating way to handle trial-and-error. Artificial intelligence could provide students with a method to learn and experiment in a comparatively lenient environment, especially when artificial intelligence instructors can provide improvement solutions. Artificial intelligence is a seamless format for assisting this type of learning, as artificial intelligence systems mostly learn by trial and error (Carvalho et al., 2022).

Explore, Teach, and Assist Students

Intelligence data accumulation powered by smart computer systems is already modifying how faculty interact with current and prospective students. From hiring to supporting students in choosing the best subjects, smart computer systems assist in making every segment of the university experience more nearly personalised to student requirements and objectives. Data mining systems are already vital in today's higher education setting, but artificial intelligence can further modify higher education to enhance faculty engagement and success. Initiatives are already underway at some universities to provide artificial intelligence-directed instruction that can simplify the functions of faculty engagement (Chen et al., 2022).

While significant modifications may still be some years in the future, the truth is that artificial intelligence has the prospect of fundamentally altering everything required for faculty engagement and success. Students can use artificial intelligence software, systems, and software to learn from any place in the world at any time, and with these kinds of programs taking the place of specific types of classroom learning, artificial intelligence substitutes instructors in some situations for worse or better. Educational programs driven by artificial intelligence are already support students in acquiring basic skills. However, these programs progress, and developers research more, possibly providing students and faculty with a broad range of services (Wilson, 2022).

Transformative artificial intelligence power can be witnessed in every sector, including the higher education sector. Artificial intelligence is modifying the method instructors teach and students learn. Quality learning is the right of every student; however, due to educational partiality, vital obstacles exist in guaranteeing access to quality and affordable learning. Artificial intelligence's prospects in the higher education industry can be modified so that governments around the globe are seeking to guarantee reasonable access to quality learning. University competence can be improved by implementing data and analytics in the classroom. Artificial intelligence is the future of higher education. It is estimated that international artificial intelligence use in higher education will reach $5.80 billion by 2025. It is also estimated that the international market share of artificial intelligence in higher education may reach up to $3.68 billion by 2023, as it represents a CAGR of 47%. While there are doubts that technology can replace instructors, critics agree that artificial intelligence can enhance educational best tasks. According to researchers, artificial intelligence can significantly affect present learners "from how they learn to the services in their accessibility, and the careers they will be taught for". Artificial intelligence can be utilised to enhance accessibility to quality education, enhance students' learning results, develop customised learning experiences, bridge any gaps in teaching and learning, and decrease the non-teaching management workload of faculty (Bhardwaj et al., 2021).

ARTIFICIAL INTELLIGENCE BENEFITS FOR FACULTY ENGAGEMENT AND SUCCESS

The following are how artificial learning is beneficial for faculty engagement and success:

Automation of Education-Related Administration Procedures

Instructors spend considerable time on non-teaching relevant work such as grading assessment papers, marking homework, preparing progress reports, preparing reports, handling teaching content, and arranging resources and content for lessons. All of these tasks are tiring for instructors and leave them feeling tired. Artificial intelligence can help automate these tasks, leaving instructors to emphasise their fundamental teaching responsibility, freeing their time, and saving effort. Artificial intelligence can be utilised to grade essays via augmented intelligence support, which can leave instructors free to spend time on their students. This will help them become better teachers and enhance the faculty's success and engagement (Schiff, 2022).

Customised Learning

Customised learning, which depends on an individual student's requirements, has been a priority for instructors for years. This can be attained through artificial intelligence, which will allow a differentiation level impossible for teachers to attain, as they manage approximately 30 students in every class. Smart educational design and digital media use artificial intelligence to offer learning, feedback, and testing to students from college to university levels, which provides them with the challenges they are prepared for, recognises gaps in learning, and readdresses novel topics when suitable. Artificial intelligence can support emphasising particular topics that a learner is weak in, and repeating courses they have not understood. Customised learning can become a reality with artificial intelligence (Nazari et al., 2021).

Enhanced Student Engagement

Artificial intelligence can enhance student-teacher engagement using innovative technologies, such as virtual reality and gamification. These technologies enhance students' engagement in class by making the education enjoyable. Various artificial intelligence-driven algorithms can assess a student's interest and knowledge, thereby supporting the development of personalized learning programs. Instructors can assess learners' weaknesses and strengths and offer them additional time to enhance their learning, if required (Williams et al., 2021).

Intelligent Content Preparation

Instructors spend a lot of time preparing exercises and assignments for their students. Artificial intelligence can support instructors by preparing intelligent content, such as exercises and study guides. It can support the preparation of content that makes learning and teaching more convenient for them and learners. It can be an electronic book guide, lectures on smart TVs, or video lessons. Instructors can utilize artificial intelligence to engage in digital content and update content regularly (Williams et al., 2021).

An Instructor's Best Friend

The instructor's learning journey has never ended. Artificial intelligence can support instructors in continuously educating themselves on subjects they do not know. This will support instructors in becoming more efficient at teaching. Artificial intelligence can even work as a decision support for instructors. They can use data to make more knowledgeable decisions. Artificial intelligence in higher education has evolved as a challenge. It has enhanced the digital divide-the gap between those who have access to tools and those who do not. However, the advantages of artificial intelligence must be accessible to all the students. Most artificial intelligence advancements in higher education have emerged in the private sector. The government will have to explore solutions to develop an environment to extract limitless prospects that artificial intelligence provides to the higher education sector. This is the most vital factor in enhancing university faculty engagement and success. This can be attained by framing a widespread public policy on artificial intelligence to develop an environment that serves sustainable progress. Inclusion and equity should be fundamental values when enrolling in such a policy (Schiff, 2022).

Learners Today, Leaders Tomorrow

All learners must be taught certain technical skills which will allow them to interact and program with artificial intelligence in the future. Courses and subjects in philosophy and ethics also focus on abilities that artificial intelligence cannot benefit from. Such complicated decision-making, emotional intelligence, entrepreneurship, and critical thinking will become a segment of fundamental education offering tools that will support them live and function with artificial intelligence. The faculty should also consider what students study today may modify well. Students across the globe will have the possibility that what they are investing their time in the present may soon become outdated. Every sector is implementing and modifying digital transformation, and industry 4.0 university faculty must embrace education 4.0 to remain relevant. In time, institutes which struggle with change and are unable to transform and those that do not implement artificial intelligence will not remain competitive. They will have to make dismissals to attempt survival, but in the end, they will indeed become terminated. Changes are the only constants in the world. Accepting change is vital for faculty members in higher education institutes (Carvalho et al., 2022).

DISCOVERING CLASSROOM VULNERABILITIES

One of the vital artificial intelligence technologies used in higher education is upholding the positive effect of remote learning on the environmental outline. However, many professionals assume that artificial intelligence will soon substitute for human touch in education. This might be the case for other sectors, but not the academic domain. Education and artificial intelligence go hand-in-hand, supplementing virtual and manual teaching. Artificial intelligence assists faculty by automating various functions and enhancing the learning and teaching process for people (Thiry & Hug, 2021).

Closing Skills Gap

Upskilling learners is a valuable solution for higher education institutions facing a technology gap. Artificial intelligence and machine-learning-driven software and application development solutions deliver broadly accessible and cost-efficient prospects for students to upskill. It is not restricted to learners; training and upskilling the faculty can also boost morale and spark institute-wide commitment to innovation and development. In addition, machine learning and deep learning in higher education affect the learning and development field by assessing how people attain their skills. As soon as the system adjusts to human learning and studying, it helps automate the teaching procedure (Kumar et al., 2021).

Personalized Data-Based Feedback

Feedback is critical when designing learning experiences, whether in the classroom or the workplace. The essential variability between efficient teaching and simply providing the material is that efficient teaching involves constant feedback. Feedback must come from a trusted source, so artificial intelligence in higher education determines and assesses work reports based on regular data. A data-based feedback system supports student satisfaction, eradicates bias elements from learning, and supports comprehension where skills are lacking. This feedback is customized based on every student's and faculty's performance noted in the system (Abbas et al., 2022).

24/7 SUPPORT WITH CONVERSATIONAL ARTIFICIAL INTELLIGENCE

Chatbots are an increasingly known instance of how artificial intelligence in higher education uses data to inform itself and assist the faculty accordingly. It benefits teaching and non-teaching faculties for user engagement in personalized learning (Wijayati et al., 2022).

Universal Accessibility

Artificial intelligence in higher education departments makes information accessible globally. A current survey projects that more than 60 percent of education businesses depend on artificial intelligence and machine learning-based education app development, assisted by contemporary features and tools. Features such as multilingualism help translate information into different languages, making it comfortable for each faculty member to learn and teach. Artificial intelligence also plays a prominent role in audiences with hearing and visual impairments. Artificial intelligence-driven converter tools like presentation translators offer real-time subtitles for virtual lessons (Hannan & Liu, 2021).

Regular Content Updates

Artificial intelligence also allows faculty members to update and create information regularly to keep the lectures updated over time. Users are also alerted whenever new information is added, which supports their preparation for future tasks (Nikita and Velicheti, 2022).

THE FUTURE OF AI FOR FACULTY SUCCESS AND ENGAGEMENT

Using manufactured insights (AI) in higher instruction is rapidly advancing, advertising promising roads for improving staff victory and engagement. This point-by-point note investigates long-standing AI applications in the scholarly community, focusing on inventive instructing hones, enquiries about headways, proficient improvement, collaborative apparatuses, moral contemplations, and the overarching effect on workforce engagement and regulatory victory. By synthesising current enquiries and projecting future patterns, this audit provides a comprehensive perspective on the potential of AI to convert to higher instruction.

Personalized Learning Situations

One of AI's foremost promising future applications of AI in instruction is the improvement of personalised learning situations. These AI-driven stages can analyse tremendous amounts of understudied information to tailor directions to a person's learning styles and needs. Personalised learning situations adjust in real time, giving custom criticism and assets to optimise learning involvement (Luckin et al., 2016). As these frameworks become more modern, they will empower the workforce to address different under-study needs more successfully, driving instructive results to move forward. For example, AI can track under-study advances over diverse courses and recognise regions where they battle, proposing personalised mediations and supplementary materials (Nguyen et al., 2020). This level of customisation makes a significant difference. Staff centre their endeavours on understudies who require the foremost support to improve general education and learning encounters.

Brilliantly Mentoring Frameworks

Cleverly Coaching Frameworks (ITS) speak to another noteworthy headway in AI-driven instruction. These frameworks use machine learning calculations to supply understudies with personalised mentoring and real-time feedback. As ITS innovation advances, it will become more proficient at mimicking human mentors and advertising nuanced directions and backs (VanLehn, 2011). The workforce can use ITS to supplement their teaching, guaranteeing that students get outside conventional classroom hours nonstop. For occasion, ITS instance monotonous enquiries and give point-by-point point-by-point responses on complex themes, permitting the workforce to commit more time to higher-order education, which not only moveonlyunderstudy learning but also decreases tattooed on staff, contributing to their general victory and overall (Graesser et al., 2012).

Increased Reality (AR) and Virtual Reality (VR)

Integrating AR and VR in instructive settings offers immersive learning encounters that can upgrade under-study engagement and understanding. AI-driven AR and VR innovations can make intuitive reenactments and virtual labs, permitting understudies to investigate complex concepts (Kukulska-Hulme, 2020). The workforce can utilise these instruments to plan inventive educational modules that lock in students more profoundly and cater to different learning inclinations. For example, a biology professor might utilise VR textbooks on a virtual human-to-day visit, providing students with virtual involvement that goes past intuitive course readings. Such experience that goes beyond upgrade understudy learning but moreover strengthen upgrades student learning but also strengthens staff education

Quickened Information Investigation

AI's capacity of AI to quickly handle and analyse expansive datasets is changing investigation techniques across disciplines. Progressed AI calculations can filter through tremendous sums of information to recognise designs, produce speculations, and reveal experiences that would be inconceivable to observe physically (Jordan

& Mitchell, 2015). This capability allows the staff to conduct more advanced and impactful enquiries quickly.

In the future, AI-driven information examination instruments will become more capable of combining advanced methods such as profound learning and fortification learning. These instruments will empower the workforce to investigate unused enquiries about the wilderness and address complex questions with more prominent accuracy and speed (LeCun et al., 2015). AI can assist in recognising biological markers for illnesses, analysing climate-altering information, or showing financial patterns, encouraging groundbreaking enquiries in various areas. AI can also facilitate enhanced collaboration between analysts within and beyond education. AI-driven stages can analyse scholarly distributions, social media intuition, and institutional information to distinguish potential collaborators with complementary skill skills (Li et al., 2018). By cultivating these associations, AI advances in intrigues, enquiry, and development. For illustration, an AI platform might recognise an etymologist and a computer researcher working on related themes from internal colleges and propose a collaboration that combines linguistic dialect-preparing strategies with phonetic hypotheses. Such intriguing collaborations can lead to novel bits of knowledge and propel scholastic enquiry about forward and improving staff victory.

Computerized Writing Audits and Composing

Robotising schedules but time-consuming errands, such as writing audits and composing, is another zone where AI can affect staff victory. AI devices can check and summarise tremendous sums of scholastic writing, highlighting key ponders and rising patterns (Halevy et al., 2009). This, not as it were, spared time but guaranteed that staff remained current with the most recent enquiries about advancements.

In addition, AI can help compose effective applications and distinguish common elements that contribute to their victory (Stone et al., 2019). These apparatuses can provide templates and recommendations, help the workforce, and provide more competitive recommendations. As a result, the workforce can focus more on their enquiry about ideas and less on authoritative errands, thus improving efficiency and victory.

Personalized Proficient Improvement Plans

AI has the potential to revolutionise faculty professional advancement by providing personalised learning plans custom-made according to a person's career objectives and needs. AI-driven platforms can analyse workforce execution information and investigate interface and career earnings to prescribe significant courses, workshops, and assets (Daniela & Lytras, 2019). These personalised plans guarantee that the workforce is focused on bolstering to upgrade their aptitudes and improve their careers. For example, an AI stage might prescribe an unused partner teacher to attend a particular instruction workshop based on their understudy input and regions of change. This focused approach to proficient improvement makes a difference in staff development and guarantees that they receive the support they need to succeed in and remain locked in their parts.

Ceaseless Input and Change

AI-driven analytics can provide critical feedback to the workforce on their education hones and enquiries about exercises. By analysing under-study execution, engagement levels, and peer surveys, AI can offer actionable insights that assist the workforce in refining their approaches (Viberg et al., 2020). This progressive criticism circle advances the culture of continuous enhancement and proficient development. For instance, AI might recognise that a specific teaching strategy is not resounding with students, and propose elective approaches based on effective hones utilised by other workforces. Such experiences empower the workforce to adapt and progress their teaching techniques, driving better student results and expanding work fulfilment.

Mentorship and Peer Learning Systems

AI can improve staff mentorship and peer-learning systems by encouraging associations between teachers with complementary abilities and encounters. AI-driven stages can coordinate guides and mentees based on their profiles and cultivate meaningful and beneficial mentoring connections (Baldwin and De Zure, 2001). Moreover, AI can recognise staff with comparable enquiries about the interface or instructing challenges, thereby advancing peer learning and back systems.

For example, a mid-career staff member looking to improve their grant writing skills may be coordinated with a senior colleague with an effective track record of securing financing. Such mentorship openings improve workforce proficiency and engagement, thus creating a steady scholastic community.

COLLABORATIVE APPARATUSES AND REGULATION BACK

AI-Driven Collaboration Platforms

AI-driven collaboration platforms are balanced to convert how staff associate and collaborate in research and instructing ventures. These stages can encourage consistent communication, venture administration, resource sharing, and upgrading collaboration within and over teaching (Blau et al., 2020). AI can analyse communication patterns to identify potential zones for collaboration and bolster intrigue ventures. In this case, an AI-driven stage might propose collaboration openings between staff based on their investigative yields and ability ranges, even if they are completely different offices or colleges. Such stages were not only to cultivate a collaborative culture, but also to drive development and scholarly victory.

Decision Making

AI can support organizational decision making by providing data-driven experiences in workforce execution, student results, and asset allotment. By analysing organizational information, AI can help chairpersons recognise opportunities for advancement and execute targeted interventions (Huang et al., 2020). This data-driven approach guarantees that education can provide necessary support to upgrade workforce victory and engagement. For example, AI might distinguish a decay in under-study engagement in a specific office and propose strategies to address the issue, such as staff improvement programs or educational module modifications. Such insights enable teachers to create a steady environment that cultivates staff victory and student achievements.

Staff Prosperity and Work-Life Adjust

AI can also advance staff well-being and work-life adjustment by distinguishing stressors and prescribing medications. AI-driven wellness platforms can screen staff workloads, stretch levels, and work fulfilment, providing personalised proposals to improve prosperity (Ozkula & Reiner, 2020). These instruments can assist in creating a beneficial and steady work environment. For instance, an AI stage may propose mindfulness hones, workload alterations, or peer-back groups for a highly stretched workforce. By proactively tending toward prosperity, education can upgrade workforce engagement and maintenance.

Ethical Contemplations and Challenges

As AI becomes more coordinated with higher instruction, tending to algorithmic inclination is pivotal to guarantee impartial results. AI frameworks can inadvertently perpetuate existing inclinations displayed in the data they are prepared on, driving the out-of-line treatment of certain bunches (O'Neil, 2016). Teachers must actualise thorough testing and approval strategies to recognise and relieve inclination toward AI applications. For example, ensuring diversity in the preparation of datasets and consolidating decency calculations can help decrease the inclination of AI systems. Progressive monitoring and auditing of AI applications are essential for preserving reasonableness and transparency in their utilisation.

Guaranteeing Information Protection and Security

Information privacy and security are basic concerns regarding the use of AI in higher education. Faculty and under-study information must be ensured to maintain beliefs and compliance with regulations (Gibbs et al., 2013). Educate must receive vigorous information security measures, count encryption, get to control, and normal security audits. For instance, AI-driven stages should comply with information assurance laws, such as the Common Information Security Control (GDPR) in Europe or the Family Instructive Rights and Protection Act (FERPA) within the Joined Together States. Guaranteeing that information is dealt with dependably and safely is fundamental to the moral utilisation of AI.

Bridging the Advanced Isolate

The digital divide remains a significant challenge in the adoption of AI innovations in higher education. Disparities in obtaining innovation and computerised assets can worsen disparities among staff and understudies (van Dijk, 2020). Teachers must contribute to the foundation and provide preparation and bolsters to guarantee enhanced access to advanced AI. For example, providing workforce access to AI tools and preparing programs can help bridge the digital divide and ensure that all teachers take advantage of these technologies. Promoting computerised education and inclusivity is essential for cultivating a reasonable and equitable academic environment. Thus, AI in higher instruction has immense potential for enhancing faculty victory and engagement. AI offers various opportunities to convert instructing, investigating, and proficient improvement, from personalised learning situations and intelligent tutoring frameworks to progressed enquiries about instruments and collaborative platforms. Be that as it may, tending to moral contemplations such as algorithmic bias, data protection, and advanced isolation is vital to ensuring the capable and impartial utilisation of AI.

By grasping AI innovations and adapting to these challenges, higher education can create a dynamic, steady, and imaginative environment for faculty members. This enhances faculty victory and engagement and contributes to the progression of information and education.

CONCLUSION

Higher education faculty do not need to be worried about replacing AI. Although artificial intelligence is becoming a beneficial tool for educational faculty members, there are several ways in which computers cannot substitute human touch in in-class sessions. The international market for artificial intelligence in higher education is anticipated to read $3.68 billion 2023. Although most professionals believe that the crucial existence of instructors is exceptional, there will be various modifications to instructors' jobs and academic best practice. Artificial intelligence can help with monotonous tasks, inform the academic process by tracking student performance, and enhance the experience of faculty members. Artificial intelligence is becoming a valued instructor aid and is modifying classrooms; thus, sooner faculty members can be utilized to work alongside artificial intelligence and smart robots, the better. Artificial intelligence in higher education has come a long way, but it is argued that technology will not replace instructors anytime soon. As artificial intelligence and machine learning progress, human interaction has become even more vital. Only faculty members can recognize the shades of what is happening in their students' minds during class. Encouraging students to learn, grow, and practice is an ability beyond the range of artificial intelligence. High-grade human teachers have a broad range of motivational strategies that they can use to provide students with a jump start and encourage them throughout the university year. Even young students quickly comprehend that the rewards and penalties provided by systems are similar to those provided by faculty members alongside their classmates. General media is full of stories about technology's prospects to substitute faculty staff, involving instructors, but the reality is that there is more to teaching than just knowledge sharing. A machine cannot substitute the human touch required in universities, which can only be provided by high-quality faculty staff. Rather than feeling scared of artificial intelligence, educational professionals and teachers can see it as a valuable tool for providing enhanced, customized learning experiences and lifting some of the administrative load on faculty shoulders. Progression in information technology has led to new progress in domains, such as online assessments, which has decreased some of the pressure students might experience around assessments. This method helps to make the test more pervasive and beneficial for instructors because the approaches are interlinked with the learning procedure and are invisible to learners. However, to obtain a space where all faculty members have access to such assessments, there must be a significant investment in research and development that results in enhanced systems of formative and diagnostic assessments (Williams et al., 2021).

CASE STUDY: THE USE OF AI FOR FACULTY SUCCESS AND ENGAGEMENT AT GEORGIA STATE UNIVERSITY

Georgia State College (GSU) has been experimenting with using artificial intelligence (AI) to improve staff victory and engagement. This case briefly investigates how GSU coordinates AI to bolster staff in education, enquiry, proficient improvement, and regulation collaboration, giving knowledge to other teachers to receive comparable innovations. GSU, an open enquire-about college in Atlanta, Georgia, is known for its assorted under-study body and commitment to making strides in instructive results. The university's key centre on AI points to improving instruction and learning, back enquiry about cultivating proficient advancement, and moving forward regulation productivity.

Key Goals

1. Upgrading education and learning: Utilising AI for personalised learning situations.
2. Supporting Investigation and Advancement: Encourage advanced information examination and intrigue collaboration.
3. Proficient Advancement: Provide AI-driven apparatuses for nonstop learning.
4. Organisation Proficiency: Progress Decision-and-Asset Assets through AI Experiences.

GSU's current analytics framework recognises at-risk understudies by analysing participation and grades, permitting the workforce to mediate early. For occurrence, if an understudy misses numerous classes or performs ineffectively on assignments, the framework alarms the workforce, empowering convenient back to make strides in understudy results (Nguyen et al., 2020). Personalised Learning Implements AI-driven versatile learning stages in basic tailoring directions for individual students to monitor progress. Staff can screen advances through analytics dashboards, permitting them to address students' challenges in upgrading under-study learning and workforce adequacy (Luckin et al., 2016). Cleverly Mentoring Frameworks (ITS) give personalized back exterior lesson hours, advertising real-time assignment input. The workforce can utilise ITS analytics to obtain common understudied blunders, refine their instruction techniques, and diminish their workload by off-loading schedule assignments to AI frameworks (Graesser et al., 2012). AI devices encourage progress in information investigation and cultivate information at GSU. For example, AI-driven stages analyse workforce distributions and enquire about interfaces to coordinate potential collaborators, improve efficiency, and cultivate development (LeCun et al., 2015).

GSU employs AI to create personalised proficient improvement plans, suggesting pertinent courses and workshops based on staff execution information and career objectives. Ceaseless criticism frameworks analyse understudy execution and provide noteworthy experiences to the workforce, making a difference in refining their instruction strategies (Daniela & Lytras, 2019).

AI-driven decision-making instruments improve regulation effectiveness by imparting knowledge to workforce execution and asset assignments. This data-driven approach makes a difference in GSU, as it recognises and addresses issues proactively, supporting staff victory and engagement (Huang et al., 2020).

Challenges and Moral Contemplations

GSU addresses algorithmic predisposition by executing decency calculations and routinely examining AI frameworks to guarantee the evenhanded treatment of all workforce and understudies (O'Neil, 2016). GSU guarantees information protection and security through strong measures such as encryption and get-to controls, complying with directions such as GDPR and FERPA to ensure staff and under-study information (Gibbs et al., 2013). To bridge the computerised divide, GSU provides training and support to guarantee that all staff have access to and can utilise AI instruments, advancing computerised proficiency and inclusivity (van Dijk, 2020).

Results and Impact

AI-driven frameworks have progressed under study maintenance and execution, with a workforce able to supply focused on bolstering at-risk understudies (Nguyen et al., 2020). AI apparatuses have boosted investigative efficiency by encouraging progress in information investigation and intriguing collaboration, thereby driving high-impact distributions (LeCun et al., 2015). Personalised proficient advancement plans and persistent inputs have upgraded staff aptitudes and work fulfilment, supporting their proficient development (Daniela & Lytras, 2019). AI-driven decision-making has made strides in regulation productivity, permitting GSU to address challenges proactively and successfully support the workforce. (Huang et al, 2020)

GSU's integration with AI has upgraded its workforce victory and engagement. By tending to challenges such as algorithmic inclination and information protection, GSU provides a solid example for other educators. The GSU case study illustrates AI's transformative potential in higher instruction and advertising important knowledge for leveraging AI to bolster the workforce and achieve better instructional results.

REFERENCES

Abbas, N., Whitfield, J., Atwell, E., Bowman, H., Pickard, T., & Walker, A. (2022). Online chat and chatbots to enhance mature student engagement in higher education. *International Journal of Lifelong Education*, 41(3), 1–19. DOI:10.1080/02601370.2022.2066213

Alam, A., & Mohanty, A. (2022, December). Facial Analytics or Virtual Avatars: Competencies and Design Considerations for Student-Teacher Interaction in AI-Powered Online Education for Effective Classroom Engagement. In *International Conference on Communication, Networks and Computing* (pp. 252-265). Cham: Springer Nature Switzerland.

Bhardwaj, P., Gupta, P. K., Panwar, H., Siddiqui, M. K., Morales-Menendez, R., & Bhaik, A. (2021). Application of Deep Learning on Student Engagement in e-learning environments. *Computers & Electrical Engineering*, 93, 107277. DOI:10.1016/j.compeleceng.2021.107277 PMID:36567679

Carvalho, L., Martinez-Maldonado, R., Tsai, Y. S., Markauskaite, L., & De Laat, M. (2022). How can we design for learning in an AI world? *Computers and Education: Artificial Intelligence*, 3, 100053. DOI:10.1016/j.caeai.2022.100053

Chen, Y., Jensen, S., Albert, L. J., Gupta, S., & Lee, T. (2022). Artificial Intelligence (AI) Student Assistants in the Classroom: Designing Chatbots to Support Student Success. *Information Systems Frontiers*, 1–22.

Cukurova, M., Miao, X., & Brooker, R. (2023, June). Adoption of artificial intelligence in schools: unveiling factors influencing teachers' engagement. In *International conference on artificial intelligence in education* (pp. 151-163). Cham: Springer Nature Switzerland. DOI:10.1007/978-3-031-36272-9_13

Fazil, A. W., Hakimi, M., Shahidzay, A. K., & Hasas, A. (2024). Exploring the Broad Impact of AI Technologies on Student Engagement and Academic Performance in University Settings in Afghanistan. *RIGGS: Journal of Artificial Intelligence and Digital Business*, 2(2), 56–63. DOI:10.31004/riggs.v2i2.268

Hannan, E., & Liu, S. (2021). AI: New source of competitiveness in higher education. *Competitiveness Review*.

Hooda, M., Rana, C., Dahiya, O., Rizwan, A., & Hossain, M. S. (2022). Artificial intelligence for assessment and feedback to enhance student success in higher education. *Mathematical Problems in Engineering*, 2022, 1–19. DOI:10.1155/2022/5215722

Kumar, P., Dwivedi, Y. K., & Anand, A. (2021). Responsible artificial intelligence (AI) for value formation and market performance in healthcare: The mediating role of patient's cognitive engagement. *Information Systems Frontiers*, 1–24. PMID:33948105

Naidoo, D. T. (2023). Integrating TAM and IS success model: Exploring the role of blockchain and AI in predicting learner engagement and performance in e-learning. *Frontiers of Computer Science*, 5, 1227749. DOI:10.3389/fcomp.2023.1227749

Nazari, N., Shabbir, M. S., & Setiawan, R. (2021). Application of Artificial Intelligence powered digital writing assistant in higher education: Randomized controlled trial. *Heliyon*, 7(5), e07014. DOI:10.1016/j.heliyon.2021.e07014 PMID:34027198

Nguyen, A., Kremantzis, M., Essien, A., Petrounias, I., & Hosseini, S. (2024). Enhancing Student Engagement Through Artificial Intelligence (AI): Understanding the Basics, Opportunities, and Challenges. *Journal of University Teaching & Learning Practice*, 21(06). Advance online publication. DOI:10.53761/caraaq92

Nikita, G., & Velicheti, S. N. (2022). AI as a Tool in Internal Communication to Reduce Employee Attrition Rate in India. In *Achieving $5 Trillion Economy of India* (pp. 43–62). Springer. DOI:10.1007/978-981-16-7818-9_3

Ramasamy, V., Singsen, D., & Walia, G. S. (2024). Fostering Student Engagement and Success in STEM Education: An AI-Driven Exploration of High Impact Practices from Cross-Disciplinary General Education Courses. *Journal of Engineering Education Transformations, 37*(Special Issue 2).

Schiff, D. (2022). Education for AI, not AI for Education: The role of education and ethics in national AI policy strategies. *International Journal of Artificial Intelligence in Education*, 32(3), 527–563. DOI:10.1007/s40593-021-00270-2

Singer, A. M., DeBenedectis, C. M., & Rosen, M. P. (2021). Integrating art museum visits into the radiology curriculum: A program to encourage engagement, observation and analytic skills among millennial learners. *Clinical Imaging*, 79, 204–206. DOI:10.1016/j.clinimag.2021.05.019 PMID:34116296

Talwar, P. (2023). *The Strategic Use of Virtual Teacher Assistants to Increase Faculty Engagement and Job Satisfaction* (Doctoral dissertation, Trident University International).

Tariq, M. U. (2024a). AI and the future of talent management: Transforming recruitment and retention with machine learning. In Christiansen, B., Aziz, M., & O'Keeffe, E. (Eds.), *Global practices on effective talent acquisition and retention* (pp. 1–16). IGI Global. DOI:10.4018/979-8-3693-1938-3.ch001

Tariq, M. U. (2024b). Application of blockchain and Internet of Things (IoT) in modern business. In Sinha, M., Bhandari, A., Priya, S., & Kabiraj, S. (Eds.), *Future of customer engagement through marketing intelligence* (pp. 66–94). IGI Global. DOI:10.4018/979-8-3693-2367-0.ch004

Tariq, M. U. (2024c). The role of AI ethics in cost and complexity reduction. In Tennin, K., Ray, S., & Sorg, J. (Eds.), *Cases on AI ethics in business* (pp. 59–78). IGI Global. DOI:10.4018/979-8-3693-2643-5.ch004

Tariq, M. U. (2024d). Challenges of a metaverse shaping the future of entrepreneurship. In Inder, S., Dawra, S., Tennin, K., & Sharma, S. (Eds.), *New business frontiers in the metaverse* (pp. 155–173). IGI Global. DOI:10.4018/979-8-3693-2422-6.ch011

Tariq, M. U. (2024e). Neurodiversity inclusion and belonging strategies in the workplace. In J. Vázquez de Príncipe (Ed.), *Resilience of multicultural and multigenerational leadership and workplace experience* (pp. 182-201). IGI Global. DOI:10.4018/979-8-3693-1802-7.ch009

Tariq, M. U. (2024f). AI and IoT in flood forecasting and mitigation: A comprehensive approach. In Ouaissa, M., Ouaissa, M., Boulouard, Z., Iwendi, C., & Krichen, M. (Eds.), *AI and IoT for proactive disaster management* (pp. 26–60). IGI Global. DOI:10.4018/979-8-3693-3896-4.ch003

Tariq, M. U. (2024g). Empowering student entrepreneurs: From idea to execution. In Cantafio, G., & Munna, A. (Eds.), *Empowering students and elevating universities with innovation centers* (pp. 83–111). IGI Global. DOI:10.4018/979-8-3693-1467-8.ch005

Thiry, H., & Hug, S. T. (2021, March). Sustaining student engagement and equity in computing departments during the covid-19 pandemic. In *Proceedings of the 52nd ACM Technical Symposium on Computer Science Education* (pp. 987-993). DOI:10.1145/3408877.3432381

Wang, W., Chen, L., Xiong, M., & Wang, Y. (2021). Accelerating AI adoption with responsible AI signals and employee engagement mechanisms in health care. *Information Systems Frontiers*, •••, 1–18.

Wijayati, D. T., Rahman, Z., Rahman, M. F. W., Arifah, I. D. C., & Kautsar, A. (2022). A study of artificial intelligence on employee performance and work engagement: The moderating role of change leadership. *International Journal of Manpower*, 43(2), 486–512. DOI:10.1108/IJM-07-2021-0423

Williams, R., Kaputsos, S. P., & Breazeal, C. (2021, May). Teacher Perspectives on How To Train Your Robot: A Middle School AI and Ethics Curriculum. *Proceedings of the AAAI Conference on Artificial Intelligence*, 35(17), 15678–15686. DOI:10.1609/aaai.v35i17.17847

Wilson, C. (2022). Public engagement and AI: A values analysis of national strategies. *Government Information Quarterly*, 39(1), 101652. DOI:10.1016/j.giq.2021.101652

ADDITIONAL READING

Babar, M., Tariq, M. U., Alshehri, M. D., Ullah, F., & Uddin, M. I. (2022). Smart teledentistry healthcare architecture for medical big data analysis using IoT-enabled environment. *Sustainable Computing : Informatics and Systems*, 35, 100719. DOI:10.1016/j.suscom.2022.100719

Banu, S. R., Thulasi, V. V. Y. R., Tariq, M. U., & Sethi, S. (2023). Relationship between leadership effectiveness and organizational performance and its effect on human resource management. *Journal of Informatics Education and Research*, 3(2).

Bhardwaj, S., Nair, K., Tariq, M. U., Ahmad, A., & Chitnis, A. (2023). The state of research in green marketing: A bibliometric review from 2005 to 2022. *Sustainability (Basel)*, 15(4), 2988. DOI:10.3390/su15042988

Kaleem, S., Sohail, A., Babar, M., Ahmad, A., & Tariq, M. U. (2023). Ensemble learning for multi-class COVID-19 detection from big data. *PLoS One*, 18(10), e0292587. DOI:10.1371/journal.pone.0292587 PMID:37819992

Kaleem, S., Sohail, A., Tariq, M. U., & Asim, M. (2023). An improved big data analytics architecture using federated learning for IoT-enabled urban intelligent transportation systems. *Sustainability (Basel)*, 15(21), 15333. DOI:10.3390/su152115333

Kaleem, S., Sohail, A., Tariq, M. U., & Asim, M. (2024). A hybrid model for energy-efficient green Internet of Things enabled intelligent transportation systems using federated learning. *Internet of Things : Engineering Cyber Physical Human Systems*, 25, 101038. DOI:10.1016/j.iot.2023.101038

KEY TERMS AND DEFINITIONS

Adaptive Learning Systems: AI-powered platforms that adjust the difficulty and content of educational material in real time based on a student's performance.

AI-Driven Analytics: The use of AI to analyse large datasets in educational settings, providing insights into student performance.

Cleverly Mentoring Systems (ITS): Intelligent Tutoring Systems that use AI to offer personalized guidance and feedback to students outside of traditional classroom settings.

Personalised Learning: An educational approach where AI tailors learning experiences to individual student needs, preferences, and performance.

Proficient Development: The process of continuous learning and skill enhancement for faculty members, often facilitated by AI-driven platforms that recommend relevant courses.

Chapter 14
Artificial Intelligence for General Administration

ABSTRACT

Artificial intelligence implements automation beyond physical intelligence. It infers the automation of tasks that currently require the human brain to conclude things, such as driving, discussion, and data assessment. Similarly, artificial intelligence is new, and computer experts have been discussing and developing it over the years. The evolved aspects include the accessibility of cost-effective computing, advancements in algorithm coding, and profusion of recently accessible data. The world already had this better synergy as advancement progressed, and the algorithms were both designed simultaneously. What sustains the implementation of artificial intelligence for general objectives? In addition, people are doing so, and in and outside the administration, it is only difficult to inform at times. Artificial intelligence, as stimulating as the term is at this moment, functions as a significant element of a product for most segments.

INTRODUCTION

Artificial intelligence is only one phase; it does not include accumulating information or doing anything vital. Artificial intelligence sustains the probability of significantly enhancing government function. It supports addressing the problems of citizens in a refined manner, ranging from healthcare delivery to traffic management, to the processing of tax systems. While public domain authorities are gradually becoming aware of the transformational impact of information and artificial powered solutions, the data needed for artificial intelligence solutions to

DOI: 10.4018/979-8-3693-4074-5.ch014

be developed and implemented are routinely neither accessible nor ascertainable (Ponkin & Redkina, 2018).

Administrating authorities may similarly not have the suitable knowledge and proficiency to settle on fundamental purchasing choices for artificial-powered tools. The susceptibility to moral inspection involves further complexity. Later, authorities generally delayed purchasing choices or decreased perceived risk by emphasizing their purchases on a couple of recognized providers. Authorities feel that artificial intelligence can handle the challenges of the governing authorities today. The private sector is now using different artificial intelligence devices and developments, such as chatbots, for enhanced and increasingly collaborative customer service (Henman, 2020). The general administration sector has different domains that can benefit from artificial intelligence. There are different citizen-facing aspects such as social services and health, social security, policing and justice, revenue, pension, and administration, where artificial intelligence can assist the public sector. For example, the fundamental innovations of the UAE government include biometrics, machine learning, identity analysis, process automation, and IoT. One of the fundamental reasons that artificial intelligence has not been recognized in the government sector is the fear of losing jobs. This will support people in disposing of routine and monotonous tasks. Emphasis should be placed on more crucial and decision-oriented tasks. One primary domain of government applications is customer service chatbots. As local and state governments started positioning data on sites in recent decades, they explored the use of those media as a means for replying to queries that element utilized to require making a call to the office to ask, in a perfect world, that ends up in a recurring victory. Government offices did not have a similar number of calls to respond to, so they could provide supplementary assets and time for diversified capacities (Etscheid, 2019).

Moreover, when someone calls them, they may be addressed more quickly. According to a survey, almost 80 percent of customer service calls were required to change their passwords. A chatbot can accelerate a process with minimal support from artificial intelligence, where the process is comprehensive each time. At that stage, like the government online portal, employees are opened to respond to more complex calls more quickly. In any situation, there is more than one (Senthiil et al., 2019).

Regarding a customer service-type situation, artificial intelligence can ease the process by obtaining data from a guest while waiting for a person to accept their call. Others use artificial intelligence to distinguish and report objects in images and videos, cracked concrete, weapons, pedestrians, semi-tracks, and waterfowls. Others have used artificial intelligence to actively support translations between languages. Some required it to break down the email load. Some use it to remain conscious of cybersecurity risks, as they evolve and transform. The use of data analytics is another domain of intelligence that can greatly benefit administrative authorities (Boburbek et al., 2022). For example, a fire department can use data analytics for advanced medical emergency response. It recommends dispatchers as an appropriate response to medical emergency requirements. It can support settling on a choice recognized by a patient to be treated near or taken to a medical hospital. The current system allows them to address an average of eighty-five thousand medical emergencies annually. Their vision has lessened the running of the emergency response groups. Presently, the profession of government digital services as a significant characteristic of cabinet offices apprehends the digital transformation of the government. They are a principal point of excellence in digital, data, and technology, coordinating with departments to support their evolution (Surden, 2019). Its function is to develop digital platforms, services, and standards. In a manual for using artificial intelligence in the general administration, they revealed that artificial intelligence can alter how people work and live; for example, some general administration offices utilize artificial intelligence for tasks from fraud detection to replying to consumer questions efficaciously today. While it is assessed that artificial intelligence could subsidize five percent of the UAE's GDP by 2030, safety, moral, and fairness considerations must be measured. In any situation, with an artificial intelligence venture, one must consider a few aspects of artificial intelligence safety and ethics such as costs, fairness, accountability, data quality, transparency, privacy, and explainability (Jaikaew et al., 2022).

Artificial intelligence is becoming more widespread in every facet of modern life (Tariq, 2024). In particular, the growing usage of artificial intelligence technologies and assistants for decision-making in public affairs, in taking authoritative decisions or policy decisions relevant to the rights or burdens of specific citizens, has sparked a dynamic debate on the advantages and probable threats of self-learning technologies (Morkhat et al., 2019). The discussion varied from objective and informed decisions to threats of the ruin of humankind. To avert adverse outcomes and create responsible systems that people can trust, many have argued that people must open up the black box of artificial intelligence decision making and make it more see-through. This opening up will make it easy for us to recognize and interpret the operations of artificial intelligence and obtain explanations for specific decisions. Although much stimulating work has been done in the domain of transparency, far less attention has been devoted to the role of transparency in how those who are eventually affected, which is the general public, come to observe artificial intelligence decision-making as valid and worthy of acceptance (Robertson et al., 2021). Scholars have noted the significance of public acceptance of AI implementation. Various models can make artificial intelligence systems less biased and fairer, leading to an upsurge in perceived legitimacy. However, these models do not openly involve empirical findings and theories from the social sciences concerning how individuals' legitimacy perceptions are impacted by various aspects, such as decisions, process transparency, and reasons behind decisions. In addition, no regular model is available to assess the perceived validity of artificial intelligence in the wider context of the socio-technological system to clarify the present and future problems relevant to perceived validity and transparency (Young et al., 2019).

COMPLETE TRANSPARENCY IN ARTIFICIAL INTELLIGENCE AND PUBLIC DECISION-MAKING

Social experts and policymakers have promoted confirmation transparency in administrative affairs to increase trust and perceived validity among administrations. This has led to a broad range of transparency revolutions, from making records openly accessible on the internet to broadcasting all meetings (Wirtz et al., 2019). Therefore, it is not strange to think, as those included in the discussion about artificial intelligence in public decision-making have done, that the interpretation of artificial intelligence decision-making procedures that are more transparent will enhance the public's trust in these procedures and decisions, even though not all types of transparency may have optimistic impacts on perceived validity, some favor transparency which is both transparency and rationale in the process (Busuioc, 2021). Perceiving that the debate relevant to the employment of artificial intelligence generally follows the logic of public discussion on transparency, those voices may emerge stronger as artificial intelligence techniques create and become more broadly applied in society. It is believed that if perceived validity is the objective, the general administration should choose transparency in rationale and not in the procedure. Transparency in rationale refers to the public getting information for the explanation or justification of a decision and details of who can be held responsible for it (Yan et al., 2021). The rationale for transparency is the same as that of explicability. This infers that the public receives the justification or explanation for the decision taken, a portrayal of the procedure leading up to it, and a record of who is responsible for it. However, suppose explicability means that the general administration makes the decision-making procedures completely transparent. In such cases, it is not believed to be appropriate for producing perceived validity (Dymitruk, 2019). Still, if decision-makers should explain the form of a narrative where it describes how the decision is taken, this might be valid for perceived legitimacy. The idea that artificial intelligence assistants should be capable of providing explanations or justifications for decisions is not new. This finding is consistent with the fundamental components of the progressively evolving research domain of explainable artificial intelligence.

Some authors have surveyed various explanations that impact the public's impartial judgments (Bignami, 2022; Tariq, 2024).

Similarly, organisations such as Microsoft, Google, and the Defense Advanced Research Projects Agency have worked toward explainable artificial intelligence development. The decision-making procedure is divided into three stages to appreciate what transparency in artificial intelligence and public decision-making would add up (Zbuchea et al., 2019). The first phase is the objective-setting phase, also known as goal-setting, the second phase is the coding stage, and the third is the implementation phase. During the first phase, which is the goal-setting stage, regulators determine the objectives of the artificial intelligence, how they should be evaluated against each other when at odds, and the features and data accessible to draw implications. For example, suppose you want your artificial intelligence to choose which buildings you should prioritize when beginning a large renovation project. In this case, one may want it to have a feature that knows each building was last refurbished and which renovation procedure would be the most cost-efficient to start (Padurean et al., 2021). Indeed, these features might attract various directions, inferring that one will have to provide the values of various weights to guide artificial intelligence in what to do when the features conflict. These decisions are mostly highly political, as they require decision-makers to openly differentiate between pros and cons with a high level of accuracy. In the second phase, the coding stage, the artificial intelligence is created and functions to ensure that it meets the required standards. This is mainly the point of introduction for issues relevant to biases and bugs and is mentioned correctly in the literature (Biryukov & Antonova, 2018). In this stage, we discuss what the precision rates are, what they should be, how these and other performance metrics vary, and how they should be permitted to differ across various subpopulations when determining individuals and groups, and what data to utilize when training and cleaning the algorithm (Koch, 2018). With public decision making, the vital challenge is guaranteeing that artificial intelligence is sufficient to address these issues. It may be challenging or even impossible for decision makers to know whether the artificial intelligence they have legalized is up to the standard without depending on programmers (Valle-Cruz et al., 2020). This is not an issue limited to artificial decision making, as decision makers depend on expert opinions in almost all policy domains. This issue may be emphasized in artificial decision making, as some political agents are trained in programming or reading (Pang et al., 2022). In addition, setting goals and ensuring that their respective significance is suitable for programmer requirements may be difficult. In the third implementation phase, artificial intelligence is implemented in general administrative decision-making procedures, and the results generated by artificial intelligence are utilized in actual decision-making (Krasteva, 2021). It can be done by having the artificial intelligence decide by itself, more reasonably, by having a human properly make the decision based on the results or suggestions of the artificial intelligence. Logically, this phase is mostly the one scholar refer to when debating artificial intelligence and transparency. This phase also feeds back into the first and second phases (Rahayu, 2021; Matibag, 2020). For instance, when artificial intelligence assistance has been deployed in real-world settings, it is sometimes unintentionally biased and later requires modifications (van de Sande et al., 2021). Likewise, if left unsupervised, they might have bad habits that modify the intentions of decision makers (Engstrom et al., 2020). In addition, conceptual shifts among decision-makers might need alterations in prioritization and goals to complicate things further; these alterations among decision-makers might be flickered by their more profound recognition of the realization of the artificial intelligence assistant's objectives. Therefore, there is a continuous merger between the first and third phases, with all phases being strongly associated (Pesapane et al., 2018). To make the procedure of the first phase, which is goal-setting, and the second phase, coding, entirely transparent to the public, decision-makers must discuss prioritization and objectives and the discussions of programmers accessible to the general public along with the testing and training data (Amann et al., 2020). In the third phase, when artificial intelligence is applied in the decision-making procedure, the source code and records relevant to how the artificial intelligence is utilized in decision-making procedures are required to make it publicly available. The assurance of transparency of the reasons is that decisions are dependent on the decision-makers who should offer reasons for their decisions, which can be done in every phase (Tariq, 2024. Transparency concerning these reasons will probably comprise an attempt to validate the functionality of artificial intelligence, such as the weights, methods in different scenarios, and goals (Wirtz et al., 2020).

Why More Transparency Is Not Essentially Better

For artificial intelligence in general administration decision-making, there are voices favoring transparency. This indicates the transparency of all three phases in the decision-making process. Even though some favor transparency, the discussion relevant to transparency in artificial intelligence and general administration decision-making is presently biased to partial transparency, which means that transparency is the rationale, which is observed as a fundamental element of validity and perceived validity (Corvalán, 2018). Even though we tend to agree with this, there are persuasive arguments in favor of full transparency that have not yet been fully marshalled in the debate. Consequently, in this section, we present arguments in favor of why, for example, releasing the source code could lead to higher perceived legitimacy, even though the public will not understand it. We then explain why we believe that these arguments fail (Reis et al., 2019). The first argument for interpreting decision-making in the first to third phases as entirely transparent is that transparency makes decision-makers conscious of the general public eye, thus making them conscious of their responsibility to work for the public good instead of their self-interests (Zhang, 2021). This is true for decision-makers when setting objectives and programmers writing the code, such as opting for classifiers, training, and testing data. This makes them conscious that the general public is watching by monitoring their meetings in actual time or by revealing the source code.

Transparency in a procedure can result in optimistic outcomes (He & Wang, 2020). It is believed that this is not relevant to artificial intelligence in administrative decision-making. Starting with the third phase, assuming that the public requires a chance to recognize the code, it will possibly have to be much easier than it is in present-day systems. This could possibly make it simpler to game the system and offer the industry less motivation for innovation. Thus, in this sense, even transparency demands would possibly produce a lower quality in decisions and, thus, less perceived validity (Luchini et al., 2022). Likewise, convincing arguments are presented against the perception that transparency would lead to better decisions in the first and second phases. One reason for this is that transparency about a procedure provides incentives for decision-makers to look reliable in the eyes of viewers during their discussions, but this is not important in terms of the opportunity to lead to a good decision (Lu & Gao, 2022). In addition, as artificial intelligence assistants function quickly, generating possibly negative and positive results in a short timeframe, fast and effective decision-making may be essential when deploying artificial intelligence assistants in the first and second phases and regulating them in the third phase. Therefore, the ability to act or reach a decision and apply it is even more essential in artificial decision-making than in routine policymaking (Huang & Chen, 2020).

However, when the procedure is transparent, decision-makers may be more concerned with gesticulating loyalty to their elements or following the specific interests they represent than exploring a solution to an emerging issue. This means that vital decisions may be delayed or dependent on an inexact account of the information at hand, resulting in a lower perceived validity. The second argument favoring complete transparency is that it should increase the general public's recognition of decision-making procedures and decisions (Benjamens et al., 2020). This argument has some issues, but the most pertinent one is what is sometimes known as the information overload or transparency paradox. It holds that if we obtain all of the information from the first and second phases, we will have a lot of information to integrate, and this issue worsens in the third phase. Exploring pertinent information would be as difficult as exploring familiar needles in a haystack-something to which the public and decision makers will recognize and adapt. Later, we did not observe optimistic results in making information accessible (Moglia et al., 2022). Thus, there are strong arguments favoring not being completely transparent but rather providing public information about what they want and require knowing to assure that they are sufficiently informed about decisions. The third argument favoring full transparency is that it enhances perceived validity by encouraging feelings of control among the public. The close association between accountability and transparency has inspired various debates on transparency (Angin, 2021). Transparency allows the general public to control the irregularity of information relevant to a representative's work, leading to transformed instructions about what to do or eliminate from office (Ke, 2021). Decreased uncertainty makes it possible to concentrate the principal more poised in delegating powers to the representative and assuring that it sticks to its decision and regards it as valid. There are reasons for believing that this is not the case. Transparency, as a supporter of accountability, can subsidize the myth of concealed politics, where the public does not trust that it has access to the decision-making procedure (Balakrishnan et al., 2020). Therefore, when data and code are transparent, the general public might assume that this release conceals the real code in true use, or that there is some kind of backdoor in the code to confirm that it functions in another method from what is anticipated (Bullock, 2019).

Likewise, the data and source code on which artificial intelligence has been tested and trained are mostly too complicated for most people to completely recognize, meaning that entire transparency might actually make the general public less viable to suppose that they have more control over artificial intelligence than they did before they had access to the data. Intrinsically, because of the astounding amount of data availability, it may be tough to recognize who to hold responsible for what. The last argument favoring full transparency is that transparency produces optimistic outcomes relevant to perceived validity, as the general public will perceive the decision-making procedures to be fair, which will also impact their assessments of decision makers and decisions (Talapina, 2021). From almost every standardizing perspective, transparency is more significant than non-transparency, and at present, data transparency has become a slogan in general administration. Thus, transparency itself might have an optimistic self-governing impact on perceived validity, regardless of the content of the procedure that is accessible to the general public. Therefore, even if a person cannot recognize the working of a classifier, such as a deep neural network, or how the input produces the output, they can escalate the fact that the general administration has made the procedure transparent (Collins & Moons, 2019). However, it is intuitive that transparent institutions are prioritized over non-transparent institutions and that they produce higher perceived validity. Some known research has shown that it is far from evident that enhanced transparency engenders acceptance or trust of general public policies. In certain situations, this impact can be adverse. The issue is that full transparency discloses the reality of decision-making, and real-world decision-making infrequently or never lives up to the professional or democratic ideals. In other words, the general public may become dissatisfied when they comprehend those decision-making procedures are, more than rarely, classified by a procedure of muddling through instead of a normal process of detecting the issues, accumulating related information, and prudently weighing all the substitutes (Reis et al., 2019). By contrast, the formula for such disappointments is to enhance the procedure. Alternatively, an actual-world political and private decision-making procedure with which the public is thoroughly pleased is unlikely because of inherent inefficiencies and conflicts in political affairs. In the third phase, the possible adverse impacts of the data and code can be implemented (Meskó et al., 2018).

There are many indications that complete transparency in decision-making procedures does not essentially make decision-making about or by artificial intelligence valid in the eyes of the general public. On the other hand, there are reasons to trust that transparency can negatively affect public confidence or the reception of decisions, not least because of possible issues with setting below-average-quality algorithms. It is not to say that we should not provide access to researchers, auditors, or any other participants who can decode algorithms. Providing these groups with accessibility may lead to improved quality decisions and a greater degree of perceived validity. Moreover, there may be good reasons favoring the demand for transparency in decision-making procedures in the workings of artificial intelligence when it comes to other representatives, such as decision-makers. This is because they might utilize the information to make more informed decisions, leading to higher-quality decisions that increase the perceived validity among the general public. However, this does not imply that there are fine reasons favoring information sharing with the general public if perceived legitimacy is the objective (Girasa, 2020).

The Advantages of a Justified Approach to Artificial Intelligence Transparency

In view of the previous discussion on the possible disadvantages of transparency in the process, it is argued that a strategy that emphasizes justifications for decisions has the prospect of producing perceived validity among the public, both for decisions relevant to the design of the artificial intelligence in the first and second phases and the decision made by artificial intelligence in the third phase. Additionally, it is argued that a justification approach can eliminate various possible issues that arise from far more challenging forms of transparency that represent the risk of failing in perceived validity. A policy justifying the decision will notify the public of what the decision is, on what basis the decision is taken, and, in doing so, recognize who the accountable actor is (Larsson & Heintz, 2020). In various situations, this information is sufficient to get participants from the public to generate an opinion about the appeal of the decision and, if they so like, demand that the accountable participant be responsible. Therefore, we may desire decision makers to provide favorable reasons for the objectives and priorities in the first and second phases. They have set for artificial intelligence and guarantee that these reasons are made accessible to the public in a manner that they can recognize (Nurjaman, 2022). In the third phase, the artificial intelligence assistants should be able to explain their decisions or suggestions in the available language. It should be evident who is responsible for the decision and where to switch if a person wants to make the decision.

The Role of Justifications in AI Transparency

Explanations of AI systems serve as a means of connecting the technical intricacy of such systems with the general public's comprehension. Unlike complete transparency, which might involve the disclosure of source code or intricate algorithmic procedures, explanations concentrate on providing reasons for decisions in a manner that is comprehensible to individuals who lack technical expertise. This approach acknowledges that, for the majority of people, the primary concern is not necessarily the technical process by which a decision was reached but rather the rationale behind the decision and the individuals who are accountable for it.

By offering clear explanations, decision-makers can make the decision-making process more accessible and relatable to the general public. This is crucial during the first two stages of AI development, where objectives are established and coding decisions are made. These phases often involve complex trade-offs and decisions that require careful consideration, which can be politically sensitive and technically intricate. An approach that emphasises justification allows decision-makers to articulate the values and priorities that guide these decisions, making the process more transparent in a manner that is meaningful to the public.

Additionally, during the third stage, when AI systems are implemented and start making autonomous decisions or providing recommendations, explanations become increasingly important. At this point, AI systems must be capable of explaining their decisions in language that is both understandable and relevant to the end-users. This requirement ensures that users can comprehend the basis for AI-driven decisions, which is essential for maintaining trust in the system.

Addressing the Limitations of Full Transparency

One of the key benefits of adopting a justified approach is its capacity to mitigate the risks associated with full transparency. While full transparency may seem desirable, it can sometimes lead to information overload, whereby the sheer volume of data and technical detail becomes overwhelming for the public. This, in turn, reduces transparency, making it difficult for individuals to distinguish relevant information from noise. Additionally, full transparency can sometimes lead to increased scepticism, as the public might perceive the disclosed information as a smokescreen, concealing the actual workings of the AI system. In contrast, a justified approach concentrates on the most pertinent aspects of decision-making, namely the reasons behind decisions and the accountability of the stakeholders involved. This method does not inundate the public with technical details but instead provides a more comprehensible and evaluable narrative. It also enables decision-makers to control the narrative, highlighting the ethical considerations and value judgments that guided the decision-making process.

Moreover, by clearly identifying who is accountable for decisions, a justified approach reinforces the concept of responsibility. This aspect is of particular importance in AI systems, where the decision-making process might be dispersed across various stakeholders, including developers, regulators, and the AI systems themselves. Clear justifications help to clarify where responsibility lies, thus making it easier for the public to hold the appropriate stakeholders accountable.

Enhancing Public Trust and Perceived Validity

Trust is a fundamental aspect of any successful AI implementation, particularly in the context of public administration. A justifiable approach towards AI transparency can significantly bolster public trust by making the decision-making process more comprehensible and relatable. When the public is able to discern that decisions are based on clear, ethical considerations, and when they are cognizant of the individuals responsible for these decisions, they are more likely to perceive the system as legitimate and worthy of trust. This approach also aligns with the growing demand for ethical AI. In recent years, there has been a heightened recognition of the need for AI systems to not only be effective, but also fair, accountable, and transparent. A justifiable approach meets these demands by ensuring that AI decisions are not opaque, but rather accompanied by clear, understandable explanations. This transparency in rationale, as opposed to process, ensures that the public's focus is on the ethical and practical implications of AI decisions, rather than on the technical intricacies.

Furthermore, the provision of justifications can also facilitate more informed public discourse. When the public is aware of the reasons behind AI decisions, they are better equipped to participate in meaningful discussions about the implications of those decisions. This can lead to a more knowledgeable and engaged citizenry, which is essential for the democratic governance of AI technologies.

FUTURE RESEARCH DIRECTIONS

The field of artificial intelligence (AI) transparency, particularly in the context of justifications for decision-making, presents numerous avenues for future research. As AI continues to permeate various aspects of society, understanding how to best implement and communicate transparency will be crucial for fostering public trust, ensuring ethical outcomes, and enabling accountable governance. Below are key directions for future research that can significantly contribute to advancing this area.

Developing Standardised Frameworks for Justification

One pressing area for future research is the development of standardised frameworks that can guide the formulation of justifications across different AI systems and contexts. Such frameworks should address the diverse needs of stakeholders, including policymakers, developers, and the general public. Research should focus on identifying the core elements that make justifications clear, relevant, and accessible, while also ensuring that they are sufficiently comprehensive to cover the ethical and technical aspects of AI decision-making. Additionally, these frameworks should be adaptable to various domains, from healthcare to public administration, where AI is increasingly being deployed.

Empirical Studies on Public Perception of AI Justifications

Another important research direction involves empirical studies that explore how different forms of justifications are perceived by the public. While theoretical discussions provide valuable insights, it is crucial to understand how actual users and citizens interpret and react to justifications provided by AI systems. Research should examine factors such as the level of detail, language complexity, and the perceived fairness of justifications. These studies can help refine the approaches used to communicate AI decisions, ensuring that they are both effective and trustworthy from the perspective of end-users.

Exploring the Role of Context in Justification Effectiveness

Context plays a significant role in how justifications are received and understood. Future research should explore how different contexts—such as cultural, social, or political environments—impact the effectiveness of AI justifications. For instance, justifications that are effective in one cultural setting might not resonate in another due to different societal values or levels of technological literacy. Comparative studies across different regions and populations could provide valuable insights into how AI transparency strategies need to be tailored to specific contexts to enhance their effectiveness.

Integrating AI Justifications With Human Oversight Mechanisms

As AI systems increasingly operate autonomously, there is a growing need to integrate AI justifications with human oversight mechanisms. Future research should investigate how justifications can be designed to not only inform the public but also support human supervisors in monitoring and controlling AI systems. This includes exploring how justifications can be used to trigger human intervention when AI decisions deviate from expected norms or when ethical dilemmas arise. Research in this area could lead to the development of hybrid models where AI and human oversight work in tandem to ensure responsible decision-making.

Ethical Implications of AI Justifications

The ethical dimensions of AI justifications also warrant further exploration. Future research should examine the potential ethical risks associated with how justifications are framed, such as the possibility of manipulating public perception or oversimplifying complex decisions. Additionally, there is a need to investigate the balance between transparency and privacy, especially in contexts where providing detailed justifications might involve disclosing sensitive information. Research should aim to develop ethical guidelines that can inform the design and implementation of AI justifications, ensuring that they contribute to fairness, accountability, and the overall public good.

Longitudinal Studies on the Impact of Justifications on Trust and Legitimacy

Finally, longitudinal studies are needed to assess the long-term impact of AI justifications on public trust and the perceived legitimacy of AI systems. While short-term studies can provide initial insights, understanding how trust evolves over time in response to ongoing interactions with AI systems is crucial. Research should focus on tracking changes in public attitudes, trust levels, and the acceptance of AI decisions as justification practices are implemented and refined. Such studies will provide a deeper understanding of the sustainability and effectiveness of justification-based transparency strategies.

CONCLUSION

The discussion surrounding artificial intelligence (AI) transparency has brought to light the intricate issues and challenges associated with entirely transparent systems, particularly in terms of public comprehension and confidence. While transparency is frequently regarded as a panacea for ethical concerns in AI, this method can sometimes result in information overload, increased scepticism, and a paradoxical reduction in perceived legitimacy. In response to these challenges, a justified approach to AI transparency presents a more effective and practical alternative.

A justified approach prioritises providing clear, accessible justifications for AI decisions, focusing on the reasons behind a decision and the person responsible for it, rather than on the intricate technical details of the decision-making process. This approach addresses the limitations of full transparency by making the decision-making process more comprehensible and relatable to the general public. By emphasising justifications, decision-makers can enhance public trust, ensure accountability, and foster a sense of fairness, all of which are essential for the ethical deployment of AI systems.

Additionally, the justified approach aligns with the ethical demands of contemporary AI deployment, ensuring that AI systems are not only effective but also transparent in a manner that is meaningful to non-experts. This approach also facilitates more informed public discourse, empowering citizens to engage more deeply with the implications of AI decisions and thus contributing to more democratic governance of AI technologies.

However, implementing this approach requires careful consideration and ongoing refinement. Future research must focus on developing standardised frameworks for justifications, exploring public perceptions, and understanding the role of context in shaping the effectiveness of AI justifications. Additionally, integrating AI justifications with human oversight mechanisms and addressing the ethical implications of how justifications are framed are essential for ensuring that AI systems remain accountable and trusted.

In summary, while full transparency has its merits, a justified approach to AI transparency provides a more balanced and effective strategy for enhancing public trust and perceived legitimacy. By focusing on clear and accessible justifications, this approach can help bridge the gap between complex AI systems and the public's understanding, ultimately contributing to the responsible and ethical use of AI in society.

CASE STUDY: IMPLEMENTING AI IN PUBLIC HEALTH DECISION-MAKING: THE COVID-19 RESPONSE

The global COVID-19 pandemic presented unprecedented challenges to public health systems worldwide. In response, many governments turned to artificial intelligence (AI) to manage the crisis, particularly in areas such as disease tracking, resource allocation, and decision-making. This case study examines the deployment of AI in the public health response to COVID-19, focusing on how a justified approach to AI transparency played a crucial role in fostering public trust and ensuring the ethical use of AI technologies.

The Role of AI in the COVID-19 Response

During the COVID-19 pandemic, AI was leveraged in various ways to support public health efforts. AI models were used to predict the spread of the virus, optimize the allocation of medical resources, and assist in the development of vaccines. For instance, machine learning algorithms were employed to analyse large datasets, including mobility data, to predict infection hotspots and inform lockdown measures. AI was also used to manage the distribution of ventilators and personal protective equipment (PPE), ensuring that resources were directed to areas with the greatest need.

However, the rapid deployment of AI systems raised concerns about transparency, accountability, and public trust. As AI systems made critical decisions that impacted millions of lives, questions arose about how these decisions were made and who was responsible for them. This situation underscored the importance of a justified approach to AI transparency, where the reasons behind AI-driven decisions are clearly communicated to the public.

The Justified Approach in Action

In several countries, governments and health authorities adopted a justified approach to AI transparency to address these concerns. This approach involved providing clear and accessible explanations for how AI models were used in decision-making processes, particularly in areas where public understanding and trust were critical.

One of the key areas where AI was used during the pandemic was in predicting the spread of COVID-19. Governments used AI models to analyse data on population movements, social interactions, and health records to forecast potential outbreaks and inform lockdown decisions. For example, in South Korea, AI-powered models were instrumental in identifying clusters of infections and predicting their spread.

To maintain public trust, the South Korean government adopted a justified approach by explaining the rationale behind lockdown measures. Instead of merely presenting the AI predictions, authorities provided context, explaining how the models worked, what data they used, and how predictions were validated against real-world outcomes. This transparency helped the public understand why certain areas were subject to stricter lockdowns and why others were not, reducing resistance to government measures and fostering compliance.

Resource Allocation

AI also played a crucial role in allocating scarce medical resources during the pandemic. In Italy, one of the hardest-hit countries during the early stages of the pandemic, AI models were used to optimize the distribution of ventilators and PPE to hospitals based on real-time data on infection rates and hospital capacity.

The Italian government recognized the ethical implications of AI-driven resource allocation and the need for transparency. A justified approach was implemented by ensuring that the criteria used by AI systems were publicly disclosed. Authorities explained how decisions were made, emphasizing the ethical considerations involved, such as prioritizing regions with the highest mortality rates or where hospitals were closest to capacity. This approach not only enhanced the perceived fairness of the distribution process but also helped alleviate public concerns about potential biases or inequalities in resource allocation.

Vaccine Distribution

AI was also utilized in the logistics of vaccine distribution, particularly in countries like the United States and the United Kingdom, where the scale of the operation was enormous. AI systems helped to manage the distribution networks, ensuring that vaccines were delivered efficiently to where they were needed most.

In the United Kingdom, the government took a justified approach to AI transparency by providing detailed explanations of how vaccine distribution decisions were made. Public briefings and reports outlined the factors considered by the AI systems, such as population demographics, infection rates, and logistical constraints. The government also made efforts to explain the limitations of AI, acknowledging that while the systems were designed to optimize distribution, they were not infallible and that human oversight was an essential component of the decision-making process. This transparency helped build public confidence in the vaccine rollout, particularly in communities that were initially sceptical of the government's distribution strategy.

Challenges and Lessons Learned

While the justified approach to AI transparency was largely successful in fostering public trust during the COVID-19 pandemic, it also highlighted several challenges and areas for improvement.

Complexity of AI Models

One of the main challenges was the inherent complexity of AI models, which made it difficult to communicate the decision-making process to the general public. Even with simplified explanations, some members of the public struggled to understand how AI systems worked, leading to confusion and, in some cases, mistrust. This challenge underscores the need for ongoing research into how AI justifications can be made more accessible without oversimplifying critical details.

Balancing Transparency and Privacy

Another challenge was balancing transparency with the need to protect individual privacy. AI systems used during the pandemic often relied on sensitive personal data, such as health records and location information. Providing justifications for AI decisions required disclosing some of this data, which raised concerns about privacy. In South Korea, for example, the use of detailed contact tracing data in AI models was met with criticism from privacy advocates, even though the government took steps to anonymize the data. This highlights the need for clear guidelines on how to balance transparency with privacy, ensuring that justifications do not inadvertently compromise personal data.

Public Perception and Trust

Finally, the effectiveness of a justified approach depends heavily on public perception and trust in government institutions. In countries where trust in government was already low, such as the United States, justifications provided by authorities were sometimes met with scepticism, regardless of their transparency. This indicates that while a justified approach to AI transparency is crucial, it must be part of a broader strategy to build and maintain public trust in institutions. The COVID-19 pandemic provided a unique context for testing the effectiveness of AI in public decision-making and highlighted the critical importance of transparency and accountability. A justified approach to AI transparency, which focuses on providing clear and accessible explanations for AI-driven decisions, proved to be a valuable strategy for fostering public trust and ensuring ethical decision-making.

This case study demonstrates that while full transparency in AI systems can be challenging, particularly given the complexity of the models and the need to protect privacy, a justified approach can mitigate these challenges by focusing on what matters most to the public: understanding the reasons behind decisions and knowing who is accountable. However, the experience also underscores the need for continued research into improving how justifications are communicated and how they can be balanced with other ethical considerations, such as privacy.

REFERENCES

Angin, R. (2021, March). Artificial Intelligence and Human Resources: A Challenge in Implementing Artificial Intelligence in Village Government. *IOP Conference Series. Earth and Environmental Science*, 717(1), 012044. DOI:10.1088/1755-1315/717/1/012044

Balakrishnan, S., Janet, J., & Aswin, G. (2020). Artificial Intelligence and Robotics: A Research Overview. *CSI Communications Magazine,* (44), 24-26.

Benjamens, S., Dhunnoo, P., & Meskó, B. (2020). The state of artificial intelligence-based FDA-approved medical devices and algorithms: An online database. *NPJ Digital Medicine*, 3(1), 1–8. DOI:10.1038/s41746-020-00324-0 PMID:32984550

Bignami, F. (2022). Artificial Intelligence Accountability of Public Administration. *The American Journal of Comparative Law*, 70(Supplement_1), i312–i346. DOI:10.1093/ajcl/avac012

Biryukov, A., & Antonova, N. (2018, October). Expert systems of real time as key tendency of artificial intelligence in tax administration. In *The 2018 International Conference on Digital Science* (pp. 111-118). Springer.

Boburbek, B., Sanjarbek, R., Elmurod, U., & Satimov, A. (2022). The importance of artificial intelligence in modern technology. *Journal of Advanced Scientific Research, 2*(1).

Bullock, J. B. (2019). Artificial intelligence, discretion, and bureaucracy. *American Review of Public Administration*, 49(7), 751–761. DOI:10.1177/0275074019856123

Busuioc, M. (2021). Accountable artificial intelligence: Holding algorithms to account. *Public Administration Review*, 81(5), 825–836. DOI:10.1111/puar.13293 PMID:34690372

Collins, G. S., & Moons, K. G. (2019). Reporting of artificial intelligence prediction models. *Lancet*, 393(10181), 1577–1579. DOI:10.1016/S0140-6736(19)30037-6 PMID:31007185

Corvalán, J. G. (2018). Digital and intelligent public administration: transformations in the era of artificial intelligence. *A&C-Revista de Direito Administrativo & Constitucional, 18*(71), 55-87.

Dymitruk, M. (2019). Artificial Intelligence as a Tool to Improve the Administration of Justice? *Acta Universitatis Sapientiae. Legal Studies*, 8(2), 179–189.

Engstrom, D. F., Ho, D. E., Sharkey, C. M., & Cuéllar, M. F. (2020). Government by algorithm: Artificial intelligence in federal administrative agencies. *NYU School of Law, Public Law Research Paper*, (20-54).

Etscheid, J. (2019, September). Artificial intelligence in public administration. In *International Conference on Electronic Government* (pp. 248-261). Springer.

Girasa, R. (2020). *Artificial intelligence as a disruptive technology*. Springer International Publishing. DOI:10.1007/978-3-030-35975-1

He, H., & Wang, T. (2020, June). Application of Blended Teaching in Public Administration Courses under the Background of Artificial Intelligence. *Journal of Physics: Conference Series*, 1575(1), 012174. DOI:10.1088/1742-6596/1575/1/012174

Henman, P. (2020). Improving public services using artificial intelligence: Possibilities, pitfalls, governance. *Asia Pacific Journal of Public Administration*, 42(4), 209–221. DOI:10.1080/23276665.2020.1816188

Huang, H., & Chen, M. (2020, October). Research on the Construction of Practice Teaching System of Business Administration Specialty Based on Artificial Intelligence. *Journal of Physics: Conference Series*, 1648(4), 042055. DOI:10.1088/1742-6596/1648/4/042055

Jaikaew, P., Suntawan, T., & Yafu, S. (2022). A Model of the Need for Artificial Intelligence Using on the Administration of World-Class Standard Secondary School. *Journal of Positive School Psychology*, 6417–6424.

Jia, D. M., Yuan, C. F., Guo, S., Jiang, Z. Z., Xu, D., & Wang, D. A. (2019, October). Application of" Artificial Intelligence and Big Data" in Sports Rehabilitation for Chinese Judicial Administrative Drug Addicts. In *Proceedings of the 2019 International Conference on Artificial Intelligence and Advanced Manufacturing* (pp. 1-5). DOI:10.1145/3358331.3358336

Ke, Y. (2021, September). Application of Artificial Intelligence in Large-scale International Wushu (Taolu) Events. In *2021 2nd International Conference on Big Data & Artificial Intelligence & Software Engineering (ICBASE)* (pp. 575-578). IEEE.

Koch, M. (2018). Artificial intelligence is becoming natural. *Cell*, 173(3), 533. DOI:10.1016/j.cell.2018.04.007 PMID:29677502

Krasteva, N. (2021). The Artificial Intelligence And Contemporary Marketing. *Yearbook of the Faculty of Economics and Business Administration. Sofia University*, 20(1), 109–129.

Larsson, S., & Heintz, F. (2020). Transparency in artificial intelligence. *Internet Policy Review*, 9(2). Advance online publication. DOI:10.14763/2020.2.1469

Lu, Y., & Gao, X. (2022). The Impact of Artificial Intelligence Technology on Market Public Administration in a Complex Market Environment. *Wireless Communications and Mobile Computing*, 2022, 2022. DOI:10.1155/2022/5646234

Luchini, C., Pea, A., & Scarpa, A. (2022). Artificial intelligence in oncology: Current applications and future perspectives. *British Journal of Cancer*, 126(1), 4–9. DOI:10.1038/s41416-021-01633-1 PMID:34837074

Matibag, T. (2020). Artificial intelligence for local governance. *The Urban Lawyer*, 50, 415–435.

Meskó, B., Hetényi, G., & Győrffy, Z. (2018). Will artificial intelligence solve the human resource crisis in healthcare? *BMC Health Services Research*, 18(1), 1–4. DOI:10.1186/s12913-018-3359-4 PMID:30001717

Moglia, A., Georgiou, K., Morelli, L., Toutouzas, K., Satava, R. M., & Cuschieri, A. (2022). Breaking down the silos of artificial intelligence in surgery: Glossary of terms. *Surgical Endoscopy*, 36(11), 1–12. DOI:10.1007/s00464-022-09371-y PMID:35729406

Morkhat, P. M., Ponkin, I. V., Markhgeym, M. V., Botnev, V. K., & Turganbayev, A. O. (2019). Artificial intelligence versus public administration: limitations of application.

Nurjaman, A. (2022). Artificial intelligence as an instrument to improve the quality of public service. In *Social and Political Issues on Sustainable Development in the Post Covid-19 Crisis* (pp. 121–130). Routledge. DOI:10.1201/9781003263586-15

Padurean, A. I., Daniel, M. N., & Claudiu, C. (2021). On smart city, artificial intelligence and the evolution of public administration digitalization in the COVID-19 pandemic. *Timisoara Journal of Economics and Business, 14*(1).

Pang, S., Pang, C., Zeng, D., & Chen, X. (2022, June). Exploration on the Talent Training Path of "Post, Course, Competition, Certificate" for Artificial Intelligence Technology Application Major Based on Huawei 1+ X Certificate. In *2022 8th International Conference on Humanities and Social Science Research (ICHSSR 2022)* (pp. 2212-2215). Atlantis Press.

Pesapane, F., Volonté, C., Codari, M., & Sardanelli, F. (2018). Artificial intelligence as a medical device in radiology: Ethical and regulatory issues in Europe and the United States. *Insights Into Imaging*, 9(5), 745–753. DOI:10.1007/s13244-018-0645-y PMID:30112675

Ponkin, I. V., & Redkina, A. I. (2018). Artificial intelligence from the point of view of law. *RUDN Journal of Law*, 22(1), 91–109. DOI:10.22363/2313-2337-2018-22-1-91-109

Rahayu, S. K. (2021). Utilization of artificial intelligence in tax audit in Indonesia. *Management Accounting Research*, 20(3), 135–157.

Reis, J., Santo, P. E., & Melão, N. (2019, April). Artificial intelligence in government services: A systematic literature review. In *World conference on information systems and technologies* (pp. 241-252). Springer. DOI:10.1007/978-3-030-16181-1_23

Reis, J., Santo, P. E., & Melão, N. (2019, June). Impacts of artificial intelligence on public administration: A systematic literature review. In *2019 14th Iberian conference on information systems and technologies (CISTI)* (pp. 1-7). IEEE. DOI:10.23919/CISTI.2019.8760893

Robertson, J., Fossaceca, J. M., & Bennett, K. W. (2021). A cloud-based computing framework for artificial intelligence innovation in support of multidomain operations. *IEEE Transactions on Engineering Management.*

Senthiil, P. V., Sirusshti, V. A., & Sathish, T. (2019). Artificial Intelligence Based Green Manufacturability quantification of a unit production process. *International Journal of Mechanical and Production Engineering Research and Development*, 9(2), 841–852. DOI:10.24247/ijmperdapr201981

Surden, H. (2019). Artificial intelligence and law: An overview. *Georgia State University Law Review*, 35, 19–22.

Talapina, E. V. (2021). Artificial Intelligence and Legal Expertise in Public Administration. *Vestnik Saint Petersburg UL*, 865.

Tariq, M. U. (2024a). The transformation of healthcare through AI-driven diagnostics. In Sharma, A., Chanderwal, N., Tyagi, S., Upadhyay, P., & Tyagi, A. (Eds.), *Enhancing medical imaging with emerging technologies* (pp. 250–264). IGI Global. DOI:10.4018/979-8-3693-5261-8.ch015

Tariq, M. U. (2024b). The role of emerging technologies in shaping the global digital government landscape. In Guo, Y. (Ed.), *Emerging developments and technologies in digital government* (pp. 160–180). IGI Global. DOI:10.4018/979-8-3693-2363-2.ch009

Tariq, M. U. (2024c). Equity and inclusion in learning ecosystems. In Al Husseiny, F., & Munna, A. (Eds.), *Preparing students for the future educational paradigm* (pp. 155–176). IGI Global. DOI:10.4018/979-8-3693-1536-1.ch007

Tariq, M. U. (2024d). Empowering educators in the learning ecosystem. In Al Husseiny, F., & Munna, A. (Eds.), *Preparing students for the future educational paradigm* (pp. 232–255). IGI Global. DOI:10.4018/979-8-3693-1536-1.ch010

Tariq, M. U. (2024e). Revolutionizing health data management with blockchain technology: Enhancing security and efficiency in a digital era. In Garcia, M., & de Almeida, R. (Eds.), *Emerging technologies for health literacy and medical practice* (pp. 153–175). IGI Global. DOI:10.4018/979-8-3693-1214-8.ch008

Tariq, M. U. (2024f). Emerging trends and innovations in blockchain-digital twin integration for green investments: A case study perspective. In Jafar, S., Rodriguez, R., Kannan, H., Akhtar, S., & Plugmann, P. (Eds.), *Harnessing blockchain-digital twin fusion for sustainable investments* (pp. 148–175). IGI Global. DOI:10.4018/979-8-3693-1878-2.ch007

Valle-Cruz, D., Criado, J. I., Sandoval-Almazán, R., & Ruvalcaba-Gomez, E. A. (2020). Assessing the public policy-cycle framework in the age of artificial intelligence: From agenda-setting to policy evaluation. *Government Information Quarterly*, 37(4), 101509. DOI:10.1016/j.giq.2020.101509

van de Sande, D., van Genderen, M. E., Huiskens, J., Gommers, D., & van Bommel, J. (2021). Moving from bytes to bedside: A systematic review on the use of artificial intelligence in the intensive care unit. *Intensive Care Medicine*, 47(7), 750–760. DOI:10.1007/s00134-021-06446-7 PMID:34089064

Wirtz, B. W., Weyerer, J. C., & Geyer, C. (2019). Artificial intelligence and the public sector—Applications and challenges. *International Journal of Public Administration*, 42(7), 596–615. DOI:10.1080/01900692.2018.1498103

Wirtz, B. W., Weyerer, J. C., & Sturm, B. J. (2020). The dark sides of artificial intelligence: An integrated AI governance framework for public administration. *International Journal of Public Administration*, 43(9), 818–829. DOI:10.1080/01900692.2020.1749851

Yan, B., Hao, F., & Meng, X. (2021). When artificial intelligence meets building energy efficiency, a review focusing on zero energy building. *Artificial Intelligence Review*, 54(3), 2193–2220. DOI:10.1007/s10462-020-09902-w

Young, M. M., Bullock, J. B., & Lecy, J. D. (2019). Artificial discretion as a tool of governance: A framework for understanding the impact of artificial intelligence on public administration. *Perspectives on Public Management and Governance*, 2(4), 301–313. DOI:10.1093/ppmgov/gvz014

Zbuchea, A., Vidu, C., & Pinzaru, F. (2019). Is Artificial Intelligence Changing Knowledge Management. *Strategica*, 445-452.

Zhang, D. (2021, December). Research on the Innovative Development of Chinese Mixed Martial Arts (MMA) Events Based on Artificial Intelligence. In *2021 3rd International Conference on Machine Learning, Big Data and Business Intelligence (MLBDBI)* (pp. 785-788). IEEE.

ADDITIONAL READING

Tsietso, D., Yahya, A., Samikannu, R., Tariq, M. U., Babar, M., Qureshi, B., & Koubaa, A. (2023). Multi-input deep learning approach for breast cancer screening using thermal infrared imaging and clinical data. *IEEE Access : Practical Innovations, Open Solutions*, 11, 52101–52116. DOI:10.1109/ACCESS.2023.3280422

Xu, S., Alturki, R., Rehman, A. U., & Tariq, M. U. (2021). BP neural network combination prediction for big data enterprise energy management system. *Mobile Networks and Applications*, 26(1), 184–190. DOI:10.1007/s11036-020-01698-x

Zhang, H., Babar, M., Tariq, M. U., Jan, M. A., Menon, V. G., & Li, X. (2020). Safe-City: Toward safe and secured data management design for IoT-enabled smart city planning. *IEEE Access : Practical Innovations, Open Solutions*, 8, 145256–145267. DOI:10.1109/ACCESS.2020.3014622

Zhu, X., Zhu, Y., Li, L., Pan, S., Tariq, M. U., & Jan, M. A. (2021). Ioht-enabled gliomas disease management using fog computing computing for sustainable societies. *Sustainable Cities and Society*, 74, 103215. DOI:10.1016/j.scs.2021.103215

Ziyambe, B., Yahya, A., Mushiri, T., Tariq, M. U., Abbas, Q., Babar, M., Albathan, M., Asim, M., Hussain, A., & Jabbar, S. (2023). A deep learning framework for the prediction and diagnosis of ovarian cancer in pre- and post-menopausal women. *Diagnostics (Basel)*, 13(10), 1703. DOI:10.3390/diagnostics13101703 PMID:37238188

KEY TERMS AND DEFINITIONS

Accountability in AI: The principle that assigns responsibility to specific actors for decisions made by AI systems.

AI Transparency: The practice of making the processes, algorithms, and decision-making criteria of artificial intelligence systems accessible and understandable to users and stakeholders.

AI-Driven Decision-Making: The process in which artificial intelligence systems analyze data and make decisions or recommendations.

Information Overload: A situation where the sheer volume of information provided, particularly in the context of AI transparency, overwhelms individuals.

Justified Approach: A method of AI transparency that focuses on providing clear and accessible explanations for decisions made by AI systems.

Perceived Validity: The degree to which the public views decisions made by AI systems as legitimate and trustworthy.

Public Trust in AI: The confidence that the general public has in the fairness, reliability, and ethical use of AI systems.

Chapter 15
AI for Human Resources and Talent Acquisition

ABSTRACT

Artificial intelligence (AI) has become disruptive in many industries, revolutionising how businesses function and make choices. Human resources (HR) and talent acquisition are areas where AI is gaining traction. This chapter will focus on the use of AI in HR and talent acquisition, outlining its history and analysing the urgent demand for AI-driven HR solutions. Understanding AI's function in HR begins by acknowledging its capacity to improve and complement human resource management procedures. Systems can perform a variety of previously labour- and time-intensive operations for HR experts owing to machine learning algorithms, natural language processing (NLP), and data analytics. These duties include finding candidates, assessing resumes, onboarding new employees, analysing performance, and forecasting attrition.

INTRODUCTION

HR teams can make judgments using data, because AI systems are excellent for data analysis. For example, AI can analyze enormous volumes of historical data to identify recruitment patterns and trends, thereby helping HR managers improve their hiring tactics. Additionally, AI-powered chatbots and virtual assistants improve employee experience by responding quickly to questions, facilitating quicker issue resolution, and freeing HR employees for more strategic duties. Additionally, AI-enabled HR solutions may point out any biases in recruitment procedures and suggest remedies to foster diversity and inclusion in the workplace. Owing to AI, which essentially functions as a force multiplier in the field, HR personnel can concentrate on higher-value duties such as talent development, employee engagement, and culture-building. Several revolutionary developments have characterized talent acquisition using AI.

DOI: 10.4018/979-8-3693-4074-5.ch015

The AI's function in HR was first restricted to automating routine operations such as monitoring personnel data and payments. Nevertheless, as AI technologies have developed, they have begun to play a more strategic role in hiring.

The development of application tracking systems (ATS), which use AI to scan and rank resumes based on keywords and credentials, has been a significant turning point in history. As the initial screening process was considerably reduced, recruiters were able to concentrate on the most promising individuals. Additional developments in AI, notably machine learning and NLP, have enabled the creation of increasingly complex tools. These tools evaluate a candidate's suitability based on their credentials, interpersonal skills, and cultural fit with the company. AI systems frequently conduct video interviews to evaluate the candidates' body language and verbal communication abilities (Tariq, 2024).

Predictive analytics is now part of the use of AI in hiring. AI systems have started predicting which applicants would perform best in particular positions, assisting with succession and staff planning. Additionally, AI-powered chatbots began interacting with applicants during the application process, providing quick feedback, and enhancing the overall applicant experience. Currently, AI is sufficiently advanced to fully automate the employment process, including finding individuals, performing preliminary interviews, and even making job offers. In addition to improving efficiency, this development sparked a debate over the moral implications of AI in hiring, particularly concerning fairness and prejudice.

HR and the Need for AI

The complexity and evolution of human resource management in contemporary corporate environments create a demand for AI in HR. The following factors influenced this surge.

- **Scale and amount:** HR personnel frequently feel overworked because of the overwhelming number of job applications they receive. AI systems can swiftly process massive amounts of data and assist HR departments in managing enormous amounts of hiring.
- **Efficiency and Accuracy:** AI-driven automation shortens the time required to complete repetitive HR processes such as data input and candidate screening. This also reduces human error. This effectiveness increases the accuracy of the HR operations and saves time.
- **Data-driven decision-making:** Organisations are beginning to appreciate the importance of data-driven decision-making in the age of big data. AI empowers HR practitioners to use data insights for personnel management, strategic planning, and employee engagement.

- **Improved Candidate Experience**: AI-driven chatbots and virtual assistants provide candidates with a smooth and responsive experience by responding to their questions and giving them feedback immediately. An organization's employer brand may be strengthened through good candidate experience.
- **Enhanced Candidate Experience:** AI can assist organisations in reducing prejudice in their employment procedures. AI can detect and reduce prejudice by examining previous data and by encouraging inclusion and diversity in the workplace.
- **Competitive Advantage:** Companies that adopt AI in HR are at a competitive advantage as they fight for top personnel. With the help of AI, recruitment choices can be made quickly and accurately, guaranteeing that businesses can hire top individuals before their rivals.
- **Cost savings:** AI-powered HR solutions may significantly reduce the overhead expenses. Routine duties may be automated to help organisations deploy resources more effectively and concentrate on key HR projects (Ramesh and Das, 2022).

AI can rapidly change how HR and talent acquisition are conducted. It combines effectiveness, data-driven insights, and better candidate experience in a formidable package. However, technology also creates difficulties that must be addressed properly in terms of ethics, justice, and privacy. In this chapter, we thoroughly understand how AI has revolutionized the HR domain by examining many aspects of AI in terms of HR and talent acquisition. We also understand why the adoption of AI is becoming increasingly crucial for businesses worldwide (Tariq, 2024.

BACKGROUND

Organisations must perform the crucial task of talent acquisition to recruit and maintain talent. Artificial intelligence (AI) has become a potent ally in this area in recent years, providing several advantages that boost the effectiveness of hiring procedures and enhance the applicant experience. AI also adds the capacity for data-driven decision making and can help advance diversity and inclusion in recruiting procedures. In this section, we explore the essential advantages of AI for hiring.

Enhanced Recruitment Effectiveness

AI-driven recruitment tools and technology have revolutionized the effectiveness of talent acquisition procedures. The automation of time-consuming and repetitive processes is one of the greatest benefits. According to predetermined criteria, AI algorithms can quickly scan and analyze many resumes and select the most suitable applicants. Using this screening procedure, HR workers can save numerous hours by manually examining resumes. Additionally, AI-driven chatbots and virtual assistants changed candidate interactions and communication. AI-powered applications can arrange interviews, respond to applicant questions, and provide real-time status updates. This immediate communication improves the candidates' hiring experience and accelerates the process of filling open positions.

AI can also help with job-posting optimization. By examining historical data and job descriptions, AI algorithms can suggest adjustments and modifications to job advertisements to make them more interesting candidates. The recruitment process is streamlined, and the chance of attracting the best candidates increases owing to the fine-tuning of job advertisements (Tariq, 2024).

Superior Candidate Experience

A key element in luring and maintaining top personnel is the candidate's experience. AI is crucial for improving this experience at various points during the recruitment process. Candidates may receive prompt solutions to questions through AI-powered chatbots and virtual assistants, avoiding an inconvenient wait for email or phone conversations. AI may also customize an applicant's experience. AI may offer specialised job suggestions and insights into career prospects within a company by examining candidate data and behavior. This personalization shows a firm's dedication to its applicants and encourages them to apply for more than one position in the same company.

AI-powered systems that perform video interviews have become standard practices in the applicant experience. These platforms examine candidates' body language, facial expressions, and speech patterns to obtain important information about their soft skills and cultural fit with their companies. With the help of this data-driven methodology, recruitment decisions that consider a candidate's overall appropriateness for the position and corporate culture are made. AI also supports smooth and open communication throughout the employment process. Candidates can sign up for automated notifications regarding the status of their applications, interview dates, and performance reviews. Even if a candidate is eventually not chosen for the position, this openness promotes trust and a favorable view of the company (Tariq, 2024).

Making Decisions Based on Data

Owing to AI's data-driven approach to talent acquisition, businesses can now make strategic and informed hiring decisions. AI analyzes enormous volumes of past recruiting data as one of its primary methods. AI can help HR professionals improve their hiring tactics by spotting patterns and trends. For instance, using criteria such as credentials, talent, and cultural fit, AI may analyze the success rates of prior recruits. Based on this data, AI algorithms may provide prediction models that assist in identifying people who have the best chances of succeeding in particular jobs. By streamlining the applicant screening process using predictive analytics, businesses are more likely to choose employees who match their positions and businesses well. AI helps workforce planning by foreseeing future talent requirements. AI systems may assist organisations in proactively identifying skill gaps and formulating strategies for personnel acquisition and development by examining turnover rates, predicted growth, and other variables. An organization's talent pool is ensured to align with its long-term objectives using this strategic strategy. AI also aids data-driven programs for diversity and inclusion. AI can identify possible biases in the recruitment process and advise changes to encourage a more diverse and inclusive workforce by analysing hiring data. Making decisions about hiring new employees based on data is effective and consistent with the organization's values and larger aims.

Inclusion and Diversity in Hiring

Success in a contemporary organization depends on its diversity and inclusion. AI plays a crucial role in advancing diversity and inclusion in talent acquisition by minimizing prejudice and boosting objectivity during recruitment. Artificial intelligence (AI)-driven technologies are used to assess applicants using objective standards to minimize the impact of unconscious biases that might affect human decision making. These prejudices may be influenced by factors such as the candidate's alma mater, age, sex, or ethnicity. AI ensures that candidates are judged to be fairly independent of personal traits by concentrating only on qualifications and skills.

AI can also actively identify and correct biases in the hiring procedures. Machine-learning algorithms can examine historical hiring data to identify bias in applicant selection. AI can recommend altering job descriptions or broadening the candidate pool if particular groups are persistently underrepresented in the workforce. When using AI, applicant profiles may remain anonymous during the preliminary screening stage. This allows recruiters to concentrate entirely on credentials and abilities because it prevents them from seeing personal information such as names and addresses. Anonymization aids in reducing prejudices that may result from stereotypes connected to places or names.

AI has several advantages for recruiting people, such as higher effectiveness, improved applicant experience, data-driven decision making, and more diversity and inclusion. Organisations may streamline their hiring procedures, entice top talent and create a more diverse and inclusive workforce utilizing AI-powered tools and technology. These benefits help improve recruitment results and support the overarching objective of making the workplace more productive and equitable.

Issues and Moral Considerations

Organisations face various difficulties and ethical issues as they progressively use artificial intelligence (AI) in their hiring procedures, which must be properly handled. The fairness, privacy, and adherence to ethical standards depend on these factors.

Fairness and Bias in AI Recruiting

The possibility of prejudice in AI algorithms is one of the biggest problems in hiring an AI. Bias can develop from biased training data, which reflects previous employment choices and could maintain inequities already present. For instance, an AI system educated on this data may unintentionally bias against other groups if historical employment choices favor specific demographics. Such prejudices must be mitigated to maintain fairness during the hiring process. To overcome this issue, organisations must engage in diversity and fairness audits of their AI recruitment systems. To identify and correct bias, these audits use meticulous testing and monitoring. Additionally, AI systems must be clear and understandable in order to comprehend and evaluate decision-making processes for fairness.

Privacy Issues

The frequent collection and analysis of enormous volumes of applicant data using AI recruitment technologies has raised significant privacy concerns. During the employment process, candidates give prospective employers access to sensitive information. Therefore, it is crucial to safeguard against exploitation and security breach. Organisations must establish strong data protection measures and comply with strict data privacy laws such as the GDPR or CCPA. This involves safeguarding candidate data, obtaining informed consent for data processing, and ensuring that AI systems do not base their judgments on protected traits or private information.

BEST PRACTISES AND ETHICAL RULES

Organisations must set and abide by ethical standards and best practices in AI recruitment to successfully manage these issues. Transparency, responsibility, and ensuring that AI boosts human decision-making rather than completely replacing it are ethical issues. Collaboration with stakeholders such as HR specialists, data scientists, and legal professionals should be encouraged while developing ethical rules. These principles ensure that AI recruitment procedures support an organization's ideals, uphold applicants' rights, and foster equity and diversity. Additionally, organisations should regularly examine and update their ethical standards to keep up with the development of AI technology and the shifting legal environment (Kaur and Gandolfi, 2023).

AI Implementation in Hiring

To fully realize the promise of AI tools and technologies to improve recruitment results, it is necessary to take several strategic measures when implementing AI in recruitment.

Choosing the Correct AI Technologies and Tools

A crucial first step is to choose the appropriate AI tools and technology for recruitment. A detailed requirements study must be conducted to determine the precise issues that AI is intended to solve for an organization. Predictive analytics for talent forecasts, chatbots for applicant interaction, and resume screening are only a few recruitment-related uses of AI tools.

When choosing AI solutions, organisations should consider aspects such as scalability, simplicity of interaction with current HR systems, and compliance with data-protection laws. Collaboration between HR professionals and IT specialists is essential to evaluate and choose AI technologies that support an organization's recruitment objectives (Perello-Marin, 2022).

Including AI in Current HR Processes

AI in recruiting must be seamlessly integrated with current HR procedures to be successful. Establishing clear protocols and lines of communication between AI systems and HR departments are necessary for this integration. For instance, HR teams must work with data scientists to set the selection criteria for an AI algorithm when using it to screen resumes. The understanding, verification, and alignment of

AI suggestions with the organization's recruitment goals are made possible through clear communication channels.

The integration should be flexible and iterative. Organisations should continually improve their procedures to maximize AI's potential and adapt to shifting recruiting demands, as AI systems gather more data and insights.

HR Teams Training for AI Adoption

HR personnel must upgrade their skills and expertise to adopt AI-driven hiring procedures. For AI to be used successfully, HR personnel must be trained. Understanding how AI algorithms function, deciphering insights produced by AI, and utilizing AI technologies to improve decision making should all be included in training. HR professionals should be proficient in using AI for data analysis, applicant engagement, and performance forecasting. Workshops, online classes, and collaborations with AI training providers are all ways organisations can provide this training. HR teams can confidently leverage the capabilities of AI in recruiting while preserving human touch during the hiring process by investing in ongoing learning and upskilling.

Incorporating AI into recruitment is a complex process that includes resolving ethical issues, choosing appropriate technologies, integrating AI into current processes, and educating human resource (HR) professionals. Companies that successfully negotiate these difficulties and uphold moral standards to improve efficiency, objectivity, and diversity in their hiring processes may unlock AI's full potential.

Candidate Sourcing and Screening Powered by AI

AI has been a game changer in talent acquisition, especially during the early applicant sourcing and screening phases. To illuminate the procedures for automated resume screening, AI-powered job matching, applicant sourcing, and outreach, this chapter discusses the revolutionary influence of AI in these fields. These developments have revolutionized how businesses find and assess potential individuals, making hiring more effective and accurate than ever before.

Screening of Automated Resumes

For HR professionals, reviewing resumes is often labor- and time-intensive. Identifying applicants who satisfy certain employment requirements requires manually going through many resumes. However, AI has intervened to transform this procedure and provide automated resume screening as a remedy. Machine learning algorithms are used in automated resume screening to swiftly and effectively analyze resumes. These algorithms are taught using historical data, such as records of successful and unsuccessful hiring decisions, to recognize trends and keywords connected to desirable credentials and competencies. Speed is one of the main benefits of automated resumption screening. Human recruiters require days or even weeks to process thousands of resumes, whereas AI can process it in a matter of minutes. Because of quick processing, organisations may find and engage in top talent before their rivals, drastically reducing the time to employ. Objectivity is an important advantage of this approach. The evaluation of resumes by AI algorithms is based on predetermined standards and is unaffected by individual preferences or subjective opinions. This impartiality encourages fairness in the hiring procedure and helps businesses avoid discrimination and bias-related issues. Automated resume screening further improves precision. When AI algorithms are used to discover pertinent credentials and abilities, it is less likely to ignore competent applicants or wrongly advance unqualified applicants. This accuracy leads to better hiring quality.

Businesses must work with their HR departments and data scientists to enable automated resumption of screening. HR specialists are essential for developing standards and certifications that AI algorithms should prioritize. To fine-tune the system and ensure that it is in line with the unique needs and culture of the organization, it is crucial to obtain ongoing feedback and revisions.

Intelligent Job Matching

A key component of efficient talent acquisition is job matching, which involves matching individuals with openings that suit their interests and capabilities. AI-powered job matching uses cutting-edge algorithms to improve the precision and effectiveness of a procedure. AI-driven job matching begins with compiling comprehensive data on candidates, such as their qualifications, experience, and preferences. Simultaneously, it compiles thorough information on open positions, including job descriptions, prerequisites, and organizational culture. When AI uses this information to provide highly customized job suggestions for candidates, its power is used. These suggestions not only rely on keyword matching but also consider the specifics of each employment opportunity and a candidate's profile. Therefore, candidates received employment recommendations that closely matched their qualifications and career goals. This tailored approach improves applicant experience, because identifying appropriate employment requires less time and effort.

In addition, individuals are more likely to submit applications for jobs that interest them. AI-driven job matching optimizes recruitment from an organizational standpoint. A well-curated list of qualified prospects is sent to recruiters to minimize the need for time-consuming manual screening and to improve the effectiveness of the recruiting process. AI may also help increase employee retention rates by matching applicants based on qualifications and cultural fit. It is important to note that the AI-powered job matching is not universal. Aligning algorithms with each organization's unique industry, workplace culture, and job positions requires customization. HR specialists, data scientists, and AI experts collaborate throughout this customization to guarantee that the system appropriately represents the organization's employment needs.

Recruiting and Outreach for Candidates

The sourcing and outreach of qualified candidates are essential components of talent acquisition. Finding appropriate people and communicating with them effectively may be difficult, but AI answers these problems. Finding suitable applicants requires searching for job boards, social media, and professional networks among other sources. AI improves this process by automating the search for applicants who meet specific job needs and credentials. The time and effort required for human sourcing have decreased because AI algorithms can continually search Internet platforms for possible talent, even in passive candidate pools. After identifying individuals, AI may speed up the outreach procedure. Virtual assistants and AI-powered chatbots may interact with candidates, respond to their initial questions, and organize interviews. Candidates obtain a smooth and responsive experience thanks to these automated exchanges, which boost the company's opinions. AI also makes it possible to customize outreach for specific prospects. By examining the candidate data and behavior, AI algorithms can offer personalized messages and content that speak to each applicant's particular history and taste. This personalization increases the possibility of luring top talent and cultivating successful interactions with the applicants.

AI-driven sourcing and outreach are more than just actively looking for job candidates. Additionally, they can help locate passive applicants who may not be actively looking for new jobs but could be persuaded by a proper offer. Thanks to this proactive strategy, the talent pool is widened, and organisations can access untapped talent markets. Organisations should spend money on reliable AI platforms and technologies to successfully adopt AI-driven talent sourcing and outreach. HR teams should work closely with AI specialists to create sourcing and outreach tactics, and these technologies should be included in the organization's current hiring procedures. To respond to shifting candidate preferences and market realities, it is crucial to regularly assess and modify these techniques.

Thus, AI-driven candidate sourcing and screening are crucial for talent acquisition. The efficiency, objectivity, and personalization benefits of these technologies are substantial. Organisations may speed up their hiring procedures, identify top talent more accurately, and provide applicants with improved experience by utilizing AI, eventually resulting in better hiring results and more organizational success.

ANALYTICS FOR THE FUTURE OF HR

Predictive analytics in HR have completely changed how human resource professionals approach decision making. Future trends, behaviors, and results relating to workers and the workforce may now be predicted by HR teams by utilizing modern statistical approaches and machine learning algorithms. This chapter examines the various uses of predictive analytics in HR, such as employee attrition forecasting, performance forecasting, talent development, and workforce planning.

How to Foresee Employee Attrition

Employee attrition, also known as turnover, is a major business challenge. High attrition rates can be expensive due to lost production, training, and recruitment. Organisations can predict and reduce attrition using predictive analytics. The variables considered by the predictive models in HR include historical attrition statistics, employee demographics, job satisfaction surveys, and performance evaluations. Machine learning algorithms analyze these data to identify patterns and correlations that can be used to forecast which employees are most likely to leave the company. The ability of predictive analytics to recognize early warning indicators is one of the primary benefits of attrition prediction. HR departments may take proactive steps to keep people prized by spotting patterns and the variables that contribute to turnover. For instance, organisations may concentrate on career development and advancement opportunities if the study shows that employees who obtain promotions are less likely to quit.

Predictive analytics can also be used to design retention efforts for each employee. HR can better deliver tailored interventions, such as individualized training, mentorship, or work role changes, by recognizing the elements contributing to the attrition risk for each employee. Attrition prediction should be approached ethically and openly. Employee trust must be maintained while respecting employees' privacy rights and using data responsibly to make appropriate decisions. Additionally, organisations should exercise caution when depending only on predictive algorithms because human judgement and qualitative insights continue to be important in the decision-making process for HR.

Performance Analysis and Talent Identification

Predictive analytics are also essential for predicting employee performance and identifying areas where talent development possibilities exist. HR personnel may learn which employees are likely to perform well, which would benefit from additional help by examining past performance data, training records, and other pertinent indicators. In this situation, predictive algorithms can assist HR professionals in identifying high-potential individuals and developing specialised development plans. These initiatives include stretch assignments, mentorship opportunities, and individualized training that pushes staff members to realize their maximum potential.

Predictive analytics may facilitate succession planning by identifying workers suitable for leadership positions. HR can develop future leaders and guarantee a seamless transition when senior roles become available by identifying the abilities and qualities associated with effective organizational leadership. The HR department can become nimbler and more proactive through predictive analytics, performance prediction, and talent development. Organisations may adopt a proactive approach to nurturing and growing their staff rather than responding to performance concerns or talent gaps as they occur, which will eventually enhance employee engagement and retention.

AI-Based Workforce Planning

Workforce planning is the strategic process of aligning an organization's staff with its long-term goals and objectives. Predictive analytics powered by AI are useful tools for workforce planning because they enable businesses to anticipate workforce requirements, maximize talent allocation, and prepare for new problems. Artificial intelligence (AI) systems can estimate future talent demands by analysing past workforce data, economic trends, and external influences. Organisations may make wise choices regarding hiring, training, and people development programmes by considering factors such as retirement rates, turnover, and skill gaps (Kshetri, 2022).

For instance, HR can start focused training programs or look into external employment alternatives if the data indicates a scarcity of workers with certain technical capabilities over the next few years. However, if the study predicts a talent shortage in some sectors, HR may modify recruitment methods and better deploy resources. AI-driven labor planning goes beyond predicting talent surpluses or shortages. Additionally, it considers wider developments in the workforce, such as how automation and artificial intelligence affect job positions. HR may proactively reskill and upskill people to prepare them for changing organizational roles by assessing job tasks that are most susceptible to automation (Tariq, 2024).

AI workforce planning also promotes organizational flexibility. HR may swiftly modify workforce strategies to address these difficulties or seize new opportunities when unanticipated events arise, such as economic downturns or unforeseen growth opportunities.

Predictive analytics in HR offers a revolutionary method for workforce planning and talent management. It gives HR professionals more control and foresight over predicting and handling problems such as employee attrition, performance enhancement, and talent development. Organizations can optimize their personnel, strengthen their competitive edge, and develop a more flexible and adaptive HR function using the potential of AI-driven predictive analytics (Tariq, 2024).

AI-ENHANCED ONBOARDING OF NEW WORKERS

A crucial stage in an employee's journey inside an organization is employee onboard. This establishes a tone for their experiences and greatly influences their retention and long-term engagement. In recent years, AI has improved onboarding, making it more individualized, effective, and interesting. This chapter examines the idea of personalized onboard experiences and the use of artificial intelligence (AI) to streamline administrative processes and enhance onboard employee engagement.

Individualized Onboarding Processes

Each new employee's requirements, tastes, and history are considered when creating a personalized onboarding experience. To make an introduction to the organization that is more relevant and interesting, they go beyond the "one size fits all" philosophy and consider individual characteristics. AI. AI is essential for personalizing onboarding processes through automation and data. This is how it goes:

- **Tailored Training Paths:** Using an employee's abilities, experience, and job as inputs, AI algorithms may suggest a specific training path. For instance, a salesperson can be instructed on sales skills and product expertise, whereas a software developer may receive training modules tailored to their programming language.
- **Content Recommendations:** AI may suggest pertinent resources such as articles, videos, and training materials based on employees' work functions and learning preferences. By doing this, it is made sure that recruits have access to the knowledge they need to flourish in their positions.

- **Mentor Matching** It can help mentorship programmes by pairing new hires with seasoned mentors according to their goals, hobbies, and personalities. This encourages a collaborative work environment.
- **Feedback and development Tracking:** AI-driven feedback systems provide new employees with instantaneous insight into their development. Managers can monitor their progress and steps when necessary to ensure seamless integration into a company.
- **Personalized Communications:** AI can automatically send each recruit-specific welcome message, check-ins, and reminders. Employees were informed and involved throughout the onboarding process.

The benefits of a personalized onboarding process extend beyond employees' first impressions of the company to their continued engagement and retention. Employees are likely to stay devoted to their jobs and the company when they believe that their needs and goals are respected.

Automating Office Procedures

Although administrative duties can be time-consuming and take away from the overall employee experience, they are an important element of the onboarding process. AI saves the day by automating these procedures, expediting them, and lessening administrative strain on HR and new recruits. During onboarding, AI may automate a variety of routine administrative duties, including

- **Document management:** AI-driven document management solutions may help in gathering, validating, and archiving personnel papers, including contracts, tax forms, and proofs of identity.
- **Filling-out forms:** Chatbots and virtual assistants may aid staff members in filling out various forms and documentation, ensuring accuracy and compliance.
- **IT Setup:** AI can automate the allocation of hardware, software tools, email accounts, and other IT resources.
- **Benefit Enrolment:** AI-driven solutions may help employees choose and sign up for benefit plans, making the process easier to use and comprehend.
- **Planning and Coordination:** AI may plan meetings, training sessions, and orientation sessions to ensure that recruits obtain correct knowledge at the right time.

In addition to saving time, automating these administrative activities lowers the risk of mistakes and delays during onboarding. Employees can transition to new positions faster and HR teams may focus on more strategic onboarding initiatives.

Increasing Worker Engagement

A strong and fruitful employee-employer relationship is built based on employee engagement throughout the onboarding phase. Engaged employees are likely to stick to the company and help it succeed. AI-driven solutions provide several strategies for boosting employee engagement during onboarding.

- **Interactive training:** AI-driven e-learning systems design interactive and captivating training materials to accommodate various learning preferences. Using gamified information, tests, and simulations makes learning interesting and effective.
- **Real-time Feedback:** AI chatbots and virtual assistants gather real-time input from new recruits while onboarding, who can then swiftly handle any issues or queries. This two-way communication increases engagement and makes it easier for new hires to feel appreciated and heard.
- **Social Integration:** AI may identify relationships between coworkers based on shared jobs or interests by analysing social interactions between staff members inside the organization's collaboration platforms. This fosters a sense of community and belonging to the right away.
- **Personalized Resources:** As already mentioned, AI may customize the materials given to recruits. Employees are more likely to engage in information when they believe their learning path suits their requirements.
- **Recognition and Rewards:** During onboarding, AI-driven recognition and reward programs may recognize and celebrate new hires' accomplishments and milestones, reinforcing their positive experiences. These programs will be covered in more detail later in this paper.

Organisations may create a favorable atmosphere for employees' employment by concentrating on engagement during onboarding. Engaged employees are more likely to become passionate brand ambassadors and to contribute to an organization's success.

AI IN EMPLOYEE RETENTION AND ENGAGEMENT

Organizations must prioritize employee engagement and retention to have a stable and engaged workforce. With its sophisticated skills in employee feedback, sentiment analysis, recognition and incentive schemes, and AI-enabled career planning, AI has emerged as a crucial tool.

Analysis of Feelings and Employee Comments

Sentiment analysis is a technology that aids organisations in learning about sentiments, emotions, and viewpoints of their workforce. They are frequently powered by artificial intelligence-driven (AI)-driven NLP algorithms. Understanding how workers see their work environment and experiences entails analysing various employee feedback sources, including surveys, reviews, social media, and internal communications. In addition to classifying inputs into good, negative, or neutral feelings, AI-driven sentiment analysis technologies may identify certain themes or areas of concern. HR departments may benefit from these insights on employee morale, job satisfaction, and developmental opportunities.

The ability of sentiment analysis to identify early warning indications of employee disengagement or unhappiness is one of its main benefits. Organisations may reduce the risk of attrition by recognizing these signs in real time, taking proactive steps to fix problems, and enhancing employee experience. Additionally, sentiment analysis may assist HR departments in tracking the results of various activities including modifications to corporate policies, employee engagement initiatives, and leadership changes. Organisations may measure the efficiency of their strategies and make necessary adjustments by tracking sentiment patterns over time. To analyze sentiments effectively, a combination of AI technology and human interpretation is required. Human specialists are necessary for contextual interpretation and decision making based on the insights gained, even if AI processes vast amounts of data efficiently.

Programmes for Rewards and Recognition

Programs for recognizing and rewarding employees are essential for increasing employee engagement, motivation, and morale. These programs are becoming more efficient because AI-driven solutions make them more timely, personalized, and data-driven. A real-time AI analysis of employee milestones and accomplishments is possible. For instance, it may acknowledge finished projects, sales that surpassed expectations, or client feedback. When AI recognizes such achievements, it may immediately acknowledge them and offer prizes such as digital badges, custom thank-you notes, or cash bonuses.

AI-enabled recognition and reward programs emphasize personalization as a crucial component. These programs may consider each employee's preferences, values, and performance history when creating incentives. For instance, a worker who prioritizes professional growth could have the chance to take on more training, but someone who prioritizes work-life balance would get more vacation time. AI can be used to monitor the effects of rewards and recognition on staff engagement and retention. Organisations may learn which tactics best inspire workers and promote a healthy workplace culture by analysing data on the frequency and types of recognition provided. The scalability of AI-powered recognition and reward programs makes it possible to show appreciation to staff members at all levels, and among geographically scattered teams. This inclusiveness leads to a culture of appreciation and acknowledgement, which raises levels of engagement and retention.

AI-POWERED CAREER PLANNING

Employee engagement and retention were significantly influenced by career development and advancement. AI-enabled career pathing uses data and algorithms to assist staff members in locating prospective career paths within the company and outlining the actions necessary to achieve their objectives.

AI can analyze a worker's abilities, competencies, and performance history to pinpoint the strengths and areas needing development. This can suggest options for pertinent training and development.

- **Role matching:** AI may recommend prospective career changes that match an employee's talent and objectives by examining previous data on successful career routes inside the company. This could suggest jobs in which workers with comparable backgrounds have performed well.
- **Personalized Development Plans:** AI can provide development plans for each individual with suggested training programs, credentials, mentorship opportunities, and work rotations. These programs are based on each individual's career objectives and transferable skills.
- **Real-time Updates:** AI may deliver real-time updates on employees' growth, emphasizing accomplishments and milestones as they move along their career pathways. This feedback fosters a sense of success and drive.

Job matching

AI may match employees with open positions that fit their talent and career objectives when preparing to investigate new employment options within the company. This facilitates internal mobility and motivates the staff to remain with the company to follow their preferred career routes. Employees are given more control over their professional development thanks to AI-enabled career pathing, which also helps them to match their goals with those of the company. This demonstrates that the company recognizes and supports workers' long-term professional growth, which increases their job satisfaction, engagement, and retention. AI has completely transformed the onboarding process for new employees, making it more individualized, effective, and enjoyable. Automation of administrative processes, increased staff engagement, and improved employee retention are benefits of AI-driven solutions. AI also plays a critical role in employee engagement and retention by allowing sentiment analysis, recognition, incentive programs, and AI-enabled career paths. These AI-driven methodologies foster a supportive and effective work environment that ultimately benefits organisations and people.

AI IN HR: USEFUL APPLICATIONS

AI has substantially impacted human resource (HR) practices across several sectors, thereby improving workflow. The application of chatbots for employee support is a real-world example of AI in HR. Today, many businesses use AI-powered chatbots to answer common HR questions, such as leave requests, benefit details, and policy clarifications. This frees HR professionals up for more difficult jobs and provides them with 24/7 access to rapid and available help. An AI-driven resume screening was performed. Large organisations sometimes obtain hundreds of resumes for open positions, making the manual screening process time-consuming. AI algorithms can scan resumes, which can then determine the necessary abilities, credentials, and rank applicants appropriately. By streamlining the initial screening procedure, HR professionals can concentrate on the most qualified applicants, while conserving time and money.

Additionally, predictive analytics in HR uses AI to forecast probable employee churn. AI can identify which employees are most likely to depart from the organization by analyzing multiple data sources, including past turnover rates, employee satisfaction surveys, and performance measures. HR may then take proactive actions to lower turnover and keep valued employees on the board, such as focused retention initiatives.

Increasing ROI in Talent Acquisition With AI

Organisations engaging in AI for hiring have seen significant returns on their investment (ROI). Utilizing platforms with AI-powered talent sourcing is an example of success. These platforms use machine learning algorithms to find applicants for positions from various sources, including job sites, social media, and internal databases. Companies may reduce recruiting expenses and fill positions more rapidly by automating the applicant sourcing process and enhancing ROI.

AI-driven interview scheduling is another example of such a problem. Organizing interviews with several parties may require time and effort. AI algorithms can look up acceptable timeslots in the calendars of participants, analyze the data, and automatically issue invitations. This improves the applicant's experience and guarantees that interviews are completed swiftly, thereby saving overall time and reducing the time it takes to employ someone. AI has been shown to be helpful for promoting diversity and inclusion. AI technologies assist businesses in creating more inclusive job advertisements by analysing job descriptions and spotting biased wording. This broadens the recruitment pool and improves the organization's reputation, boosting employee engagement and creativity and increasing ROI.

FUTURE RESEARCH DIRECTIONS

The field of artificial intelligence (AI) transparency, particularly in the context of justifications for decision making, presents numerous avenues for future research. As AI continues to permeate various aspects of society, understanding how to best implement and communicate transparency is crucial for fostering public trust, ensuring ethical outcomes, and enabling accountable governance. The following are the key directions for future research that can significantly contribute to advancing this area. HR AI adoption has accelerated owing to the workplace's continuing transition fuelled by remote employment. Organisations use AI and cutting-edge technology to address the difficulties and possibilities of remote work as they adjust to a more scattered workforce. In this study, we examined emerging trends and technologies that affect the interaction between HR AI and remote employment.

Virtual Onboarding and Training

The conventional onboarding procedure has been impacted by the growth of remote employment. Businesses rely on AI powered virtual onboarding solutions to greet new hires, acquaint them with the workplace, and offer training. These solutions generate immersive and engaging onboarding experiences using chatbots, virtual reality (VR), and gamification to make distant recruits feel included immediately.

AI-Driven Employee Engagement

Keeping employees engaged in remote work environments is extremely difficult. AI is used to track employee satisfaction, degree of engagement, and work-life balance. Machine learning algorithms analyze data from communication platforms, employee surveys, and collaboration tools to give HR insights into employee well-being. To increase participation, predictive analytics may also identify prospective problems and provide suggestions for interventions.

Feedback and Performance Management

Yearly performance review, formerly the norm, is a continual process. Remote teams benefit from AI-driven performance management systems that offer real-time feedback and performance insights. HR may provide individualized coaching and assistance using natural language processing (NLP) algorithms to analyze written and spoken communication and evaluate teamwork, leadership, and productivity.

AI Powered Collaboration Tools

Collaboration platforms use AI to make it easier for teams to collaborate remotely. Intelligent document classification, automatic work assignment, and preemptive meeting scheduling are the AI-driven features. With these solutions, remote workers will have less administrative work, freeing them to work on innovative and strategic projects.

Remote Employee Monitoring

Although working remotely provides flexibility, it also poses issues regarding employee privacy and productivity. Artificial intelligence (AI) tools, such as time-tracking software, screen capture analysis, and keystroke monitoring, can shed light on the actions of remote workers. To preserve trust and privacy, surveillance techniques must be used ethically and transparently.

AI-Enhanced Communication

AI-powered chatbots are becoming increasingly important in distance communication. They can coordinate virtual team building exercises, plan meetings, and respond to commonly requested enquiries. Language obstacles can also be overcome through AI-driven language translation and transcription services that encourage inclusion in remote international teams.

Predictive Workforce Planning

Using machine learning and predictive analytics, HR can accurately estimate the human resource requirements. To determine the best workforce composition, trends in remote work, employee preferences, and skill shortages should be examined. This ensures that businesses can tackle upcoming problems.

AI in Recruitment and On-Demand Talent

Organisations now have access to a larger talent pool owing to the remote workforce. AI-powered platforms may find and connect gig or freelance employees with certain project requirements. These tools allow HR to swiftly construct remote project teams by evaluating individuals' abilities, availability, and work history.

Recapture of How AI Affects Hiring and Human Resources

Human Resources (HR) and recruiting practices have undergone substantial changes owing to artificial intelligence (AI). In the past several years, AI has been used in various HR activities to improve decision making, increase efficiency, and simplify processes. This summary will explore how AI has affected hiring and HR and the lessons that may be drawn from these advancements.

Automating monotonous jobs is one of AI's most obvious consequences of AI in HR. In HR organisations, AI-powered chatbots and virtual assistants are already widespread; they assist with onboarding, handling routine questions, and scheduling interviews. In addition to lessening the workload of HR specialists, automation has provided staff members access to HR assistance around the clock. AI is also crucial in hiring new employees. AI algorithms accelerate the once lengthy and labor-intensive process of reviewing resumes. These algorithms review resumes, extract pertinent data, and forecast candidate fits for a given position. This results in faster hiring cycles and a more effective use of HR resources.

Furthermore, staff turnover was predicted using predictive analytics driven by AI. AI models can identify trends and variables that cause turnover by examining historical data and employee indicators. As a result, HR departments may more effectively handle problems, place retention measures, and lessen the expenses and inconvenience brought about by high turnover rates. The rise of platforms that link jobs with AI-driven algorithms is another important trend. These platforms use machine learning to match job seekers with relevant employment that matches their talent, credentials, and preferences. This helps job searchers and companies to uncover people who are a better fit for their organisations by offering more individualized job suggestions.

CONCLUSION

AI is anticipated to be crucial in assisting organisations in preparing for the changing nature of the workplace, as we look to the future of HR. Here, we examine the lessons that may be implemented to prepare for the future from AI's past and present implementations in HR. The success of AI in automating commonplace HR functions emphasizes the significance of accepting automation for efficiency improvements. To free up time for strategic and value-added tasks, HR departments must continue looking for procedures that can be automated. HR professionals must adapt by concentrating on duties that require human judgement and empathy as their work progresses. AI has succeeded in predictive analytics and data analyses. In the future, HR should use AI to make data-driven choices regarding hiring, retaining, and training of new employees. Utilizing the AI's capacity to analyze massive amounts of data, HR can see patterns, foresee employee requirements, and proactively handle problems. Past experiences with AI have taught us the value of ethical concerns.

Prioritizing ethical AI practices is important for HR departments, particularly with regard to recruitment and employee welfare. This entails eliminating prejudice in AI systems, ensuring that decision-making is transparent, and protecting the privacy and data of employees. Ethical AI minimizes legal and reputational concerns while aligning with company values. Application of AI to HR should improve employee satisfaction. AI-driven technologies should be created with the employees in mind, offering them individualized assistance, possibilities for professional advancement, and a sense of community. HR should seek novel ways to leverage AI to enhance employee performance, engagement, and wellbeing. Because of work automation, increased productivity, and improved decision making, AI has fundamentally changed how HR and hiring practices are carried out. The lessons learned from AI's past and present implementations of AI provide important insights into the future of HR. HR can position itself as a prosper in an ever-changing work environment by embracing automation, placing ethics first, and strategically using AI. Successful AI integration in HR ultimately involves the use of technology to enhance human capacity and establish a more effective, inclusive, and employee-centric work environment.

REFERENCES

Albert, E. T. (2019). AI in talent acquisition: A review of AI-applications used in recruitment and selection. *Strategic HR Review*, 18(5), 215–221. DOI:10.1108/SHR-04-2019-0024

Arora, M., Prakash, A., Mittal, A., & Singh, S. (2021, December). HR analytics and artificial intelligence-transforming human resource management. In *2021 International Conference on Decision Aid Sciences and Application (DASA)* (pp. 288-293). IEEE. DOI:10.1109/DASA53625.2021.9682325

Chowdhury, S., Dey, P., Joel-Edgar, S., Bhattacharya, S., Rodriguez-Espindola, O., Abadie, A., & Truong, L. (2023). Unlocking the value of artificial intelligence in human resource management through AI capability framework. *Human Resource Management Review*, 33(1), 100899. DOI:10.1016/j.hrmr.2022.100899

Gethe, R. K. (2022). Extrapolation of talent acquisition in AI aided professional environment. *International Journal of Business Innovation and Research*, 27(4), 462–479. DOI:10.1504/IJBIR.2022.122510

Johnson, R. D., Stone, D. L., & Lukaszewski, K. M. (2020). The benefits of eHRM and AI for talent acquisition. *Journal of Tourism Futures*, 7(1), 40–52. DOI:10.1108/JTF-02-2020-0013

Kaur, M., & Gandolfi, F. (2023). Artificial Intelligence in Human Resource Management-Challenges and Future Research Recommendations. *Revista de Management Comparat International*, 24(3), 382–393.

Kinkel, S., Baumgartner, M., & Cherubini, E. (2022). Prerequisites for the adoption of AI technologies in manufacturing–Evidence from a worldwide sample of manufacturing companies. *Technovation*, 110, 102375. DOI:10.1016/j.technovation.2021.102375

Kshetri, N. (2021). Evolving uses of artificial intelligence in human resource management in emerging economies in the global South: Some preliminary evidence. *Management Research Review*, 44(7), 970–990. DOI:10.1108/MRR-03-2020-0168

Paramita, D. (2020). Digitalization in talent acquisition: A case study of AI in recruitment.

Perello-Marin, M. R. (2022). Adoption Factors of Artificial intelligence in Human Resources Management. *Future of Business Administration*, 1(1), 1–12. DOI:10.33422/fba.v1i1.140

Pillai, R., & Sivathanu, B. (2020). Adoption of artificial intelligence (AI) for talent acquisition in IT/ITeS organizations. *Benchmarking*, 27(9), 2599–2629. DOI:10.1108/BIJ-04-2020-0186

Ramesh, S., & Das, S. (2022, January). Adoption of AI in Talent Acquisition: A Conceptual Framework. In *International Conference on Digital Technologies and Applications* (pp. 12-20). Cham: Springer International Publishing. DOI:10.1007/978-3-031-01942-5_2

Rao, R., & Hill, B. (2019). How is the Role of AI in Talent Acquisition Evolving?

Tariq, M. U. (2024a). Emotional intelligence in understanding and influencing consumer behavior. In Musiolik, T., Rodriguez, R., & Kannan, H. (Eds.), *AI impacts in digital consumer behavior* (pp. 56–81). IGI Global. DOI:10.4018/979-8-3693-1918-5.ch003

Tariq, M. U. (2024b). Fintech startups and cryptocurrency in business: Revolutionizing entrepreneurship. In Kankaew, K., Nakpathom, P., Chnitphattana, A., Pitchayadejanant, K., & Kunnapapdeelert, S. (Eds.), *Applying business intelligence and innovation to entrepreneurship* (pp. 106–124). IGI Global. DOI:10.4018/979-8-3693-1846-1.ch006

Tariq, M. U. (2024c). Multidisciplinary service learning in higher education: Concepts, implementation, and impact. In S. Watson (Ed.), *Applications of service learning in higher education* (pp. 1-19). IGI Global. DOI:10.4018/979-8-3693-2133-1.ch001

Tariq, M. U. (2024d). Enhancing cybersecurity protocols in modern healthcare systems: Strategies and best practices. In Garcia, M., & de Almeida, R. (Eds.), *Transformative approaches to patient literacy and healthcare innovation* (pp. 223–241). IGI Global. DOI:10.4018/979-8-3693-3661-8.ch011

Tariq, M. U. (2024e). Advanced wearable medical devices and their role in transformative remote health monitoring. In Garcia, M., & de Almeida, R. (Eds.), *Transformative approaches to patient literacy and healthcare innovation* (pp. 308–326). IGI Global. DOI:10.4018/979-8-3693-3661-8.ch015

Tariq, M. U. (2024f). Leveraging artificial intelligence for a sustainable and climate-neutral economy in Asia. In Ordóñez de Pablos, P., Almunawar, M., & Anshari, M. (Eds.), *Strengthening sustainable digitalization of Asian economy and society* (pp. 1–21). IGI Global. DOI:10.4018/979-8-3693-1942-0.ch001

Tariq, M. U. (2024g). Metaverse in business and commerce. In Kumar, J., Arora, M., & Erkol Bayram, G. (Eds.), *Exploring the use of metaverse in business and education* (pp. 47–72). IGI Global. DOI:10.4018/979-8-3693-5868-9.ch004

ADDITIONAL READING

Abonamah, A. A., Tariq, M. U., & Shilbayeh, S. (2021). On the commoditization of artificial intelligence. *Frontiers in Psychology*, 12, 696346. Advance online publication. DOI:10.3389/fpsyg.2021.696346 PMID:34659012

Ashfaq, M., Khan, I., Alzahrani, A., Tariq, M. U., Khan, H., & Ghani, A. (2024). Accurate wheat yield prediction using machine learning and climate-NDVI data fusion. *IEEE Access : Practical Innovations, Open Solutions*, 12, 40947–40961. DOI:10.1109/ACCESS.2024.3376735

Babar, M., Ahmad, A., Tariq, M. U., & Kaleem, S. (2023). Real-time fake news detection using big data analytics and deep neural network. *IEEE Transactions on Computational Social Systems*. Advance online publication. DOI:10.1109/TCSS.2023.3309704

Babar, M., Alshehri, M. D., Tariq, M. U., Ullah, F., Khan, A., Uddin, M. I., & Almasoud, A. S. (2021). IoT-enabled big data analytics architecture for multimedia data communications. *Wireless Communications and Mobile Computing*, 2021(1), 1–9. DOI:10.1155/2021/5283309

Babar, M., Jan, M. A., He, X., Tariq, M. U., Mastorakis, S., & Alturki, R. (2023). An optimized IoT-enabled big data analytics architecture for edge–cloud computing. *IEEE Internet of Things Journal*, 10(5), 3995–4005. DOI:10.1109/JIOT.2022.3157552 PMID:38046398

Babar, M., Kaleem, S., Sohail, A., Asim, M., & Tariq, M. U. (2023). An improved big data analytics architecture for intruder classification using machine learning. *Security and Communication Networks*, 2023, 2023. DOI:10.1155/2023/1216192

Babar, M., Khattak, A. S., Jan, M. A., & Tariq, M. U. (2021). Energy aware smart city management system using data analytics and internet of things. *Sustainable Energy Technologies and Assessments*, 44, 100992. Advance online publication. DOI:10.1016/j.seta.2021.100992

Babar, M., Tariq, M. U., & Jan, M. A. (2020). Secure and resilient demand side management engine using machine learning for IoT-enabled smart grid. *Sustainable Cities and Society*, 62, 102370. Advance online publication. DOI:10.1016/j.scs.2020.102370

KEY TERMS AND DEFINITIONS

Accountability in AI: The principle that assigns responsibility to specific actors for decisions made by AI systems.

AI Transparency: The practice of making the processes, algorithms, and decision-making criteria of artificial intelligence systems accessible and understandable to users and stakeholders.

AI-Driven Decision-Making: The process in which artificial intelligence systems analyze data and make decisions or recommendations.

Information Overload: A situation where the sheer volume of information provided, particularly in the context of AI transparency, overwhelms individuals.

Justified Approach: A method of AI transparency that focuses on providing clear and accessible explanations for decisions made by AI systems.

Perceived Validity: The degree to which the public views decisions made by AI systems as legitimate and trustworthy.

Public Trust in AI: The confidence that the general public has in the fairness, reliability, and ethical use of AI systems.

Conclusion

As we reach the culmination of *AI-Driven Learning and Engagement in Higher Education*, it is evident that the integration of Artificial Intelligence (AI) in the academic landscape is not merely a fleeting trend but a profound shift poised to redefine the future of education. This book has navigated through various dimensions of AI applications, offering a comprehensive understanding of how these technologies can enhance learning experiences, streamline administrative processes, and foster innovative R&D.

Exploration began with foundational concepts, equipping readers with essential AI terminology and theoretical frameworks. This groundwork is crucial to understanding the sophisticated applications and implications of AI in higher education. From personalised learning systems and intelligent tutoring to advanced learning analytics, AI's capability to tailor education to individual needs marks a significant leap towards inclusive and effective teaching methodologies.

One of the most striking advantages of AI is its potential to personalise education. Adaptive learning technologies and intelligent tutoring systems can cater to diverse learning styles and paces, ensuring that each student receives customised support. This personalised approach not only enhances student engagement, but also improves academic outcomes, making education more accessible and equitable.

Beyond personalised learning, AI's role of AI in administrative efficiency cannot be overlooked. Automating routine tasks, such as admission processing, grading, and scheduling, allows educators and administrators to focus on more strategic initiatives. AI-driven chatbots and virtual assistants provide continuous support to students, enhance their overall experience, and ensure that they receive timely and accurate information. These advancements have led to the creation of more efficient and responsive educational institutions.

The application of AI in learning analytics has also been proven transformative. By analysing vast amounts of data, AI can uncover patterns and insights that inform decision-making processes at all levels of education. Predictive analytics helps to identify at-risk students, enabling early intervention and support. This data-driven approach optimises resource allocation and improves the student retention and success rates.

Ethical considerations are a recurrent theme in this book. The responsible implementation of AI in education requires careful attention to issues, such as data privacy, algorithmic bias, and transparency. The discussions presented emphasise the importance of developing ethical frameworks and policies to ensure that AI technologies are used fairly and equitably. Addressing these challenges is crucial for building trust and fostering an environment in which AI can be leveraged to its full potential, without compromising ethical standards.

The case studies and real-world examples provided in the chapters illustrate the practical applications and benefits of AI in various educational contexts. These success stories, along with the lessons learned from the challenges and setbacks, offer valuable insights for educators, administrators, and policymakers seeking to implement AI in their institutions.

The future of AI in higher education is promising. As AI technologies continue to evolve, their potential for transforming education will expand. This book offers a forward-looking perspective on emerging trends and future directions, encouraging readers to remain informed and engage with the latest developments in AI and education.

In conclusion, *AI-Driven Learning and Engagement in Higher Education* provides a thorough and insightful examination of the opportunities and challenges presented by AI integration in education. By carefully addressing theoretical concepts, practical applications, and ethical considerations, this book provides the knowledge and tools necessary to navigate the complexities of AI in higher education. Responsible and informed adoption of AI technologies can significantly enhance educational outcomes, streamline administrative functions, and prepare students for future demands. As we embrace this technological evolution, the ultimate goal remains clear–to create a more effective, inclusive, and engaging educational landscape for all learners.

Compilation of References

Abad-Segura, E., González-Zamar, M. D., Infante-Moro, J. C., & Ruipérez García, G. (2020). Sustainable management of digital transformation in higher education: Global research trends. *Sustainability (Basel)*, 12(5), 2107. DOI: 10.3390/su12052107

Abbas, N., Whitfield, J., Atwell, E., Bowman, H., Pickard, T., & Walker, A. (2022). Online chat and chatbots to enhance mature student engagement in higher education. *International Journal of Lifelong Education*, 41(3), 1–19. DOI: 10.1080/02601370.2022.2066213

Abdelghany, S. Z. A. (2022). Students' attitudes Towards Using Duolingo As A Self-Learning Artificial Intelligence-Based App In Distance Learning During The Pandemic In The United Arab Emirates.

Abdelghany, S. Z. A. (2022). Students'attitudes Towards Using Duolingo As A Self-Learning Artificial Intelligence-Based App In Distance Learning During The Pandemic In The United Arab Emirates.

Ahmad, S. F., Rahmat, M. K., Mubarik, M. S., Alam, M. M., & Hyder, S. I. (2021). Artificial intelligence and its role in education. *Sustainability (Basel)*, 13(22), 12902. DOI: 10.3390/su132212902

Ahmad, T. (2020). Scenario based approach to re-imagining future of higher education which prepares students for the future of work. *Higher Education. Skills and Work-Based Learning*, 10(1), 217–238. DOI: 10.1108/HESWBL-12-2018-0136

Ahmed, S. I., Radhakrishnan, S., Nair, B. B., & Thiruvengadathan, R. (2021). Efficient hyperparameter-tuned machine learning approach for estimation of supercapacitor performance attributes. *Journal of Physics Communications*, 5(11), 115011. DOI: 10.1088/2399-6528/ac3574

Alam, A., & Mohanty, A. (2022, December). Facial Analytics or Virtual Avatars: Competencies and Design Considerations for Student-Teacher Interaction in AI-Powered Online Education for Effective Classroom Engagement. In *International Conference on Communication, Networks and Computing* (pp. 252-265). Cham: Springer Nature Switzerland.

Alam, A., & Mohanty, A. (2022, November). Business models, business strategies, and innovations in EdTech companies: integration of learning analytics and artificial intelligence in higher education. In *2022 IEEE 6th Conference on Information and Communication Technology (CICT)* (pp. 1-6). IEEE. DOI: 10.1109/CICT56698.2022.9997887

Alam, A. (2022). Employing Adaptive Learning and Intelligent Tutoring Robots for Virtual Classrooms and Smart Campuses: Reforming Education in the Age of Artificial Intelligence. In *Advanced Computing and Intelligent Technologies* (pp. 395–406). Springer. DOI: 10.1007/978-981-19-2980-9_32

Albert, E. T. (2019). AI in talent acquisition: A review of AI-applications used in recruitment and selection. *Strategic HR Review*, 18(5), 215–221. DOI: 10.1108/SHR-04-2019-0024

Aleven, V., Blankestijn, J., Lawrence, L., Nagashima, T., & Taatgen, N. (2022, September). A dashboard to support teachers during students' self-paced AI-supported problem-solving practice. In *European Conference on Technology Enhanced Learning* (pp. 16-30). Cham: Springer International Publishing. DOI: 10.1007/978-3-031-16290-9_2

Alexander, B., Ashford-Rowe, K., Barajas-Murph, N., Dobbin, G., Knott, J., McCormack, M., . . . Weber, N. (2019). *Horizon report 2019 higher education edition* (pp. 3-41). EDU19.

Algabri, H. K., Kharade, K., & Kamat, R. (2021). Promise, threats, and personalization in higher education with artificial intelligence. *Webology, 18*(6).

Al-Kumaim, N. H., Alhazmi, A. K., Mohammed, F., Gazem, N. A., Shabbir, M. S., & Fazea, Y. (2021). Exploring the impact of the COVID-19 pandemic on university students' learning life: An integrated conceptual motivational model for sustainable and healthy online learning. *Sustainability (Basel)*, 13(5), 2546. DOI: 10.3390/su13052546

Allil, K. (2024). Integrating AI-driven marketing analytics techniques into the classroom: pedagogical strategies for enhancing student engagement and future business success. *Journal of Marketing Analytics*, 1-27.

Almusaed, A., Almssad, A., Yitmen, I., & Homod, R. Z. (2023). Enhancing student engagement: Harnessing "AIED"'s power in hybrid education—A review analysis. *Education Sciences*, 13(7), 632. DOI: 10.3390/educsci13070632

Al-Sartawi, M. (2021). *Big Data-Driven Digital Economy: Artificial and Computational Intelligence*. Springer. DOI: 10.1007/978-3-030-73057-4

Alsobeh, A., & Woodward, B. (2023, October). AI as a Partner in Learning: A Novel Student-in-the-Loop Framework for Enhanced Student Engagement and Outcomes in Higher Education. In *Proceedings of the 24th Annual Conference on Information Technology Education* (pp. 171-172). DOI: 10.1145/3585059.3611405

Alt, D., Kapshuk, Y., & Dekel, H. (2023). Promoting perceived creativity and innovative behavior: Benefits of future problem-solving programs for higher education students. *Thinking Skills and Creativity*, 47, 101201. DOI: 10.1016/j.tsc.2022.101201

Alyahyan, E., & Düştegör, D. (2020). Predicting academic success in higher education: Literature review and best practices. *International Journal of Educational Technology in Higher Education*, 17(1), 1–21. DOI: 10.1186/s41239-020-0177-7

Angin, R. (2021, March). Artificial Intelligence and Human Resources: A Challenge in Implementing Artificial Intelligence in Village Government. *IOP Conference Series. Earth and Environmental Science*, 717(1), 012044. DOI: 10.1088/1755-1315/717/1/012044

Anwar, M. (2021). Designing an expert system for determining student learning styles using forward chaining in engineering education. *Jurnal Konseling dan Pendidikan, 9*(1), 93-101.

Arabnia, H. R., Ferens, K., de la Fuente, D., Kozerenko, E. B., Varela, J. A. O., & Tinetti, F. G. (2021). *Advances in Artificial Intelligence and Applied Cognitive Computing*. Springer International Publishing. DOI: 10.1007/978-3-030-70296-0

Arora, M., Prakash, A., Mittal, A., & Singh, S. (2021, December). HR analytics and artificial intelligence-transforming human resource management. In *2021 International Conference on Decision Aid Sciences and Application (DASA)* (pp. 288-293). IEEE. DOI: 10.1109/DASA53625.2021.9682325

Bai, X., Wang, X., Liu, X., Liu, Q., Song, J., Sebe, N., & Kim, B. (2021). Explainable deep learning for efficient and robust pattern recognition: A survey of recent developments. *Pattern Recognition*, 120, 108102. DOI: 10.1016/j.patcog.2021.108102

Balakrishnan, S., Janet, J., & Aswin, G. (2020). Artificial Intelligence and Robotics: A Research Overview. *CSI Communications Magazine,* (44), 24-26.

Bangalore Seetharam, S. (2020). Developing a digital AI roadmap for retail.

Bao, Y., Ma, L., & Chen, W. (2018, November). SSL: Synchronous Self-paced Learning for Internet-of-Things Devices. In *Proceedings of the 1st ACM International Workshop on Smart Cities and Fog Computing* (pp. 13-18). DOI: 10.1145/3277893.3277898

Barclay, R. C., Cudney, E. A., Shetty, S., & Antony, J. (2022). Determining critical success factors for lean implementation. *Total Quality Management & Business Excellence*, 33(7-8), 818–832. DOI: 10.1080/14783363.2021.1894919

Bashir, A., Bashir, S., Rana, K., Lambert, P., & Vernallis, A. (2021, August). Post-COVID-19 adaptations; the shifts towards online learning, hybrid course delivery and the implications for biosciences courses in the higher education setting. *Frontiers in Education*, 6, 711619. DOI: 10.3389/feduc.2021.711619

Bees, J. (2022). How Artificial Intelligence Use Is Expanding in Health Care. *NEJM Catalyst Innovations in Care Delivery*, 3(4), CAT.22.0089. DOI: 10.1056/CAT.22.0089

Beghetto, R. A. (2019). Large-scale assessments, personalized learning, and creativity: Paradoxes and possibilities. *ECNU Review of Education*, 2(3), 311–327. DOI: 10.1177/2096531119878963

Bejani, M. M., & Ghatee, M. (2021). A systematic review on overfitting control in shallow and deep neural networks. *Artificial Intelligence Review*, 54(8), 6391–6438. DOI: 10.1007/s10462-021-09975-1

Benjamens, S., Dhunnoo, P., & Meskó, B. (2020). The state of artificial intelligence-based FDA-approved medical devices and algorithms: An online database. *NPJ Digital Medicine*, 3(1), 1–8. DOI: 10.1038/s41746-020-00324-0 PMID: 32984550

Berg, M. (2022). Hate It? Automate It! Thinking and doing robotic process automation and beyond. In *Everyday Automation* (pp. 157-170). Routledge.

Bhardwaj, P., Gupta, P. K., Panwar, H., Siddiqui, M. K., Morales-Menendez, R., & Bhaik, A. (2021). Application of Deep Learning on Student Engagement in e-learning environments. *Computers & Electrical Engineering*, 93, 107277. DOI: 10.1016/j.compeleceng.2021.107277 PMID: 36567679

Bhutoria, A. (2022). Personalized education and artificial intelligence in the United States, China, and India: A systematic review using a human-in-the-loop model. *Computers and Education: Artificial Intelligence*, 3, 100068. DOI: 10.1016/j.caeai.2022.100068

Bignami, F. (2022). Artificial Intelligence Accountability of Public Administration. *The American Journal of Comparative Law*, 70(Supplement_1), i312–i346. DOI: 10.1093/ajcl/avac012

Biryukov, A., & Antonova, N. (2018, October). Expert systems of real time as key tendency of artificial intelligence in tax administration. In *The 2018 International Conference on Digital Science* (pp. 111-118). Springer.

Biswas, S., Carson, B., Chung, V., Singh, S., & Thomas, R. (2020). *AI-bank of the future: Can banks meet the AI challenge*. McKinsey & Company.

Blankenberger, B., & Williams, A. M. (2020). COVID and the impact on higher education: The essential role of integrity and accountability. *Administrative Theory & Praxis*, 42(3), 404–423. DOI: 10.1080/10841806.2020.1771907

Boburbek, B., Sanjarbek, R., Elmurod, U., & Satimov, A. (2022). The importance of artificial intelligence in modern technology. *Journal of Advanced Scientific Research, 2*(1).

Bonk, C. J., Zhu, M., Kim, M., Xu, S., Sabir, N., & Sari, A. R. (2018). Pushing toward a more personalized MOOC: Exploring instructor selected activities, resources, and technologies for MOOC design and implementation. *International Review of Research in Open and Distance Learning*, 19(4). Advance online publication. DOI: 10.19173/irrodl.v19i4.3439

Bratasanu, V. (2018). Leadership Decision-Making Processes in the Context of Data Driven Tools. *Quality - Access to Success*, 19.

Bryson, J., & Winfield, A. (2017). Standardizing ethical design for artificial intelligence and autonomous systems. *Computer*, 50(5), 116–119. DOI: 10.1109/MC.2017.154

Buck, B., & Morrow, J. (2018). AI, performance management and engagement: Keeping your best their best. *Strategic HR Review*, 17(5), 261–262. DOI: 10.1108/SHR-10-2018-145

Bullock, J. B. (2019). Artificial intelligence, discretion, and bureaucracy. *American Review of Public Administration*, 49(7), 751–761. DOI: 10.1177/0275074019856123

Busuioc, M. (2021). Accountable artificial intelligence: Holding algorithms to account. *Public Administration Review*, 81(5), 825–836. DOI: 10.1111/puar.13293 PMID: 34690372

Cai, Y., Ma, J., & Chen, Q. (2020). Higher education in innovation ecosystems. *Sustainability (Basel)*, 12(11), 4376. DOI: 10.3390/su12114376

Cao, L. (2022). A new age of AI: Features and futures. *IEEE Intelligent Systems*, 37(1), 25–37. DOI: 10.1109/MIS.2022.3150944

Carter, R. A.Jr, Rice, M., Yang, S., & Jackson, H. A. (2020). Self-regulated learning in online learning environments: Strategies for remote learning. *Information and Learning Science*, 121(5/6), 321–329. DOI: 10.1108/ILS-04-2020-0114

Carvalho, L., Martinez-Maldonado, R., Tsai, Y. S., Markauskaite, L., & De Laat, M. (2022). How can we design for learning in an AI world? *Computers and Education: Artificial Intelligence*, 3, 100053. DOI: 10.1016/j.caeai.2022.100053

Castro, R. (2019). Blended learning in higher education: Trends and capabilities. *Education and Information Technologies*, 24(4), 2523–2546. DOI: 10.1007/s10639-019-09886-3

Cermann, H., Kern, S., Bertram, F., Sander, M., Heimann, T., & Proctor, R. (2021). Towards an agile and adaptive Enterprise. *INFORMATIK 2021*.

Cesco, S., Zara, V., De Toni, A. F., Lugli, P., Betta, G., Evans, A. C., & Orzes, G. (2021). Higher education in the first year of COVID-19: Thoughts and perspectives for the future. *International Journal of Higher Education*, 10(3), 285–294. DOI: 10.5430/ijhe.v10n3p285

Chahal, H., Fedasiuk, R., & Flynn, C. (2020). Messier than Oil: Assessing Data Advantage in Military AI. *Center for Security and Emerging Technology*.

Chaipidech, P., Srisawasdi, N., Kajornmanee, T., & Chaipah, K. (2022). A personalized learning system-supported professional training model for teachers' TPACK development. *Computers and Education: Artificial Intelligence*, 3, 100064. DOI: 10.1016/j.caeai.2022.100064

Chan, C. K. Y., & Hu, W. (2023). Students' voices on generative AI: Perceptions, benefits, and challenges in higher education. *International Journal of Educational Technology in Higher Education*, 20(1), 43. DOI: 10.1186/s41239-023-00411-8

Chang, C. L., & Fang, M. (2020, June). E-Learning and online instructions of higher education during the 2019 novel coronavirus diseases (COVID-19) epidemic. *Journal of Physics: Conference Series*, 1574(1), 012166. DOI: 10.1088/1742-6596/1574/1/012166

Chan, K. S., & Zary, N. (2019). Applications and challenges of implementing artificial intelligence in medical education: Integrative review. *JMIR Medical Education*, 5(1), e13930. DOI: 10.2196/13930 PMID: 31199295

Chan, L., Hogaboam, L., & Cao, R. (2022). Artificial Intelligence in Education. In *Applied Artificial Intelligence in Business* (pp. 265–278). Springer. DOI: 10.1007/978-3-031-05740-3_17

Chassignol, M., Khoroshavin, A., Klimova, A., & Bilyatdinova, A. (2018). Artificial Intelligence trends in education: A narrative overview. *Procedia Computer Science*, 136, 16–24. DOI: 10.1016/j.procs.2018.08.233

Chatterjee, S., & Bhattacharjee, K. K. (2020). Adoption of artificial intelligence in higher education: A quantitative analysis using structural equation modelling. *Education and Information Technologies*, 25(5), 3443–3463. DOI: 10.1007/s10639-020-10159-7

Cheng, Y., & Jiang, H. (2021). Customer–brand relationship in the era of artificial intelligence: Understanding the role of chatbot marketing efforts. *Journal of Product and Brand Management.*

Chen, J. S., Tran-Thien-Y, L., & Florence, D. (2021). Usability and responsiveness of artificial intelligence chatbot on online customer experience in e-retailing. *International Journal of Retail & Distribution Management*, 49(11), 1512–1531. DOI: 10.1108/IJRDM-08-2020-0312

Chen, L., Chen, P., & Lin, Z. (2020). Artificial intelligence in education: A review. *IEEE Access : Practical Innovations, Open Solutions*, 8, 75264–75278. DOI: 10.1109/ACCESS.2020.2988510

Chen, L., & Ifenthaler, D. (2021). The Adoption of Intelligent and Virtual Teams in Online Entrepreneurship Education Courses. In *International Conference. The Future of Education* (pp. 8-11).

Chen, M., Zhang, H., Ning, Q., Li, M., Ji, H., McKeown, K., & Roth, D. (2021). Event-centric natural language understanding. *Proceedings of the 59th Annual Meeting of the Association for Computational Linguistics.*

Chen, Q., Leaman, R., Allot, A., Luo, L., Wei, C. H., Yan, S., & Lu, Z. (2021). Artificial intelligence in action: Addressing the COVID-19 pandemic with natural language processing. *Annual Review of Biomedical Data Science*, 4(1), 313–339. DOI: 10.1146/annurev-biodatasci-021821-061045 PMID: 34465169

Chen, X., Xie, H., Zou, D., & Hwang, G. J. (2020). Application and theory gaps during the rise of artificial intelligence in education. *Computers and Education: Artificial Intelligence*, 1, 100002. DOI: 10.1016/j.caeai.2020.100002

Chen, Y., Jensen, S., Albert, L. J., Gupta, S., & Lee, T. (2022). Artificial Intelligence (AI) Student Assistants in the Classroom: Designing Chatbots to Support Student Success. *Information Systems Frontiers*, 1–22.

Chen, Y., Jensen, S., Albert, L. J., Gupta, S., & Lee, T. (2023). Artificial intelligence (AI) student assistants in the classroom: Designing chatbots to support student success. *Information Systems Frontiers*, 25(1), 161–182. DOI: 10.1007/s10796-022-10291-4

Choi, D., & Lee, S. (2021). Comparison of machine learning algorithms for predicting lane changing intent. *International Journal of Automotive Technology*, 22(2), 507–518. DOI: 10.1007/s12239-021-0047-x

Chou, Y. L., Moreira, C., Bruza, P., Ouyang, C., & Jorge, J. (2022). Counterfactuals and causability in explainable artificial intelligence: Theory, algorithms, and applications. *Information Fusion*, 81, 59–83. DOI: 10.1016/j.inffus.2021.11.003

Chowdhury, S., Dey, P., Joel-Edgar, S., Bhattacharya, S., Rodriguez-Espindola, O., Abadie, A., & Truong, L. (2023). Unlocking the value of artificial intelligence in human resource management through AI capability framework. *Human Resource Management Review*, 33(1), 100899. DOI: 10.1016/j.hrmr.2022.100899

Christensen, R., Hillaire, G., Marvez, G. R., Azukas, M. E., Holben, D., Gregory, S., & Ledger, S. (2022, April). Using Virtual Simulations in Teacher Education to Develop Equitable Teaching Strategies. In *Society for Information Technology & Teacher Education International Conference* (pp. 412-416). Association for the Advancement of Computing in Education (AACE).

Chu, H. C., Hwang, G. H., Tu, Y. F., & Yang, K. H. (2022). Roles and research trends of artificial intelligence in higher education: A systematic review of the top 50 most-cited articles. *Australasian Journal of Educational Technology*, 38(3), 22–42.

Ciolacu, M., Tehrani, A. F., Binder, L., & Svasta, P. M. (2018, October). Education 4.0-Artificial Intelligence assisted higher education: early recognition system with machine learning to support students' success. In *2018 IEEE 24th International Symposium for Design and Technology in Electronic Packaging (SIITME)* (pp. 23-30). IEEE.

Clancey, W. J., Bennett, J., & Cohen, P. R. (1979). *Applications-oriented AI research: Education*. Computer Science Department, Stanford University.

Clinton, L. (2021). International principles for boards of directors and cyber security. *Cyber Security: A Peer-Reviewed Journal, 4*(3), 243-250.

Collins, G. S., & Moons, K. G. (2019). Reporting of artificial intelligence prediction models. *Lancet*, 393(10181), 1577–1579. DOI: 10.1016/S0140-6736(19)30037-6 PMID: 31007185

Cook-Sather, A. (2018). Listening to equity-seeking perspectives: How students' experiences of pedagogical partnership can inform wider discussions of student success. *Higher Education Research & Development*, 37(5), 923–936. DOI: 10.1080/07294360.2018.1457629

Cooperrider, D. L., & Fry, R. (2020). Appreciative inquiry in a pandemic: An improbable pairing. *The Journal of Applied Behavioral Science*, 56(3), 266–271. DOI: 10.1177/0021886320936265

Corrin, L., & Bakharia, A. (2020). Re-imagining Peer Assessment in Self-Paced Online Learning Environments. In *Re-imagining University Assessment in a Digital World* (pp. 197–212). Springer. DOI: 10.1007/978-3-030-41956-1_14

Corvalán, J. G. (2018). Digital and intelligent public administration: transformations in the era of artificial intelligence. *A&C-Revista de Direito Administrativo & Constitucional, 18*(71), 55-87.

Crompton, H., & Burke, D. (2023). Artificial intelligence in higher education: The state of the field. *International Journal of Educational Technology in Higher Education*, 20(1), 22. DOI: 10.1186/s41239-023-00392-8

Cukurova, M., Miao, X., & Brooker, R. (2023, June). Adoption of artificial intelligence in schools: unveiling factors influencing teachers' engagement. In *International conference on artificial intelligence in education* (pp. 151-163). Cham: Springer Nature Switzerland. DOI: 10.1007/978-3-031-36272-9_13

Danesh, M. H. (2021, May). Reducing Neural Network Parameter Initialization Into an SMT Problem (Student Abstract). *Proceedings of the AAAI Conference on Artificial Intelligence*, 35(18), 15775–15776. DOI: 10.1609/aaai.v35i18.17884

Daniels, L. M., Goegan, L. D., & Parker, P. C. (2021). The impact of COVID-19 triggered changes to instruction and assessment on university students' self-reported motivation, engagement and perceptions. *Social Psychology of Education*, 24(1), 299–318. DOI: 10.1007/s11218-021-09612-3 PMID: 33613084

De Stefano, V. (2019). "Negotiating the Algorithm": Automation, Artificial Intelligence, and Labor Protection. *Comp. Lab. L. & Pol'y J.*, 41, 15.

De Wit, H., & Altbach, P. G. (2021). Internationalization in higher education: Global trends and recommendations for its future. *Policy Reviews in Higher Education*, 5(1), 28–46. DOI: 10.1080/23322969.2020.1820898

Deeva, G., Bogdanova, D., Serral, E., Snoeck, M., & De Weerdt, J. (2021). A review of automated feedback systems for learners: Classification framework, challenges and opportunities. *Computers & Education*, 162, 104094. DOI: 10.1016/j.compedu.2020.104094

Dekker, I., De Jong, E. M., Schippers, M. C., De Bruijn-Smolders, M., Alexiou, A., & Giesbers, B. (2020). Optimizing students' mental health and academic performance: AI-enhanced life crafting. *Frontiers in Psychology*, 11, 1063. DOI: 10.3389/fpsyg.2020.01063 PMID: 32581935

Dhawan, S., & Batra, G. (2020). Artificial intelligence in higher education: Promises, perils, and perspective. *Expanding Knowledge Horizon.OJAS*, 11, 11–22.

Dignum, V. (2019). *Responsible artificial intelligence: how to develop and use AI in a responsible way*. Springer Nature. DOI: 10.1007/978-3-030-30371-6

Dilmurod, R., & Fazliddin, A. (2021). Prospects for the introduction of artificial intelligence technologies in higher education. *ACADEMICIA: an international multidisciplinary research journal, 11*(2), 929-934.

Dogan, A., & Birant, D. (2021). Machine learning and data mining in manufacturing. *Expert Systems with Applications*, 166, 114060. DOI: 10.1016/j.eswa.2020.114060

Dong, B., Huang, Z., Guo, Y., Wang, Q., Niu, Z., & Zuo, W. (2021). Boosting Weakly Supervised Object Detection via Learning Bounding Box Adjusters. In *Proceedings of the IEEE/CVF International Conference on Computer Vision* (pp. 2876-2885). DOI: 10.1109/ICCV48922.2021.00287

Duran, A., Orozco, R. C., & Gonzalez, S. A. (2020). Imagining the future of jotería studies as a framework in the field of higher education. *Association of Mexican American Educators Journal*, 14(2), 67–86. DOI: 10.24974/amae.14.2.360

Dymitruk, M. (2019). Artificial Intelligence as a Tool to Improve the Administration of Justice? *Acta Universitatis Sapientiae. Legal Studies*, 8(2), 179–189.

Eimer, T., Biedenkapp, A., Hutter, F., & Lindauer, M. (2021, July). Self-paced context evaluation for contextual reinforcement learning. In *International Conference on Machine Learning* (pp. 2948-2958). PMLR.

Eitle, V., Zöll, A., & Buxmann, P. (2022). Organizational Readiness Concept for AI: A Quantitative Analysis of a Multi-stage Adoption Process from the Perspective of Data Scientists.

Ejdys, J., Gudanowska, A., Halicka, K., Kononiuk, A., Magruk, A., Nazarko, J., Nazarko, L., Szpilko, D., & Widelska, U. (2019). Foresight in higher education institutions: Evidence from Poland. *Форсайт*, 13(1), 77–89. DOI: 10.17323/2500-2597.2019.1.77.89

El Said, G. R. (2021). How Did the COVID-19 Pandemic Affect Higher Education Learning Experience? An Empirical Investigation of Learners' Academic Performance at a University in a Developing Country. *Advances in Human-Computer Interaction*, 2021(1), 6649524. DOI: 10.1155/2021/6649524

Engstrom, D. F., Ho, D. E., Sharkey, C. M., & Cuéllar, M. F. (2020). Government by algorithm: Artificial intelligence in federal administrative agencies. *NYU School of Law, Public Law Research Paper*, (20-54).

Eriksson, T., Bigi, A., & Bonera, M. (2020). Think with me, or think for me? On the future role of artificial intelligence in marketing strategy formulation. *The TQM Journal*, 32(4), 795–814. DOI: 10.1108/TQM-12-2019-0303

Eringfeld, S. (2021). Higher education and its post-coronial future: Utopian hopes and dystopian fears at Cambridge University during Covid-19. *Studies in Higher Education*, 46(1), 146–157. DOI: 10.1080/03075079.2020.1859681

Etscheid, J. (2019, September). Artificial intelligence in public administration. In *International Conference on Electronic Government* (pp. 248-261). Springer.

Fahimirad, M., & Kotamjani, S. S. (2018). A review on application of artificial intelligence in teaching and learning in educational contexts. *International Journal of Learning and Development*, 8(4), 106–118. DOI: 10.5296/ijld.v8i4.14057

Fazil, A. W., Hakimi, M., Shahidzay, A. K., & Hasas, A. (2024). Exploring the Broad Impact of AI Technologies on Student Engagement and Academic Performance in University Settings in Afghanistan. *RIGGS: Journal of Artificial Intelligence and Digital Business*, 2(2), 56–63. DOI: 10.31004/riggs.v2i2.268

Finlayson, S. G., Subbaswamy, A., Singh, K., Bowers, J., Kupke, A., Zittrain, J., Kohane, I. S., & Saria, S. (2021). The clinician and dataset shift in artificial intelligence. *The New England Journal of Medicine*, 385(3), 283–286. DOI: 10.1056/NEJMc2104626 PMID: 34260843

Fisher, R., Porod, C., & Peterson, S. (2021). Motivating employees and organizations to adopt a cybersecurity-focused culture. *Journal of Organizational Psychology*, 21(1), 114–131.

Fitzgerald, H. E., Karen, B., Sonka, S. T., Furco, A., & Swanson, L. (2020). The centrality of engagement in higher education. In *Building the field of higher education engagement* (pp. 201–219). Routledge.

Gaebel, M., Zhang, T., Stoeber, H., & Morrisroe, A. (2021). Digitally enhanced learning and teaching in European higher education institutions. *Survey Report.*

Gallagher, S. E., & Savage, T. (2023). Challenge-based learning in higher education: An exploratory literature review. *Teaching in Higher Education*, 28(6), 1135–1157. DOI: 10.1080/13562517.2020.1863354

Gao, P., Li, J., & Liu, S. (2021). An introduction to key technology in artificial intelligence and big data driven e-learning and e-education. *Mobile Networks and Applications*, 26(5), 2123–2126. DOI: 10.1007/s11036-021-01777-7

Garcia-Silva, A., Denaux, R., & Gomez-Perez, J. M. (2021). On the impact of knowledge-based linguistic annotations in the quality of scientific embeddings. *Future Generation Computer Systems*, 120, 26–35. DOI: 10.1016/j.future.2021.02.019

Gethe, R. K. (2022). Extrapolation of talent acquisition in AI aided professional environment. *International Journal of Business Innovation and Research*, 27(4), 462–479. DOI: 10.1504/IJBIR.2022.122510

Ghai, B., Liao, Q. V., Zhang, Y., Bellamy, R., & Mueller, K. (2021). Explainable active learning (xal) toward ai explanations as interfaces for machine teachers. *Proceedings of the ACM on Human-Computer Interaction, 4*(CSCW3), 1-28.

Girasa, R. (2020). *Artificial intelligence as a disruptive technology*. Springer International Publishing. DOI: 10.1007/978-3-030-35975-1

Goel, A. K., & Joyner, D. A. (2017). Using AI to teach AI: Lessons from an online AI class. *AI Magazine*, 38(2), 48–59. DOI: 10.1609/aimag.v38i2.2732

Goel, P. M., Kumar, P., Johri, P., Srivastava, S. K., & Suhag, S. (2020). A comparative study of Industry 4.0 with Education 4.0. *Available atSSRN* 3553215.

Govindarajan, V., & Srivastava, A. (2020). What the shift to virtual learning could mean for the future of higher ed. *Harvard Business Review*, 31(1), 3–8.

Greene, D., Hoffmann, A. L., & Stark, L. (2019). Better, nicer, clearer, fairer: A critical assessment of the movement for ethical artificial intelligence and machine learning.

Gröger, C. (2021). There is no AI without data. *Communications of the ACM*, 64(11), 98–108. DOI: 10.1145/3448247

Guan, C., Mou, J., & Jiang, Z. (2020). Artificial intelligence innovation in education: A twenty-year data-driven historical analysis. *International Journal of Innovation Studies*, 4(4), 134–147. DOI: 10.1016/j.ijis.2020.09.001

Guàrdia, L., Crisp, G., & Alsina, I. (2020). Trends and challenges of e-assessment to enhance student learning in higher education. *Learning and Performance Assessment: Concepts, Methodologies, Tools, and Applications*, 1575-1595.

Gupta, R., Srivastava, D., Sahu, M., Tiwari, S., Ambasta, R. K., & Kumar, P. (2021). Artificial intelligence to deep learning: Machine intelligence approach for drug discovery. *Molecular Diversity*, 25(3), 1315–1360. DOI: 10.1007/s11030-021-10217-3 PMID: 33844136

Gutiérrez, M., & Tomás, J. M. (2019). The role of perceived autonomy support in predicting university students' academic success mediated by academic self-efficacy and school engagement. *Educational Psychology*, 39(6), 729–748. DOI: 10.1080/01443410.2019.1566519

Hallunovi, A. (2021). Money, finance and credit. *Research and Innovation*, 90.

Handini, B. S., Nurhasanah, N., & Panly, F. I. (2022). The Effect of Artificial Intelligent Technology Used (Duolingo Application) To Enhance English Learning. *ELLITE: Journal of English Language, Literature, and Teaching*, 7(2), 86–94. DOI: 10.32528/ellite.v7i2.8354

Hannan, E., & Liu, S. (2021). AI: New source of competitiveness in higher education. *Competitiveness Review*.

Harris, J. C., & Patton, L. D. (2019). Un/doing intersectionality through higher education research. *The Journal of Higher Education*, 90(3), 347–372. DOI: 10.1080/00221546.2018.1536936

Hashim, S., Omar, M. K., Ab Jalil, H., & Sharef, N. M. (2022). Trends on Technologies and Artificial Intelligence in Education for Personalized Learning: Systematic Literature. *Journal of Acdemic Research in Progressive Education and Development*, 12(1), 884–903. DOI: 10.6007/IJARPED/v11-i1/12230

Hasyim, M., Saleh, F., Yusuf, R., & Abbas, A. (2021). Artificial Intelligence: Machine Translation Accuracy in Translating French-Indonesian Culinary Texts. *Available atSSRN* 3816594.

He, H., & Wang, T. (2020, June). Application of Blended Teaching in Public Administration Courses under the Background of Artificial Intelligence. *Journal of Physics: Conference Series*, 1575(1), 012174. DOI: 10.1088/1742-6596/1575/1/012174

He, L., Bai, L., Dionysiou, D. D., Wei, Z., Spinney, R., Chu, C., Lin, Z., & Xiao, R. (2021). Applications of computational chemistry, artificial intelligence, and machine learning in aquatic chemistry research. *Chemical Engineering Journal, 426*, 131810. DOI: 10.1016/j.cej.2021.131810

Helbekkmo, H., Levy, C., & White, O. (2019). Creating the bank enterprise risk management function of the future. *Journal of Risk Management in Financial Institutions*, 12(4), 297–310. DOI: 10.69554/IFVQ1353

Henke, N., Puri, A., & Saleh, T. (2020). *Accelerating analytics to navigate COVID-19 and the next normal.* Mckinsey.

Henman, P. (2020). Improving public services using artificial intelligence: Possibilities, pitfalls, governance. *Asia Pacific Journal of Public Administration*, 42(4), 209–221. DOI: 10.1080/23276665.2020.1816188

Herskovits, B. (2018). 'Build it and they will come'is a myth: Building a digital activation strategy. *Journal of Digital Banking*, 3(2), 102–113. DOI: 10.69554/NWVV2163

Hinojo-Lucena, F. J., Aznar-Díaz, I., Cáceres-Reche, M. P., & Romero-Rodríguez, J. M. (2019). Artificial intelligence in higher education: A bibliometric study on its impact in the scientific literature. *Education Sciences*, 9(1), 51. DOI: 10.3390/educsci9010051

Holmes, W., Porayska-Pomsta, K., Holstein, K., Sutherland, E., Baker, T., Shum, S. B., Santos, O. C., Rodrigo, M. T., Cukurova, M., Bittencourt, I. I., & Koedinger, K. R. (2022). Ethics of AI in education: Towards a community-wide framework. *International Journal of Artificial Intelligence in Education*, 32(3), 504–526. DOI: 10.1007/s40593-021-00239-1

Hong, C., & Ma, W. W. (2020). Introduction: Education 4.0: Applied degree education and the future of work. In *Applied Degree Education and the Future of Work: Education 4.0* (pp. 1–13). Springer Singapore. DOI: 10.1007/978-981-15-3142-2_1

Hooda, M., Rana, C., Dahiya, O., Rizwan, A., & Hossain, M. S. (2022). Artificial intelligence for assessment and feedback to enhance student success in higher education. *Mathematical Problems in Engineering*, 2022, 1–19. DOI: 10.1155/2022/5215722

Huallpa, J. J. (2023). Exploring the ethical considerations of using Chat GPT in university education. *Periodicals of Engineering and Natural Sciences*, 11(4), 105–115. DOI: 10.21533/pen.v11i4.3770

Huang, A. Y., Lu, O. H., & Yang, S. J. (2023). Effects of artificial Intelligence–Enabled personalized recommendations on learners' learning engagement, motivation, and outcomes in a flipped classroom. *Computers & Education*, 194, 104684. DOI: 10.1016/j.compedu.2022.104684

Huang, H., & Chen, M. (2020, October). Research on the Construction of Practice Teaching System of Business Administration Specialty Based on Artificial Intelligence. *Journal of Physics: Conference Series*, 1648(4), 042055. DOI: 10.1088/1742-6596/1648/4/042055

Hudson, C., Archibald, A., & Heap, T. (2020, June). Integrating an AI-driven discussion platform: The impact of platform on engagement and quality. In *EDEN Conference Proceedings* (No. 1, pp. 117-126). DOI: 10.38069/edenconf-2020-ac0009

Huff, E., & Bonde, A. (2022). AI meets consumer insights.

Hu, K. H. (2023). An exploration of the key determinants for the application of AI-enabled higher education based on a hybrid Soft-computing technique and a DEMATEL approach. *Expert Systems with Applications*, 212, 118762. DOI: 10.1016/j.eswa.2022.118762

Hwang, G. J., Xie, H., Wah, B. W., & Gašević, D. (2020). Vision, challenges, roles and research issues of Artificial Intelligence in Education. *Computers and Education: Artificial Intelligence*, 1, 100001. DOI: 10.1016/j.caeai.2020.100001

Ilkka, T. (2018). The impact of artificial intelligence on learning, teaching, and education. *European Union*.

Jackson, N. C. (2019). Managing for competency with innovation change in higher education: Examining the pitfalls and pivots of digital transformation. *Business Horizons*, 62(6), 761–772. DOI: 10.1016/j.bushor.2019.08.002

Jaikaew, P., Suntawan, T., & Yafu, S. (2022). A Model of the Need for Artificial Intelligence Using on the Administration of World-Class Standard Secondary School. *Journal of Positive School Psychology*, 6417–6424.

Janjanam, D., Ganesh, B., & Manjunatha, L. (2021, February). Design of an expert system architecture: An overview. *Journal of Physics: Conference Series*, 1767(1), 012036. DOI: 10.1088/1742-6596/1767/1/012036

Jelonek, D., Mesjasz-Lech, A., Stępniak, C., Turek, T., & Ziora, L. (2020). The artificial intelligence application in the management of contemporary organization: Theoretical assumptions, current practices and research review. In *Advances in Information and Communication:Proceedings of the 2019 Future of Information and Communication Conference (FICC),* Volume 1 (pp. 319-327). Springer International Publishing.

Jena, B., Saxena, S., Nayak, G. K., Saba, L., Sharma, N., & Suri, J. S. (2021). Artificial intelligence-based hybrid deep learning models for image classification: The first narrative review. *Computers in Biology and Medicine*, 137, 104803. DOI: 10.1016/j.compbiomed.2021.104803 PMID: 34536856

Jia, D. M., Yuan, C. F., Guo, S., Jiang, Z. Z., Xu, D., & Wang, D. A. (2019, October). Application of" Artificial Intelligence and Big Data" in Sports Rehabilitation for Chinese Judicial Administrative Drug Addicts. In *Proceedings of the 2019 International Conference on Artificial Intelligence and Advanced Manufacturing* (pp. 1-5). DOI: 10.1145/3358331.3358336

Johnson, K., Pasquale, F., & Chapman, J. (2019). Artificial intelligence, machine learning, and bias in finance: Toward responsible innovation. *Fordham Law Review*, 88, 499.

Johnson, R. D., Stone, D. L., & Lukaszewski, K. M. (2020). The benefits of eHRM and AI for talent acquisition. *Journal of Tourism Futures*, 7(1), 40–52. DOI: 10.1108/JTF-02-2020-0013

Johnson, S. R., & Stage, F. K. (2018). Academic engagement and student success: Do high-impact practices mean higher graduation rates? *The Journal of Higher Education*, 89(5), 753–781. DOI: 10.1080/00221546.2018.1441107

Kabudi, T., Pappas, I., & Olsen, D. H. (2021). AI-enabled adaptive learning systems: A systematic mapping of the literature. *Computers and Education: Artificial Intelligence*, 2, 100017. DOI: 10.1016/j.caeai.2021.100017

Kahu, E. R., & Nelson, K. (2018). Student engagement in the educational interface: Understanding the mechanisms of student success. *Higher Education Research & Development*, 37(1), 58–71. DOI: 10.1080/07294360.2017.1344197

Kairu, C. (2020, June). Students' attitude towards the use of artificial intelligence and machine learning to measure classroom engagement activities. In *EdMedia+ Innovate Learning* (pp. 793-802). Association for the Advancement of Computing in Education (AACE).

Kaplan, A., & Haenlein, M. (2020). Rulers of the world, unite! The challenges and opportunities of artificial intelligence. *Business Horizons*, 63(1), 37–50. DOI: 10.1016/j.bushor.2019.09.003

Kaur, M., & Gandolfi, F. (2023). Artificial Intelligence in Human Resource Management-Challenges and Future Research Recommendations. *Revista de Management Comparat International*, 24(3), 382–393.

Kavoya, J. (2020). Machine Learning for Intelligence Driven Customs Management. *African Tax and Customs Review*, 3(2), 1–8.

Kazemitabaar, M., Hou, X., Henley, A., Ericson, B. J., Weintrop, D., & Grossman, T. (2023, November). How novices use LLM-based code generators to solve CS1 coding tasks in a self-paced learning environment. In *Proceedings of the 23rd Koli Calling International Conference on Computing Education Research* (pp. 1-12). DOI: 10.1145/3631802.3631806

Ke, Y. (2021, September). Application of Artificial Intelligence in Large-scale International Wushu (Taolu) Events. In *2021 2nd International Conference on Big Data & Artificial Intelligence & Software Engineering (ICBASE)* (pp. 575-578). IEEE.

Khonturaev, S. I. (2023). The Evolution Of Artificial Intelligence: A Comprehensive Exploration For Higher Education. *Best Journal of Innovation in Science. Research for Development*, 2(11), 700–706.

Kim, B., Suh, H., Heo, J., & Choi, Y. (2020). AI-driven interface design for intelligent tutoring system improves student engagement. *arXiv preprint arXiv:2009.08976.*

Kim, J., & Maloney, E. J. (2020). *Learning innovation and the future of higher education*. JHU Press. DOI: 10.1353/book.71965

Kim, K., & Kim, B. (2022). Decision-Making Model for Reinforcing Digital Transformation Strategies Based on Artificial Intelligence Technology. *Information (Basel)*, 13(5), 253. DOI: 10.3390/info13050253

Kinkel, S., Baumgartner, M., & Cherubini, E. (2022). Prerequisites for the adoption of AI technologies in manufacturing–Evidence from a worldwide sample of manufacturing companies. *Technovation*, 110, 102375. DOI: 10.1016/j.technovation.2021.102375

Klašnja-Milićević, A., & Ivanović, M. (2021). E-learning personalization systems and sustainable education. *Sustainability (Basel)*, 13(12), 6713. DOI: 10.3390/su13126713

Knox, J. (2020). Artificial intelligence and education in China. *Learning, Media and Technology*, 45(3), 298–311. DOI: 10.1080/17439884.2020.1754236

Koch, M. (2018). Artificial intelligence is becoming natural. *Cell*, 173(3), 533. DOI: 10.1016/j.cell.2018.04.007 PMID: 29677502

Kocielnik, R., Amershi, S., & Bennett, P. N. (2019, May). Will you accept an imperfect ai? exploring designs for adjusting end-user expectations of ai systems. In *Proceedings of the 2019 CHI Conference on Human Factors in Computing Systems* (pp. 1-14).

Kordon, A. (2020, August). Applied Artificial Intelligence-Based Systems as Competitive Advantage. In *2020 IEEE 10th International Conference on Intelligent Systems (IS)* (pp. 6-18). IEEE. DOI: 10.1109/IS48319.2020.9200097

Kordon, A. K. (2020). How to Operate AI-Based Data Science in a Business. In *Applying Data Science* (pp. 433–451). Springer. DOI: 10.1007/978-3-030-36375-8_16

Krasteva, N. (2021). The Artificial Intelligence And Contemporary Marketing. *Yearbook of the Faculty of Economics and Business Administration. Sofia University*, 20(1), 109–129.

Krejci, D., Küng, L., & Missonier, S. (2022). A Case Study of Enterprise-wide Digital Innovation: Involving Non-IT Employees.

Kshetri, N. (2021). Evolving uses of artificial intelligence in human resource management in emerging economies in the global South: Some preliminary evidence. *Management Research Review*, 44(7), 970–990. DOI: 10.1108/MRR-03-2020-0168

Kuang, L., He, L. I. U., Yili, R. E. N., Kai, L. U. O., Mingyu, S. H. I., Jian, S. U., & Xin, L. I. (2021). Application and development trend of artificial intelligence in petroleum exploration and development. *Petroleum Exploration and Development*, 48(1), 1–14. DOI: 10.1016/S1876-3804(21)60001-0

Kuleto, V., Ilić, M., Dumangiu, M., Ranković, M., Martins, O. M., Păun, D., & Mihoreanu, L. (2021). Exploring opportunities and challenges of artificial intelligence and machine learning in higher education institutions. *Sustainability (Basel)*, 13(18), 10424. DOI: 10.3390/su131810424

Kumar, M., Sharma, S., Chaudhary, D., & Prakash, S. (2021, March). Image Recognition Using Artificial Intelligence. In *2021 International Conference on Advance Computing and Innovative Technologies in Engineering (ICACITE)* (pp. 760-763). IEEE.

Kumar, P., Dwivedi, Y. K., & Anand, A. (2021). Responsible artificial intelligence (AI) for value formation and market performance in healthcare: The mediating role of patient's cognitive engagement. *Information Systems Frontiers*, 1–24. PMID: 33948105

Kumar, V., Rajan, B., Venkatesan, R., & Lecinski, J. (2019). Understanding the role of artificial intelligence in personalized engagement marketing. *California Management Review*, 61(4), 135–155. DOI: 10.1177/0008125619859317

Kuziemski, M., & Misuraca, G. (2020). AI governance in the public sector: Three tales from the frontiers of automated decision-making in democratic settings. *Telecommunications Policy*, 44(6), 101976. DOI: 10.1016/j.telpol.2020.101976 PMID: 32313360

Lacy, P., Long, J., & Spindler, W. (2020). Culture & Organization. In *The Circular Economy Handbook* (pp. 259–281). Palgrave Macmillan. DOI: 10.1057/978-1-349-95968-6_19

Lai, C. L. (2021). Exploring university students' preferences for AI-assisted learning environment. *Journal of Educational Technology & Society*, 24(4), 1–15.

Lameras, P. (2022, March). A Vision of Teaching and Learning with AI. In *2022 IEEE Global Engineering Education Conference (EDUCON)* (pp. 1796-1803). IEEE. DOI: 10.1109/EDUCON52537.2022.9766718

Lantz, J. L., Liu, J. C., & Basnyat, I. (2022). Piloting Artificial Intelligence (AI) to Facilitate Online Discussion in Large Online Classes: A Case Study. In *Cases on Innovative and Successful Uses of Digital Resources for Online Learning* (pp. 204-222). IGI Global.

Larsson, S., & Heintz, F. (2020). Transparency in artificial intelligence. *Internet Policy Review*, 9(2). Advance online publication. DOI: 10.14763/2020.2.1469

Latinovic, Z., & Chatterjee, S. C. (2022). Achieving the promise of AI and ML in delivering economic and relational customer value in B2B. *Journal of Business Research*, 144, 966–974. DOI: 10.1016/j.jbusres.2022.01.052

Lauder, H. (2020). The roles of higher education, further education and lifelong learning in the future economy. *Journal of Education and Work*, 33(7-8), 460–467. DOI: 10.1080/13639080.2020.1852499

Lauriola, I., Lavelli, A., & Aiolli, F. (2022). An introduction to deep learning in natural language processing: Models, techniques, and tools. *Neurocomputing*, 470, 443–456. DOI: 10.1016/j.neucom.2021.05.103

Lawry, T. (2020). *AI in health: a leader's guide to winning in the new age of intelligent health systems*. CRC Press. DOI: 10.4324/9780429321214

Lazarevic, B., & Bentz, D. (2021). Student perception of stress in online and face-to-face learning: The exploration of stress determinants. *American Journal of Distance Education*, 35(1), 2–15. DOI: 10.1080/08923647.2020.1748491

Lee, S., & Miller, S. (2019). AI gets real at Singapore's Changi Airport (Part 1).

Lee, C. A., Tzeng, J. W., Huang, N. F., & Su, Y. S. (2021). Prediction of student performance in Massive Open Online Courses using deep learning system based on learning behaviors. *Journal of Educational Technology & Society*, 24(3), 130–146.

Lee, D., Huh, Y., Lin, C. Y., & Reigeluth, C. M. (2018). Technology functions for personalized learning in learner-centered schools. *Educational Technology Research and Development*, 66(5), 1269–1302. DOI: 10.1007/s11423-018-9615-9

Li, K., Xu, B., Gao, K., Yang, D., & Chen, M. (2018, May). Self-paced learning with identification refinement for SPOC student grading. In *Proceedings of ACM Turing Celebration Conference*-China (pp. 79-84). DOI: 10.1145/3210713.3210732

Li, L., Zhao, K., Li, S., Sun, R., & Cai, S. (2020). Extreme learning machine for supervised classification with self-paced learning. *Neural Processing Letters*, 52(3), 1723–1744. DOI: 10.1007/s11063-020-10286-9

Limani, Y., Hajrizi, E., Stapleton, L., & Retkoceri, M. (2019). Digital transformation readiness in higher education institutions (HEI): The case of Kosovo. *IFAC-PapersOnLine*, 52(25), 52–57. DOI: 10.1016/j.ifacol.2019.12.445

Limonova, V., dos Santos, A. M. P., Mamede, J. H. P. S., & de Jesus Filipe, V. M. (2024, March). Maximising Attendance in Higher Education: How AI and Gamification Strategies Can Boost Student Engagement and Participation. In *World Conference on Information Systems and Technologies* (pp. 64-70). Cham: Springer Nature Switzerland. DOI: 10.1007/978-3-031-60224-5_7

Liu, S. Y. (2021). Harnessing Artificial Intelligence to Transform Agricultural. *Case Studies: Insights on Agriculture Innovation 2020 (IAAS Series)*, 13.

Liu, Y., & Quan, Q. (2022). AI Recognition Method of Pronunciation Errors in Oral English Speech with the Help of Big Data for Personalized Learning. *Journal of Information & Knowledge Management*, 2240028.

Liu, Z., Feng, X., Wang, Y., & Zuo, W. (2021). Self-paced learning enhanced neural matrix factorization for noise-aware recommendation. *Knowledge-Based Systems*, 213, 106660. DOI: 10.1016/j.knosys.2020.106660

Li, W., & Liu, F. (2022). Exploration on College Ideological and Political Education Integrating Artificial Intelligence-Intellectualized Information Technology. *Computational Intelligence and Neuroscience*, 2022, 2022. DOI: 10.1155/2022/4844565 PMID: 35634053

Li, Z., & Bonk, C. J. (2023). Self-directed language learning with Duolingo in an out-of-class context. *Computer Assisted Language Learning*, 1–23. DOI: 10.1080/09588221.2023.2206874

Locke, S., Bashall, A., Al-Adely, S., Moore, J., Wilson, A., & Kitchen, G. B. (2021). Natural language processing in medicine: A review. *Trends in Anaesthesia & Critical Care*, 38, 4–9. DOI: 10.1016/j.tacc.2021.02.007

Looi, K. H. (2024). Ameliorating emergency Web-enabled teaching in higher education institutions and implications for future emergencies. *Information Discovery and Delivery*, 52(3), 289–304. DOI: 10.1108/IDD-01-2023-0005

Luan, H., & Tsai, C. C. (2021). A review of using machine learning approaches for precision education. *Journal of Educational Technology & Society*, 24(1), 250–266.

Luchini, C., Pea, A., & Scarpa, A. (2022). Artificial intelligence in oncology: Current applications and future perspectives. *British Journal of Cancer*, 126(1), 4–9. DOI: 10.1038/s41416-021-01633-1 PMID: 34837074

Luckin, R., & Holmes, W. (2016). Intelligence unleashed: An argument for AI in education.

Luger, G. F. (1998). *Artificial Intelligence: Structures and Strategies for Complex Problem Solving, 5/e*. Pearson Education India.

Lu, Y., & Gao, X. (2022). The Impact of Artificial Intelligence Technology on Market Public Administration in a Complex Market Environment. *Wireless Communications and Mobile Computing*, 2022, 2022. DOI: 10.1155/2022/5646234

Lynch, D., Christensen, U. J., & Howe, N. J. (2020). AI Technology and Personalized Learning Design—Uncovering Unconscious Incompetence. In *Radical Solutions and Learning Analytics* (pp. 157–172). Springer. DOI: 10.1007/978-981-15-4526-9_10

Lytras, M. D., & Visvizi, A. (2021). Artificial intelligence and cognitive computing: Methods, technologies, systems, applications and policy making. *Sustainability (Basel)*, 13(7), 3598. DOI: 10.3390/su13073598

Ma, Y., Wang, Z., Yang, H., & Yang, L. (2020). Artificial intelligence applications in the development of autonomous vehicles: a survey. *IEEE/CAA Journal of Automatica Sinica, 7*(2), 315-329.

Maddox, T. M., Rumsfeld, J. S., & Payne, P. R. (2019). Questions for artificial intelligence in health care. *Journal of the American Medical Association*, 321(1), 31–32. DOI: 10.1001/jama.2018.18932 PMID: 30535130

Maghsudi, S., Lan, A., Xu, J., & van Der Schaar, M. (2021). Personalized education in the artificial intelligence era: What to expect next. *IEEE Signal Processing Magazine*, 38(3), 37–50. DOI: 10.1109/MSP.2021.3055032

Magomadov, V. S. (2020, November). The application of artificial intelligence and Big Data analytics in personalized learning. *Journal of Physics: Conference Series*, 1691(1), 012169. DOI: 10.1088/1742-6596/1691/1/012169

Malik, A. R., Pratiwi, Y., Andajani, K., Numertayasa, I. W., Suharti, S., Darwis, A., & Marzuki, . (2023). Exploring Artificial Intelligence in Academic Essay: Higher Education Student's Perspective. *International Journal of Educational Research Open*, 5, 100296. DOI: 10.1016/j.ijedro.2023.100296

Marcinkowski, F., Kieslich, K., Starke, C., & Lünich, M. (2020, January). Implications of AI (un-) fairness in higher education admissions: the effects of perceived AI (un-) fairness on exit, voice and organizational reputation. In *Proceedings of the 2020 conference on fairness, accountability, and transparency* (pp. 122-130). DOI: 10.1145/3351095.3372867

Martin, S. M., Casey, J. R., & Kane, S. (2021). History of Artificial Intelligence and Personalized Learning. In *Serious Games in Personalized Learning* (pp. 27–47). Routledge. DOI: 10.4324/9781003042709-2

Martins, R. M., & Gresse Von Wangenheim, C. (2022). *Findings on Teaching Machine Learning in High School: A Ten-Year Systematic Literature Review*. Informatics in Education.

Matibag, T. (2020). Artificial intelligence for local governance. *The Urban Lawyer*, 50, 415–435.

Meera, S., & Geerthik, S. (2022). Natural language processing. *Artificial Intelligent Techniques for Wireless Communication and Networking*, 139-153.

Meskó, B., Hetényi, G., & Győrffy, Z. (2018). Will artificial intelligence solve the human resource crisis in healthcare? *BMC Health Services Research*, 18(1), 1–4. DOI: 10.1186/s12913-018-3359-4 PMID: 30001717

Mirdad, K., Daeli, O. P. M., Septiani, N., Ekawati, A., & Rusilowati, U. (2024). Optimizing Student Engagement and Performance usingAI-Enabled Educational Tools. *CORISINTA*, 1(1), 53–60.

Moglia, A., Georgiou, K., Morelli, L., Toutouzas, K., Satava, R. M., & Cuschieri, A. (2022). Breaking down the silos of artificial intelligence in surgery: Glossary of terms. *Surgical Endoscopy*, 36(11), 1–12. DOI: 10.1007/s00464-022-09371-y PMID: 35729406

Mohammed, A. A., Al-ghazali, A., & Alqohfa, K. A. (2023). Exploring ChatGPT uses in higher studies: A case study of Arab postgraduates in India. *Journal of English Studies in Arabia Felix*, 2(2), 9–17. DOI: 10.56540/jesaf.v2i2.55

Mohiuddin Babu, M., Akter, S., Rahman, M., Billah, M. M., & Hack-Polay, D. (2022). The role of artificial intelligence in shaping the future of Agile fashion industry. *Production Planning and Control*, 1–15. DOI: 10.1080/09537287.2022.2060858

Montebello, M. (2021, August). Personalized Learning Environments. In *2021 International Symposium on Educational Technology (ISET)* (pp. 134-138). IEEE. DOI: 10.1109/ISET52350.2021.00036

Morkhat, P. M., Ponkin, I. V., Markhgeym, M. V., Botnev, V. K., & Turganbayev, A. O. (2019). Artificial intelligence versus public administration: limitations of application.

Mullen, J., Milechin, L., & Reuther, A. (2019, October). Cultivating professional technical skills and understanding through hands-on online learning experiences. In *2019 IEEE Learning With MOOCS (LWMOOCS)* (pp. 150-155). IEEE. DOI: 10.1109/LWMOOCS47620.2019.8939637

Murphy, R. F. (2019). Artificial intelligence applications to support K-12 teachers and teaching. *Rand Corporation, 10.*

Naidoo, D. T. (2023). Integrating TAM and IS success model: Exploring the role of blockchain and AI in predicting learner engagement and performance in e-learning. *Frontiers of Computer Science*, 5, 1227749. DOI: 10.3389/fcomp.2023.1227749

Nazari, N., Shabbir, M. S., & Setiawan, R. (2021). Application of Artificial Intelligence powered digital writing assistant in higher education: Randomized controlled trial. *Heliyon*, 7(5), e07014. DOI: 10.1016/j.heliyon.2021.e07014 PMID: 34027198

Nelson, G. S. (2019). Bias in artificial intelligence. *North Carolina Medical Journal*, 80(4), 220–222. DOI: 10.18043/ncm.80.4.220 PMID: 31278182

Neuwirth, L. S., Jović, S., & Mukherji, B. R. (2021). Reimagining higher education during and post-COVID-19: Challenges and opportunities. *Journal of Adult and Continuing Education*, 27(2), 141–156. DOI: 10.1177/1477971420947738

Ng, T. K. (2021). New interpretation of extracurricular activities via social networking sites: A case study of artificial intelligence learning at a secondary school in Hong Kong. *Journal of Education and Training Studies*, 9(1), 49–60. DOI: 10.11114/jets.v9i1.5105

Nguyen, A., Kremantzis, M., Essien, A., Petrounias, I., & Hosseini, S. (2024). Enhancing Student Engagement Through Artificial Intelligence (AI): Understanding the Basics, Opportunities, and Challenges. *Journal of University Teaching & Learning Practice*, 21(06). Advance online publication. DOI: 10.53761/caraaq92

Nguyen, N. D. (2023). Exploring the role of AI in education. *London Journal of Social Sciences*, (6), 84–95. DOI: 10.31039/ljss.2023.6.108

Nieminen, J. H., Bearman, M., & Tai, J. (2023). How is theory used in assessment and feedback research? A critical review. *Assessment & Evaluation in Higher Education*, 48(1), 77–94. DOI: 10.1080/02602938.2022.2047154

Nikita, G., & Velicheti, S. N. (2022). AI as a Tool in Internal Communication to Reduce Employee Attrition Rate in India. In *Achieving $5 Trillion Economy of India* (pp. 43–62). Springer. DOI: 10.1007/978-981-16-7818-9_3

Nurjaman, A. (2022). Artificial intelligence as an instrument to improve the quality of public service. In *Social and Political Issues on Sustainable Development in the Post Covid-19 Crisis* (pp. 121–130). Routledge. DOI: 10.1201/9781003263586-15

Ogude, N. A., Meyer, I. J., Mwambakana, J., & Mthethwa, N. E. (2019). Can extended curriculum programmes be improved through engagement with students using appreciative inquiry? *South African Journal of Higher Education*, 33(4), 219–236. DOI: 10.20853/33-4-2835

Oke, A., & Fernandes, F. A. P. (2020). Innovations in teaching and learning: Exploring the perceptions of the education sector on the 4th industrial revolution (4IR). *Journal of Open Innovation*, 6(2), 31. DOI: 10.3390/joitmc6020031

Okunlaya, R. O., Syed Abdullah, N., & Alias, R. A. (2022). Artificial intelligence (AI) library services innovative conceptual framework for the digital transformation of university education. *Library Hi Tech*, 40(6), 1869–1892. DOI: 10.1108/LHT-07-2021-0242

Ortagus, J. C., Kelchen, R., Rosinger, K., & Voorhees, N. (2020). Performance-based funding in American higher education: A systematic synthesis of the intended and unintended consequences. *Educational Evaluation and Policy Analysis*, 42(4), 520–550. DOI: 10.3102/0162373720953128

Padurean, A. I., Daniel, M. N., & Claudiu, C. (2021). On smart city, artificial intelligence and the evolution of public administration digitalization in the COVID-19 pandemic. *Timisoara Journal of Economics and Business, 14*(1).

Pang, S., Pang, C., Zeng, D., & Chen, X. (2022, June). Exploration on the Talent Training Path of "Post, Course, Competition, Certificate" for Artificial Intelligence Technology Application Major Based on Huawei 1+ X Certificate. In *2022 8th International Conference on Humanities and Social Science Research (ICHSSR 2022)* (pp. 2212-2215). Atlantis Press.

Pan, L., Ai, S., Ren, Y., & Xu, Z. (2020). Self-paced deep regression forests with consideration on underrepresented examples. *Computer Vision–ECCV 2020: 16th European Conference, Glasgow, UK, August 23–28, 2020Proceedings*, 16, 271–287.

Papa, R., & Jackson, K. M. (2021). AI Transforms Twentieth-Century Learning. In *Artificial Intelligence, Human Agency and the Educational Leader* (pp. 1–32). Springer. DOI: 10.1007/978-3-030-77610-7_1

Paramita, D. (2020). Digitalization in talent acquisition: A case study of AI in recruitment.

Parikh, R. B., Teeple, S., & Navathe, A. S. (2019). Addressing bias in artificial intelligence in health care. *Journal of the American Medical Association*, 322(24), 2377–2378. DOI: 10.1001/jama.2019.18058 PMID: 31755905

Parvin, S. (2021, December). Success Factors of an Enterprise-Wide Digital Twin Strategy. In *Abu Dhabi International Petroleum Exhibition & Conference*. OnePetro.

Pedro, F., Subosa, M., Rivas, A., & Valverde, P. (2019). Artificial intelligence in education: Challenges and opportunities for sustainable development.

Pedró, F. (2020). Applications of Artificial Intelligence to higher education: Possibilities, evidence, and challenges. *IUL Research*, 1(1), 61–76. DOI: 10.57568/iulres.v1i1.43

Penprase, B. E. (2018). The fourth industrial revolution and higher education. *Higher education in the era of the fourth industrial revolution, 10*, 978-981.

Perello-Marin, M. R. (2022). Adoption Factors of Artificial intelligence in Human Resources Management. *Future of Business Administration*, 1(1), 1–12. DOI: 10.33422/fba.v1i1.140

Pesapane, F., Volonté, C., Codari, M., & Sardanelli, F. (2018). Artificial intelligence as a medical device in radiology: Ethical and regulatory issues in Europe and the United States. *Insights Into Imaging*, 9(5), 745–753. DOI: 10.1007/s13244-018-0645-y PMID: 30112675

Pillai, R., & Sivathanu, B. (2020). Adoption of artificial intelligence (AI) for talent acquisition in IT/ITeS organizations. *Benchmarking*, 27(9), 2599–2629. DOI: 10.1108/BIJ-04-2020-0186

Ponkin, I. V., & Redkina, A. I. (2018). Artificial intelligence from the point of view of law. *RUDN Journal of Law*, 22(1), 91–109. DOI: 10.22363/2313-2337-2018-22-1-91-109

Popenici, S. A., & Kerr, S. (2017). Exploring the impact of artificial intelligence on teaching and learning in higher education. *Research and Practice in Technology Enhanced Learning*, 12(1), 22. DOI: 10.1186/s41039-017-0062-8 PMID: 30595727

Prakash, K. B., & Kanagachidambaresan, G. R. (2021). Pattern Recognition and Machine Learning. In *Programming with TensorFlow* (pp. 105–144). Springer. DOI: 10.1007/978-3-030-57077-4

Pratama, M. P., Sampelolo, R., & Lura, H. (2023). Revolutionizing education: harnessing the power of artificial intelligence for personalized learning. *Klasikal: Journal of Education. Language Teaching and Science*, 5(2), 350–357.

Radianti, J., Majchrzak, T. A., Fromm, J., & Wohlgenannt, I. (2020). A systematic review of immersive virtual reality applications for higher education: Design elements, lessons learned, and research agenda. *Computers & Education*, 147, 103778. DOI: 10.1016/j.compedu.2019.103778

Rad, P., Roopaei, M., Beebe, N., Shadaram, M., & Au, Y. (2018, January). AI thinking for cloud education platform with personalized learning. *Proceedings of the 51st Hawaii international conference on system sciences*. DOI: 10.24251/HICSS.2018.003

Rahayu, S. K. (2021). Utilization of artificial intelligence in tax audit in Indonesia. *Management Accounting Research*, 20(3), 135–157.

Ramasamy, V., Singsen, D., & Walia, G. S. (2024). Fostering Student Engagement and Success in STEM Education: An AI-Driven Exploration of High Impact Practices from Cross-Disciplinary General Education Courses. *Journal of Engineering Education Transformations, 37*(Special Issue 2).

Ramesh, S., & Das, S. (2022, January). Adoption of AI in Talent Acquisition: A Conceptual Framework. In *International Conference on Digital Technologies and Applications* (pp. 12-20). Cham: Springer International Publishing. DOI: 10.1007/978-3-031-01942-5_2

Rampersad, G. (2020). Robot will take your job: Innovation for an era of artificial intelligence. *Journal of Business Research*, 116, 68–74. DOI: 10.1016/j.jbusres.2020.05.019

Rao, R., & Hill, B. (2019). How is the Role of AI in Talent Acquisition Evolving?

Rasul, T., Nair, S., Kalendra, D., Robin, M., de Oliveira Santini, F., Ladeira, W. J., & Heathcote, L. (2023). The role of ChatGPT in higher education: Benefits, challenges, and future research directions. *Journal of Applied Learning and Teaching*, 6(1), 41–56.

Reis, J., Santo, P. E., & Melão, N. (2019, June). Impacts of artificial intelligence on public administration: A systematic literature review. In *2019 14th Iberian conference on information systems and technologies (CISTI)* (pp. 1-7). IEEE. DOI: 10.23919/CISTI.2019.8760893

Reis, J., Santo, P. E., & Melão, N. (2019, April). Artificial intelligence in government services: A systematic literature review. In *World conference on information systems and technologies* (pp. 241-252). Springer. DOI: 10.1007/978-3-030-16181-1_23

Reis, T., Bornschlegl, M. X., & Hemmje, M. L. (2021). Toward a Reference Model for Artificial Intelligence Supporting Big Data Analysis. In *Advances in Data Science and Information Engineering* (pp. 561–572). Springer. DOI: 10.1007/978-3-030-71704-9_38

Ren, Y., Xu, N., Ling, M., & Geng, X. (2022). Label distribution for multimodal machine learning. *Frontiers of Computer Science*, 16(1), 1–11. DOI: 10.1007/s11704-021-0611-6

Renz, A., & Hilbig, R. (2020). Prerequisites for artificial intelligence in further education: Identification of drivers, barriers, and business models of educational technology companies. *International Journal of Educational Technology in Higher Education*, 17(1), 1–21. DOI: 10.1186/s41239-020-00193-3

Rerhaye, L., Altun, D., Krauss, C., & Müller, C. (2021, July). Evaluation Methods for an AI-Supported Learning Management System: Quantifying and Qualifying Added Values for Teaching and Learning. In *International Conference on Human-Computer Interaction* (pp. 394-411). Springer. DOI: 10.1007/978-3-030-77857-6_28

Rismani, S., & Moon, A. (2022). What does it mean to be an AI Ethicist: An ontology of existing roles. *arXiv preprint arXiv:2205.03946.*

Rivers, C., & Holland, A. (2022). Management Education and Artificial Intelligence: Toward Personalized Learning. In *The Future of Management Education* (pp. 184-204). Routledge.

Roberts, H., Cowls, J., Morley, J., Taddeo, M., Wang, V., & Floridi, L. (2021). The Chinese approach to artificial intelligence: An analysis of policy, ethics, and regulation. *AI & Society*, 36(1), 59–77. DOI: 10.1007/s00146-020-00992-2

Robertson, J., Fossaceca, J. M., & Bennett, K. W. (2021). A cloud-based computing framework for artificial intelligence innovation in support of multidomain operations. *IEEE Transactions on Engineering Management.*

Rudolph, J., Tan, S., & Tan, S. (2023). ChatGPT: Bullshit spewer or the end of traditional assessments in higher education? *Journal of Applied Learning and Teaching, 6*(1), 342-363.

Ruel, H., & Njoku, E. (2020). AI redefining the hospitality industry. *Journal of Tourism Futures.*

Rydén, P., & El Sawy, O. (2022). Real-Time Management: When AI Goes Fast and Flow. In *Platforms and Artificial Intelligence* (pp. 225–243). Springer. DOI: 10.1007/978-3-030-90192-9_11

Sakharov, A. (2021). A Best-first Backward-chaining Search Strategy based on Learned Predicate Representations. In *ICAART (2)* (pp. 982-989). DOI: 10.5220/0010299209820989

Salas-Pilco, S. Z., Yang, Y., & Zhang, Z. (2022). Student engagement in online learning in Latin American higher education during the COVID-19 pandemic: A systematic review. *British Journal of Educational Technology*, 53(3), 593–619. DOI: 10.1111/bjet.13190 PMID: 35600418

Samek, W., Montavon, G., Lapuschkin, S., Anders, C. J., & Müller, K. R. (2021). Explaining deep neural networks and beyond: A review of methods and applications. *Proceedings of the IEEE*, 109(3), 247–278. DOI: 10.1109/JPROC.2021.3060483

Sanz, J. L., & Zhu, Y. (2021, September). Toward Scalable Artificial Intelligence in Finance. In *2021 IEEE International Conference on Services Computing (SCC)* (pp. 460-469). IEEE. DOI: 10.1109/SCC53864.2021.00067

Sarker, I. H., Hoque, M. M., Uddin, M., & Alsanoosy, T. (2021). Mobile data science and intelligent apps: Concepts, ai-based modeling and research directions. *Mobile Networks and Applications*, 26(1), 285–303. DOI: 10.1007/s11036-020-01650-z

Schiff, D. (2022). Education for AI, not AI for Education: The role of education and ethics in national AI policy strategies. *International Journal of Artificial Intelligence in Education*, 32(3), 527–563. DOI: 10.1007/s40593-021-00270-2

Schwartz, R., Vassilev, A., Greene, K., Perine, L., Burt, A., & Hall, P. (2022). Towards a Standard for Identifying and Managing Bias in Artificial Intelligence.

Sekeroglu, B., Dimililer, K., & Tuncal, K. (2019, March). Student performance prediction and classification using machine learning algorithms. In *Proceedings of the 2019 8th International Conference on Educational and Information Technology* (pp. 7-11). DOI: 10.1145/3318396.3318419

Senthiil, P. V., Sirusshti, V. A., & Sathish, T. (2019). Artificial Intelligence Based Green Manufacturability quantification of a unit production process. *International Journal of Mechanical and Production Engineering Research and Development*, 9(2), 841–852. DOI: 10.24247/ijmperdapr201981

Shang, Y., Nguyen, H., Bui, X. N., Tran, Q. H., & Moayedi, H. (2020). A novel artificial intelligence approach to predict blast-induced ground vibration in open-pit mines based on the firefly algorithm and artificial neural network. *Natural Resources Research*, 29(2), 723–737. DOI: 10.1007/s11053-019-09503-7

Sherman, M., Puhovskiy, E., Kambalova, Y., & Kdyrova, I. (2022). The future of distance education in war or the education of the future (the Ukrainian case study). *Futurity Education*, 2(3), 15–24.

Shi, C., Gu, Z., Duan, C., & Tian, Q. (2020). Multi-view adaptive semi-supervised feature selection with the self-paced learning. *Signal Processing*, 168, 107332. DOI: 10.1016/j.sigpro.2019.107332

Shin, H., Rim, D., Kim, H., Park, S., & Shon, S. (2019). Educational characteristics of virtual simulation in nursing: An integrative review. *Clinical Simulation in Nursing*, 37, 18–28. DOI: 10.1016/j.ecns.2019.08.002

Shu, W. (2021, April). Combined Forecasting Model Method Based on Python and Artificial Intelligence Algorithm. In *International Conference on Application of Intelligent Systems in Multi-modal Information Analytics* (pp. 636-643). Springer, Cham. DOI: 10.1007/978-3-030-74811-1_91

Singer, A. M., DeBenedectis, C. M., & Rosen, M. P. (2021). Integrating art museum visits into the radiology curriculum: A program to encourage engagement, observation and analytic skills among millennial learners. *Clinical Imaging*, 79, 204–206. DOI: 10.1016/j.clinimag.2021.05.019 PMID: 34116296

Sircar, A., Yadav, K., Rayavarapu, K., Bist, N., & Oza, H. (2021). *Application of machine learning and artificial intelligence in oil and gas industry*. Petroleum Research. DOI: 10.1016/j.ptlrs.2021.05.009

Slimi, Z., & Carballido, B. V. (2023). Navigating the Ethical Challenges of Artificial Intelligence in Higher Education: An Analysis of Seven Global AI Ethics Policies. *TEM Journal, 12*(2).

Sobocińska, M. (2021). Artificial Intelligence and Human Talent in Decision Making in the Sphere of Marketing in an Enterprise. *Problemy Zarządzania*, 19(1 (91)), 65–75. DOI: 10.7172/1644-9584.91.5

Somasundaram, M., Junaid, K. M., & Mangadu, S. (2020). Artificial intelligence (AI) enabled intelligent quality management system (IQMS) for personalized learning path. *Procedia Computer Science*, 172, 438–442. DOI: 10.1016/j.procs.2020.05.096

Soni, N., Sharma, E. K., Singh, N., & Kapoor, A. (2019). Impact of artificial intelligence on businesses: from research, innovation, market deployment to future shifts in business models. *arXiv preprint arXiv:1905.02092*.

Souza, J., & Leung, C. K. (2021). Explainable Artificial Intelligence for Predictive Analytics on Customer Turnover: A User-Friendly Interface for Non-expert Users. In *Explainable AI Within the Digital Transformation and Cyber Physical Systems* (pp. 47–67). Springer. DOI: 10.1007/978-3-030-76409-8_4

Soviany, P., Ionescu, R. T., Rota, P., & Sebe, N. (2021). Curriculum self-paced learning for cross-domain object detection. *Computer Vision and Image Understanding*, 204, 103166. DOI: 10.1016/j.cviu.2021.103166

Staszak, M., Staszak, K., Wieszczycka, K., Bajek, A., Roszkowski, K., & Tylkowski, B. (2022). Machine learning in drug design: Use of artificial intelligence to explore the chemical structure–biological activity relationship. *Wiley Interdisciplinary Reviews. Computational Molecular Science*, 12(2), e1568. DOI: 10.1002/wcms.1568

Sunil, A., Sheth, M. H., & Shreyas, E. (2021, September). Usual and Unusual Human Activity Recognition in Video using Deep Learning and Artificial Intelligence for Security Applications. In *2021 Fourth International Conference on Electrical, Computer and Communication Technologies (ICECCT)* (pp. 1-6). IEEE. DOI: 10.1109/ICECCT52121.2021.9616791

Sun, T. Q., & Medaglia, R. (2019). Mapping the challenges of Artificial Intelligence in the public sector: Evidence from public healthcare. *Government Information Quarterly*, 36(2), 368–383. DOI: 10.1016/j.giq.2018.09.008

Surden, H. (2019). Artificial intelligence and law: An overview. *Georgia State University Law Review*, 35, 19–22.

Talapina, E. V. (2021). Artificial Intelligence and Legal Expertise in Public Administration. *Vestnik Saint Petersburg UL*, 865.

Talent, L. A. (2021). The DOD's Hidden Artificial Intelligence Workforce.

Talwar, P. (2023). *The Strategic Use of Virtual Teacher Assistants to Increase Faculty Engagement and Job Satisfaction* (Doctoral dissertation, Trident University International).

Tang, Y., Liang, J., Hare, R., & Wang, F. Y. (2020). A personalized learning system for parallel intelligent education. *IEEE Transactions on Computational Social Systems*, 7(2), 352–361. DOI: 10.1109/TCSS.2020.2965198

Tapalova, O., & Zhiyenbayeva, N. (2022). Artificial intelligence in education: AIEd for personalised learning pathways. *Electronic Journal of e-Learning*, 20(5), 639–653. DOI: 10.34190/ejel.20.5.2597

Tariq, M. U. (2024a). Harnessing Persuasive Technologies for Enhanced Learner Engagement and Motivation. In M. Sanmugam, D. Lim, N. Mohd Barkhaya, W. Wan Yahaya, & Z. Khlaif (Eds.), *Power of Persuasive Educational Technologies in Enhancing Learning* (pp. 30-62). IGI Global. DOI: 10.4018/979-8-3693-6397-3.ch002

Tariq, M. U. (2024c). Multidisciplinary service learning in higher education: Concepts, implementation, and impact. In S. Watson (Ed.), *Applications of service learning in higher education* (pp. 1-19). IGI Global. DOI: 10.4018/979-8-3693-2133-1.ch001

Tariq, M. U. (2024e). Neurodiversity inclusion and belonging strategies in the workplace. In J. Vázquez de Príncipe (Ed.), *Resilience of multicultural and multigenerational leadership and workplace experience* (pp. 182-201). IGI Global. DOI: 10.4018/979-8-3693-1802-7.ch009

Tariq, M. U. (2024). Crafting Authentic Narratives for Sustainable Branding. In *Compelling Storytelling Narratives for Sustainable Branding* (pp. 194–229). IGI Global. DOI: 10.4018/979-8-3693-3326-6.ch011

Tariq, M. U. (2024). Cybersecurity Risk Assessment Models and Theories in the Travel and Tourism Industry. In Thealla, P., Nadda, V., Dadwal, S., Oztosun, L., & Cantafio, G. (Eds.), *Corporate Cybersecurity in the Aviation, Tourism, and Hospitality Sector* (pp. 1–17). IGI Global. DOI: 10.4018/979-8-3693-2715-9.ch001

Tariq, M. U. (2024). Integration of IoMT for Enhanced Healthcare: Sleep Monitoring, Body Movement Detection, and Rehabilitation Evaluation. In Liu, H., Tripathy, R., & Bhattacharya, P. (Eds.), *Clinical Practice and Unmet Challenges in AI-Enhanced Healthcare Systems* (pp. 70–95). IGI Global. DOI: 10.4018/979-8-3693-2703-6.ch004

Tariq, M. U. (2024). Leading Smart Technologies and Innovations for E-Business 5.0: Applications and Management Frameworks. In Popkova, E. (Ed.), *Smart Technologies and Innovations in E-Business* (pp. 25–46). IGI Global. DOI: 10.4018/978-1-6684-7840-0.ch002

Tariq, M. U. (2024). Leveraging AI for Entrepreneurial Innovation in Healthcare. In Özsungur, F. (Ed.), *Generating Entrepreneurial Ideas With AI* (pp. 192–216). IGI Global. DOI: 10.4018/979-8-3693-3498-0.ch009

Tariq, M. U. (2024). Multi-Agent Models in Healthcare System Design. In Dall'Acqua, L. (Ed.), *Bioethics of Cognitive Ergonomics and Digital Transition* (pp. 143–170). IGI Global. DOI: 10.4018/979-8-3693-2667-1.ch008

Tariq, M. U. (2024). Navigating the Personalization Pathway: Implementing Adaptive Learning Technologies in Higher Education. In Minh Tung, T. (Ed.), *Adaptive Learning Technologies for Higher Education* (pp. 265–291). IGI Global. DOI: 10.4018/979-8-3693-3641-0.ch012

Tariq, M. U. (2024). Smart Transportation Systems: Paving the Way for Sustainable Urban Mobility. In Munuhwa, S. (Ed.), *Contemporary Solutions for Sustainable Transportation Practices* (pp. 254–283). IGI Global., DOI: 10.4018/979-8-3693-3755-4.ch010

Tariq, M. U. (2024). The role of AI in skilling, upskilling, and reskilling the workforce. In Doshi, R., Dadhich, M., Poddar, S., & Hiran, K. (Eds.), *Integrating generative AI in education to achieve sustainable development goals* (pp. 421–433). IGI Global. DOI: 10.4018/979-8-3693-2440-0.ch023

Tariq, M. U. (2024a). AI and the future of talent management: Transforming recruitment and retention with machine learning. In Christiansen, B., Aziz, M., & O'Keeffe, E. (Eds.), *Global practices on effective talent acquisition and retention* (pp. 1–16). IGI Global. DOI: 10.4018/979-8-3693-1938-3.ch001

Tariq, M. U. (2024a). Emotional intelligence in understanding and influencing consumer behavior. In Musiolik, T., Rodriguez, R., & Kannan, H. (Eds.), *AI impacts in digital consumer behavior* (pp. 56–81). IGI Global. DOI: 10.4018/979-8-3693-1918-5.ch003

Tariq, M. U. (2024a). The transformation of healthcare through AI-driven diagnostics. In Sharma, A., Chanderwal, N., Tyagi, S., Upadhyay, P., & Tyagi, A. (Eds.), *Enhancing medical imaging with emerging technologies* (pp. 250–264). IGI Global. DOI: 10.4018/979-8-3693-5261-8.ch015

Tariq, M. U. (2024b). Application of blockchain and Internet of Things (IoT) in modern business. In Sinha, M., Bhandari, A., Priya, S., & Kabiraj, S. (Eds.), *Future of customer engagement through marketing intelligence* (pp. 66–94). IGI Global. DOI: 10.4018/979-8-3693-2367-0.ch004

Tariq, M. U. (2024b). Enhancing Students and Learning Achievement as 21st-Century Skills Through Transdisciplinary Approaches. In Kumar, R., Ong, E., Anggoro, S., & Toh, T. (Eds.), *Transdisciplinary Approaches to Learning Outcomes in Higher Education* (pp. 220–257). IGI Global. DOI: 10.4018/979-8-3693-3699-1.ch007

Tariq, M. U. (2024b). Fintech startups and cryptocurrency in business: Revolutionizing entrepreneurship. In Kankaew, K., Nakpathom, P., Chnitphattana, A., Pitchayadejanant, K., & Kunnapapdeelert, S. (Eds.), *Applying business intelligence and innovation to entrepreneurship* (pp. 106–124). IGI Global. DOI: 10.4018/979-8-3693-1846-1.ch006

Tariq, M. U. (2024b). The role of emerging technologies in shaping the global digital government landscape. In Guo, Y. (Ed.), *Emerging developments and technologies in digital government* (pp. 160–180). IGI Global. DOI: 10.4018/979-8-3693-2363-2.ch009

Tariq, M. U. (2024c). Equity and inclusion in learning ecosystems. In Al Husseiny, F., & Munna, A. (Eds.), *Preparing students for the future educational paradigm* (pp. 155–176). IGI Global. DOI: 10.4018/979-8-3693-1536-1.ch007

Tariq, M. U. (2024c). Social Innovations for Improving Healthcare. In Chandan, H. (Ed.), *Social Innovations in Education, Environment, and Healthcare* (pp. 302–317). IGI Global. DOI: 10.4018/979-8-3693-2569-8.ch015

Tariq, M. U. (2024c). The role of AI ethics in cost and complexity reduction. In Tennin, K., Ray, S., & Sorg, J. (Eds.), *Cases on AI ethics in business* (pp. 59–78). IGI Global. DOI: 10.4018/979-8-3693-2643-5.ch004

Tariq, M. U. (2024d). Challenges of a metaverse shaping the future of entrepreneurship. In Inder, S., Dawra, S., Tennin, K., & Sharma, S. (Eds.), *New business frontiers in the metaverse* (pp. 155–173). IGI Global. DOI: 10.4018/979-8-3693-2422-6.ch011

Tariq, M. U. (2024d). Enhancing cybersecurity protocols in modern healthcare systems: Strategies and best practices. In Garcia, M., & de Almeida, R. (Eds.), *Transformative approaches to patient literacy and healthcare innovation* (pp. 223–241). IGI Global. DOI: 10.4018/979-8-3693-3661-8.ch011

Tariq, M. U. (2024e). Revolutionizing health data management with blockchain technology: Enhancing security and efficiency in a digital era. In Garcia, M., & de Almeida, R. (Eds.), *Emerging technologies for health literacy and medical practice* (pp. 153–175). IGI Global. DOI: 10.4018/979-8-3693-1214-8.ch008

Tariq, M. U. (2024f). AI and IoT in flood forecasting and mitigation: A comprehensive approach. In Ouaissa, M., Ouaissa, M., Boulouard, Z., Iwendi, C., & Krichen, M. (Eds.), *AI and IoT for proactive disaster management* (pp. 26–60). IGI Global. DOI: 10.4018/979-8-3693-3896-4.ch003

Tariq, M. U. (2024f). Emerging trends and innovations in blockchain-digital twin integration for green investments: A case study perspective. In Jafar, S., Rodriguez, R., Kannan, H., Akhtar, S., & Plugmann, P. (Eds.), *Harnessing blockchain-digital twin fusion for sustainable investments* (pp. 148–175). IGI Global. DOI: 10.4018/979-8-3693-1878-2.ch007

Tariq, M. U. (2024f). Leveraging artificial intelligence for a sustainable and climate-neutral economy in Asia. In Ordóñez de Pablos, P., Almunawar, M., & Anshari, M. (Eds.), *Strengthening sustainable digitalization of Asian economy and society* (pp. 1–21). IGI Global. DOI: 10.4018/979-8-3693-1942-0.ch001

Tariq, M. U. (2024g). Empowering student entrepreneurs: From idea to execution. In Cantafio, G., & Munna, A. (Eds.), *Empowering students and elevating universities with innovation centers* (pp. 83–111). IGI Global. DOI: 10.4018/979-8-3693-1467-8.ch005

Tariq, M. U. (2024g). Metaverse in business and commerce. In Kumar, J., Arora, M., & Erkol Bayram, G. (Eds.), *Exploring the use of metaverse in business and education* (pp. 47–72). IGI Global. DOI: 10.4018/979-8-3693-5868-9.ch004

Thiry, H., & Hug, S. T. (2021, March). Sustaining student engagement and equity in computing departments during the covid-19 pandemic. In *Proceedings of the 52nd ACM Technical Symposium on Computer Science Education* (pp. 987-993). DOI: 10.1145/3408877.3432381

Thomas, R., & Zikopoulos, P. (2020). *The AI Ladder: Accelerate your journey to AI*. O'Reilly Media.

Trivedi, S., & Patel, N. (2020). Clustering Students Based on Virtual Learning Engagement, Digital Skills, and E-learning Infrastructure: Applications of K-means, DBSCAN, Hierarchical, and Affinity Propagation Clustering. *Sage Science Review of Educational Technology*, 3(1), 1–13.

Tsai, S. C., Chen, C. H., Shiao, Y. T., Ciou, J. S., & Wu, T. N. (2020). Precision education with statistical learning and deep learning: A case study in Taiwan. *International Journal of Educational Technology in Higher Education*, 17(1), 1–13. DOI: 10.1186/s41239-020-00186-2

Valle-Cruz, D., Criado, J. I., Sandoval-Almazán, R., & Ruvalcaba-Gomez, E. A. (2020). Assessing the public policy-cycle framework in the age of artificial intelligence: From agenda-setting to policy evaluation. *Government Information Quarterly*, 37(4), 101509. DOI: 10.1016/j.giq.2020.101509

van de Sande, D., van Genderen, M. E., Huiskens, J., Gommers, D., & van Bommel, J. (2021). Moving from bytes to bedside: A systematic review on the use of artificial intelligence in the intensive care unit. *Intensive Care Medicine*, 47(7), 750–760. DOI: 10.1007/s00134-021-06446-7 PMID: 34089064

Vargas, M. A., & Comuzzi, M. (2020). A multi-dimensional model of Enterprise Resource Planning critical success factors. *Enterprise Information Systems*, 14(1), 38–57. DOI: 10.1080/17517575.2019.1678072

Vartiainen, H., Tedre, M., & Valtonen, T. (2020). Learning machine learning with very young children: Who is teaching whom? *International Journal of Child-Computer Interaction*, 25, 100182. DOI: 10.1016/j.ijcci.2020.100182

Vazhayil, A., Shetty, R., Bhavani, R. R., & Akshay, N. (2019, December). Focusing on teacher education to introduce AI in schools: Perspectives and illustrative findings. In *2019 IEEE tenth international conference on Technology for Education (T4E)* (pp. 71-77). IEEE.

Waheed, H., Hassan, S. U., Nawaz, R., Aljohani, N. R., Chen, G., & Gasevic, D. (2023). Early prediction of learners at risk in self-paced education: A neural network approach. *Expert Systems with Applications*, 213, 118868. DOI: 10.1016/j.eswa.2022.118868

Wang, D. (2021, March). Construction of Knowledge Graph Corpus Under the Framework of Artificial Intelligence. In *The International Conference on Cyber Security Intelligence and Analytics* (pp. 41-48). Springer. DOI: 10.1007/978-3-030-69999-4_6

Wang, H., Wu, W., Dou, Z., He, L., & Yang, L. (2023). Performance and exploration of ChatGPT in medical examination, records and education in Chinese: Pave the way for medical AI. *International Journal of Medical Informatics*, 177, 105173. DOI: 10.1016/j.ijmedinf.2023.105173 PMID: 37549499

Wang, W., Chen, L., Xiong, M., & Wang, Y. (2021). Accelerating AI adoption with responsible AI signals and employee engagement mechanisms in health care. *Information Systems Frontiers*, 1–18.

Warner, K. S., & Wäger, M. (2019). Building dynamic capabilities for digital transformation: An ongoing process of strategic renewal. *Long Range Planning*, 52(3), 326–349. DOI: 10.1016/j.lrp.2018.12.001

Wei, L. (2023). Artificial intelligence in language instruction: Impact on English learning achievement, L2 motivation, and self-regulated learning. *Frontiers in Psychology*, 14, 1261955. DOI: 10.3389/fpsyg.2023.1261955 PMID: 38023040

Weisz, J. D., Jain, M., Joshi, N. N., Johnson, J., & Lange, I. (2019, March). BigBlueBot: teaching strategies for successful human-agent interactions. In *Proceedings of the 24th International Conference on Intelligent User Interfaces* (pp. 448-459). DOI: 10.1145/3301275.3302290

Wijayati, D. T., Rahman, Z., Rahman, M. F. W., Arifah, I. D. C., & Kautsar, A. (2022). A study of artificial intelligence on employee performance and work engagement: The moderating role of change leadership. *International Journal of Manpower*, 43(2), 486–512. DOI: 10.1108/IJM-07-2021-0423

Williamson, B. (2019). Policy networks, performance metrics and platform markets: Charting the expanding data infrastructure of higher education. *British Journal of Educational Technology*, 50(6), 2794–2809. DOI: 10.1111/bjet.12849

Williams, R., Kaputsos, S. P., & Breazeal, C. (2021, May). Teacher Perspectives on How To Train Your Robot: A Middle School AI and Ethics Curriculum. *Proceedings of the AAAI Conference on Artificial Intelligence*, 35(17), 15678–15686. DOI: 10.1609/aaai.v35i17.17847

Wilson, C. (2022). Public engagement and AI: A values analysis of national strategies. *Government Information Quarterly*, 39(1), 101652. DOI: 10.1016/j.giq.2021.101652

Wirtz, B. W., Weyerer, J. C., & Geyer, C. (2019). Artificial intelligence and the public sector—Applications and challenges. *International Journal of Public Administration*, 42(7), 596–615. DOI: 10.1080/01900692.2018.1498103

Wirtz, B. W., Weyerer, J. C., & Sturm, B. J. (2020). The dark sides of artificial intelligence: An integrated AI governance framework for public administration. *International Journal of Public Administration*, 43(9), 818–829. DOI: 10.1080/01900692.2020.1749851

Wise, J., de Barron, A. G., Splendiani, A., Balali-Mood, B., Vasant, D., Little, E., Mellino, G., Harrow, I., Smith, I., Taubert, J., van Bochove, K., Romacker, M., Walgemoed, P., Jimenez, R. C., Winnenburg, R., Plasterer, T., Gupta, V., & Hedley, V. (2019). Implementation and relevance of FAIR data principles in biopharmaceutical R&D. *Drug Discovery Today*, 24(4), 933–938. DOI: 10.1016/j.drudis.2019.01.008 PMID: 30690198

Wong, C. H. (2021). *Applications of Data Science and Artificial Intelligence to Decision Making in Healthcare and Finance* (Doctoral dissertation, Massachusetts Institute of Technology).

Woods, T. M. (2022). Examining the Effects of Learning Theory Implemented Within an Online and Self-Paced Learning Path.

Yan, B., Hao, F., & Meng, X. (2021). When artificial intelligence meets building energy efficiency, a review focusing on zero energy building. *Artificial Intelligence Review*, 54(3), 2193–2220. DOI: 10.1007/s10462-020-09902-w

Yang, A. C., Flanagan, B., & Ogata, H. (2022). Adaptive formative assessment system based on computerized adaptive testing and the learning memory cycle for personalized learning. *Computers and Education: Artificial Intelligence*, 100104.

Yang, C., Huan, S., & Yang, Y. (2020). A practical teaching mode for colleges supported by artificial intelligence. *International Journal of Emerging Technologies in Learning*, 15(17), 195–206. DOI: 10.3991/ijet.v15i17.16737

Yang, S. J. (2021). Precision education-a new challenge for AI in education. *Journal of Educational Technology & Society*, 24(1).

Yang, S. J., Ogata, H., Matsui, T., & Chen, N. S. (2021). Human-centered artificial intelligence in education: Seeing the invisible through the visible. *Computers and Education: Artificial Intelligence*, 2, 100008. DOI: 10.1016/j.caeai.2021.100008

Yang, Y. C., Islam, S. U., Noor, A., Khan, S., Afsar, W., & Nazir, S. (2021). Influential usage of big data and artificial intelligence in healthcare. *Computational and Mathematical Methods in Medicine*, 2021, 2021. DOI: 10.1155/2021/5812499 PMID: 34527076

Yan, H., Lin, F., & Kinshuk, . (2021). Including learning analytics in the loop of self-paced online course learning design. *International Journal of Artificial Intelligence in Education*, 31(4), 878–895. DOI: 10.1007/s40593-020-00225-z

Yigitcanlar, T., Desouza, K. C., Butler, L., & Roozkhosh, F. (2020). Contributions and risks of artificial intelligence (AI) in building smarter cities: Insights from a systematic review of the literature. *Energies*, 13(6), 1473. DOI: 10.3390/en13061473

Younes, S. S. (2021). Examining the Effectiveness of Using Adaptive AI-Enabled e-Learning during the Pandemic of COVID-19. *Journal of Healthcare Engineering*, 2021, 2021. DOI: 10.1155/2021/3928326 PMID: 34567481

Young, M. M., Bullock, J. B., & Lecy, J. D. (2019). Artificial discretion as a tool of governance: A framework for understanding the impact of artificial intelligence on public administration. *Perspectives on Public Management and Governance*, 2(4), 301–313. DOI: 10.1093/ppmgov/gvz014

Zawacki-Richter, O., Marín, V. I., Bond, M., & Gouverneur, F. (2019). Systematic review of research on artificial intelligence applications in higher education–where are the educators? *International Journal of Educational Technology in Higher Education*, 16(1), 1–27. DOI: 10.1186/s41239-019-0171-0

Zbuchea, A., Vidu, C., & Pinzaru, F. (2019). Is Artificial Intelligence Changing Knowledge Management. *Strategica*, 445-452.

Zhang, D. (2021, December). Research on the Innovative Development of Chinese Mixed Martial Arts (MMA) Events Based on Artificial Intelligence. In *2021 3rd International Conference on Machine Learning, Big Data and Business Intelligence (MLBDBI)* (pp. 785-788). IEEE.

Zhang, C., & Lu, Y. (2021). Study on artificial intelligence: The state of the art and future prospects. *Journal of Industrial Information Integration*, 23, 100224. DOI: 10.1016/j.jii.2021.100224

Zhang, Q. (2022). Construction of Personalized Learning Platform Based on Collaborative Filtering Algorithm. *Wireless Communications and Mobile Computing*, 2022, 2022. DOI: 10.1155/2022/5878344

Zhao, T., Yan, Z., Cao, Y., & Li, Z. (2021, January). Asking effective and diverse questions: a machine reading comprehension based framework for joint entity-relation extraction. In *Proceedings of the Twenty-Ninth International Conference on International Joint Conferences on Artificial Intelligence* (pp. 3948-3954).

Zhao, Y., Llorente, A. M. P., & Gómez, M. C. S. (2021). Digital competence in higher education research: A systematic literature review. *Computers & Education*, 168, 104212. DOI: 10.1016/j.compedu.2021.104212 PMID: 36568577

Zhou, J. (2020, October). Design of AI-based self-learning platform for college english listening. In *2020 2nd International Conference on Machine Learning, Big Data and Business Intelligence (MLBDBI)* (pp. 544-547). IEEE. DOI: 10.1109/MLBDBI51377.2020.00114

Zhou, J., Su, B., & Wu, Y. (2022). Discriminative Self-Paced Group-Metric Adaptation for Online Visual Identification. *IEEE Transactions on Pattern Analysis and Machine Intelligence*, 1–16. DOI: 10.1109/TPAMI.2022.3200036 PMID: 35984798

About the Author

Muhammad Usman Tariq has more than 16 years of experience in industry and academia. He has authored more than 200+ research articles, 100+ case studies, 95+ book chapters and several books other than 4 patents. He is founder and CEO of The Case HQ courses, text and video case studies center. He has been working as a consultant and trainer for industries representing six sigma, quality, health and safety, environmental systems, project management, and information security standards. His work has encompassed sectors in aviation, manufacturing, food, hospitality, education, finance, research, software and transportation. He has diverse and significant experience working with accreditation agencies of ABET, ACBSP, AACSB, WASC, CAA, EFQM and NCEAC. Additionally, Dr. Tariq has operational experience in incubators, research labs, government research projects, private sector startups, program creation and management at various industrial and academic levels. He is Certified Higher Education Teacher from Harvard University, USA, Certified Online Educator from HMBSU, Certified Six Sigma Master Black Belt, Lead Auditor ISO 9001 Certified, ISO 14001, IOSH MS, OSHA 30, and OSHA 48. He has been awarded Principal Fellowship from Advance HE UK, Chartered Fellowship of CIPD UK, and certified business and management educator recognition.

Index

A

B

C

D

L

M

N

O

P

R

S